Becker™

MW01590968

This textbook contains information that was current at the time of printing. Your course software will be updated on a regular basis as the content that is tested on the CPA Exam evolves and as we improve our materials. Note the version reference below and select your replacement textbook at **becker.com/cpa-replacements-upgrades** to learn if a newer version of this book is available to be ordered.

CPA Exam Review

Information Systems and Controls (ISC)

For Exams Scheduled
After December 31, 2024

V 1.1

Your future is just four parts away.

Welcome to the Becker CPA Exam Review! Congratulations on taking the first step to becoming a CPA. As the industry's leading partner in CPA Exam preparation, we know you're not just studying for an exam – you are preparing for your future. To help you get there, Becker CPA Exam Review is as close as you can get to the real thing. So let's get started.

Access Becker's CPA Exam Review course

Log in to your CPA Exam Review course anytime at **cpa.becker.com**. Watch our orientation video and download the mobile app to access your studies on the go. Your progress will automatically sync among all your devices, so you can pick up where you left off. For more on getting started, visit **becker.com/cpa-review/getting-started**.

Utilize the Becker resources

Make studying more organized with our study planner. With interactive tools to help you determine your ideal study schedule and to recommend your ideal exam-taking time, it's easy to plan your preparation so you can become Exam Day Ready℠. Here are the added benefits of Becker:

- Take advantage of unlimited practice tests, personalized by Adapt2U Technology

- Access 1-on-1 academic support from our experienced CPA instructors

- Test your knowledge with our simulated exams – the closest thing you can get to the actual CPA Exam itself

You're not in it alone!

For tips, stories and advice, visit our blog at **becker.com/blog**. You can also collaborate with other Becker students studying ISC on our Facebook study group at **facebook.com/groups/BeckerISCStudyGroup/**.

Becker.

Join the community!

Information Systems and Controls (ISC)
Table of Contents

NOTES

Introduction

ISC

NOTES

Information Systems and Controls (ISC) Overview

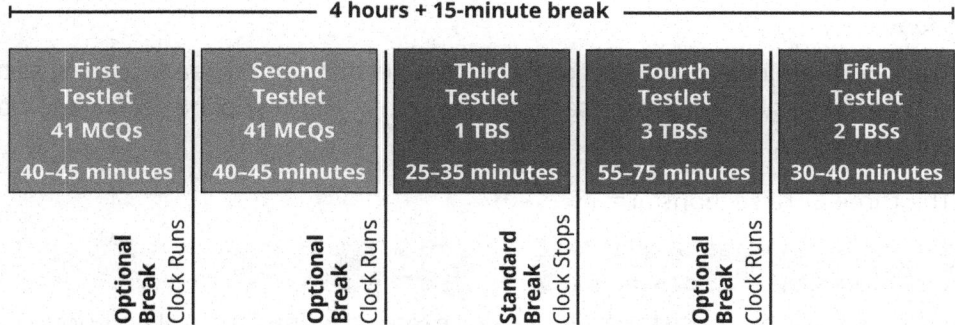

ISC Exam: Summary Blueprint

Content Area Allocation	Weight
Information Systems and Data Management	35–45%
Security, Confidentiality and Privacy	35–45%
Considerations for System and Organization Controls (SOC) Engagements	15–25%
Skill Allocation	Weight
Evaluation	—
Analysis	10–20%
Application	20–30%
Remembering and Understanding	55–65%

Becker's CPA Exam Review: Course Introduction

Becker Professional Education's CPA Exam Review products were developed with you, the candidate, in mind. To that end we have developed a series of tools designed to tap all of your learning and retention capabilities. The Becker lectures, comprehensive tests, and course software are designed to be fully integrated to give you the best chance of passing the CPA Exam.

Passing the CPA Exam is difficult, but the professional rewards a CPA enjoys make this a worthwhile challenge. We created our CPA Exam Review after evaluating the needs of CPA candidates and analyzing the CPA Exam over the years. Our course materials comprehensively present topics you must know to pass the examination, teaching you the most effective tactics for learning the material.

The Uniform CPA Exam: Overview

Exam Sections

The CPA Examination consists of three Core sections and three Discipline sections. You must pass all three Core sections and one of the Discipline sections to become a licensed CPA.

The three Core sections are:

Financial Accounting and Reporting (FAR)

The FAR section consists of a four-hour exam covering financial accounting and reporting for commercial entities under U.S. GAAP, not-for-profit accounting, and the basics of government accounting.

Auditing and Attestation (AUD)

The AUD section consists of a four-hour exam. This section covers all topics related to auditing, including audit reports and procedures, generally accepted auditing standards, attestation and other engagements, and government auditing.

Taxation and Regulation (REG)

The REG section consists of a four-hour exam, combining topics from business law and federal taxation, including the taxation of property transactions, individuals, and entities.

The three Discipline sections (you must pass one) are:

Business Analysis and Reporting (BAR)

The BAR section consists of a four-hour exam covering advanced financial accounting and reporting, government accounting, financial management, operations management, and managerial and cost accounting.

Information Systems and Controls (ISC)

The ISC section consists of a four-hour exam and includes topics related to information systems and data management, security, confidentiality and privacy, and system and organization controls (SOC) engagements.

Tax Compliance and Planning (TCP)

The TCP section consists of a four-hour exam and includes topics related to personal financial planning, entity tax compliance, entity tax planning, and property transactions.

Question Formats

The chart below illustrates the question format breakdown by exam section.

Section	Multiple-Choice Questions (MCQs)		Task-Based Simulations (TBSs)	
	Percentage	Number	Percentage	Number
FAR	50%	50	50%	7
AUD	50%	78	50%	7
REG	50%	72	50%	8
BAR	50%	50	50%	7
ISC	60%	82	40%	6
TCP	50%	68	50%	7

Each exam will contain testlets. A testlet is either a series of multiple-choice questions or a set of task-based simulations. For example, the Systems examination will contain five testlets. The first two testlets will be multiple-choice questions and the third, fourth, and fifth testlets will contain task-based simulations. Each testlet must be finished and submitted before continuing to the next testlet. Candidates cannot go back to view a previously completed testlet or go forward to view a subsequent testlet before closing and submitting the earlier testlet. Our simulated exams contain these types of restrictions so that you can familiarize yourself with the functionality of the CPA Exam.

Exam Schedule

Candidates can schedule an exam date directly with Prometric (www.prometric.com/cpa) after receiving a notice to schedule.

Eligibility and Application Requirements

Each state sets its own rules of eligibility for the examination. Please visit www.becker.com/cpa-review/requirements as soon as possible to determine your eligibility to sit for the exam.

Application Deadlines

With the computer-based exam format, set application deadlines generally do not exist. You should apply as early as possible to ensure that you are able to schedule your desired exam dates. Each state has different application requirements and procedures, so be sure to gain a thorough understanding of the application process for your state.

Grading System

You must pass all three Core exams and one of the Discipline exams to become a CPA. You must score 75 or better on a part to receive a passing grade.

Becker Customer and Academic Support

You can access Becker's Customer and Academic Support from within the course software by clicking Help Center at the top at:

cpa.becker.com

You can also access customer service and technical support by calling 1-877-CPA-EXAM (outside the U.S. +1-630-472-2213).

Regulations, Standards, and Frameworks

Module

Overview

The application of information technology (IT) in an organization is the systematic implementation of hardware and software so that data can be transmitted, modified, accessed, and stored both securely and efficiently. As the field of information science advances, the speed at which IT devices can perform these tasks has rapidly increased, and organizations must reevaluate their technology on a regular basis.

Organizations adopt technology to enhance or support business operations, protect digital records and assets, and safeguard physical assets. This makes the selection and deployment of management information systems critical to the success of any organization.

1 National Institute of Standards and Technology (NIST) Cybersecurity Framework (CSF)

1.1 NIST Background

The National Institute of Standards and Technology (NIST) was established in 1901 to remove barriers to industrial competitiveness and improve access to resources to promote U.S. research capabilities. In 1995, the NIST branched out into the cybersecurity field with the NIST Special Publication 800-12, *An Introduction to Information Security*. To date, three of the most prolific sets of standardized frameworks promulgated by NIST include the NIST Cybersecurity Framework (CSF), NIST Privacy Framework, and NIST SP 800-53 Security and Privacy Controls for Information Systems and Organizations.

1.2 Cybersecurity Framework

Introduction

The NIST Cybersecurity Framework is designed to help organizations of all sizes and sectors to manage and reduce their cybersecurity risks. It is a voluntary framework that includes three primary components to manage cybersecurity risk:

1. CSF Core
2. CSF Tiers
3. CSF Organizational Profiles

1.2.1 CSF Core

The NIST CSF Core describes cybersecurity outcomes that can be used by an organization of any size to reduce its cybersecurity risks. These outcomes create a taxonomy and structure to help organizations understand, assess, prioritize, and communicate critical cybersecurity risks.

The framework core consists of six functions, which represent different points in the security risk management life cycle that help enhance cybersecurity protection. These components are not ordered steps; they are functions that should be performed concurrently. The six functions are Govern, Identify, Protect, Detect, Respond, and Recover.

1. **Govern (GV):** This function establishes, communicates, and monitors the organization's cybersecurity risk management strategy, expectations, and policy. This function assists an organization in achieving and prioritizing outcomes of the other five functions in relation to the organization's mission and stakeholder expectations.

2. **Identify (ID):** This function focuses on understanding the assets and suppliers of an organization and the cybersecurity risks related to these assets and suppliers. This function also includes identifying improvement opportunities related to the organization's cybersecurity risk management policies, plans, processes, procedures and practices.

3. **Protect (PR):** This function focuses on an organization's ability to secure its assets to prevent or reduce the likelihood and impact of adverse cybersecurity events. Examples of the safeguards used to manage cybersecurity risks include identity management, authentication, and access control; awareness and training; data security; platform security; and infrastructure resiliency.

4. **Detect (DE):** This function focuses on the timely discovery of cybersecurity attacks and incidents by analyzing anomalies, indicators of compromise, and other potentially adverse events that may indicate that a cybersecurity attack or incident is occurring.

5. **Respond (RS):** This function focuses on a company's ability to contain the effects of cybersecurity incidents. Outcomes within this function cover incident management, analysis, mitigation, reporting, and communication.

6. **Recover (RC):** This function focuses on supporting the timely restoration of a company's normal operations to reduce the impact of cybersecurity incidents and communicate recovery efforts effectively and appropriately.

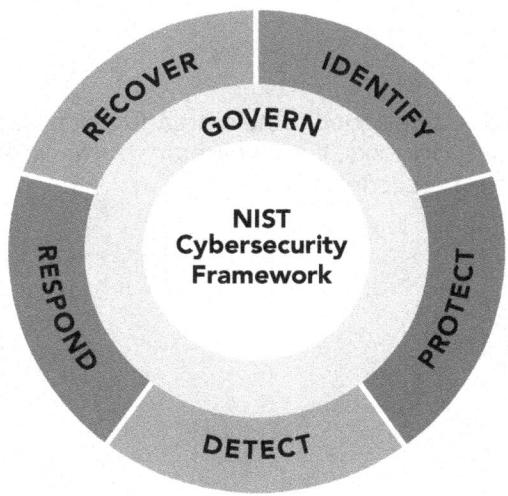

Source: Reprinted courtesy of the National Institute of Standards and Technology, U.S. Department of Commerce. Not copyrightable in the United States.

These six functions define the high-level framework and are subdivided into categories and, subsequently, into subcategories.

Categories: Tie outcomes to specific activities and company needs.

Subcategories: Divide categories into management and technical activities that help achieve the category outcomes.

Function	Category	ID
GOVERN (GV)	Organizational Context	GV.OC
	Risk Management Strategy	GV.RM
	Roles, Responsibilities, and Authorities	GV.RR
	Policy	GV.PO
	Oversight	GV.OV
	Cybersecurity Supply Chain Risk Management	GV.SC
IDENTIFY (ID)	Asset Management	ID.AM
	Risk Assessment	ID.RA
	Improvement	ID.IM
PROTECT (PR)	Identity Management, Authentication, and Access Control	PR.AA
	Awareness and Training	PR.AT
	Data Security	PR.DS
	Platform Security	PR.PS
	Technology Infrastructure Resilience	PR.IR
DETECT (DE)	Continuous Monitoring	DE.CM
	Adverse Event Analysis	DE.AE
RESPOND (RS)	Incident Management	RS.MA
	Incident Analysis	RS.AN
	Incident Response Reporting and Communication	RS.CO
	Incident Mitigation	RS.MI
RECOVER (RC)	Incident Recovery Plan Execution	RC.RP
	Incident Recovery Communication	RC.CO

Subcategory	Implementation Examples
GV.RM-01: Risk management objectives are established and agreed to by organizational stakeholders	**1st:** 1st Party Risk **Ex1:** Update near-term and long-term cybersecurity risk management objectives as part of annual strategic planning and when major changes occur **Ex2:** Establish measurable objectives for cybersecurity risk management (e.g., manage the quality of user training, ensure adequate risk protection for industrial control systems) **Ex3:** Senior leaders agree about cybersecurity objectives and use them for measuring and managing risk and performance

Source: Reprinted courtesy of the National Institute of Standards and Technology, U.S. Department of Commerce. Not copyrightable in the United States.

| Illustration 1 | **Cybersecurity Framework Core: Detect, Respond, and Recover** |

Falcon CPAs and Associates is a large accounting and IT auditing firm that has several clients for whom it provides bookkeeping, tax work, and IT audit services. Falcon decided to run a scan using its new NIST-based security software for a client. The application scans various applications and devices, generating a report with findings.

The report came back with high-risk employee behavior and the use of high-risk devices as potential red flags. The employee behavior included access to records on the weekends and after business hours. The use of high-risk devices included excessive use of USB drives that were being plugged into the network to transfer data. Both were related to an individual who was later determined to be stealing employee banking information from the payroll department outside of normal working business hours.

Falcon's utilization of the application helped to detect high-risk areas and behaviors, including those determined to be from an individual committing theft of banking information. Falcon's response may include the analysis of impact, communication to those employees impacted by the stolen information, and mitigation strategies to reduce the risk of similar breaches. Falcon's recovery may include restoring any stolen data, improving protections to restrict unauthorized access, and taking necessary disciplinary or legal action against the individual committing the data theft.

| Illustration 2 | **Detective Measures as Concurrent Protections** |

A locked door on an empty house is a preventive measure: if the criminal knows no one is home, the criminal is free to break the lock and steal from the house. If the same locked door has a webcam pointed at it to identify the thief and simultaneously alert the police, the presence of the camera may deter the thief from breaking into the house. The camera is not a preventive measure; it does nothing to stop a break-in, but because the thief can see the detective measure put in place, the camera may deter the crime.

This concept applies to the NIST Framework Core. Detection processes may be included as part of the protection process as a way to protect information and data. Similar to the webcam in the empty house, if detection tools are in place to identify individuals who access information or data, such detection tools may serve as a deterrent and protect sensitive information.

1.2.2 CSF Tiers

The NIST CSF provides a measure of an organization's information security infrastructure sophistication in the form of four Tiers. These tiers do not serve to implement the six functions. Rather, the tiers categorize the degree to which information security practices are integrated throughout an organization. The tiers should complement an organization's existing cybersecurity risk management methodology and can be used as a benchmark to communicate its organization-wide approach to managing cybersecurity risks.

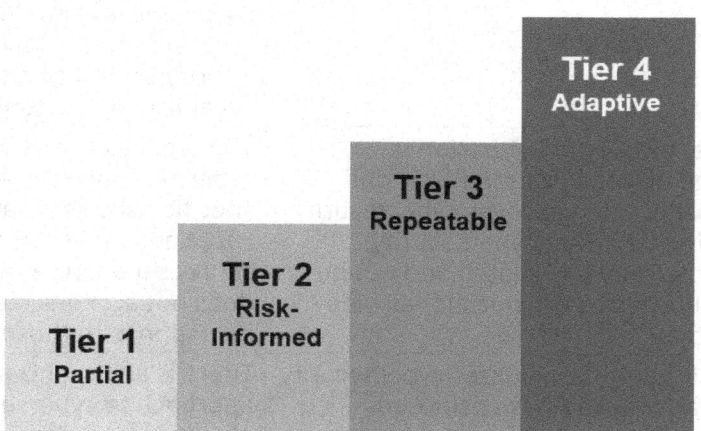

Source: Reprinted courtesy of the National Institute of Standards and Technology, U.S. Department of Commerce. Not copyrightable in the United States.

The CSF Organizational Profiles determine success or failure of information security implementation, whereas the CSF Tiers inform an organization as to the rigor of the governance and management practices associated with those profiles. Tiers are divided by level and then subdivided into cybersecurity risk governance and cybersecurity risk management.

CSF Tiers		
	Cybersecurity Risk Governance	**Cybersecurity Risk Management**
Tier 1 (Partial)	Risk management is ad hoc and reactive where prioritization of information security efforts is not formally based on organizational objectives or threat environment.	There is limited awareness of cybersecurity risks at the organizational level. The organization implements cybersecurity risk management on an irregular, case-by-case basis and does not have processes that allow cybersecurity information to be shared within the organization for general awareness.
Tier 2 (Risk-Informed)	Cybersecurity prioritization is based on organizational risk, and management approves cybersecurity efforts; however, cybersecurity policies may be isolated and not be established as organizational-wide policies.	The organization is aware of the cybersecurity risks in general and specific risks associated with its suppliers, as well as the products and services it acquires and uses, but it does not act consistently or formally in response to those risks.
Tier 3 Repeatable)	The organization utilizes cybersecurity in planning and has enshrined cybersecurity practices in formal, documented policies. These policies are frequently updated based on shifts in business requirements, threats, and technological landscape.	There is an organization-wide risk approach to cybersecurity where risks of assets, suppliers, and products and services are consistently and accurately monitored, as well as regularly communicated among senior leadership.
Tier 4 (Adaptive)	A risk-informed, organization-wide approach in managing cybersecurity risks. Senior executives monitor cybersecurity risks in the same context as financial and other organizational risks and cybersecurity risk management is part of the organizational culture.	Through a process of continuous improvement that incorporates advanced cybersecurity technologies and practices, the organization actively adapts to a changing technological landscape and responds in a timely, effective manner to evolving, sophisticated threats.

1.2.3 CSF Organizational Profiles

CSF Organizational Profiles are the mechanisms by which NIST recommends companies measure cybersecurity risk and establish a road map to ensure the organization can minimize such risk. An Organizational Profile should include one or both of the following:

▪ A Current Profile that specifies the outcome that an organization is achieving (or is attempting to achieve) based on the current cybersecurity posture.

▪ A Target Profile that specifies the desired outcome that an organization has prioritized achieving, and that considers anticipated changes to the organization's cybersecurity posture.

In addition, there are also Community Profiles which are different than organizational profiles. Community Profiles are baseline outcomes developed among a number of organizations due to the shared interest and goals of a particular industry sector, topic, or use case. These profiles can be used by organizations to develop their own Target Profile.

Organizational Profiles should factor organizational mission objectives, stakeholder expectations, threat landscape, and risk management priorities.

NIST provides a repeatable five-step approach in using Organizational Profiles to help inform continuous improvement of an organization's cybersecurity posture:

- Scope the Organizational Profile.

- Gather the information needed to prepare the Organizational Profile.

- Create the Organization Profile.

- Analyze the gaps between the Current and Target Profiles and create an action plan.

- Implement the action plan, and update the Organizational Profile.

2   National Institute of Standards and Technology (NIST) Privacy Framework

2.1   Privacy Framework

The NIST Privacy Framework was published in early 2020 to protect individuals' data as used in data processing applications. The Privacy Framework provides a common language for understanding, managing, and communicating privacy risk with internal and external stakeholders. The framework can be adaptable to organizations in any industry and is a tool that is used to align policy, business, and technological approaches to managing and reducing privacy risk.

Leveraging a similar structure to NIST CSF, the Privacy Framework expresses control objectives in the form of a Framework Core, with sophistication measures in Framework Profiles, and finally mechanisms to drive organizational change and success through Framework Implementation Tiers.

In addition to the similar structure, there is a degree of overlap between the CSF and Privacy Frameworks. The following graphic shows concepts present in both, meaning they have similar risk management approaches, but they are applied to each subject matter differently. Additionally, the Privacy Framework can apply elements in practice that are only found in the Cybersecurity framework. For instance, the guidance in the NIST Privacy Framework suggests that the Cybersecurity Framework risks—Detect, Respond, and Recover—can be applied to the Privacy Framework risks to further support the management of cybersecurity-related privacy events.

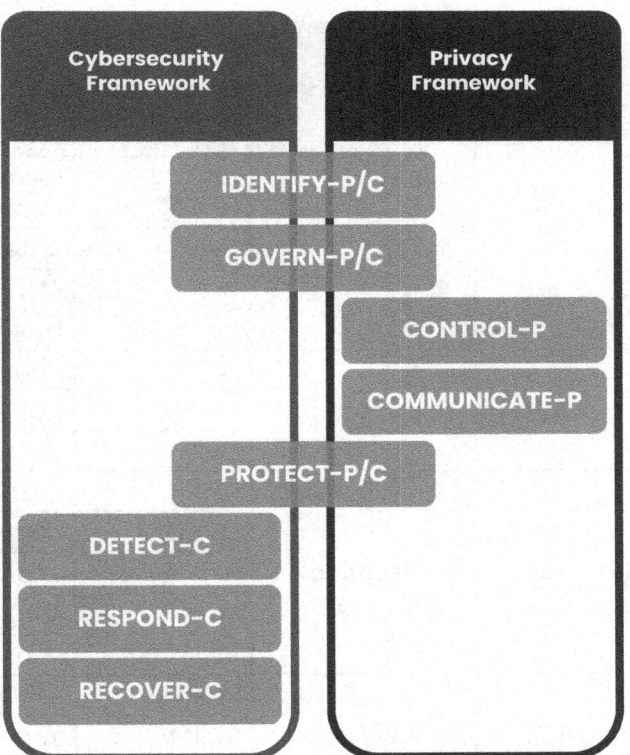

Framework Core

The Privacy Framework Core is contained in Appendix A of the Privacy Framework and is divided into the following eight Framework Functions:

Function Unique Identifier	Function	Category Unique Identifier	Category
ID-P	Identify-P	ID.IM-P	Inventory and Mapping
		ID.BE-P	Business Environment
		ID.RA-P	Risk Assessment
		ID.DE-P	Data Processing Ecosystem Risk Management
GV-P	Govern-P	GV.PO-P	Governance Policies, Processes, and Procedures
		GV.RM-P	Risk Management Strategy
		GV.AT-P	Awareness and Training
		GV.MT-P	Monitoring Review
CT-P	Control-P	CT.PO-P	Data Processing Policies, Processes, and Procedures
		CT.DM-P	Data Processing Management
		CT.DP-P	Disassociated Processing
CM-P	Communicate-P	CM.PO-P	Communication Policies, Processes, and Procedures
		CM.AW-P	Data Processing Awareness
PR-P	Protect-P	PR.PO-P	Data Protection Policies, Processes, and Procedures
		PR.AC-P	Identity Management, Authentication, and Access Control
		PR.DS-P	Data Security
		PR.MA-P	Maintenance
		PR.PT-P	Protective Technology
DE	Detect	DE.AE	Anomalies and Events
		DE.CM	Security Continuous Monitoring
		DE.DP	Detection Processes
RS	Respond	RS.RP	Response Planning
		RS.CO	Communications
		RS.AN	Analysis
		RS.MI	Mitigation
		RS.IM	Improvements
RC	Recover	RC.RP	Recovery Planning
		RC.IM	Improvements
		RC.CO	Communications

Source: Reprinted courtesy of the National Institute of Standards and Technology, U.S. Department of Commerce. Not copyrightable in the United States.

These Functions help organizations answer the following questions:

- **Identify-P:** What are the company's privacy risks related to data processing activities?

- **Govern-P:** What is the best governance structure for privacy risks related to the company's data processing activities?

- **Control-P:** What is the best management structure for privacy risks related to data processing activities?

- **Communicate-P:** How should the organization drive dialogue around privacy risks related to data processing activities?

- **Protect-P:** What are the safeguards that should be in place around privacy risks related to data processing activities?

- **Detect:** How should the organization detect data privacy risks and events?

- **Respond:** How should the organization respond to data privacy events?

- **Recover:** How should the company continue business after data privacy events?

The Functions are subdivided into 29 categories to address privacy program considerations. Those categories, in turn, are divided into 100 subcategories. As with the NIST CSF, the subcategories in the NIST Privacy Framework are individual controls resulting in successfully addressing the 29 controls and the eight Framework Functions.

- **Framework Profiles**

  NIST Privacy Framework Profiles operate identically to NIST CSF Framework Profiles. NIST identified a successful model in the NIST CSF and replicated that same platform for other control sets.

  The NIST Privacy Framework recommends creating a Current and Target Profile and using those to gauge maturity and sophistication while developing a gap analysis and road map for improvement. As with the NIST CSF, the Privacy Framework Current Profile refers to current state privacy practices, while Target Profile refers to future privacy practices.

- **Framework Implementation Tiers**

  The Privacy Framework Tiers mirror those found in NIST CSF. There are four Tiers: Partial, Risk- Informed, Repeatable, and Adaptive. Also, similar to the NIST CSF is the utility of those Tiers, which is gauging performance and communicating internally about how to allocate resources based on current and target Tiers.

  As with the CSF, the subdivisions in the Privacy Framework are divided into four Tiers. For the risk management process, risk management program integration, and ecosystem relationships, the implementation statements are materially identical and reframed for privacy.

  One key difference is the addition of workforce as a Tier subdivision. As part of the measurement of Tier maturity, NIST added the measurement of workforce dedicated to an organization's privacy function. At the Partial end of the spectrum, no one is assigned to privacy, and training is ad hoc. At the Adaptive end of the spectrum, there are dedicated privacy personnel throughout the organization and regular broad-based training.

  Another difference between the NIST CSF and Privacy Framework Tiers is the expression of progression through the Tiers. In the Privacy Framework, progression is recommended based on accomplishing goals in prior Tiers. In the Privacy Framework, Tiers are used more as a gauge of privacy maturity.

3 NIST Security and Privacy Controls

3.1 NIST SP 800-53

NIST SP 800-53 Security and Privacy Controls for Information Systems and Organizations has evolved into a set of security and privacy controls applicable to all information systems and has become the standard for federal information security systems.

NIST SP 800-53 is a stricter standard compared to the NIST CSF or Privacy Frameworks. While the CSF and Privacy Frameworks are designed for cost-effectiveness and best-practice implementation, the controls in NIST SP 800-53 are designed for protecting information systems against sophisticated threats. Even though there is a cost-based approach to NIST SP 800-53 implementation, organizations must carefully evaluate adopting the framework because it can become burdensome given that there are nearly 1,200 detailed controls.

Purpose and Applicability

NIST SP 800-53 establishes controls for systems and organizations that can be implemented within organizations or systems that process, store, or transmit information. These standards are designed to help organizations identify the security and privacy controls needed to manage risk and satisfy the following security and privacy requirements:

- **Office of Management and Budget (OMB) Circular A-130:** Requires the controls for federal information systems.

- **The Federal Information Security Modernization Act (FISMA):** Requires the implementation of minimum controls to protect federal information and information systems.

Target Audience

The following audience is intended for the NIST SP 800-53:

- Individuals with system, information security, privacy, or risk management and oversight responsibilities, including authorizing officials, chief information officers, senior agency information security officers, and senior agency officials for privacy

- Individuals with system development responsibilities, including mission owners, program managers, system engineers, system security engineers, privacy engineers, hardware and software developers, system integrators, and acquisition or procurement officials

- Individuals with logistical or disposition-related responsibilities, including program managers, procurement officials, system integrators, and property managers

- Individuals with security and privacy implementation and operations responsibilities, including mission or business owners, system owners, information owners or stewards, system administrators, continuity planners, and system security or privacy officers

- Individuals with security and privacy assessment and monitoring responsibilities, including auditors, inspectors general, system evaluators, control assessors, independent verifiers and validators, and analysts

- Commercial entities, including industry partners, producing component products and systems, creating security and privacy technologies, or providing services or capabilities that support information security or privacy

▧ **Organizational Responsibilities**

When managing security and privacy risks, the following are required by the organization:

- Well-defined security and privacy requirements for systems and organizations

- The use of trustworthy information system components based on state-of-the-practice hardware, firmware, and software development and acquisition processes

- Rigorous security and privacy planning and system development life cycle management

- The application of system security and privacy engineering principles and practices to securely develop and integrate system components into information systems

- The employment of security and privacy practices that are properly documented and integrated into, and supportive of, the institutional and operational processes of organizations

- Continuous monitoring of information systems and organizations to determine the ongoing effectiveness of controls, changes in information systems and environments of operation, and the state of security and privacy organization-wide

NIST SP 800-53 is subdivided into 20 different control families that cover organizational risk. Those families are listed below with the organizational questions they seek to answer.

▧ **AC–Access Control:** How does the organization manage application and resource access?

▧ **AT–Awareness and Training:** How should the company deliver training on information security risk?

▧ **AU–Audit and Accountability:** How does the company evaluate information security controls?

▧ **CA–Assessment, Authorization, and Monitoring:** How does the organization collect information security telemetry and use it to hunt for threats?

▧ **CM–Configuration Management:** How are assets and software configured securely?

▧ **CP–Contingency Planning:** How is the company prepared for downtime and outages?

▧ **IA–Identity and Authentication:** How is identification and authentication managed?

▧ **IR–Incident Response:** How is the organization prepared for information security and events?

▧ **MA–Maintenance:** How does the company ensure secure maintenance of infrastructure?

▧ **MP–Media Protection:** How is information on physical media managed?

▧ **PE–Physical and Environmental Protection:** How are facilities secured from intrusion or harm?

▧ **PL–Planning:** How does the organization manage information security planning?

▧ **PM–Program Management:** How does the organization securely manage its information security program?

▧ **PS–Personnel Security:** How are employees evaluated for potential compromise?

▧ **PT–PII Processing and Transparency:** How is personally identifiable information (PII) managed?

▧ **RA–Risk Assessment:** How is environmental risk evaluated?

▧ **SA–System and Services Acquisition:** How are systems securely evaluated and acquired?

▧ **SC– System and Communications Protection:** How is data securely transmitted digitally?

- **SI–System and Information Integrity:** How is the integrity of data in company systems maintained and evaluated?

- **SR–Supply Chain Risk Management:** How does the company secure its supply chain (new to NIST 800-53 Rev. 5)?

The control families are subdivided into controls and control enhancements. Controls are the objectives to be implemented for family conformance. Control enhancements are best practices, some of which are recommended, while others are necessary for conformance to a baseline.

Controls and control objectives are written as statements for implementation. Some of those statements for implementation include bracketed and italicized language, which is an organization-defined parameter. Organizations are required to enter values or compliance statements in lieu of the placeholder.

One key difference between NIST SP 800-53 Rev. 4 and NIST SP 800-53 Rev. 5 is that the latest revision dropped priority and baseline allocation. In prior iterations, NIST categorized the NIST SP 800-53 standards into low, moderate, and high control baselines. Those baselines informed the sensitivity of federal systems to which the controls applied. As those are inapplicable and potentially confusing in the private sector, the control baselines were dropped in favor of comprehensive conformance.

With respect to implementation models, NIST SP 800-53 outlines three control implementation approaches that are to be implemented on a per-control basis:

1. **Common (Inheritable):** Implement controls at the organizational level, which are adopted by information systems.

2. **System-Specific:** Implement controls at the information system level.

3. **Hybrid:** Implement controls at the organization level where appropriate and the remainder at the information system level.

1 Data Privacy

1.1 Privacy Laws

Privacy laws exist to protect an individual's private life and keep personal details out of the public domain. These laws also create trust between consumers and enterprises so that when a consumer's personal information is shared, such as with a credit card company or a health care provider, sensitive information will be safeguarded according to rules outlined in applicable privacy regulations.

Privacy laws regulate how those entrusted with private information must collect, process, maintain, and disclose it. Generally, those entrusted with the information must be clear about what data they collect, keep it confidential, and limit access to only those who need it.

Today's modern privacy laws in the United States focus on particular types of data or entities, such as health care data, financial data, or data held by federal agencies. There is no single federal law that applies generally and regulates all personal data. Unlike the United States, the European Union enacted one comprehensive data privacy law, the General Data Protection Regulation (GDPR), that applies generally and governs how all entrusted with personal data should handle such information. A few U.S. states, such as California, have enacted similar privacy laws of general applicability that apply to those doing business in the state or the data of the people in the state.

1.2 Data Breaches

With society's use of the internet and the cloud, data exchange is more prevalent than ever. The rise in available data has led to a surge in data breaches. A data breach is the exposure of confidential information to unauthorized persons. There are two categories of data breaches:

- **Unintentional:** A breach resulting from negligence or error.
- **Intentional:** A breach resulting from bad actors illegally gaining access to data.

Data breaches can create significant consequences for companies and consumers. For companies, a data breach can cause business disruption, reputational harm, financial loss, data loss, and potential legal and regulatory implications. The IBM Cost of Data Breach Report for 2022 shows that the average cost of a data breach is over $4 million. This cost includes four categories of expenditures:

- **Detection and Escalation:** The cost to detect a breach, such as forensics and investigative efforts.
- **Notification:** The cost to notify necessary parties, such as consumers and regulators.
- **Post-breach Response:** The cost to rectify the effects of the breach, such as paying regulatory fines, implementing credit-monitoring services for consumers, and providing ongoing communications to consumers.

- **Loss of Business and Revenue:** Revenue is temporarily lost during downtime caused by data breaches, and this can ultimately lead to loss of customers, which creates a more permanent loss of revenue.

For consumers, the impact is different and more personal. A data breach can mean exposure of personal information, such as name, home address, Social Security number, and payment or banking information. This exposure puts consumers at risk of identity theft and monetary theft.

2   Modern Privacy Regulations

2.1   Health Insurance Portability and Accountability Act (HIPAA)

The Health Insurance Portability and Accountability Act (HIPAA) of 1996 required the Department of Health and Human Services to adopt national standards promoting health care privacy and security. In response, the department adopted the Privacy Rule and the Security Rule. HIPAA and the rules that resulted regulate how the health care industry maintains and discloses health information.

The HIPAA Privacy Rule governs the privacy of protected health information (PHI). This rule applies to specific health care-related entities and businesses, called covered entities, which include any of the following:

- Health care providers that transmit health information electronically
- Health plans
- Health care clearing houses
- Business associates who are service providers who need access to PHI to perform services for covered entities

The Privacy Rule permits a covered entity to use and disclose PHI, with no further authorization required:

- To the individual.
- For treatment, payment, and health care operations.
- Incident to an otherwise permitted use and disclosure.
- With valid authorization.
- After giving the individual the opportunity to agree or object.
- As a limited (redacted) dataset for research, public health, or health care operations.
- For public interest and benefit activities provided by the law.

The HIPAA Security Rule specifically governs electronic PHI. Under the Security Rule, all covered entities must:

- Ensure the confidentiality, integrity, and availability of all electronic PHI;
- Protect against reasonably anticipated threats to the security of the information;
- Protect against reasonably anticipated impermissible uses or disclosures; and
- Ensure compliance by the covered entity's workforce.

HIPAA requires different safeguards for covered entities or business associates, including the following:

- **Administrative Safeguards:** Standards include security management processes, assigned security responsibility, workforce security, information access management, security awareness and training, security incident procedures, contingency plans, and evaluation.

- **Physical Safeguards:** Standards include facility access controls, workstation use, workstation security, and device and media controls.

- **Technical Safeguards:** Standards include access control, audit controls, data integrity controls, person or entity authentication, and transmission security.

2.1.1 Health Information Technology for Economic and Clinical Health (HITECH) Act of 2009

HIPAA was amended by the Health Information Technology for Economic and Clinical Health (HITECH) Act. HITECH was enacted in 2009 to promote health information technology and the transition from paper to electronic records. HITECH amended HIPAA in a few ways. Namely, it increased penalties for HIPAA violations, required that patients receive the option to obtain records in electronic form, and added "business associates" as a covered entity. The U.S. Department of Health and Human Services defines covered entities as individuals, organizations, and agencies who must comply with the Rules' requirements to protect the privacy and security of health information and must provide individuals with certain rights with respect to their health information.

The most significant change resulting from HITECH, however, is the addition of breach notification rules. HITECH requires that covered entities provide notice of a breach to impacted individuals within 60 days after discovery of the breach.

2.2 General Data Protection Regulation (GDPR)

Effective May 2018, GDPR became the European Union's general applicability law regulating the privacy of data. GDPR provides circumstances when it is lawful to process personal data, such as with proper consent or when complying with a legal obligation. This law is one of the strictest privacy laws in the world, as it imposes steep penalties for violators, with fines reaching millions of dollars. Although enacted by the EU, the law's scope extends beyond the EU. GDPR applies to any of the following:

- Data processors based in the EU, even if the actual processing takes place outside of the EU

- Data processors not based in the EU if the processor is offering goods or services to those in the EU or is monitoring the behavior of those in the EU

- Data processors not based in the EU but where EU law applies via public international law (e.g., EU embassies)

GDPR provides six principles that must be followed when processing data:

- **Lawfulness, Fairness, Transparency:** Data must be processed lawfully, fairly, and in a transparent manner.

- **Purpose Limitation:** Data must be processed for specified, explicit, and legitimate purposes. Further processing beyond the purpose is permitted for public interest archiving, scientific or historical research, or statistical purposes.

- **Data Minimization:** Data processing must be adequate, relevant, and limited to what is necessary for the purpose.

- **Accuracy:** Data must be accurate and kept updated.

- **Storage Limitation:** Data must be stored only for as long as is necessary. Storing it for longer periods is permitted for public interest archiving, scientific or historical research, or statistical purposes.

- **Integrity and Confidentiality:** Data must be processed securely and protected against unauthorized or unlawful processing, accidental loss, destruction, or damage.

2.2.1 Privacy Shield

To support transatlantic commerce, the European Union (EU) and the United States implemented the Safe Harbor Framework, allowing companies to transfer data between the EU and the United States legally. Ultimately, the EU's court declared the Framework invalid in 2015. As a result, the EU and the United States negotiated the Privacy Shield in 2016 to replace the invalidated Safe Harbor Framework agreement. Then, in July 2020, the EU court declared the Privacy Shield invalid as well.

Until the EU and the United States reach a new agreement, companies that transfer data across the Atlantic live in uncertainty. The U.S. Federal Trade Commission, responsible for enforcing the Privacy Shield in the United States, expects U.S. companies to continue complying with their obligations under the Privacy Shield until further notice.

3 Data Security Standards

3.1 Payment Card Industry Data Security Standard (PCI DSS)

With the rise of cashless transactions, financial institutions in the payment card industry created the PCI (Payment Card Industry) Security Standards Council to enhance payment security. The council created the PCI Data Security Standard (DSS), an applicable framework for entities to promote data security when processing payments. Data subject to PCI DSS includes both cardholder data (e.g., primary account number or PAN, cardholder name, expiration date, and service code) and sensitive authentication data (e.g., full track data, card verification code, PIN). Cardholder data and sensitive authentication data are collectively referred to as account data.

The PCI DSS provides the following six goals and 12 requirements:

Goals	PCI DSS Requirements
Build and Maintain a Secure Network and Systems	1. Install and maintain network security controls. 2. Apply secure configurations to all system components.
Protect Account Data	3. Protect stored account data. 4. Protect cardholder data with strong cryptography during transmission over open, public networks.
Maintain a Vulnerability Management Program	5. Protect all systems and networks from malicious software. 6. Develop and maintain secure systems and software.
Implement Strong Access Control Measures	7. Restrict access to system components and cardholder data through use of need-to-know restrictions. 8. Identify users and authenticate access to system components. 9. Restrict physical access to cardholder data.
Regularly Monitor and Test Networks	10. Log and monitor all access to system components and cardholder data. 11. Test security of systems and networks regularly.
Maintain an Information Security Policy	12. Support information security with organizational policies and programs.

Source: Material from *PCI DSS v4.0 Quick Reference Guide*, © 2022 PCI Security Standards Council.

The following diagram outlines a typical card payment processing network in which these 12 requirements must be applied, which affects retailers, banks, and the card payment processors themselves. The process starts when a customer makes a purchase at a business using either a physical or virtual debit or credit card that is processed on a third-party payment processor's network (also referred to as a card network). The transaction is sent to the business' bank (acquiring bank) using an electronic gateway supplied by the card network. The acquiring bank then submits a payment request to the card network, which routes payment from the customer's bank (issuing bank) to the acquiring bank. Note that the sequence of these steps may vary depending on the card network and payment processor, with variation in the method of authorization, transmission of data and its encryption, tokenization to mask sensitive data, transaction settlement, and compliance practices.

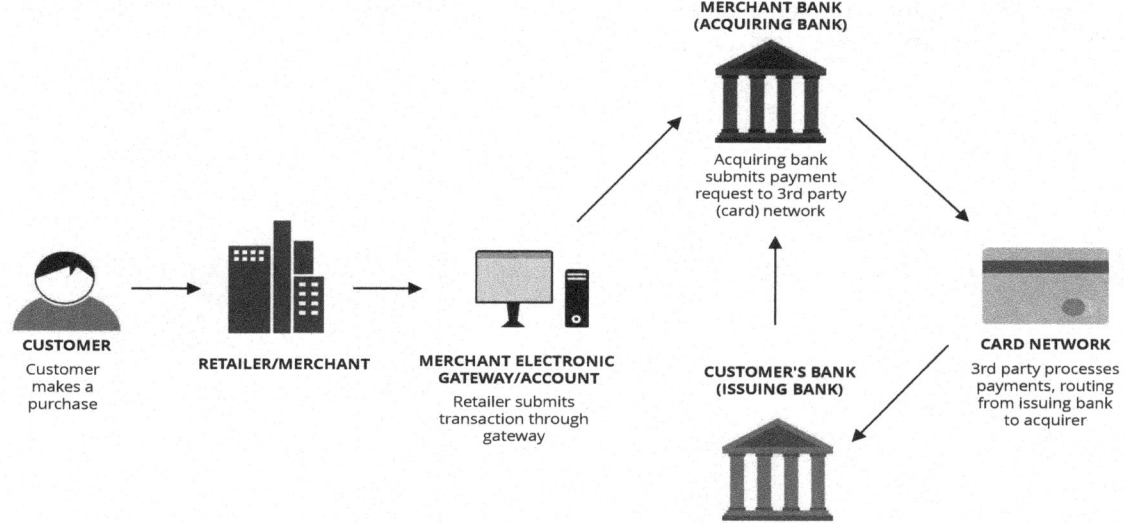

Adhering to each of the 12 PCI DSS requirements in the above payment processing network involves the following:

1. Enforcing, for both physical and software-defined networking technologies, network policies that control network traffic between two or more logical or physical network segments.

2. Establishing formalized processes and procedures to apply secure configurations to all system components and wireless environments. Examples include enforcing strict passwords and removing unnecessary software or functions, etc.

3. Minimizing the storage of account data. Sensitive authentication data should not be stored after authorization. Cardholder data, specifically PAN, should be rendered unreadable through means such as cryptography. Cryptographic keys should be secured and their life cycles should be defined and implemented.

4. Encrypting data in transit when transactions are submitted to the card network across the internet and other public networks.

5. Implementing the use of software to protect against malware and phishing attacks.

6. Ensuring all system components have the most recent critical security patches installed. Internally developed software should adhere to secure development and coding practices. Changes to system components are managed securely.

7. Applying strict requirements to grant access to cardholder data on a need-to-know basis, periodically revoking access when applicable.

8. Every user with access to the cardholder data environment (CDE) must have a unique ID. Every user should have a strong authentication mechanism—such as a strong password, biometric, or access token—and use multifactor authentication for all access to the CDE.

9. Physical access to cardholder data or systems that store, process, or transmit cardholder data should be restricted. The point-of-interaction devices utilized should be protected from tampering and unauthorized substitution.

10. Implementing network monitoring that provides audit trails and log activity that are reviewed for suspicious activity.

11. Performing external vulnerability scanning at least once every three months and achieving a passing score. Penetration testing should be performed regularly to identify both external and internal vulnerabilities.

12. Creating, enforcing, and regularly updating the written policy for each stage of the payment process that outlines the sensitivity of account data and employees' responsibilities and procedures to protect account data.

1 Center for Internet Security (CIS) Controls

1.1 Overview

The Center for Internet Security (CIS) Controls are a recommended set of actions, processes, and best practices that can be adopted and implemented by organizations to strengthen their cybersecurity defenses. CIS Controls were first developed in 2008 by an international consortium and have evolved over time. The controls are currently supported by the SANS Institute, which provides training, administers certification, and performs research. However, each iteration of control updates involves experts across industries, entity-type (government vs. public companies), and job roles (from operators to policy makers).

The controls are now task-focused and organized by activities. There are 18 CIS controls to reflect shifts in the cybersecurity ecosystem to cloud computing, remote work, and virtualization. Each control has recommendations prescribed to achieve the control objective. These recommendations are referred to as the Safeguards.

1.2 Design Principles

The CIS Controls were designed with the following principles in mind:

- **Context:** An enhancement to the scope and practical applicability of safeguards through incorporation of examples and explanations.

- **Coexistence:** Alignment with evolving industry standards and frameworks, including NIST's CSF 2.0 framework.

- **Consistency:** Disruption to controls users are minimized, limiting the impact on implementation groups.

1.3   Implementation Groups

The implementation of the CIS Controls can be tailored to an organization's size by using one of three Implementation Groups (IGs). These are self-assessed categories that identify a subset of the CIS Controls, which are critical for companies to adopt, given their size.

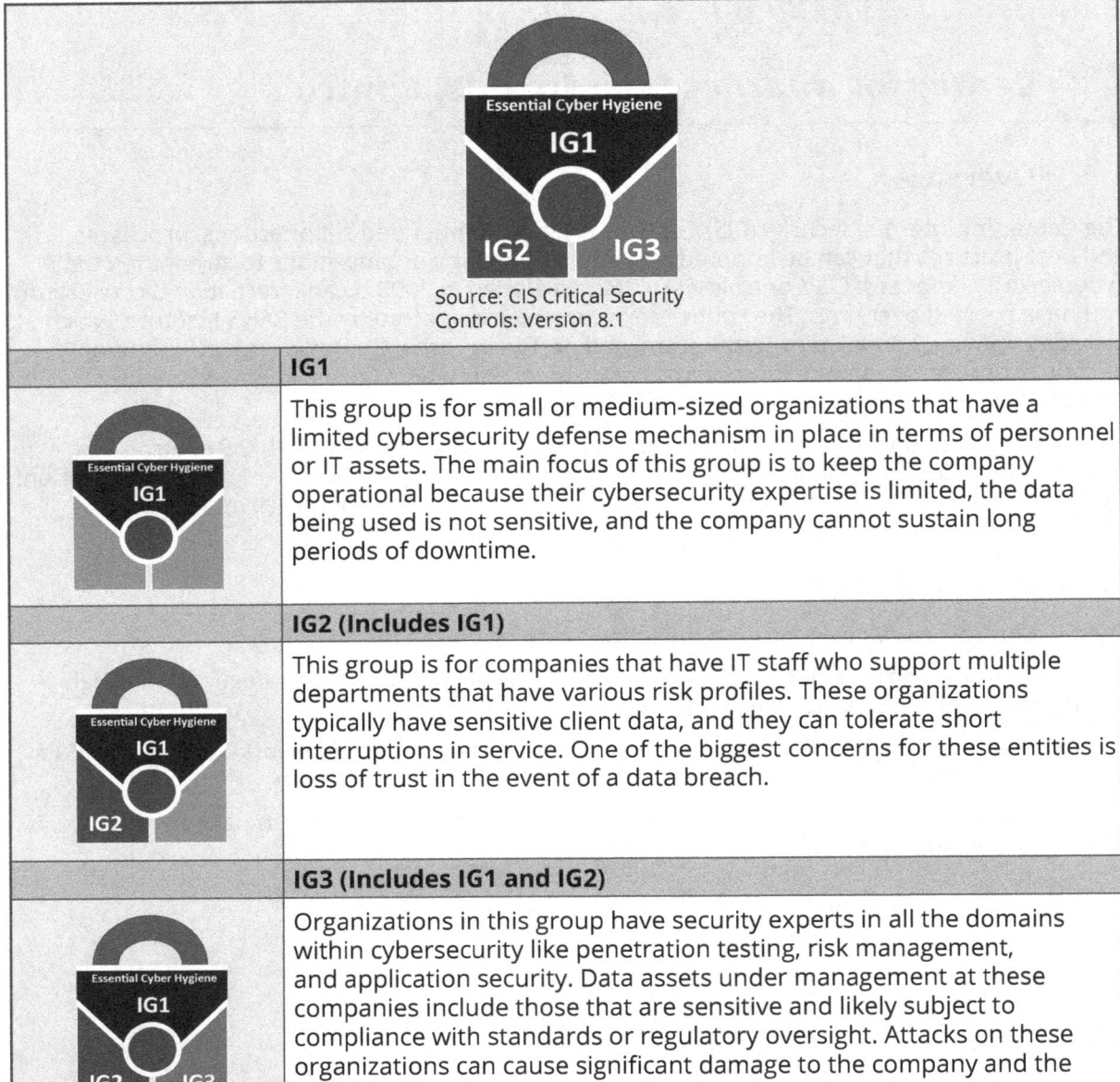

Source: CIS Critical Security Controls: Version 8.1

IG1	
	This group is for small or medium-sized organizations that have a limited cybersecurity defense mechanism in place in terms of personnel or IT assets. The main focus of this group is to keep the company operational because their cybersecurity expertise is limited, the data being used is not sensitive, and the company cannot sustain long periods of downtime.
IG2 (Includes IG1)	
	This group is for companies that have IT staff who support multiple departments that have various risk profiles. These organizations typically have sensitive client data, and they can tolerate short interruptions in service. One of the biggest concerns for these entities is loss of trust in the event of a data breach.
IG3 (Includes IG1 and IG2)	
	Organizations in this group have security experts in all the domains within cybersecurity like penetration testing, risk management, and application security. Data assets under management at these companies include those that are sensitive and likely subject to compliance with standards or regulatory oversight. Attacks on these organizations can cause significant damage to the company and the public welfare.

2   CIS Controls 01–09

2.1   Control 01: Inventory and Control of Enterprise Assets

This control helps organizations actively track and manage all IT assets connected to a company's IT infrastructure physically or virtually within a cloud environment. This allows companies to know the totality of IT assets that should be monitored and protected. Using an IT inventory list, as shown in the following example, will allow organizations to track various data points for company assets:

Asset Description	Serial Number	Model	User	Warranty Expiration	Support End-of-Life Date
Laptop	N4300008A	ProBook 500	Avery Greene	20X5	20X5
Scanner	XCH00R	DesignJet T830	Martin Glenn	20X6	20X7

Having a comprehensive view of company assets will also give visibility into how data flows throughout an organization. Knowing which devices contain sensitive information can help IT managers prioritize the security and maintenance for those devices (e.g., knowing servers and laptops that store employee records should be closely monitored for needed updates, cyber threats, and other irregularities so that unauthorized access is prevented).

Companies should also focus on the potential for external devices to connect to a company's network through means such as guest networks, even if they are segregated from the core network. Other scenarios in which external devices connect to a company's core network include temporary access granted to auditors and permanent access given to managed service providers (MSPs) to manage a company's IT operations.

One challenge organizations face is portable end-user devices that periodically connect to a company's network and then disappear, making it difficult for organizations to have a holistic view of its inventory when devices are off, paused, or otherwise disconnected from the corporate network. Having a robust IT inventory system will mitigate these issues.

The following is a list of the Safeguards (recommendations) within Control 01, along with the asset type associated with the Safeguard, security function, and whether the Safeguard is a priority for an Implementation Group:

Control		Asset Type	Security Function	IG1	IG2	IG3
1.1	Establish and Maintain Detailed Asset Inventory	Devices	Identify	●	●	●
1.2	Address Unauthorized Assets	Devices	Respond	●	●	●
1.3	Utilize an Active Discovery Tool	Devices	Detect		●	●
1.4	Use DHCP Logging to Update Company Inventory—Helps detect which devices are active on the network.	Devices	Identify		●	●
1.5	Use a Passive Asset Discovery Tool—Identifies devices connected to a company's network.	Devices	Detect			●

Source: CIS Critical Security Controls Version 8.1

2.2 Control 02: Inventory and Control of Software Assets

This control provides recommendations for organizations to track and actively manage all software applications so that only authorized software is installed on company devices. This control also provides guidance on finding unmanaged and unauthorized software already installed so that it can be removed and remediated.

Software within scope consists of operating systems, programming software and library, business applications, drivers, open-source software, application programming interface (API), and some forms of firmware, which is embedded software that comes standard in hardware such as a scanner or printer.

Allowlisting (also known as whitelisting) should be in place so that only approved software is installed on company devices. Maintaining a software inventory list keeps the company informed on whether the most current software patches are installed, applications reaching end-of-life support are renewed or transitioned out, and any additional safeguards needed are in place to compensate for software-related risks.

One popular method of managing software applications is using tools that provide an inventory check against commonly used applications in other companies. Such tools reference information regarding each application's patch level, latest version installed, and naming structure.

Control	Asset Type	Security Function	IG1	IG2	IG3
2.1 Establish and Maintain a Software Inventory	Software	Identify	○	●	●
2.2 Ensure Authorized Software Is Currently Supported	Software	Identify	○	●	●
2.3 Address Unauthorized Software	Software	Respond	○	●	●
2.4 Utilize Automated Software Inventory Tools	Software	Detect		●	●
2.5 Allowlist Authorized Software—Ensures only authorized software can be accessed or executed.	Software	Protect		●	●
2.6 Allowlist Authorized Libraries—Ensures that only specific files can be loaded into a system process.	Software	Protect		●	●
2.7 Allowlist Authorized Scripts—Ensures only authorized scripts, or lines of code, can be executed.	Software	Protect			●

Source: CIS Critical Security Controls Version 8.1

2.3 Control 03: Data Protection

This control helps organizations develop ways to securely manage the entire life cycle of their data, from the initial identification and classification data to its disposal.

Organizations must identify, archive, label, and classify their data to understand the implications of the data being lost or compromised. Classification categories are labeled at the discretion of the enterprise and should be assigned based on sensitivity, such as internal, public, sensitive, and confidential. These labels will vary by industry and each country's relevant regulations, privacy requirements, and compliance obligations.

After sensitivity is defined, data mapping should be developed that identifies the various software applications that access each of these sensitivity levels. This would allow devices and software to be consolidated into one network so that more sensitive classifications are separate from less sensitive forms of data. Retention requirements, access control lists, access logging mechanisms, and data disposal plans can also be implemented in a tailored fashion once data classification levels are assigned. Encryption can be strategically used to further secure data at rest and in transit so that data compromise is avoided.

Control	Asset Type	Security Function	IG1	IG2	IG3
3.1 Establish and Maintain a Data Management Process	Data	Govern	●	●	●
3.2 Establish and Maintain a Data Inventory	Data	Identify	●	●	●
3.3 Configure Data Access Control Lists	Data	Protect	●	●	●
3.4 Enforce Data Retention	Data	Protect	●	●	●
3.5 Securely Dispose of Data	Data	Protect	●	●	●
3.6 Encrypt Data on End-User Devices	Data	Protect	●	●	●
3.7 Establish and Maintain a Data Classification Scheme	Data	Identify		●	●
3.8 Document Data Flows	Data	Identify		●	●
3.9 Encrypt Data on Removable Media	Data	Protect		●	●
3.10 Encrypt Sensitive Data in Transit	Data	Protect		●	●
3.11 Encrypt Sensitive Data at Rest	Data	Protect		●	●
3.12 Segment Data Processing and Storage Based on Sensitivity	Data	Protect		●	●
3.13 Deploy a Data Loss Prevention Solution	Data	Protect			●
3.14 Log Sensitive Data Access	Data	Detect			●

Source: CIS Critical Security Controls Version 8.1

2.4   Control 04: Secure Configuration of Enterprise Assets and Software

This control helps organizations establish and maintain secure baseline configurations for their enterprise assets, including servers, network devices, mobile and portable end-user devices, non-computing assets such as Internet of Things (IoT) devices, operating systems, and other corporately managed hardware or software.

Many applications are sold preconfigured with default configuration settings that were designed for ease of installation or usage. However, default configurations may present vulnerabilities that can be exploited, allowing unauthorized users to gain access to an organization's core network. This means organizations should implement control activities to assess preconfigured devices at their baseline state, modify vulnerable configuration settings, and eventually move to a continuous review phase.

It is worth noting that the cloud environment provided by cloud service providers (CSPs) may not be setup in the most secure configuration in order to provide flexibility to their customers. Re-mediating the vulnerability would fall on the enterprises using the platform or services instead of the CSPs.

Publicly available security standards, such as the CIS Benchmarks Program or NIST National Checklist Program Repository, can be used by organizations as a starting point for asset reconfiguration. Adhering to these standards will also assist in complying with any applicable laws and regulations.

Security hardening, which is the process of making an organization less vulnerable to attacks, can be incorporated into adjusting target security configurations so that they are continuously "hardened" against new forms of attack. These improvements may include removing any unused or unnecessary software, closing network ports that are openly exposed to the internet, changing default passwords, and turning off nonessential services.

Security tools such as firewalls, intrusion detection/prevention systems, data loss prevention (DLP) systems, and mobile device management (MDM) software can also be used to secure networks and end-user devices. Organizations with multiple types of environments or data classification levels may have several security baselines that should be addressed. Once target configuration levels have been implemented, they should be continuously monitored for deviations and necessary updates.

Control	Asset Type	Security Function	IG1	IG2	IG3
4.1 Establish and Maintain a Secure Configuration Process	Documentation	Govern	●	●	●
4.2 Establish and Maintain a Secure Configuration Process for Network Infrastructure	Documentation	Govern	●	●	●
4.3 Configure Automatic Session Locking on Enterprise Assets	Devices	Protect	●	●	●
4.4 Implement and Manage a Firewall on Servers	Devices	Protect	●	●	●
4.5 Implement and Manage a Firewall on End-User Devices	Devices	Protect	●	●	●
4.6 Securely Manage Enterprise Assets and Software	Devices	Protect	●	●	●
4.7 Manage Default Accounts on Enterprise Assets and Software	Users	Protect	●	●	●
4.8 Uninstall or Disable Unnecessary Services on Enterprise Assets and Software	Devices	Protect		●	●
4.9 Configure Trust DNS Servers on Enterprise Assets	Devices	Protect		●	●
4.10 Enforce Automatic Device Lockout on Portable End-User Devices	Devices	Protect		●	●
4.11 Enforce Remote Wipe Capability on Portable End-User Devices	Data	Protect		●	●
4.12 Separate Enterprise Workspaces on Mobile End-User Devices	Data	Protect			●

Source: CIS Critical Security Controls Version 8.1

2.5 Control 05: Account Management

This control outlines best practices for companies to manage credentials and authorization for user accounts, privileged user accounts (such as administrator accounts), and service accounts for company hardware and software.

As with other enterprise assets, accounts must be inventoried and tracked so that appropriate controls may be applied. Centralized account management tools and services can be utilized for consolidated account management across the organization. Organizations should develop and communicate an acceptable use policy and account safety guidelines. Credentials should be treated as highly sensitive information, and formal training should be provided to educate users on account safety best practices as well as the organization's account security policies. These may include password requirements, controls for inactivity, and account lockout policies.

Administrator accounts should be restricted to specific use cases. End-users requiring administrator privileges should have separate accounts to run administrative actions to lower the risk of a user's account being compromised because these accounts are more likely to be targeted by attackers. Service accounts used to run systems and services must be well-documented, indicating ownership and purpose.

▪ Single Sign-on and Multifactor Authentication

One common and convenient form of authentication is single sign-on (SSO). This lets users use a single log-in to securely authenticate across multiple applications. While this increases the number of applications an attacker can gain access to with a single password, security can be enhanced using multifactor authentication (MFA) so that the users must have a secondary point of contact to validate their identity.

	Control	Asset Type	Security Function	IG1	IG2	IG3
5.1	Establish and Maintain an Inventory of Accounts	Users	Identify	○	●	●
5.2	Use Unique Passwords	Users	Protect	○	●	●
5.3	Disable Dormant Accounts	Users	Protect	○	●	●
5.4	Restrict Administrator Privileges to Dedicated Administrator Accounts	Users	Protect	○	●	●
5.5	Establish and Maintain an Inventory of Service Accounts	Users	Identify		●	●
5.6	Centralize Account Management	Users	Govern		●	●

Source: CIS Critical Security Controls Version 8.1

2.6 Control 06: Access Control Management

This control expands on Account Management (Control 05) by specifying the type of access that user accounts should have. Ideally, an organization's users should only have the necessary privileges required for their job role.

Organizations should follow the principles of "least privilege" and "need-to-know" role assignments. These methodologies assist with the goal that users only have access to systems, services, and data needed to perform their job duties. Accounts that do not follow these principles pose a security risk to the organization by allowing unauthorized access.

Protocols should be put in place for granting access and revoking access based on job duties, roles, and responsibilities. Access control models, such as role-based access control (RBAC) or policy-based access control (PBAC), can be utilized to help facilitate this process by defining roles within the organization and assigning appropriate access to each role to provide separation of duties. For accounts with administrator access or remote access, additional controls such as multifactor authentication (MFA) and privileged account management (PAM) can be used as an additional security layer.

A comprehensive solution, ideally centralized, for provisioning and de-provisioning employee access should also be in place. Sophisticated methods allow access to all applications across the organization to be removed synchronously within minutes of initiating such a change in the system.

	Control	Asset Type	Security Function	IG1	IG2	IG3
6.1	Establish an Access Granting Process	Documentation	Govern	○	●	●
6.2	Establish an Access Revoking Process	Documentation	Govern	○	●	●
6.3	Require Multifactor Authentication for Externally Exposed Applications	Users	Protect	○	●	●
6.4	Require Multifactor Authentication for Remote Network Access	Users	Protect	○	●	●
6.5	Require Multifactor Authentication for Administrative Access	Users	Protect	○	●	●
6.6	Establish and Maintain an Inventory of Authentication and Authorization Systems	Software	Identify		●	●
6.7	Centralize Access Control	Users	Protect		●	●
6.8	Define and Maintain Role-Based Access Control	Users	Govern			●

Source: CIS Critical Security Controls Version 8.1

2.7   Control 07: Continuous Vulnerability Management

This control assists organizations in continuously identifying and tracking vulnerabilities within their infrastructure so that they can remediate and eliminate weak points or windows of opportunity for bad actors.

An evolving cybersecurity landscape requires organizations to keep abreast of threats and vulnerabilities to be able to defend against them. Attackers can exploit and leverage vulnerabilities to compromise assets and gain a foothold into a company's network. Unknown vulnerabilities, referred to as zero-day exploits, occur when there is no known solution to a weak point. In these instances, attackers can carry out attacks for which there is not yet any remediation.

Organizations must remain proactive in scanning, monitoring, and managing vulnerabilities to reduce the window of opportunity for attackers to capitalize on them. As new vulnerabilities are discovered, they should be assessed for their likelihood of exploitation and impact if they occur so that they can be ranked and prioritized. It is preferable to use vulnerability scanning tools that map vulnerabilities to industry-recognized publications such as Common Vulnerabilities and Exposures (CVE®), Common Configuration Enumeration (CCE), Open Vulnerability and Assessment Language (OVAL®), Common Platform Enumeration (CPE), Common Vulnerability Scoring System (CVSS), and/or Extensible Configuration Checklist Description Format (XCCDF).

	Control	Asset Type	Security Function	IG1	IG2	IG3
7.1	Establish and Maintain a Vulnerability Management Process	Documentation	Govern	◐	●	●
7.2	Establish and Maintain a Remediation Process	Documentation	Govern	◐	●	●
7.3	Perform Automated Operating System Patch Management	Software	Protect	◐	●	●
7.4	Perform Automated Application Patch Management	Software	Protect	◐	●	●
7.5	Perform Automated Vulnerability Scans of Internal Enterprise Assets	Software	Identify		●	●
7.6	Perform Automated Vulnerability Scans of Externally Exposed Enterprise Assets	Software	Identify		●	●
7.7	Remediate Detected Vulnerabilities	Software	Respond		●	●

Source: CIS Critical Security Controls Version 8.1

2.8   Control 08: Audit Log Management

This control establishes an enterprise log management process so that organizations can be alerted and recover from an attack in real time, or near real time, using log collection and analytic features. There are two log categories that are frequently configured independently, system logs and audit logs, which provide valuable information that can be used for prevention, troubleshooting, incident response, discovering patterns, and detecting anomalies.

System logs provide a list of events such as start and end times, points of restoration, and system crashes. Audit logs are tied to a specific user, recording when a person logs in or out, accesses a file, or opens an application.

▦ Event Logs

Having access to event logs is critical to incident response, and it can also facilitate processes for legal matters, such as eDiscovery, accountability for auditing, lessons learned for process improvement, and data retention for compliance requirements. An enterprise log management process should address the entire life cycle of audit logs beginning with log collection and ending with log disposal. Audit logs may be captured from a variety of connection methods, whether directly to a company's network via a hard-wired connection, wirelessly, or using a virtual private network (VPN). Organizations should also be notified when failed user attempts are made to connect to resources without the appropriate privileges.

Control	Asset Type	Security Function	IG1	IG2	IG3
8.1 Establish and Maintain an Audit Log Management Process	Documentation	Govern	●	●	●
8.2 Collect Audit Logs	Data	Detect	●	●	●
8.3 Ensure Adequate Audit Log Storage	Data	Protect	●	●	●
8.4 Standardize Time Synchronization	Data	Protect		●	●
8.5 Collect Detailed Audit Logs	Data	Detect		●	●
8.6 Collect DNS Query Audit Logs	Data	Detect		●	●
8.7 Collect URL Request Audit Logs	Data	Detect		●	●
8.8 Collect Command-Line Audit Logs	Data	Detect		●	●
8.9 Centralize Audit Logs	Data	Detect		●	●
8.10 Retain Audit Logs	Data	Protect		●	●
8.11 Conduct Audit Log Reviews	Data	Detect		●	●
8.12 Collect Service Provider Logs	Data	Detect			●

Source: CIS Critical Security Controls Version 8.1

2.9   Control 09: Email and Web Browser Protections

This control provides recommendations on how to detect and protect against cybercrime attempted through email or the internet by directly engaging employees. Email clients and web browsers provide attackers direct access to users who make them vulnerable to social engineering tactics and delivering malicious payloads.

Attacks such as phishing scams and business email compromise (BEC) can be conducted by attackers using email to target senior executives who control data and financial resources or target high-value assets with data that could be used for exploitation or financial gain. Email client and web browser vulnerabilities can also be exploited to introduce malware into an organization's network, so only supported and updated versions should be used.

Web browser attacks can come in the form of exploiting vulnerabilities from insecure or unpatched browsers. Another common form is to target plugins, extensions, and add-ons. It is recommended that policies and tools be put in place to enforce URL filtering, block certain file types, and restrict options such as the ability for users to install add-ons. URL blocking can be done through domain name system (DNS) filtering, which effectively blocks users from accessing certain domains on a blacklist.

Control		Asset Type	Security Function	IG1	IG2	IG3
9.1	Ensure Use of Only Fully Supported Browsers and Email Clients	Software	Protect	●	●	●
9.2	Use DNS Filtering Services	Devices	Protect	●	●	●
9.3	Maintain and Enforce Network-Based URL Filters	Network	Protect		●	●
9.4	Restrict Unnecessary or Unauthorized Browser and Email Client Extensions	Software	Protect		●	●
9.5	Implement Domain-Based Message Authentication Reporting and Conformance	Network	Protect		●	●
9.6	Block Unnecessary File Types	Network	Protect		●	●
9.7	Deploy and Maintain Email Server Anti-Malware Protections	Network	Protect			●

Source: CIS Critical Security Controls Version 8.1

NOTES

1 CIS Controls 10–18

The Center for Internet Security (CIS) Controls are a recommended set of actions, processes, and best practices that can be adopted and implemented by organizations to strengthen their cybersecurity defenses. Within the 18 controls are 153 subcategories called Safeguards, which are the recommendations prescribed to achieve each control objective.

1.1 Control 10: Malware Defenses

This control assists companies in preventing the installation and propagation of malware onto company assets and its network.

Malware can infiltrate as viruses, worms, spyware, adware, keyloggers, and ransomware. Endpoint assets and devices can be leveraged as both entry points and targets for malware. Malware can cause substantial damage to an organization by stealing intellectual property or log-in credentials, destroying data, encrypting data for ransom, or executing other nefarious activities. Malware frequently relies on insecure end-user behavior, such as clicking links, opening attachments, installing software, or inserting flash drives to infiltrate the organization.

Anti-malware solutions should be automated, centrally managed, maintained, and deployed to all potential entry points. Security features that prevent the execution of malicious code should be enabled where possible and any software autorun or autoplay features should be disabled by default.

As malware defenses become better at defending against threats, some malicious actors have adjusted their tactics to what is known as LotL, or "living-off-the-land." This approach minimizes the likelihood that an attacker will get caught by using an organization's existing tools against itself. Existing tools and applications typically already have access to a wide variety of company applications, allowing the perpetrator a quick window into a company's systems.

Illustration 1   Malware Impacting Medical Records

Family Practice Medical Inc. (FPMI) is a national chain of health care clinics that offer primary and emergent care services to more than 50,000 patients. Through their website, a group of organized cybercriminals was able to identify an open port through which they gained access to FPMI's network. Once they were in, one of the attackers was able to open the company's Windows Management Instrumentation (WMI) interface, which is the primary means the company uses to access credentials, manage security and antivirus software, and manage file storage. Because the team of attackers was able to turn off security flags and remove files using WMI, they successfully extracted hundreds of thousands of medical records and payment information without being detected.

Control	Asset Type	Security Function	IG1	IG2	IG3
10.1 Deploy and Maintain Anti-Malware Software	Devices	Detect	○	●	●
10.2 Configure Automatic Anti-Malware Signature Updates	Devices	Protect	○	●	●
10.3 Disable Autorun and Autoplay for Removable Media	Devices	Protect	○	●	●
10.4 Configure Automatic Anti-Malware Scanning of Removable Media	Devices	Detect		●	●
10.5 Enable Anti-Exploitation Features	Devices	Protect		●	●
10.6 Centrally Manage Anti-Malware Software	Devices	Protect		●	●
10.7 Use Behavior-Based Anti-Malware Software	Devices	Detect		●	●

Source: CIS Critical Security Controls Version 8.1

1.2   Control 11: Data Recovery

This control establishes data backup, testing, and restoration processes that allow organizations to effectively recover company assets to a pre-incident state.

Organizational data is a critical resource for conducting business and can be targeted by ransomware attacks that encrypt data and leave criminals demanding ransom for its restoration. Human error, misconfigurations, and natural factors (power outages, flooding, etc.) can also cause data to become unusable or unavailable. Therefore, organizations must establish processes to enable the recovery and restoration of data to a prior trusted state.

Data value, sensitivity, classification, and retention requirements all factor into the mechanisms and cadence that will be used for backup and storage methods. Automating the backup process, utilizing off-site storage in a different geographical location, and using encryption are all recommended practices. These functions should be tested at least once per quarter to confirm the protocols and technology in place will work properly. It is also recommended to restore files using a test bed environment.

Control	Asset Type	Security Function	IG1	IG2	IG3
11.1 Establish and Maintain a Data Recovery Process	Documentation	Govern	○	●	●
11.2 Perform Automated Backups	Data	Recover	○	●	●
11.3 Protect Recovery Data	Data	Protect	○	●	●
11.4 Establish and Maintain an Isolated Instance of Recovery Data	Data	Recover	○	●	●
11.5 Test Data Recovery	Data	Recover		●	●

Source: CIS Critical Security Controls Version 8.1

1.3   Control 12: Network Infrastructure Management

This control establishes procedures and tools for managing and securing a company's network infrastructure. Network infrastructure includes both physical and virtual devices, such as firewalls, gateways, routers, switches, and wireless access points.

Network architecture documentation and diagrams should be kept up-to-date to accurately reflect the organization's network topology and layout. Additionally, that documentation should have critical vendor contact information to increase the likelihood that system upgrades or patches are implemented in a timely manner. Companies should monitor for end-of-life network components to make the appropriate upgrades prior to the end date or establish mitigating controls.

Organizations must continuously identify and remediate insecure default network configuration settings, misconfigured network settings, insecure protocol usage, and outdated network software. There are commercial tools available to help fulfill this requirement by evaluating a company's network against a set of rules to determine whether they are in conflict. These tools provide sanity checks and should be run every time a significant change is made to firewalls, access controls lists, or other filtering mechanisms in place.

Control	Asset Type	Security Function	IG1	IG2	IG3
12.1 Ensure Network Infrastructure Is Up-to-Date	Network	Protect	●	●	●
12.2 Establish and Maintain a Secure Network Architecture	Network	Protect		●	●
12.3 Securely Manage Network Infrastructure	Network	Protect		●	●
12.4 Establish and Maintain Architecture Diagram(s)	Documentation	Govern		●	●
12.5 Centralize Network Authentication, Authorization, and Auditing	Network	Protect		●	●
12.6 Use of Secure Network Management and Communication Protocols	Network	Protect		●	●
12.7 Ensure Remote Devices Utilize a VPN and Are Connecting to an Enterprise's AAA Infrastructure	Devices	Protect		●	●
12.8 Establish and Maintain Dedicated Computing Resources for All Administrative Work	Devices	Protect			●

Source: CIS Critical Security Controls Version 8.1

1.4   Control 13: Network Monitoring and Defense

This control establishes processes for monitoring and defending a company's network infrastructure against internal and external security threats. Even though network monitoring and defense software solutions may be highly proficient when purchased, there is still some degree of fine-tuning that is specific to a company's network that is required. There is, nevertheless, the possibility of human error or new attack schemes that were not common at the time of the network system's inception. Therefore, continuous monitoring is critical to keep pace with an evolving cybersecurity landscape.

■ Denial of Service (DoS) and Ransomware

Two common ways networks can be attacked include denial of service (DoS) attacks and ransomware. DoS attacks involve a perpetrator overwhelming a company's network by flooding the network with illegitimate requests so that it is effectively rendered useless. Ransomware attacks are situations in which an attacker or group of attackers gain access to a company's system, block employees from accessing it, demand payment to regain access, and threaten to either keep all systems blocked or publish sensitive data to the public (or dark web) if the company doesn't comply.

To combat these schemes, organizations should establish event logging and alerting mechanisms that can be implemented through tools such as security information and event management (SIEM) to help centralize and assist in log analysis. Traffic flow monitoring, alerting, and detection safeguards can also be implemented with tools such as network intrusion prevention systems (NIPS), next-generation firewalls (NGFW), data loss prevention (DLP) systems, and endpoint detection and response (EDR) systems.

Many organizations have their own security or network operations center (often referred to as the SOC or NOC, respectively) that is uniquely equipped to run a robust IT networking operation and champion the creation and maintenance of a knowledge base and a situation awareness program. Smaller organizations often do not have the resources to employ such a large team, so they outsource their IT function to managed service providers (MSPs) to access these services.

Control	Asset Type	Security Function	IG1	IG2	IG3
13.1 Centralize Security Event Alerting	Network	Detect		●	●
13.2 Deploy a Host-Based Intrusion Detection Solution	Devices	Detect		●	●
13.3 Deploy a Network Intrusion Detection Solution	Network	Detect		●	●
13.4 Perform Traffic Filtering Between Network Segments	Network	Protect		●	●
13.5 Manage Access Controls for Remote Assets	Devices	Protect		●	●
13.6 Collect Network Traffic Flow Logs	Network	Detect		●	●
13.7 Deploy a Host-Based Intrusion Prevention Solution	Devices	Protect			●
13.8 Deploy a Network Intrusion Prevention Solution	Network	Protect			●
13.9 Deploy Port-Level Access Control	Network	Protect			●
13.10 Perform Application Layer Filtering	Network	Protect			●
13.11 Tune Security Event Alerting Thresholds	Network	Detect			●

Source: CIS Critical Security Controls Version 8.1

1.5   Control 14: Security Awareness and Skills Training

This control guides organizations in establishing a security awareness and training program to reduce cybersecurity risk. One of the goals of this type of training is to influence employee behavior in a way that makes them conscious about the various tactics that can be employed by attackers that allow unauthorized access.

Uninformed employees pose one of the greatest risks to the security of an organization, and risks can originate externally or internally. Social engineering techniques targeting enterprise workforces can lead to significant business disruption, financial losses, and loss of reputation. Human error, negligence, and misuse of organizational assets can also introduce security issues.

Regular training is one of the best ways to establish security awareness, including educating staff on recognition of unusual behavior, social engineering tactics, best practices for handling organizational assets and data, and the risks involved with using insecure networks and devices. Staff should also understand the organization's processes for reporting incidents, issues, and concerns.

Training should not be reduced to an annual occurrence. Rather, it should be more frequent and include messages that resonate with users, such as the impact of recent data breaches at well-known companies, the rise of phishing scams during tax season, or information on phony gift rewards sent via email.

Control	Asset Type	Security Function	IG1	IG2	IG3
14.1 Establish and Maintain a Security Awareness Program	Documentation	Govern	○	●	●
14.2 Train Workforce Members to Recognize Social Engineering Attacks	Users	Protect	○	●	●
14.3 Train Workforce Members on Authentication Best Practices	Users	Protect	○	●	●
14.4 Train Workforce on Data Handling Best Practices	Users	Protect	○	●	●
14.5 Train Workforce Members on Causes of Unintentional Data Exposure	Users	Protect	○	●	●
14.6 Train Workforce Members on Recognizing and Reporting Security Incidents	Users	Protect	○	●	●
14.7 Train Workforce on How to Identify and Report if Their Enterprise Assets Are Missing Security Updates	Users	Protect	○	●	●
14.8 Train Workforce on Dangers of Connecting to and Transmitting Enterprise Data Over Insecure Networks	Users	Protect	○	●	●
14.9 Conduct Role-Specific Security Awareness and Skills Training	Users	Protect		●	●

Source: CIS Critical Security Controls Version 8.1

1.6   Control 15: Service Provider Management

This control helps organizations develop processes to evaluate third-party service providers that have access to sensitive data or that are responsible for managing some or all of a company's IT functions. Proper controls in this area enhance the likelihood that a company's data, applications, and hardware are protected adequately.

Risks can be introduced by third-party service providers that do not hold themselves to the same security standards as other organizations. Part of the reason for this disparity in organizational standards is that there are only a few industry standards available in the public domain. Examples of such standards include the Shared Assessments program for the finance industry and the Higher Education Community Vendor Assessment Toolkit (HECVAT) for higher education.

As such, it is recommended that companies establish service provider management processes to oversee the entire service provider life cycle. Service providers should be assessed, including their associated risk rating and potential impact to the business in case of an incident, and their performance and standards should be catalogued from initial engagement through decommissioning for adherence to security standards, protocols, and best practices. System and Organization Controls (SOC) audit reports can be used to assess the risks of doing business with service providers.

Control	Asset Type	Security Function	IG1	IG2	IG3
15.1 Establish and Maintain an Inventory of Service Providers	Users	Identify	●	●	●
15.2 Establish and Maintain a Service Provider Management Policy	Documentation	Govern		●	●
15.3 Classify Service Providers	Users	Govern		●	●
15.4 Ensure Service Provider Contracts Include Security Requirements	Documentation	Govern		●	●
15.5 Assess Service Providers	Users	Govern			●
15.6 Monitor Service Providers	Data	Govern			●
15.7 Securely Decommission Service Providers	Data	Protect			●

Source: CIS Critical Security Controls Version 8.1

1.7   Control 16: Application Software Security

This control establishes safeguards that manage the entire life cycle of software that is acquired, hosted, or developed in-house to detect, deter, and resolve cybersecurity weaknesses before they are exploited. This is becoming more challenging in today's environment because software development life cycles have shortened and have become more complex because software applications are often a mix of various sources of existing code, libraries, and new code. Instead of being created from scratch, many new applications are aggregations of these various sources, making it critical to understand the facets of each to thwart bad actors.

Software vulnerabilities may exist for various reasons like a flawed design, poor infrastructure, coding errors, poor authentication protocols, and the failure to test for software anomalies. Specific types of vulnerabilities mentioned in the CIS Control document for Control 16 include buffer overflows, cross-site scripting (XSS), SQL injections, and race conditions. These vulnerabilities can be leveraged by attackers to escalate privileges (the terms *escalate* and *elevate* are used somewhat interchangeably across standards in the context of privileges), compromise assets, and gain a foothold into the company network.

IT managers must consider whether best practices and safeguards are being followed, such as secure design standards and secure code reviews, and security testing tools are integrated into the software development life cycle (SDLC). It is recommended to introduce application security as early in the SDLC as possible because coding changes as development processes becomes more complex. Processes should also be in place to inventory third-party software components, tools, and applications. Suggested activities include determining whether software is up-to-date, configurations settings are reviewed, and compensating controls are in place for attack mitigation.

One common blind spot modern organizations have is the lack of visibility into Software-as-a-Service (SaaS) platforms. These platforms can be hosted anywhere across the globe and their software development and review processes usually do not involve their clients. As such, companies using SaaS should inquire about such practices and consider obtaining SOC reports to obtain assurance as to whether they operate according to the terms of service-level agreements, especially if the platform is a steward of sensitive employee or customer data.

Some larger organizations may consider implementing a bug bounty program in which employees are paid for finding flaws in company-produced or company-used software. These programs create camaraderie and healthy competition and are effective ways to find software vulnerabilities.

Control	Asset Type	Security Function	IG1	IG2	IG3
16.1 Establish and Maintain a Secure Application Development Process	Documentation	Govern		●	●
16.2 Establish and Maintain a Process to Accept and Address Software Vulnerabilities	Documentation	Govern		●	●
16.3 Perform Root Cause Analysis on Security Vulnerabilities	Software	Protect		●	●
16.4 Establish and Manage an Inventory of Third-Party Software Components	Software	Identify		●	●
16.5 Use Up-to-Date and Trusted Third-Party Software Components	Software	Protect		●	●
16.6 Establish and Maintain a Severity Rating System and Process for Application Vulnerabilities	Documentation	Govern		●	●
16.7 Use Standard Hardening Configuration Templates for Application Infrastructure	Software	Protect		●	●
16.8 Separate Production and Non-Production Systems	Network	Protect		●	●
16.9 Train Developers in Application Security Concepts and Secure Coding	Users	Protect		●	●
16.10 Apply Secure Design Principles in Application Architectures	Software	Protect		●	●
16.11 Leverage Vetted Modules or Services for Application Security Components	Software	Identify		●	●
16.12 Implement Code-Level Security Checks	Software	Protect			●
16.13 Conduct Application Penetration Testing	Software	Govern			●
16.14 Conduct Threat Modeling	Software	Protect			●

Source: CIS Critical Security Controls Version 8.1

1.8 Control 17: Incident Response Management

This control provides the recommendations necessary to establish an incident response management program to detect, respond, and prepare for potential cybersecurity attacks. When security incidents occur, their impact can be widespread throughout the organization.

In certain cases, laws and regulations may require notification of data breaches and impose fines for noncompliance, which makes it imperative to have programs in place to detect, contain, and eliminate threats. Examples include the Health Insurance Portability and Accountability Act (HIPAA), which governs medical information in the United States, or the General Data Protection Regulation (GDPR), which governs data in the European Union.

The incident response process should include the designation of a key contact, establishment of an incident response team, and the development of communication plans for notifying impacted business units, stakeholders, and regulatory agencies. It is also important to periodically carry out exercises to test the incident response process to ascertain its effectiveness and identify opportunities for improvement.

Control	Asset Type	Security Function	IG1	IG2	IG3
17.1 Designate Personnel to Manage Incident Handling	Users	Respond	◯	●	●
17.2 Establish and Maintain Contact Information for Reporting	Documentation	Govern	◯	●	●
17.3 Establish and Maintain an Enterprise Process for Reporting Incidents	Documentation	Govern	◯	●	●
17.4 Establish and Manage an Incident Response Process	Documentation	Govern		●	●
17.5 Assign Key Roles and Responsibilities	Users	Respond		●	●
17.6 Define Mechanisms for Communicating During Incident Response	Users	Respond		●	●
17.7 Conduct Routine Incident Response Exercises	Users	Recover		●	●
17.8 Conduct Post-Incident Reviews	Users	Recover		●	●
17.9 Establish and Maintain Security Incident Thresholds	Documentation	Recover			●

Source: CIS Critical Security Controls Version 8.1

1.9 Control 18: Penetration Testing

This control helps organizations test the sophistication of their cybersecurity defense system in place by simulating actual attacks in an effort to find and exploit weaknesses. Penetration testing is typically performed as a dramatic demonstration of an attack, as a method to verify whether a company's defenses work, and to make sure the company has the right defenses in place.

Penetration testing in this control is different than vulnerability testing in Control 7 in that penetration testing seeks to go beyond identifying weaknesses. It attempts to exploit those weak points and see what additional damage could be done once that first point of failure is reached.

Similar to penetration testing, "Red Team" exercises focus on specific tactics, techniques, and procedures (TTPs) to see how an organization fares against certain types of attackers. Each industry is exposed to a different mix of cybersecurity risks, with some bearing more risk simply due to the nature of the business. For instance, health care companies and financial institutions possess Social Security numbers, banking information, credit cards, and other personal information that can be used to exploit one of their customers.

Illustration 2   Penetration Testing: Payment Transactions

First Payment Network Inc. is a credit card processing company that has developed a new technology that couples biorecognition with payment transactions. First Payment wishes to see how easy it would be to either forge a fingerprint on in-person scanners used for transactions or to bypass the processing card network's code that requires the biometric for validation. To test this technology prior to launching it, First Payment engages an MSP that specializes in Red Team exercises and specifically, financial transactions.

Penetration testing generally begins with a discovery or observation of an organization's environment, followed by scanning to locate vulnerabilities that can be used to gain access. Then those vulnerabilities become targets, and the team of testers exploits those targets to demonstrate how an attacker can bypass controls. The results are then studied, and the company revises its controls accordingly. This process can, and should be, performed at least annually for large organizations with significant cybersecurity risk.

Control	Asset Type	Security Function	IG1	IG2	IG3
18.1 Establish and Maintain a Penetration Testing Program	Documentation	Govern		●	●
18.2 Perform Periodic External Penetration Tests	Network	Detect		●	●
18.3 Remediate Penetration Test Findings	Network	Protect		●	●
18.4 Validate Security Measures	Network	Protect		●	●
18.5 Perform Periodic Internal Penetration Tests	Network	Detect		●	●

Source: CIS Critical Security Controls Version 8.1

NOTES

1 Overview

1.1 Control Objectives for Information and Related Technologies (COBIT)

In 1996, the Information Systems Audit and Control Association (ISACA) developed what would become one of the most widely used enterprise IT governance standards: the Control Objectives for Information and Related Technologies (COBIT). ISACA is a nonprofit that was formed in 1967 by a small group of computing pioneers who formed to help companies and technology professionals manage, optimize, and protect information technology (IT) assets. Since then, ISACA has evolved into a standards and educational organization that spans the globe and has thousands of members.

To accomplish its mission, ISACA created the COBIT framework, which provides a road map that organizations can use to implement best practices for IT governance and management. COBIT was originally developed as a set of standards for auditors that unified multiple different and disparate standards. Over time, the COBIT standards changed and developed with different goals:

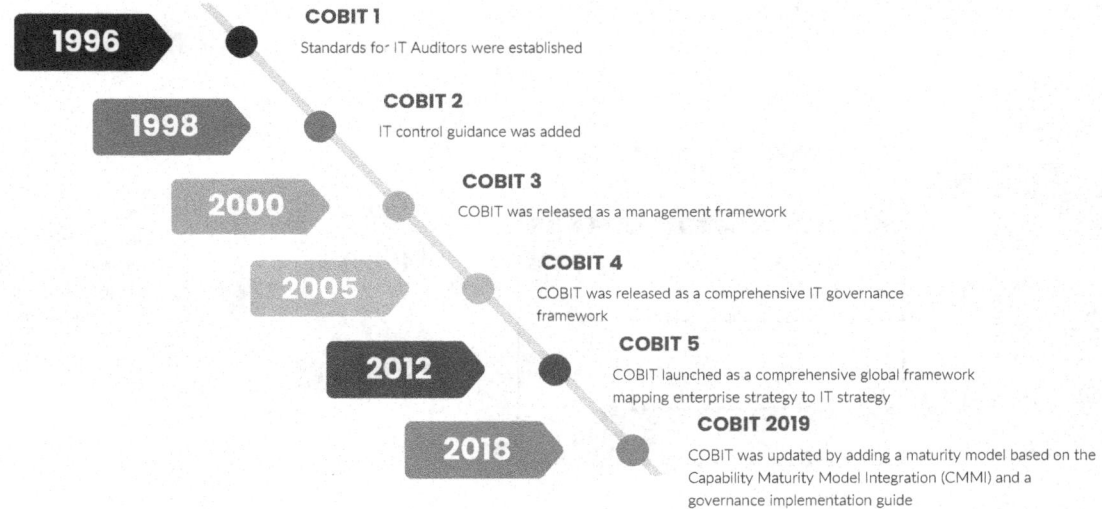

1996 — **COBIT 1**
Standards for IT Auditors were established

1998 — **COBIT 2**
IT control guidance was added

2000 — **COBIT 3**
COBIT was released as a management framework

2005 — **COBIT 4**
COBIT was released as a comprehensive IT governance framework

2012 — **COBIT 5**
COBIT launched as a comprehensive global framework mapping enterprise strategy to IT strategy

2018 — **COBIT 2019**
COBIT was updated by adding a maturity model based on the Capability Maturity Model Integration (CMMI) and a governance implementation guide

1.2 Governance Stakeholders

COBIT distinguishes between governance and management, recognizing them as two unique disciplines that each exist for different reasons and require different sets of organizational resources. Organizational governance is typically the responsibility of a company's board of directors, consisting of a chairperson and focused organizational structures (e.g., audit committee, executive committee, marketing committee).

Management is responsible for the daily planning and administration of company operations, generally consisting of a chief executive officer (CEO), chief financial officer (CFO), chief operations officer (COO), and other executive leaders. Management is selected and guided by the board of directors.

Stakeholders can be either internal or external, with the board of directors and management considered internal. Other internal stakeholders include business managers, IT managers, assurance providers, and risk managers. External stakeholders include regulators, investors, business partners, and IT vendors, parties who are entitled to some information about compliance and risk mitigation but are not entitled to the same information given to internal stakeholders.

1.3 COBIT® 2019 Overview

As part of its foundation, COBIT® 2019 was developed using the following:

- COBIT 5
- Six principles for a governance system
- Three principles for a governance framework
- Other standards and regulations
- Community contribution

These principles, standards, and regulations were used to form the COBIT core model, which can then be customized through Design Factors and Focus Areas to arrive at a tailored enterprise governance system for any organization.

The following graphic depicts the inputs of the core model, the path that organizations can take to customize the application of the model, and the underlying publications that can be used as a road map to implement the COBIT framework:

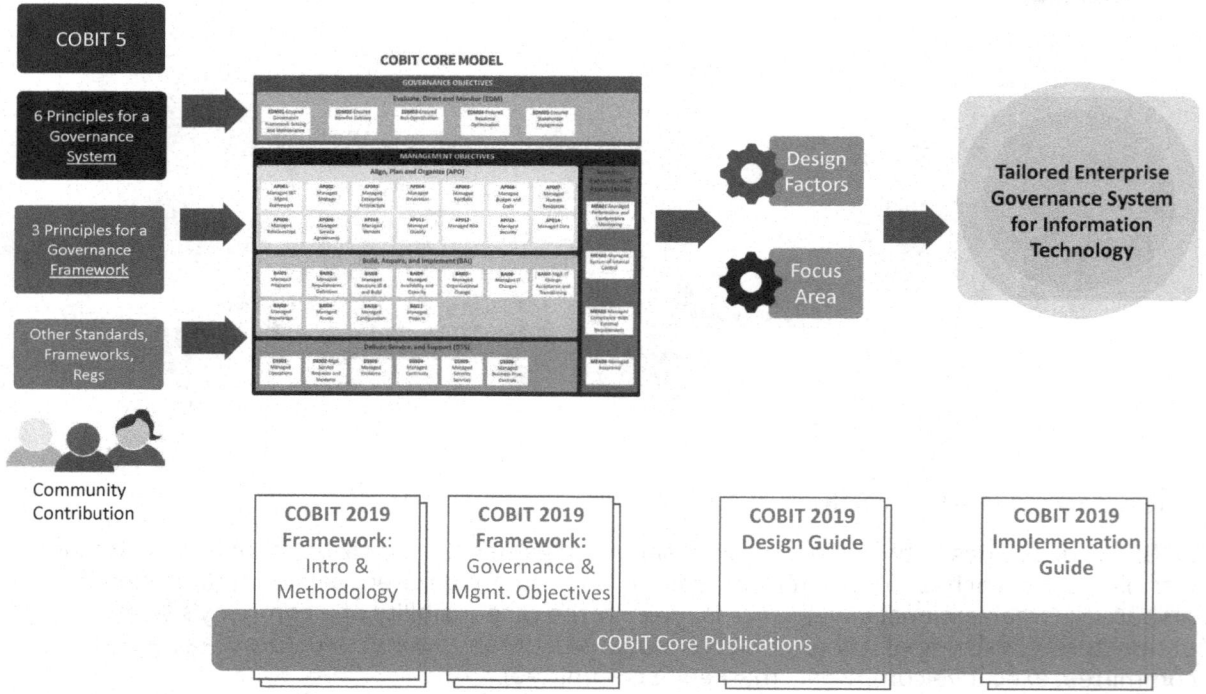

Material from COBIT®, © 2019 ISACA. All rights reserved. Used with permission.

2 Governance System Principles

2.1 Six Principles for a Governance System

The six principles outlined for a governance system that were used to develop the COBIT 2019 core model are shown below.

GOVERNANCE SYSTEM PRINCIPLES

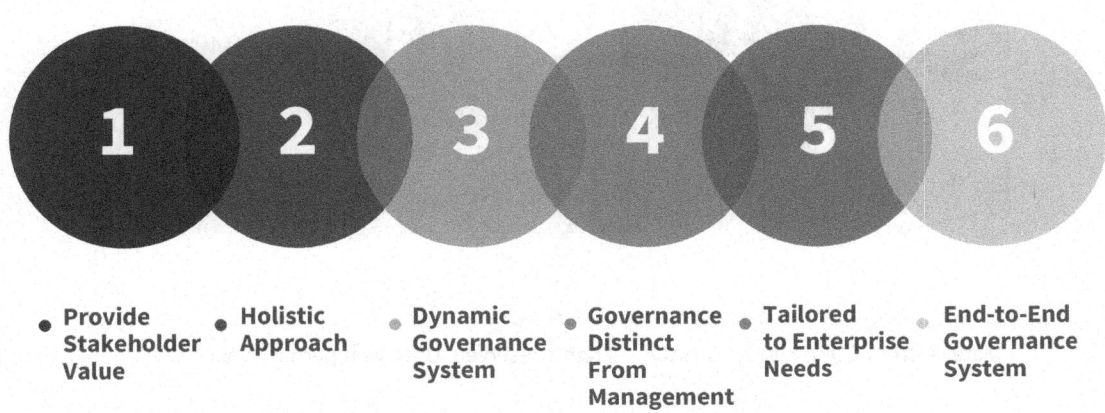

- 1 Provide Stakeholder Value
- 2 Holistic Approach
- 3 Dynamic Governance System
- 4 Governance Distinct From Management
- 5 Tailored to Enterprise Needs
- 6 End-to-End Governance System

- **Provide Stakeholder Value:** Governance systems should create value for the company's stakeholders by balancing benefits, risks, and resources. This should be accomplished through a well-designed governance system with an actionable strategy.

- **Holistic Approach:** Governance systems for IT can comprise diverse components, collectively providing a holistic model.

- **Dynamic Governance System:** When a change in one governance system occurs, the impact on all others should be considered so that the system continues to meet the demands of the organization. This means having a system that is dynamic enough that it can continue to be relevant while adjusting as new challenges arise.

- **Governance Distinct From Management:** Management activities and governance systems should be clearly distinguished from each other because they have different functions.

- **Tailored to Enterprise Needs:** Governance models should be customized to each company, using design factors to prioritize and tailor the system.

- **End-to-End Governance System:** More than just the IT function should be considered in a governance system. All processes in the organization involving information and technology should be factored into an end-to-end approach.

3 Governance Framework Principles

3.1 Three Principles for a Governance Framework

In addition to the governance system principles, there are three principles that were used to develop the COBIT 2019 core model, as follows.

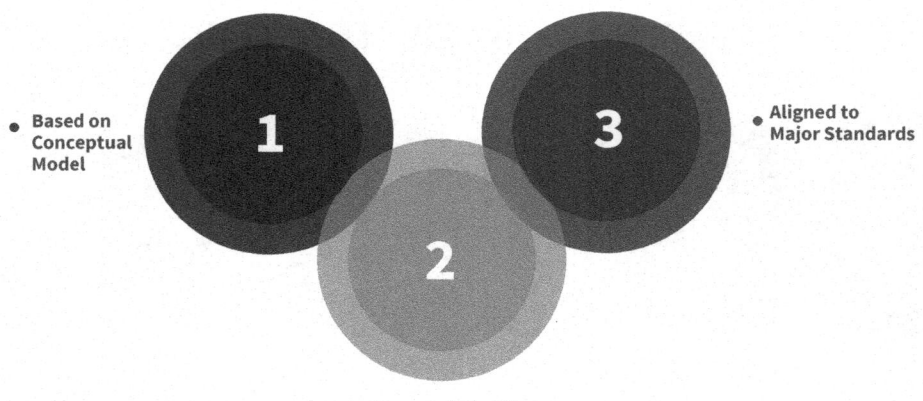

● **Based on Conceptual Model**

● **Aligned to Major Standards**

● **Open and Flexible**

Material from COBIT®, © 2019 ISACA. All rights reserved. Used with permission.

- **Based on Conceptual Model:** Governance frameworks should identify key components as well as the relationships between those components in order to provide for greater automation and to maximize consistency.

- **Open and Flexible:** Frameworks should have the ability to change, adding relevant content and removing irrelevant content, while keeping consistency and integrity.

- **Aligned to Major Standards:** Frameworks should align with regulations, frameworks, and standards.

4 Governance System Components

4.1 COBIT Core Model

According to the COBIT 2019 core model, governance and management objectives should be set so that information technology and systems contribute to company goals. Governance objectives always relate to a governance process while management objectives are always associated with management processes. Boards of directors are responsible for governance, whereas middle and senior management is responsible for management objectives.

The COBIT 2019 core model is summarized in the following graphic:

COBIT CORE MODEL

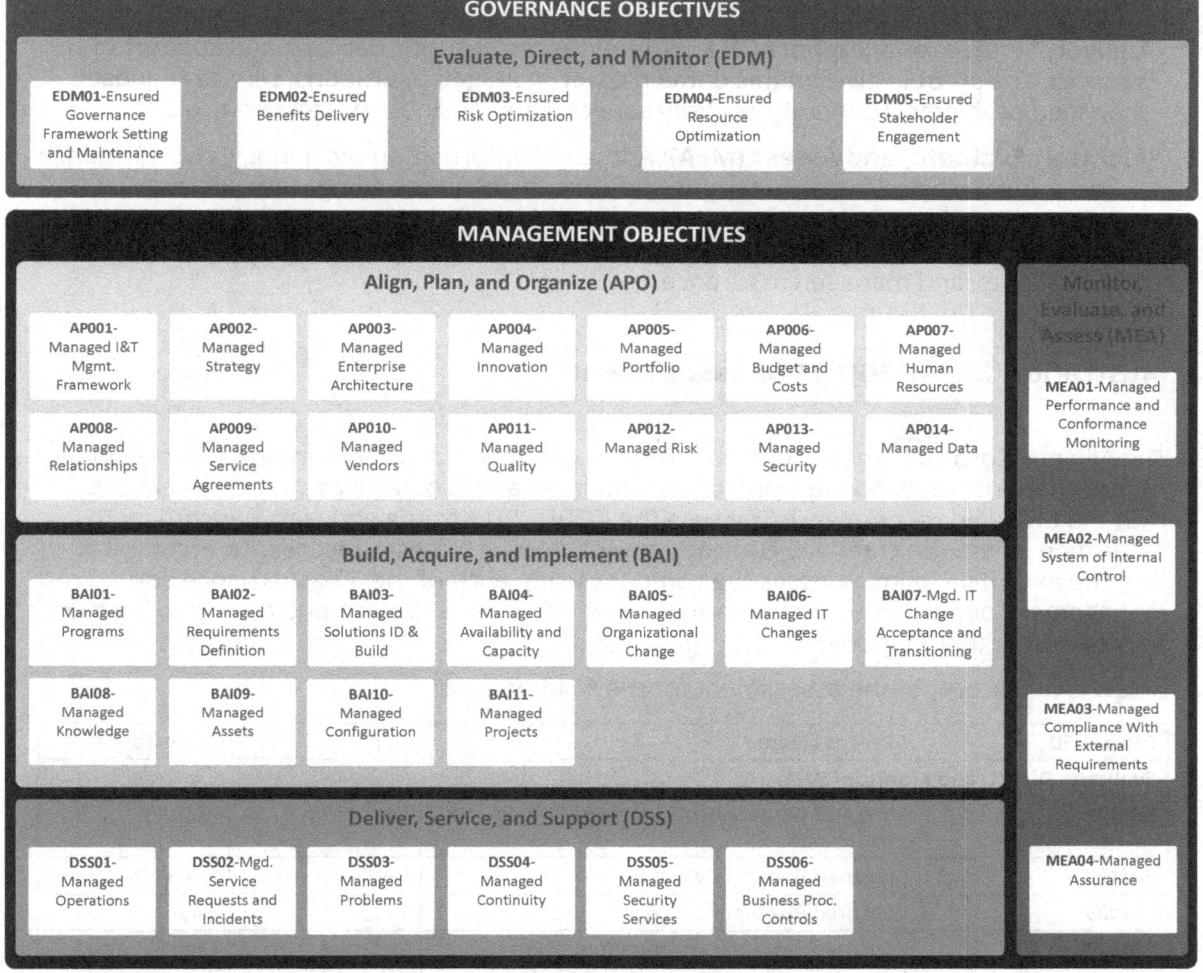

Governance objectives are grouped into one domain:

- **Evaluate, Direct, and Monitor (EDM):** Those charged with governance evaluate strategic objectives, direct management to achieve those objectives, and monitor whether objectives are being met. There are five objectives within this domain: ensuring benefits delivery, governance framework setting, risk optimization, resource optimization, and stakeholder engagement.

Management objectives have four domains:

- **Align, Plan, and Organize (APO):** Focuses on information technology's overall strategy, organization, and supporting activities. There are 14 objectives within this domain. Managed data is one of the most significant, as it ensures that critical data assets must be utilized to achieve company goals. The other objectives provide guidance on IT infrastructure and architecture, innovation, budgeting, human resources, vendors, quality, security, and managing risk.

■ **Build, Acquire, and Implement (BAI):** Addresses the implementation of information technology's solutions in the organization's business processes. This domain has 11 objectives, offering guidance on requirements definitions, identifying solutions, managing capacity, dealing with organizational and IT change, managing knowledge, administering assets, and managing configuration.

■ **Deliver, Service, and Support (DSS):** Addresses the security, delivery, and support of IT services. The six objectives in this domain cover managed operations, service requests, managed problems, continuity, security services, and business process controls.

■ **Monitor, Evaluate, and Assess (MEA):** Addresses information technology's conformance to the company's performance targets and control objectives along with external requirements. There are four objectives in this domain covering managed performance and conformance monitoring, managed system of internal control, compliance with external requirements, and managed assurance.

Illustration 1   COBIT EDM Assessment

The Alliance Corp., a high-end furniture retailer and manufacturer, is interested in aligning its information and technology processes with its strategic objectives. The CEO consults with the CIO, who recommends they use the COBIT 2019 framework as a benchmark to determine where the company currently stands relative to best practices. To accomplish this, the executive team assesses the company using each of the 40 governance and management objectives by first determining whether there is a gap and then gauging the importance of that objective.

Below is an excerpt of the assessment for the EDM domain:

Process ID	Process Name	Gap?	Importance
Evaluate, Direct, and Monitor (EDM)			
EDM01	Ensured Governance Framework Setting and Maintenance	Yes	High
EDM02	Ensured Benefits Delivery	Yes	Moderate
EDM03	Ensured Risk Optimization	Yes	High
EDM04	Ensured Resource Optimization	Yes	High
EDM05	Ensured Stakeholder Engagement	No	Very High

The executive team rates four out of five EDM processes as gaps, with the only objective not considered a gap being that stakeholders are indeed supportive and communicate effectively regarding existing IT strategy. EDM01 is rated as a gap because there is no consistent approach that aligns IT governance with the company's objectives. Compliance with legal is lacking, and processes are not effectively overseen. It rates EDM02 through EDM04 as gaps because IT services and personnel are not cost effectively delivered throughout the organization. There is significant overlap in processes and wasted expenses that could be avoided, which indicates that the company is operating at a much higher risk level than its risk appetite and tolerance threshold.

As a result, the executive team decides to overhaul the IT function by eliminating duplicative processes, placing a budget and better purchase approval process in place, requiring employees to use the company's help desk for all tasks that can be resolved remotely, and repurposing IT staff working on low-value-add tasks to activities that align with the executive team's governance objectives.

4.2   Components of the Governance System

Components of a governance system are factors that either collectively or individually contribute to the successful execution of a company's governance system over information technology and systems. These components can be of different types and interact with each other. The COBIT 2019 core model uses the following seven components to satisfy management and governance objectives:

- **Processes:** These are a set of activities or practices that produce outputs that help achieve overall information technology goals.

- **Organizational Structures:** These structures are the decision-making entities within an organization.

- **Principles, Policies, Frameworks:** These serve as the guide for turning desired behavior into practice.

- **Information:** This refers to the information needed for the governance system to function properly.

- **Culture, Ethics, and Behavior:** These factors influence the success of all management and governance activities.

- **People, Skills, and Competencies:** These are needed so that sound decisions are made, corrective actions are taken when necessary, and critical objectives are completed.

- **Services, Infrastructure, and Applications:** These are the tools required so that a well-designed governance system is in place for information technology processing.

5   Design Factors and Focus Areas

5.1   Design Factors

COBIT design factors influence the design of a company's IT governance system, with a total of 11 factors that should be considered:

- **Enterprise Strategy:** IT governance strategies generally include a primary strategy and a secondary strategy. Examples include growth/acquisition strategies, innovation/ differentiation strategies, cost leadership strategies, and client service/stability strategies.

- **Enterprise Goals:** Goals support the strategy and are structured based on the balanced scorecard dimensions, which are financial, customer, internal, and growth.

- **Risk Profile:** The risk profile addresses current risk exposure for the organization and maps out which risks exceed the organization's risk appetite. These risks include IT operational incidents, software adoption and usage problems, noncompliance, technology-based innovation, and geopolitical issues.

- **Information and Technology (I&T, or IT) Issues:** Common issues include regular IT audit findings of poor IT quality or control, insufficient IT resources, frustration between IT and different departments, hidden IT spending, problems with data quality, and noncompliance with applicable regulations.

- **Threat Landscape:** The threat landscape is the environment in which the company operates. The threat landscape may be classified as normal or high because of geopolitical threats or issues, the industry sector, or economic issues.

- **Compliance Requirements:** Compliance demands on the company can be classified as low, normal, or high. The classifications are intuitive, with low requirements implying minimal compliance demands, normal compliance indicating that the organization is typical of its industry, and high requirements meaning that the company is subject to higher-than-average compliance requirements.

- **Role of IT:** IT can be categorized as:

  - **Support**—an IT system that is not critical for operating a business or maintaining continuity.

  - **Factory**—an IT system that will have an immediate impact in business operations and continuity if it fails.

  - **Turnaround**—an IT system that drives innovation for the business but is not required for critical business operations.

  - **Strategic**—an IT system that is crucial for both innovation and business operations.

- **Sourcing Model for IT:** Sourcing is the type of IT procurement model the company adopts, ranging from outsourcing, to cloud-based (Web-based), built in-house, or a hybrid of any of these sources.

- **IT Implementation Methods:** The methods that can be used to implement new IT projects include the Agile development method, the DevOps method, the traditional (waterfall) method, or a hybrid of these methods.

- **Technology Adoption Strategy:** IT adoption falls into three categories:

  - **First-mover strategy**—emerging technologies adopted as soon as possible to gain an edge.

  - **Follower strategy**—emerging technologies are adopted after they are proven.

  - **Slow-adopter strategy**—very late to adopt new technologies.

- **Enterprise Size:** Two enterprise sizes are defined—large companies with a total full-time employee count of more than 250 (default), and small and medium companies with 50 to 250 full-time employees.

5.2   Focus Areas

Focus areas are different types of governance issues, domains, or topics that can be solved by a combination of management and governance objectives, along with their underlying components. The COBIT materials provide some examples, such as cybersecurity, cloud computing, and digital transformation, but state that the number is unlimited.

6   COBIT Core Publications

6.1   Publications Available

The COBIT 2019 framework was designed so that companies could adopt its recommendations in a way that is customized to their own organizational needs. The following publications are the road map to help achieve that customization:

- **COBIT 2019 Framework: Introduction and Methodology:** This publication introduces the core concepts of the framework.

- **COBIT 2019 Framework: Governance and Management Objectives:** This publication provides a comprehensive outline of the 40 management and governance objectives, their related components, and references to other relevant standards and frameworks.

- **COBIT 2019 Design Guide: Designing an Information and Technology Governance Solution:** This publication covers design topics that influence governance as well as a guideline for designing a customized governance system.

- **COBIT 2019 Implementation Guide: Implementing and Optimizing an Information and Technology Governance Solution:** This document provides a road map for continuous improvement when designing information technology governance systems, and it can be used in conjunction with the design guide.

NOTES

ISC

2

Information Systems and Data Management

Module

1

IT Infrastructure

1 IT Infrastructure

The supporting IT architecture within most modern companies has multiple, interconnected technological components with the core infrastructure involving a combination of on-premises and outsourced hardware, software, and specialized personnel. Some organizations manage this infrastructure themselves, but many are increasingly relying on third-party providers to support their IT operations, causing the focus on quality System and Organization Controls (SOC) 2® engagements to grow aggressively in recent years. Therefore, the topics covered throughout this module are applicable to both an organization's internal employees and those individuals auditing the organization.

SOC 2® engagements are examinations in which a third party evaluates and reports on a service organization's system controls as it relates to the AICPA's five Trust Services Criteria: security, availability, processing integrity, confidentiality, and privacy. Even though SOC 2® audits can involve any third-party company that manages or has access to sensitive data, they typically involve companies that manage the IT function of other organizations as their primary business. These third-party reports give users reasonable assurance that the service organization's controls listed in its system description are accurately depicted and effective.

SOC 2® engagements emphasize auditors to not only have an advanced understanding of information technology terminology, but also technical expertise in the way in which key components of the modern IT landscape function. This includes being conversant in a variety of operating systems, network infrastructure topologies, end-user devices, and the hardware used across all these domains.

1.1 Computer Hardware

Organizations designing their IT infrastructure must decide what hardware will be utilized to conduct business. Computers, the physical components that comprise computers, computer-related equipment, and external peripheral devices are referred to as computer hardware (or just "hardware"). This may include end-user devices such as laptops or desktops, and back-end devices such as servers, server-side equipment, switches, and routers.

1.1.1 Computers and End-User Devices

End-user devices (EUDs) are electronic machines, typically computers or minicomputers (small, low-power computing devices for specific tasks), that directly interact with employees or consumers at the "edge" of a network, meaning they are the point in a chain of applications or an organization's IT architecture that interfaces with a human. EUDs are different than devices used by programmers, administrators, and developers, who are the people responsible for building, maintaining, and repairing the underlying infrastructure on which EUDs operate.

These intermediary individuals work with non-EUDs such as switches, servers, routers, and other network support devices. Examples of EUDs include company-issued laptops, desktops, tablets, and wearables that are used by an employee who is strictly the final consumer of that device rather than an intermediary. The end user may also be a customer of the manufacturer of that device.

1.1.2 Internal Computer Hardware

Key hardware components within a computer include microprocessors; graphics and sound cards; hard drives (permanent storage); random access memory, or RAM (temporary storage); the power supply; and the motherboard, which connects most of these critical pieces.

1.1.3 External Computer Hardware

Some hardware devices may be external peripheral devices and do not need to be integrated into the machine itself. Computer mice, keyboards, speakers, microphones, disk drives, memory devices, network cards, and monitors may be built in or may be external devices that connect either wirelessly or directly to a computer through a wired connection. Other external devices include printers, scanners, and networking equipment.

1.1.4 Infrastructure Housing

Although not hardware, the facilities and the safeguards on those facilities that contain hardware, such as data centers or offices, are part of the broader IT infrastructure. This includes advanced security systems to monitor and control access. It also includes ventilation and climate control to keep temperatures down to prevent equipment from overheating.

1.2 Network Infrastructure

Network infrastructure refers to the hardware, software, layout, and topology of network resources that enable connectivity and communication between devices on a computer network.

1.2.1 Network Infrastructure Hardware

Traditional hardware found in most networks are as follows:

- **Modems:** Modems connect a network to an internet service provider's network, usually through a cable connection. It is the device that brings internet into a home or office. A modem receives analog signals from the internet service provider and translates those signals into digital signals. Each modem has a public IP address.

- **Routers:** Routers manage network traffic by connecting devices to form a network. They read the source and destination fields in information packet headers to determine the most efficient path through the network for the packet to travel. They also act as a link between a modem and the organization's switches. If there are no switches, then the router will connect directly to a user's device.

- **Switches:** Switches are similar to routers in that they connect and divide devices within a computer network. However, switches do not perform as many advanced functions as a router, such as assigning IP addresses. The same way a traditional power strip converts one electrical outlet into multiple outlets, a network switch can turn one network jack into several network jacks, so multiple devices can share one network connection.

- **Gateways:** A gateway is a computer or device that acts as an intermediary between different networks. It transforms data from one protocol into another so that information can flow between networks. A protocol is a rule, or set of rules, that governs the way in which information is transmitted, with one of the most common protocols being that which is used for the internet, known as TCP/IP (transmission control protocol/internet protocol). A gateway interprets these differing protocols and converts them into the appropriate format to facilitate network movement, usually between a company's network and the internet.

▪ **Edge-Enabled Devices:** Edge-enabled devices allow computing, storage, and networking functions closer to the devices where the data or system request originates, rather than a distant central location. The benefits of this form of distributed computing power are faster network response times and operability because data does not have to be transmitted to a remote centralized server for processing.

▪ **Servers:** Servers are physical or virtual machines that coordinate the computers, programs, and data that are part of the network. Most business networks use a client/server model in which the client sends a request to the server and it provides a response or executes some action. There are various types of servers, including Web servers, file servers, print servers, and database servers.

▪ **Firewalls:** Firewalls are software applications or hardware devices that protect a person's or a company's network traffic by filtering it through security protocols with predefined rules. For companies, these rules may be aligned with company policies and access guidelines. Firewalls are intended to prevent unauthorized access into the organization and to prevent employees from downloading malicious programs or accessing restricted sites.

Basic packet-filtering firewalls work by analyzing network traffic that is transmitted in packets (data communicated) and determining whether that firewall software is configured to accept the data. If not, the firewall blocks the packet. Firewalls can be set to only allow trusted sources (IP addresses) to transmit across the network. Other types of firewalls include:

  ▫ **Circuit-Level Gateways:** A type of firewall that verifies the source of a packet and meets rules and policies set by the security team.

  ▫ **Application-Level Gateways:** A type of firewall that inspects the packet itself. These gateways are very resource-intensive and may slow performance.

  ▫ **Network Address Translation Firewalls:** Assigns an internal network address to specific, approved external sources so that those sources are approved to be inside the firewall.

  ▫ **Stateful Multilayer Inspection Firewalls:** Combines packet-filtering and network address translation.

  ▫ **Next-Gen Firewalls:** Assigns different firewall rules to different applications as well as users. In this way, a low-threat application has more permissive rules assigned to it while a high-security application may have a highly restrictive rule set assigned.

1.2.2 Network Infrastructure Physical Layout (Topology)

Network topology refers to the physical layout of equipment, or "nodes," in a network, which is essential for understanding how to properly engineer the network for optimal performance. Each topology has different requirements for components, such as the length and type of connecting cables, data transmission rates, and physical position of each node in the network. These variables are based on the size of the network, the performance needs of the organization, and the environment in which the network is built.

The following are the four most common types of network topologies:

▪ **Bus Topology:** This layout is either in a linear or tree form, with each node connected to a single line or cable. Data can be transmitted by any node on the system at the same time, which can cause signal interference. To avoid this, cables must be terminated, or properly finished, at each end so that signal transmission is optimally managed. A disadvantage of this is if the central line is compromised, the entire network goes offline.

- **Mesh Topology:** In a mesh topology, there are numerous connections between nodes, with all nodes being connected in a full mesh topology and only some connected in a partial mesh topology. This form of layout is commonly used in wireless networks. While the number of pathways allows high levels of traffic and promotes network stability if a node is damaged, it can be costly to implement and maintain over the network's life span.

- **Ring Topology:** Nodes are connected in a circular path in ring topologies. When data is transferred to a destination device, it must first go through every other device between the source and destination. There are unidirectional ring paths that allow data transmission to move in one direction, and there are multidirectional paths that allow two-way data transmission. An advantage of ring topologies is that data transmission collision is minimized or eliminated, but this can result in very slow network performance.

- **Star Topology:** In a star topology, data passes through a central hub that acts as a switch or server, and then transmits to peripheral devices that act as clients. There can be multiple hubs so that if one fails, only the nodes connected to that hub will stop functioning. Even though the hub is a single point of failure for all connected nodes, this topology structure makes it easier to identify damaged cables.

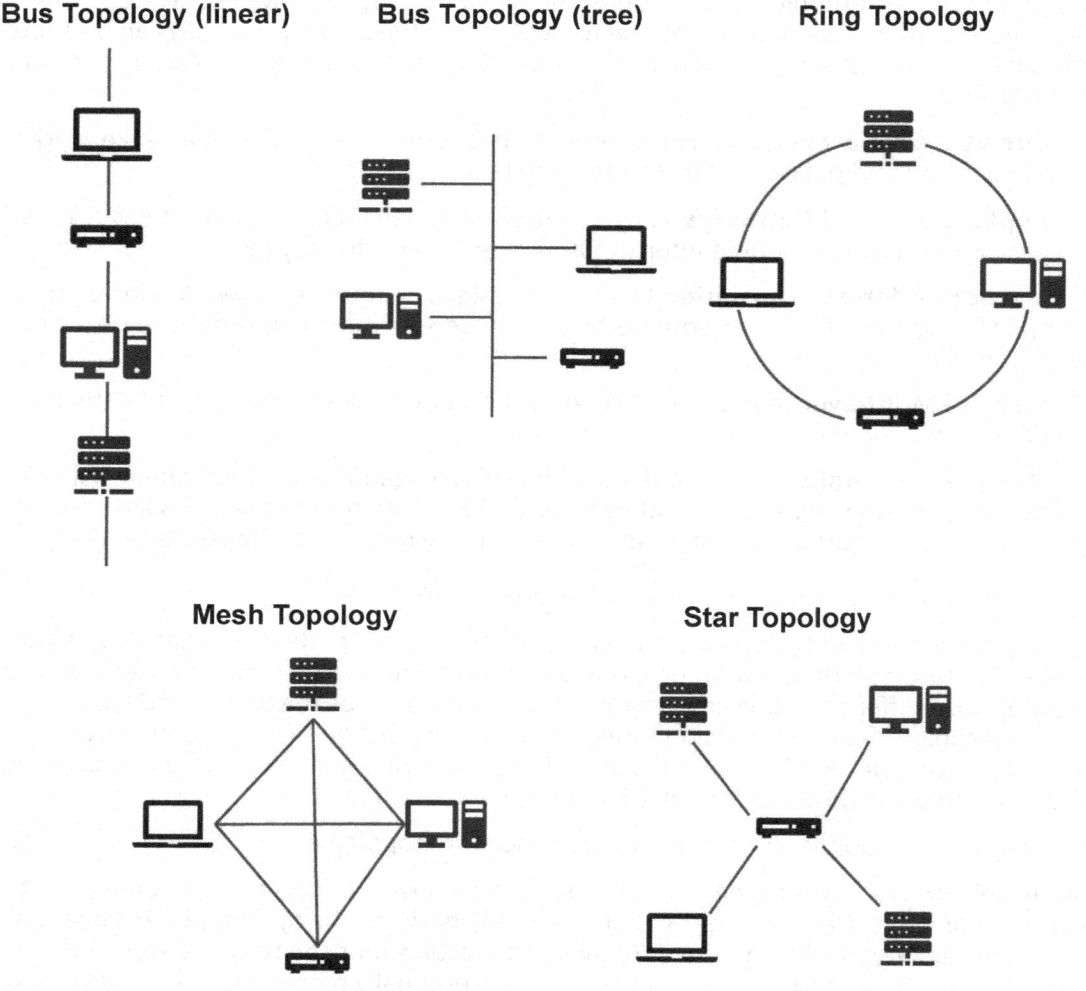

Bus Topology (linear)   **Bus Topology (tree)**   **Ring Topology**

Mesh Topology   **Star Topology**

1.2.3 Network Infrastructure Protocols

Devices in a network communicate with other devices using protocols. The type of protocol governs the way data is transmitted based on the method used, such as the type of cable, port, or wireless transmission mechanism.

The Open Systems Interconnection (OSI) model, which was developed by the International Organization for Standardization (ISO), helps explain how these protocols work as well as how networking devices communicate with each other. The OSI model segregates network functions into seven different layers, with each layer responsible for a specific data exchange function, as follows:

Application	7
Presentation	6
Session	5
Transport	4
Network	3
Data Link	2
Physical	1

Data flows through each layer using a process called encapsulation, which adds a header or a footer to the data point received from the previous layer. It starts at the Application layer with a message, which is then passed to the Presentation layer where a header or footer is added.

The data continues the encapsulation process through each layer down to the Physical layer, which represents the actual networking device that is being used to transmit the message. At the Physical layer, the message is transformed into electrical impulses that are then sent to the receiving networking device. There, the decapsulation process begins, starting with the Physical layer until it reaches the Application layer.

As the information moves through the OSI model layers from the sending network device to the receiving network device, the header that was added by each specific layer is interpreted by the same layer at the receiving device.

The following explains the purpose of each layer and the different protocols that operate within them:

- **Application Layer (Layer 7):** This layer serves as the interface between applications that a person uses and the network protocol needed to transmit a message. It does not represent that actual application being used. Some of the common and most well-known protocols used at this layer include Hypertext Transfer Protocol (HTTP), File Transfer Protocol (FTP), Simple Mail Transfer Protocol (SMTP), and Electronic Data Interchange (EDI).

- **Presentation Layer (Layer 6):** This layer transforms data received from the Application Layer into a format that other devices using the OSI model can interpret, such as standard formats for videos, images, and web pages. Encryption also occurs at this layer. Common formats used are American Standard Code for Information Interchange (ASCII), Joint Photographic Experts Group (JPEG), and Moving Picture Experts Group (MPEG).

- **Session Layer (Layer 5):** Layer 5 allows sessions between communicating devices to be established and maintained. Sessions allow networking devices to have dialogue with each other. Common protocols at this layer are Remote Procedure Call (RPC), Structured Query Language (SQL), and Network File System (NFS).

- **Transport Layer (Layer 4):** The Transport Layer supports and controls the communication connections between devices. This involves setting the rules for how devices are referenced, the amount of data that can be transmitted, validating the data's integrity, and determining whether data has been lost. Common protocols within this layer include Transmission Control Protocol (TCP), User Datagram Protocol (UDP), Secure Sockets Layer (SSL), and Transport Layer Security (TLS).

- **Network Layer (Layer 3):** The Network Layer adds routing and address headers or footers to the data, such as source and destination IP addresses, so that the message reaches the correct devices. This layer also detects errors. Common protocols include Internet Protocol (IP), Internet Protocol Security (IPSec), Network Address Translation (NAT), and Internet Group Management Protocol (IGMP).

- **Data Link Layer (Layer 2):** In the Data Link Layer, data packets are formatted for transmission. This is determined by the hardware and networking technology, which is usually Ethernet. This layer also adds Media Access Control (MAC) addresses, which are device identifiers that act as source and destination reference numbers to route messages to the correct device. Some of the protocols used are Integrated Services Digital Network (ISDN), Point-to-Point Tunneling Protocol (PPTP), Layer 2 Tunneling Protocol (L2TP), and Address Resolution Protocol (ARP).

- **Physical Layer (Layer 1):** This layer converts the message sent from the Data Link Layer into bits so it can be transmitted to other physical devices. It also receives messages from other physical devices and converts those back from bits to a format that can be interpreted by the Data Link Layer. Protocols used in this layer include High-Speed Serial Interface (HSSI), Synchronous Optical Networking (SONET), V.35, and X.21.

Illustration 1   The OSI Model

Jane would like to send a message to her best friend, Jack.

#7: The first step in applying the OSI model is to tell the Application Layer what protocols to use. Because Jane would like to send the message through the internet, the Application Layer would add the "HTTP" header to the data packet.

#6: The whole packet then enters into the Presentation Layer, where the whole package (the message along with the HTTP header) is transformed into a format that other devices using the OSI model can understand and is encrypted. The whole data packet can now be processed.

#5: The Session Layer starts by establishing and maintaining communications channels across the network devices so the packets can be delivered to Jack's tablet.

#4: The whole package then enters into the Transport Layer. This layer sets the rules on how to divide up the data packet and restitch them back together in the correct order on the receiving end. Assuming that the transmission control protocol (TCP) is selected, the TCP header will then be added to the data packet. The data packet now includes both the TCP header and the HTTP header.

#3: The data packet next enters into the Network Layer. In this layer, Jack's IP address is added to the data packet. The data packet now includes the IP address header, the TCP header, and the HTTP header along with the original message.

#2: Next, the package enters into the Data Link Layer. This layer is where the device MAC address header is added. At this point, the whole package will include four headers: MAC address, IP address, TCP, and HTTP.

#1: The last layer, the Physical Layer, converts the entire package into zeros and ones.

When the packet is delivered to Jack, it will be unwrapped in the reverse order. The Physical Layer on Jack's end will convert the zeros and ones into its data package form. Each layer will then remove its corresponding headers to eventually reveal the message Jane intends to send to Jack's tablet.

1.2.4 Network Infrastructure Architecture

A company's network infrastructure architecture refers to the way an organization structures its network from a holistic design standpoint, considering factors such as geographical layout, physical and logical layout, and network protocols used.

Networks can be wired, wireless, virtual, or on-premises; they can use a variety of hardware and software to enable connectivity, and be spread across a wide geographical area or a more narrow, concentrated area. Common types of network architecture designs include:

- **Local-Area Networks (LANs):** Provides network access to a limited geographic area such as a home or single-location office.

- **Wide-Area Networks (WANs):** Provides access to larger geographic areas such as cities, regions, or countries. WANs connect other networks such as LANs together to provide broad coverage. The largest example of a WAN is the internet.

- **Software-defined Wide Area Networks (SD-WANs):** Monitors the performance of WAN connections and manages traffic to optimize connectivity. In a WAN, the control and management of the network is integrated into the hardware. In a SD-WAN setup, control and management are separated from the hardware and included in a software.

- **Demilitarized Zone (DMZ):** A subnetwork that separates a LAN from other untrusted networks such as the internet. It is set up by creating a physical or logical subnetwork outside of the LANs' firewall.

- **Virtual Private Networks (VPNs):** These are virtual connections through a secure channel or tunnel that provide remote and secure access to an existing network. These are commonly referred to as RDCs, or remote desktop connections.

1.3 Software

Software consists of the applications, procedures, or programs that provide instructions for a computer to execute. Software is controlled by a user interacting with the program, which in turn gives instructions to the physical computer's operating system. The term *software* spans a variety of categories and can refer to programs that manage multiple applications such as an operating system, can be a standalone program, or can be local to a component of a computer or a peripheral device such as a printer.

1.3.1 Operating Systems

An operating system (OS) is software that orchestrates the global functioning of a group of applications, hardware, and their performance by acting as an intermediary between these resources to allow a user to execute specific tasks. An OS defines the parameters for managing a system's memory, processes, records, devices, and user interface. By optimizing these functions, an OS balances resources and allocates them in a way that allows the system to run seamlessly without delays or interruptions even with multiple applications running simultaneously.

1.3.2 Firmware

Software that is locally embedded in hardware instructs the hardware how to operate and is commonly known as firmware. Firmware operates like software but exists locally on the machine directing the function of the physical components, such as the motherboard and microprocessor. Firmware is not updated frequently, or at all, which is very different from how often a typical software program is updated on a frequent basis.

1.3.3   Mobile Technology

Mobile technology refers to any wireless-enabled device that is connected, or has the ability to connect, to a private network or the internet. This technology allows the user to conduct business and communicate in real time, which can sustain a business that might otherwise collapse during a crisis or a temporary inability to meet in person. Mobile technology combines hardware, such as laptops, tablets, hot spots, and mobile phones, with mobile applications and operating systems that allow connectivity to networks. This connectivity is typically done with wireless technology such as Wi-Fi, Bluetooth®, and 4G or 5G cellular technology.

Mobile devices can be EUDs (end-user devices) or non-EUDs. Mobile EUDs like laptops, tablets, and smartphones provide direct interfaces with a user. Mobile non-EUDs are wireless devices like routers, switches, firewalls, and wireless access points. These run on some form of mobile technology, but they are not direct interfaces with a person.

An extension of mobile technology is IoT (Internet of Things) devices, which typically require either Bluetooth or an internet connection to access a larger network. The mobile range for connectivity is usually more limited than first-generation (traditional) mobile technology and can be found in artificially intelligent personal assistants, smartwatches, Bluetooth earphones and speakers, lighting, electrical equipment, thermostats, and appliances such as refrigerators and dishwashers.

2   Cloud Computing

2.1   Cloud Computing Models

Cloud computing is a computing model that uses shared resources over the internet. Cloud customers rent storage space, processing power, proprietary software, or a combination of the three on remote servers from another company.

When a company acquires its own infrastructure rather than renting it, the company must purchase enough resources to cover its peak usage so the business can accommodate high-volume periods. During low-volume periods, this costly infrastructure is idle. The company would also be responsible for maintenance and tech support on its hardware.

For the customers of cloud computing, the service offers infrastructure elasticity, renting only as much as needed on a minute-to-minute basis. Processing and storage are rented in increments of computing power used per units of time, so customers pay lower amounts during low-volume periods and larger amounts during high-volume periods. Customers benefit because the provider of the cloud services usually performs all maintenance and tech support on this hardware.

Cloud computing services are offered by some companies with large computing infrastructures to either lease excess capacity during off-peak times or use purpose-built infrastructure to support their customers. Cloud computing gives customers the opportunity to gain efficiencies by allowing them to rent from cloud service providers (CSPs) instead of purchasing or building out costly solutions.

Additional efficiencies exist when a company's data is in one virtual location, especially if company operations are in many locations. Data processing can be performed more efficiently from that single virtual location, and IT hardware support may be reduced throughout the company. Because cloud service providers offer distributed redundancy among many data centers, having cloud data storage reduces the likelihood that data is lost in an attack or a disaster.

Because of its benefits, cloud computing and the variations of its use are becoming pervasive in modern society. There are three primary cloud computing models, in addition to a fully on-site or on-premises solution:

	On-Premises	IaaS	PaaS	SaaS
	Application Usage	Application Usage	Application Usage	Application Usage
	Application Design, Tools, and Data	Application Design, Tools, and Data	Application Design, Tools, and Data	Application Design, Tools, and Data
	Environment Runtime	Environment Runtime	Environment Runtime	Environment Runtime
	Virtual Management	Virtual Management	Virtual Management	Virtual Management
	Firewalls & Cybersecurity	Firewalls & Cybersecurity	Firewalls & Cybersecurity	Firewalls & Cybersecurity
	Operating Systems	Operating Systems	Operating Systems	Operating Systems
	Servers	Servers	Servers	Servers
	Storage	Storage	Storage	Storage
	Networking	Networking	Networking	Networking
	Data Center	Data Center	Data Center	Data Center

More Control → Less Control

= Managed by organization
= Managed by third-party CSP

Enterprise Risk Management—Integrating with Strategy and Performance Framework, © 2017 Committee of Sponsoring Organizations of the Treadway Commission (COSO). Used with permission.

- **IaaS (Infrastructure-as-a-Service):** The CSP provides an entire virtual data center of resources in an IaaS model, and organizations can outsource servers, storage, hardware, networking services, and networking components to third-party providers, which is generally billed on a per-use basis. The company is typically responsible for keeping the environment in which it operates consistently up and running for users, as well as virtually managing the performance of the physical infrastructure, while the CSP is responsible for the physical management of that infrastructure.

  The degree to which the organization has control over certain functions will vary across CSPs and organizations. Some companies may only use operating systems and firewalls but not update, patch, or maintain them, while other organizations may fully support those functions.

- **PaaS (Platform-as-a-Service):** The CSP provides proprietary tools or solutions remotely that are used to fulfill a specific business purpose. In a PaaS model, the tools facilitate the creation of programs and delivery of services, such as building an online platform to sell merchandise, advertise products, or build other websites, all of which run on a CSP's hosted infrastructure. The CSP is responsible for keeping the application's uptime at an acceptable level by maintaining all of the back-end infrastructure required to run that application.

- **SaaS (Software-as-a-Service):** The CSP provides a business application or software that organizations use to perform specific functions or processes. In a SaaS model, customers generally purchase the service through licensing. The CSP offers access to the application via the internet and is responsible for recurring upgrades, security enhancements, and other support functions.

A common service offered in conjunction with SaaS models are Business Processes as a Service (BPaaS) models, in which third parties use SaaS software to deliver specific business functions such as outsourced payroll, billing, or logistics services.

2.1.1 Cloud Computing Deployment Models

There are four common types of cloud computing deployment models, and how the cloud environment is shared differs with each model.

- **Public:** The cloud in this model is owned and managed by a CSP that makes the cloud services available to people or organizations who want to use or purchase them.

- **Private:** In this model, the cloud is created for a single organization and is managed by the organization or a managed service vendor. The cloud infrastructure can exist on or off the organization's premises. The organization typically owns the underlying infrastructure in this model. Use of a private cloud is popular in highly regulated industries such as the financial services industry and the health care industry.

- **Hybrid:** The cloud in a hybrid model is composed of two or more clouds, with at least one being a private cloud, that remain unique cloud entities but with technology in place that facilitates the portability of data and applications between each entity.

- **Community:** A community cloud infrastructure is shared by multiple organizations to support a common interest, such as companies banding together for regulatory compliance, a common mission, or collaboration with industry peers.

2.1.2 Cloud Service Providers (CSP)

A cloud service provider (CSP) is a third party that provides cloud computing services such as application delivery, hosting, or monitoring to customers. The CSP performs all maintenance and tech support on the hardware. CSPs often have advanced skills and experience managing cloud infrastructure and environments, and cloud computing takes advantage of this expertise.

A CSP could be a company that uses purpose-built infrastructure to support customers or one with a large computing infrastructure that leases excess capacity during off-peak times. CSPs often serve multiple cloud customers at once and use common resources and technology for all customers, which is referred to as multi-tenant.

Information about CSPs may be found in SOC 2® reports regarding compliance with regulations or standards. This could be critical for users of SOC 2® reports who are interested in controls implemented by the service organization to comply with HIPAA security requirements. It may also be of interest to potential or existing CSP clients looking for compliance with standards issued by the Cloud Security Alliance, known as the Cloud Controls Matrix, which is a framework designed for best practices regarding cloud security, data protection, and compliance in a cloud environment.

2.2   COSO Enterprise Risk Management—Integrating With Strategy and Performance

The Committee of Sponsoring Organizations (COSO), created by the Treadway Commission, has developed guidance and best practices for internal control, enterprise risk management, governance, and fraud deterrence. COSO's *Enterprise Risk Management—Integrating With Strategy and Performance* framework categorizes methods for addressing an organization's risk into five components, with 20 supporting principles:

1. **Governance and Culture:** The governance component sets the company's tone and reinforces the importance of having oversight of enterprise risk management. Culture is related to the company's target behaviors and values and involves understanding risk.

2. **Strategy and Objective-Setting:** This component is considered with enterprise risk management and strategy during the strategic planning process. A company's risk appetite should be aligned with its strategy, and business objectives should be put into place to help achieve that level of appetite through identifying risk, assessing it, and responding to it.

3. **Performance:** This component requires that organizations prioritize their risks based on risk appetite so that business objectives are assessed, met, and reported to key stakeholders.

4. **Review and Revision:** This component involves reviewing a company's performance over time and making revisions to functions when needed.

5. **Information, Communication, and Reporting:** This component recommends that a continual process be in place that supports sharing both internal and external information throughout the organization.

The set of 20 principles were designed to be practical and customizable so that organizations of any industry, size, or type can implement them. They were also designed with the thought that management and a company's board of directors could use these as a standard for reasonable expectations when managing risks associated with business objectives and strategy.

Material from *Enterprise Risk Management—Integrating with Strategy and Performance Framework,* © 2017 Committee of Sponsoring Organizations of the Treadway Commission (COSO). Used with permission.

2.3   COSO Enterprise Risk Management for Cloud Computing

COSO's *Enterprise Risk Management for Cloud Computing* publication provides specific guidance to organizations for applying the COSO framework to cloud computing. In general, an organization must integrate the governance of cloud computing into its overall risk management strategy.

COSO provides key risk management considerations for organizations using cloud service providers. When outsourcing to a CSP, ownership of risk remains with the organization. Proper governance of cloud computing and CSPs may include a Cloud Computing Steering Committee that oversees cloud computing efforts. An organization should also understand a CSP's values and culture due to a CSP becoming an extension of the organization.

An organization must consider how a CSP affects the organization's risk profile, how a CSP's risks can impact performance, what responsibilities belong to a CSP, and how a CSP's internal controls address risk. If a CSP has an outage, critical systems at the organization may be down. A CSP may provide firewall or VPN capabilities, but configuration and enforcement may be left to the organization. Finally, organizations should continuously update and reassess ERM when there are changes to the organization's cloud needs or CSP.

2.3.1   Applying the COSO Framework to Establish Computing Governance

The COSO Enterprise Risk Management (ERM) framework can help organizations establish ideal configurations for cloud options by applying eight components. This allows management to tailor the solution based on the company's own risk appetite.

COSO Framework Component	Applicability to Organization's Consideration of Cloud Computing
Internal Environment	This serves as the foundation for a company's risk appetite, helping a company understand the level at which it wants to outsource technology functions.
Objective-Setting	Management should understand how outsourcing technology functions will help it reach, or potentially hinder, its objectives.
Event Identification	Management must understand how adopting a CSP could make event identification more complex, or easier.
Risk Assessment	Management should understand the risks of its cloud strategy, understanding the impact to its risk profile, inherent and residual risk, and likelihood of the impact of all risks.
Risk Response	Management should determine whether its risk response will be to avoid a risk, reduce its likelihood, share the risk by transferring a portion of it to another entity, or accept the risk.
Control Activities	The organization should understand how traditional controls—such as detective, preventative, automated, and manual—as well as entity-level controls are modified in a cloud environment.
Information and Communication	Management should understand how operating in the cloud will affect the timeliness, availability, and dissemination of information and communication.
Monitoring	Management should modify its monitoring mechanisms to accommodate new complexities introduced by adopting a cloud solution.

2.3.2 Cloud Risks

There are multiple risks that should be considered when evaluating CSPs and their services:

1. The rate of competitor adoption
2. Being in the same risk ecosystem as the CSP and other tenants
3. Transparency
4. Reliability and performance
5. Lack of application portability (vendor lock-in)
6. Security and compliance
7. Cyber attacks
8. Data leakage
9. IT organizational change
10. CSP long-term viability

COSO also recognizes that risk increases when moving from a private model to a public deployment model. Risk also increases with less control, as is shown below, when moving from an IaaS model to a SaaS model.

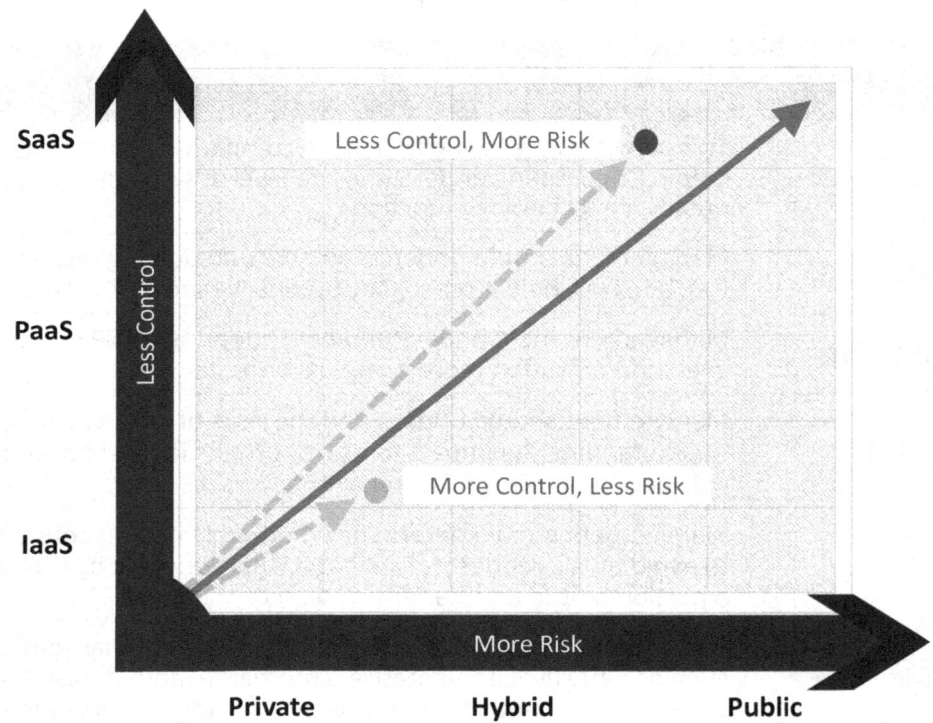

Enterprise Risk Management for Cloud Computing Publication, © 2021 Committee of Sponsoring Organizations of the Treadway Commission (COSO). Used with permission.

2.3.3 Cloud Evaluation and Adoption

Organizations evaluating various cloud options can choose among a public, private, or hybrid model, which means their computing environment may be combined with other tenants. Companies should understand the behavior and profile of those other tenants and whether their activity could have a direct impact on IT operations. In effect, the ERM composition of two companies sharing the same cloud will be combined to differing degrees, depending on the model selected.

Some cloud applications can be quickly adopted by an organization with minimal investment, whereas others require substantial time and expense to implement. Management should evaluate this prior to committing to a cloud solution as well as determine whether they fully understand any compliance risks that come with having a CSP assume certain functions within an organization. When some functions are shared or supported by a cloud application, it can remove transparency and oversight that might have otherwise existed in a company before the cloud solution was adopted.

Illustration 2   Evaluating Cloud Providers

FinGuard Financial is considering outsourcing its clearing and settlement functions to support real-time clearing for stock trades executed by its clients. FinGuard's CFO presents senior management with the following three options:

I.   MisRoq Clearinghouse platform—this company houses clients with up to 50 other companies per computing machine. Pricing is based on the relative use of the platform with a monthly minimum. If more trades are made through FinGuard than another institution sharing the same machine, then FinGuard pays more.

II. Cliff Clearinghouse Partners—this firm custom builds a clearinghouse platform that does not share physical space or computing power with any other entity. This dedicated option is the most expensive, at 5 percent of trading fees paid by investors. It is the most secure, has the most advanced computing power on the market, and has backup platforms at a separate location for redundancy if the primary platform fails.

III. R&M Group Clearinghouse—this organization offers shared cloud hosting with a maximum of two other companies on the same machine and location. Pricing is on-demand, based on the level of computing power used by FinGuard, at a fixed rate per hour. Advanced computing power has a higher price per hour than general purpose computing power.

Because it is a global market infrastructure operator, FinGuard decides to go with option II. Even though option III offers competitive pricing and reduced risk through the limited number of shared tenants, FinGuard wants a dedicated platform because it is so widespread geographically and is willing to pay a premium to get it. Option I has too much risk due to the fact that it is shared with so many other institutions. In the event of a stock-trading frenzy, a trading platform crash would prevent investors from making trades, which could magnify losses or cause them to miss out on gains.

2.3.4 Recommended Risk Responses

Given the variety of cloud computing options available to companies today, management should adapt its programs and controls so that each risk related to cloud environments has the appropriate response. To reduce the likelihood of unauthorized cloud activity, policies need to be implemented. This is particularly important for data and compliance issues, making data classification processes and policies very much a necessity.

To determine whether those safeguards are in place and working correctly, there should be periodic assessments of the CSP's control environment. There should also be management oversight, designing the way in which controls are monitored. When incidents, such as a cyberattack, do occur, an incident management plan should be in place to control and mitigate the threat.

Risks related to vendor lock-in are common but not always evident to companies with long-standing vendor relationships. CSP exit strategies give the organization a contingency plan, should an abrupt switch be required.

Monitoring the regulatory environment for changes is also critical to minimize the risk of noncompliance. Countries across the globe are rapidly implementing protective rules to restrict the use of sensitive information outside of country borders, making it important for companies operating in multiple nations to be alert. Additionally, if a company is publicly traded, noncompliance disclosures may be required if CSPs are supporting critical business processes.

1 Enterprise Resource Planning (ERP) Systems

1.1 Overview

Enterprise resource planning (ERP) systems are cross-functional systems that support different business functions and facilitate integration of information across departments such as accounting, customer management, finance, human resources, inventory management, manufacturing, marketing, and vendor management.

An ERP solution facilitates real-time communication between systems and typically operates under a centralized database and user interface. This interface may offer multiple modules that function independently or as an integrated system that allows data to be shared across different departments or divisions of an organization.

An accounting information system (AIS) is more specific in nature than an ERP and offers the particular accounting functions an organization may need. An ERP may include AIS capabilities while being more robust than a standalone AIS and integrated with other departments.

1.2 Accounting Information Systems (AIS)

The system that accountants and financial managers interact with the most is the AIS. An AIS collects, records, and stores accounting information, then compiles that information using accounting rules to report both financial and nonfinancial information to decision makers in an enterprise.

1.2.1 AIS Subsystems

An AIS typically is made up of three main subsystems (or modules):

- **Transaction Processing System (TPS):** This subsystem converts economic events into financial transactions (i.e., journal entries) and distributes the information to support daily operations. A TPS typically covers three main transaction cycles: sales cycle, conversion cycle, and expenditure cycle.

- **Financial Reporting System (FRS):** This subsystem aggregates daily financial information from the TPS and other sources for infrequent events such as mergers, lawsuit settlements, or natural disasters to enable timely regulatory and financial reporting.

- **Management Reporting System (MRS):** This subsystem provides internal financial information to solve day-to-day business problems, such as budgeting, variance analysis, or cost-volume-profit analysis.

1.2.2 Objectives of an AIS

The three subsystems of an AIS collectively achieve the following five objectives:

1. Record valid transactions.

2. Properly classify those transactions.

3. Record the transactions at their correct value.

4. Record the transactions in the correct accounting period.

5. Properly present the transactions and related information in the financial statements of the organization.

1.2.3 Sequence of Events of an AIS

An AIS processes transactions in the following order:

1. Transaction data from source documents is entered into the AIS by an end user. Alternatively, an order may be entered through the internet by a customer.

2. Original source documents, if they exist, are filed.

3. Transactions are recorded in the appropriate journal.

4. Transactions are posted to the general and subsidiary ledgers.

5. Trial balances are prepared.

6. Adjustments, accruals, and corrections are entered.

7. Financial reports are generated.

1.2.4 AIS Audit Trail

A well-designed AIS creates an audit trail for accounting transactions. The audit trail allows a user to trace a transaction from source documents to the ledger and to vouch from the ledger back to source documents. The ability to trace and vouch between records and source documents is important in auditing.

An example of a basic accounting audit trail follows. Source documents are often stored as electronic documents, thus alleviating the need to file paper documents. Sophisticated scanning systems can turn paper documents into electronic documents before they are processed.

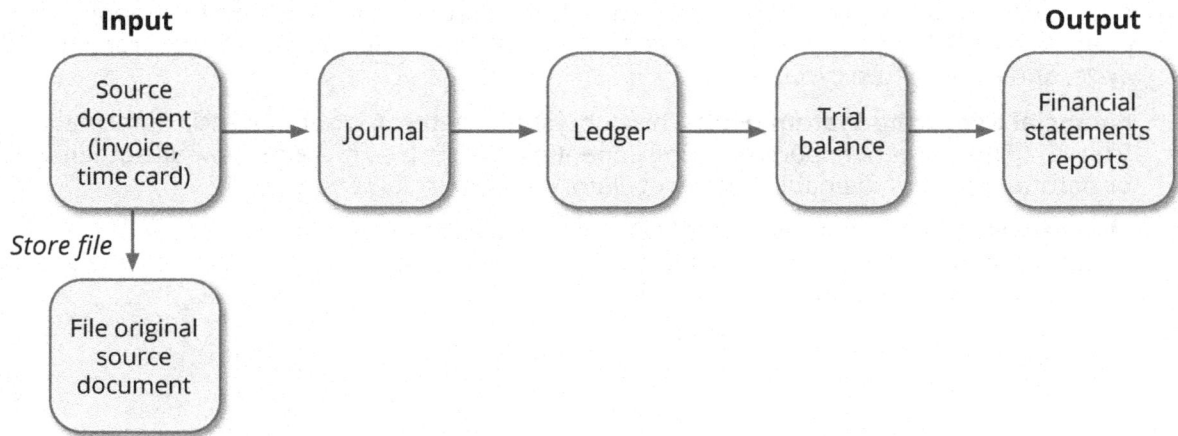

Audit trails are also useful for service auditors in a SOC 2® engagement, particularly if the service organization is an outsourced accounting firm providing bookkeeping, payroll, or other financial services. In that case, the service auditor would need a way to track transaction origination to the final output, such as a payroll check register report or financial statements.

1.3 Transaction Cycles

The transaction cycles are the core functions within an accounting department, such as the revenue cycle, purchasing and disbursement cycle, and other processes that involve the recognition and/or facilitation of transactions.

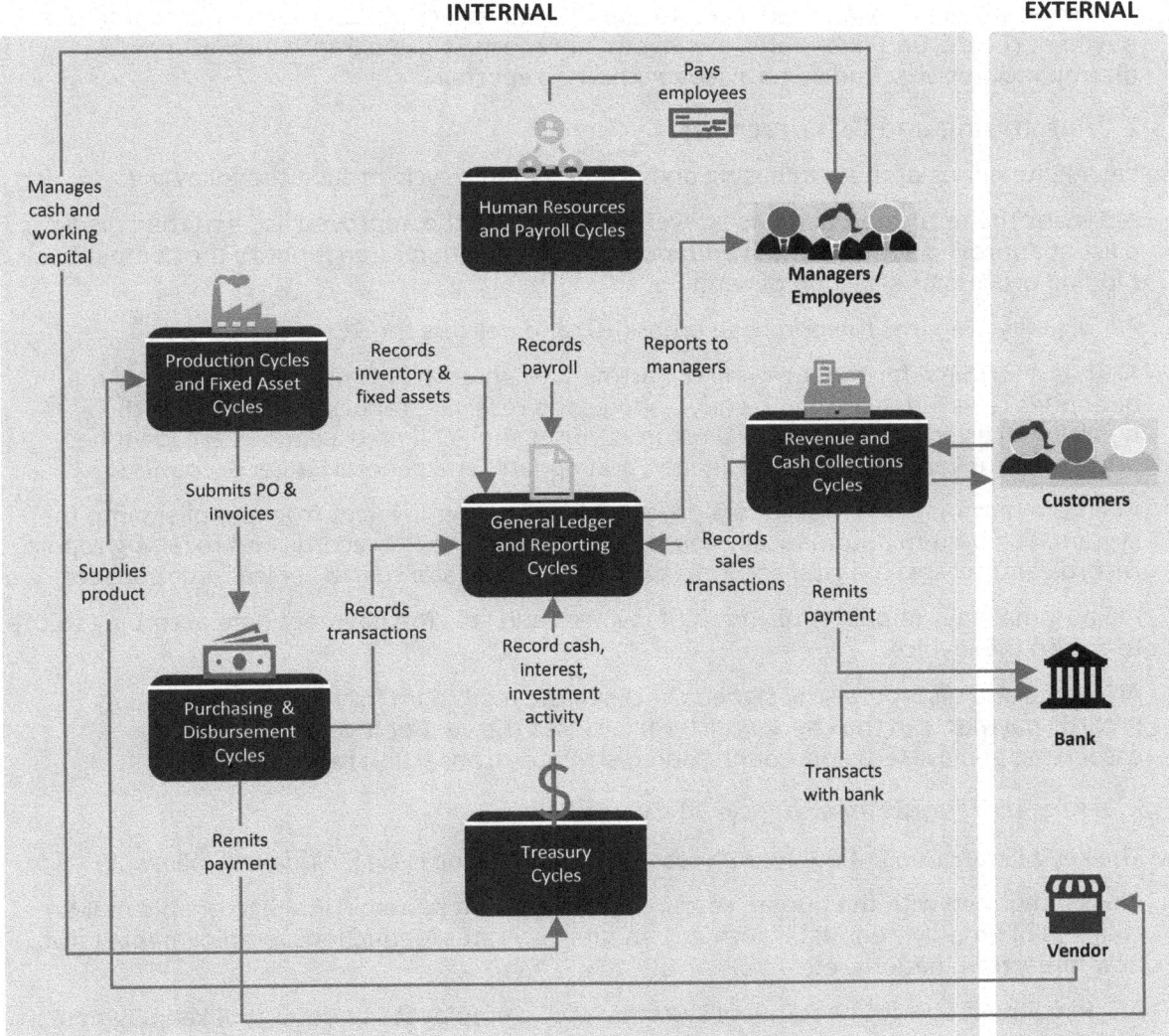

1.3.1 Revenue and Cash Collections Cycles

The key AIS functions of the revenue and cash collections cycle include the following:

▪ AIS allows real-time access to the inventory subsidiary ledger to check availability upon receiving a customer order.

▪ AIS automatically approves or denies credit based on the customer's credit record and payment history.

- AIS concurrently records sales invoices in the database, digitally transmits inventory release orders to the warehouse, and digitally sends packing slips to the shipping department.

- AIS has a terminal for the shipping department to digitally input shipping notices upon shipment. The input triggers the system to update the customer's credit record, reduce inventory subsidiary ledger records, insert the shipping date in sales invoice records, update general ledger accounts, and distribute management reports (e.g., inventory summary, sales summary).

- AIS has a terminal for the cash receipts clerk to access the cash receipt system and record the remittance.

- AIS closes the sales invoice, posts to the general ledger accounts, updates the customer's payment record, and distributes management reports (e.g., as transaction listings, discrepancy reports, and general ledger change reports).

1.3.2 Purchasing and Disbursement Cycles

The key AIS functions of the purchasing and disbursements cycle include the following:

- AIS reads the requested purchase to verify that it is on the approved list, and then displays a list of approved vendors with vendor contact information as an input to the competitive bidding process or selection of vendors.

- AIS digitally prepares the purchase order (PO) and delivers the PO to the vendor.

- AIS has a terminal for the receiving department to enter the PO number and inputs the quantities received. AIS concurrently updates the receiving report file, reconciles the quantity received against open PO records, closes the PO if no exceptions are identified, updates the inventory subsidiary ledger, and updates the general ledger accounts.

- AIS has a terminal for the accounts payable clerk to enter invoices from suppliers into the system. The system automatically links the invoices to the PO records and receiving report records and creates a digital accounts payable voucher stored in a centralized repository.

- AIS automatically approves payment of invoices and sets the payment date according to the terms on the invoice.

- AIS prints and distributes the signed checks to the mail room for mailing. The system records payments in the check register file, closes the vendor invoice, updates the associated general ledger accounts, and distributes transaction reports to users.

1.3.3 Human Resources and Payroll Cycles

- The key AIS functions of the human resources and payroll cycle include the following:

- AIS is integrated with the human resource management system (HRMS) to enable real-time changes of employment data, such as benefits, pay rates, deductions, employment status, new hires, terminations, etc.

- AIS, in connection with operational systems, allows employees to enter timekeeping data in real time to produce time and attendance files and the labor usage file.

- AIS allocates labor costs to job costs, accumulates direct and indirect labor expenses at the end of a work period (daily or weekly) on a batch basis, calculates payroll, updates employee records, and produces payroll registers for accounts payable and cash disbursement departments.

- AIS creates digital journal entries, attaches the original documents to the entries, and automatically updates the general ledger.

Illustration 1   HR and Payroll AIS

A regional commercial construction company, BuildPros, completes between 1,500 to 2,000 projects each year, building large-scale apartment complexes, office buildings, and some residential housing. Many of the employees have expertise that allows them to work across projects, and turnover is also very high, which makes an integrated human resources and payroll information system critical.

BuildPros understands this and adopts a system that streamlines onboarding due to the high frequency of new and terminated employees. The onboarding module requires the applicant to complete all paperwork prior to becoming an employee, taking the burden of completing paperwork from BuildPros. This also allows real-time updates by the employees in case they need to make changes to their W-4 for income tax withholding, elect changes in benefits, or perform supervisory tasks.

The system also has a mobile app with geo-restricted time clocks that allows employees to clock in remotely, but only from specific locations. As employees clock in and log their hours for a job, the payroll system assigns the hours to a predetermined job code that is associated with a customer list. Then before payroll is run, the payroll administrator reviews labor allocations to enhance the accuracy that customers are billed accurately. After payroll is complete, a general ledger export is created, which is automatically fed into the company's accounting information system to record payroll expense for the period.

1.3.4   Production Cycles and Fixed Asset Cycles

The key AIS functions of the production cycle include the following:

- AIS receives a work order for a production run from the production planning department. The new production order is input as a new record in the work-in-progress (WIP) subsidiary ledger.

- As labor and materials are added to the production run, documents reflecting these events, such as material requisitions and labor tickets, are sent to the AIS. AIS automatically updates the WIP account as production progresses.

- AIS tracks standard production costs for labor, materials, and manufacturing overhead (MOH). AIS records variances between standard production costs and actual costs.

- AIS closes the WIP account when it receives the final ticket marking the production move from WIP to finished goods inventory.

- AIS prepares journal entries as changes to the WIP account are recorded and automatically updates the general ledger.

Module 2   S2–23

The key AIS functions of the fixed asset cycle include the following:

- AIS has a terminal for fixed asset groups to create a record of the asset subsidiary ledger that includes each asset's useful life, salvage value, depreciation methodology, and location.

- AIS automatically updates the general ledger, prepares journal entries, and creates a depreciation schedule.

- AIS automatically calculates depreciation, accumulated depreciation, and book value at the end of the period. The system then creates a journal entry file and updates the general ledger accounts accordingly.

- When an asset is disposed of, the clerk records the disposal, prompting the system to calculate gains or losses of the disposal, prepare journal entries, and post adjusting entries to the general ledger.

1.3.5 Treasury Cycles

An AIS treasury cycle is integrated with the other transaction cycles. These other cycles provide much of the capital available to the company (revenue) that is, in turn, used to pay expenses, pay employees, and purchase fixed assets. This AIS integration allows effective cash management.

The key AIS functions of the treasury cycle include the following:

- Various source documents such as deposit slips, checks, stock market data, and interest data are used to post journal entries affecting cash balances.

- The accounting department performs bank reconciliations by using bank statements to reconcile the cash account balance at the bank with the general ledger. AIS has control features in place to help prevent fraud.

- Journal entries are posted for each change in cash, and the system automatically provides updated general ledger information.

- AIS can provide various reports to assist with cash management. These reports cover cash receipts and other trends in cash collections and disbursements. AIS can also provide changes in investments and estimates on interest and dividend payments. These reports allow the accounting department to effectively predict cash flows.

1.3.6 General Ledger and Reporting Cycles

The key AIS functions of the general ledger and reporting cycle include the following:

- AIS updates the general ledger as various transactions (discussed in the previous cycles) occur and journal entries are posted.

- At the end of an accounting period, AIS automatically produces a trial balance showing the debit and credit balances in each account. The accounting department reviews the trial balance and related worksheets to determine if any adjustments need to be made.

- The accounting department posts any necessary adjusting entries such as entries for depreciation, prepaid expenses, and unrecorded revenue.

- AIS produces final financial statements after adjusted entries are made and the debit and credit amounts in the trial balance are equal. AIS also produces reports showing variances and performance over the accounting period.

- AIS automatically closes temporary accounts so that a new accounting period can begin. AIS carries forward balance sheet accounts into the next period.

2 IT Systems and Process Improvement

2.1 Process Improvement Driven by IT Systems

An organization can improve the performance of its information systems by improving business processes that provide inputs to those systems. Improving consistency and reliability in processes results in better data. Better processes lead to fewer errors, more efficient accounting, and enhanced reporting. Four broad areas of process improvements that can enhance accounting information system performance are automation, shared services, outsourcing, and offshore operations. Additionally, there are three specific forms of technology that are gaining mass adoption in process improvement: robotic process automation (RPA), natural language processing software, and neural networks.

2.1.1 Automation

Automation is an umbrella term used to describe the process of using technology to perform tasks without human intervention. The tasks could be simple and repetitive, or complex and requiring judgment. An example of this would include business process automation for repeatable day-to-day tasks.

To implement automation, an organization must first examine an existing business process to describe the steps taken, the exchange of information, the governance of policies for each transaction, and the knowledge needed to complete each task. The goal of this analysis is to understand the process thoroughly enough to replace it with business process automation facilitated by IT systems.

2.1.2 Shared Services

Shared services refers to seeking out redundant services, combining them, and then sharing those services within a group or organization. The distinguishing feature of shared services is that they are shared within an organization or group of affiliates and almost always involve software that is designed to process large batches of data.

Illustration 2   Shared Services

Financial Group Inc. is a financial services company with three distinct lines of business including accounting, tax, and consulting. Currently, each division operates as a separate company with its own human resources, payroll, and legal departments. In order to more effectively manage the organization and reduce costs, the new CEO implements a shared services plan whereby all human resources, payroll, and legal department services will be consolidated into one centralized function. The CEO thinks that this shared services approach will eliminate redundant back-office functions and will reduce annual operating costs by $750,000.

2.1.3 Outsourcing

Outsourcing is defined as the contracting of services to an external provider. Examples include a payroll service or a call center that provide support or back-office services for a fee. A contractual relationship exists between the business and its service provider. With proper controls in place, cloud-based systems can allow external service providers to work seamlessly with an organization.

Outsourcing can provide for efficiencies, but there are also risks associated with quality of service, reduced productivity, and information security.

These risks include:

- **Quality Risk:** An outsourced product or service might be defective. Suppliers might provide substandard products or services.
- **Quality of Service:** Poorly designed service agreements may impede the quality of service.
- **Productivity:** Real productivity may be reduced even though service provider employees are paid less.
- **Staff Turnover:** Experienced and valued staff whose functions have been outsourced may leave the organization.
- **Language Skills:** Outsourced services may go offshore. Language barriers may reduce the quality of service.
- **Security:** Security of information with a third party might be compromised.
- **Qualifications of Outsourcers:** Credentials of service providers may be flawed. Offshore degrees may not include the same level of training as domestic degrees.
- **Labor Insecurity:** Labor insecurity increases when jobs move to an external service provider or, as a result of globalization, out of the country.

2.1.4 Offshore Operations

Offshore operations relate to outsourcing of services or business functions to an external party in a different country. A computer manufacturer in the United States, for example, might have its call center in India. The most common types of offshore outsourcing are:

- Information technology provided by a managed services provider (MSP)
- Business processes (call centers, accounting operations, tax compliance)
- Software research and development (software development)
- Knowledge processes (processes requiring advanced knowledge and specialized skill sets, such as reading x-rays, etc.)

2.1.5 Robotic Process Automation (RPA)

Robotic process automation is a specific form of business process automation that refers to the use of programs to perform repetitive tasks that do not require skilled human labor, such as extracting information from a user interface (e.g., a customer complaint form or a goods order form) and inputting that data into a form, moving files, sending payment reminders, and executing other commands that would be considered clerical work. RPA is different from artificial intelligence in that it focuses more on doing tasks using simple, rule-based processes rather than learning or providing analysis.

One manifestation of RPA is in web scraping tools that scour the Web looking for instances of specified text to collect all material surrounding it. This content may be forms entered by users or existing web page content. General web scraping tools often collect ancillary data unintentionally, which introduces noise into the analysis. Robotic process automation uses this as a point of refinement to yield a more highly curated collection of data yielding a more reliable analysis. Robotic process automation can mimic human interaction with many kinds of computer systems.

2.1.6   LiDAR (light detection and ranging)

LiDAR (light detection and ranging) involves emitting laser pulses toward a target and measuring the time it takes to return to the sensor. It is not considered a Robotic Process Automation technology. LiDAR is an example of how artificial intelligence and machine learning supercharged an old technology to allow it to be successful in the advancement of self-driving cars.

Illustration 3   Robotic Process Automation in Practice

A company is interested in formulating an RPA to collect the data from various inventory invoices, payment orders, and reconciling documents used in its logistics system (part of the enterprise resource planning system [ERP]), because it would be more efficient to have software collect and format this existing information than to train every employee on using existing or new systems. Because there are a limited number of forms, the company constructs a library of forms for reference by the RPA. Once the RPA has been trained to recognize each form, the company directs all forms to the RPA, which scans each form, applies the parameters set in the program, and sends the appropriate data into the ERP application database.

2.1.7   Natural Language Processing (NLP) Software

Natural language processing involves the technology developed and used to encode, decode, and interpret human languages so that the technology can perform tasks, interact with other humans, or carry out commands on other technological devices. This requires the mapping of things like pragmatics, syntax, phonetics, pitch, and tone, as well as ensuring the NLP program determines the proper response or chain of action. This is the technology needed to build a network embedded on household devices or other Internet of Things (IoT) devices so that the household has a virtual assistant to turn on the television by voice command. Accounting applications include parsing text documents or speeches made by executives to extract and catalog any financially relevant data.

2.1.8   AI and Machine Learning

Artificial intelligence (AI) is an umbrella term used to describe systems that are created to perform complex tasks typically requiring human intelligence and judgment. Examples of AI include speech recognition or natural language processing, image recognition, and various technologies used in self-driving cars.

Machine learning (ML) is a subset of Artificial Intelligence involving the use of algorithms (such as statistical models) and data sets supplied for computers to learn and make decisions. Examples of machine learning include recommendation systems (e-commerce), auto-correct, and predictive text input.

2.1.9   Neural Networks

An artificial neural network is a form of technology that is modeled after neurons that facilitate the function of human or animal memory. The basic pieces of a neural network involve an input layer, a hidden layer, and an output (results) layer. Within the input layer are the different variables that feed into the hidden layer. In the hidden layer, there are a series of weights applied based on the inputs selected, which then direct the algorithm toward a given output. A neural network is the key technology used in machine learning applications. The feedback on output becomes a key input to refine the hidden layer to generate a different outcome.

There are typically multiple layers embedded within the hidden layer acting as neurons that guide the input through to its output (result) based on the cumulative value of all weighted points. Weights may initially be predetermined but the intent of the neural network is to learn from prior trends in results based on inputs. So just as a human's response changes, its reaction is refined in the hidden layer by changes to weights, which yields a different outcome. This is the computing architecture needed to make fuzzy logic decisions for inference engines, commonly used in fraud detection. Deep learning is a specialized subset of neural networks that is used to capture patterns in large volumes of data. It can be referred to as the "engine" of the hidden layer in neural networks.

2.1.10 Managing System Changes

Whether implementing automation, outsourcing, or advanced technology to improve business processes, an organization must manage system changes methodically so that core business functions are not disrupted. While there is a myriad of methodologies that can be used to implement system changes, two well-known approaches are the waterfall model and the agile method. Both of these have phases that focus on system design, testing, deployment, change review, and maintenance.

Automation: A High-Level View

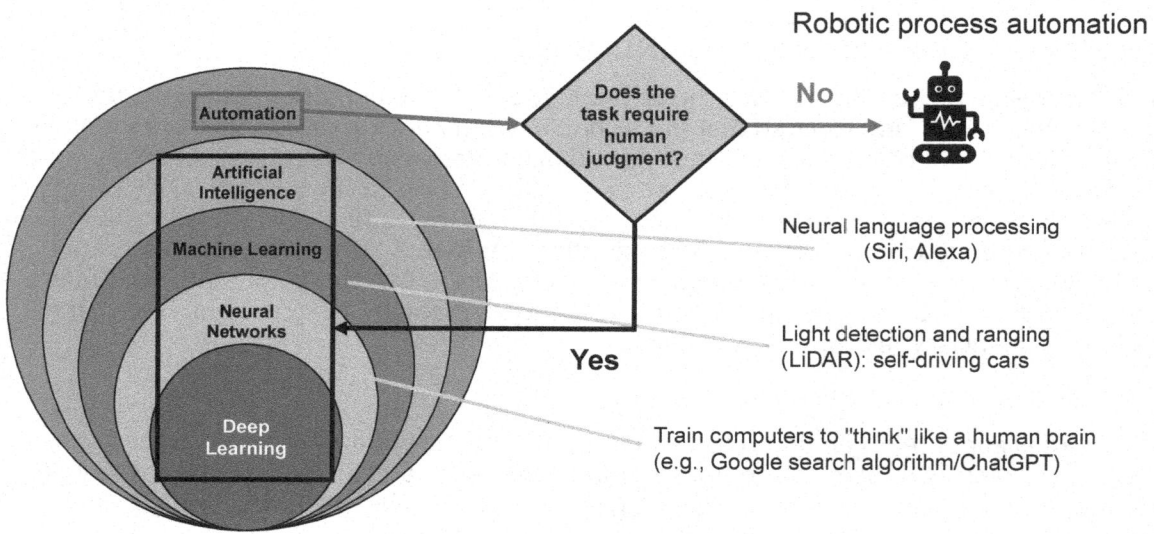

3 Detecting Design Deficiencies in Processing Integrity

3.1 Processing Integrity

Processing integrity refers to a system's ability to initiate and complete transactions so that they are valid, accurate, completed timely, and authorized to meet a company's objective. Integrity also refers to confidentiality and privacy of the details related to transactions involving data that identifies customers, patient health records, employees, or financial accounts. Additionally, processing integrity is one of the five trust services criteria.

3.2 Identifying Deficiencies in Suitability or Design

The AICPA defines deficiencies in the design of a control in a SOC 2® engagement as either:

1. necessary controls that are missing; or

2. existing controls that are not designed properly.

Identifying whether a deficiency in design exists related to processing integrity can be accomplished by applying the trust services criteria. To perform this evaluation, a service auditor must first obtain an understanding of management's risk assessment process, evaluate the link between controls in the system description and relevant trust services criteria, and determine whether the appropriate controls are in place and whether those controls were implemented.

Examples of how the trust services criteria can be used to evaluate deficiencies are as follows:

	Trust Services Criteria	Use For Detecting Deficiencies in Suitability and Design
1	Security	Identify transaction processing methods that compromise confidentiality, privacy, and availability, and that can be circumvented to allow unauthorized access.
2	Availability	Search for bottlenecks in the flow of data across the organization and identify other processes that prevent data from being available when needed.
3	Processing Integrity	Survey processing methods and transactions that do not complete timely or at all, yield faulty results, or do not meet the company's objectives.
4	Confidentiality	Evaluate employees and processes that handle transactions with confidential data to identify potential data leakage, mishandling, or other practices that expose confidential information.
5	Privacy	Analyze methods used to collect, store, use, and dispose of personal data that are being processed to identify the potential for data breaches or leakage.

Another way to identify deficiencies is by using the AICPA's *Description Criteria for a Description of a Service Organization's System in a SOC 2® Report* to compare with an organization's system design documentation. The set of benchmarks in this implementation guide serves as a strong tool for evaluating system descriptions of service organizations and can specifically be used for detecting deficiencies in the suitability or design of controls related to an information system's processing integrity.

Two items the guide recommends to review are the *principle service commitment* and the *principle system requirements*, which are required to be disclosed by management to support the understanding of the system, the services provided, and the design of the controls. Understanding how and why management disclosed certain attributes of its system within these descriptions, particularly related to processing integrity, will help assess the suitability of system control design.

3.3 Deviations in Operations of Controls

The AICPA defines a deficiency in the operation of a control in a SOC 2® engagement as a properly designed control that either:

1. does not operate as designed; or

2. is performed by a person who lacks authority or competence to perform the control effectively.

Controls are suitably designed if they meet, or have the potential to meet, the trust services criteria because the suitably designed controls provide reasonable assurance that a company's system requirements and service commitments were achieved.

3.3.1 Performing Tests of Controls

To test the operating effectiveness of controls based on the trust services criteria, the service auditor should obtain proper evidence. This will include evidence of how the controls were applied, the consistency of application, and the personnel responsible for applying them.

Changes to the service organizations should be documented and, if possible, test the controls both before and after the change to determine whether the modified control meets service commitments as they relate to the trust services criteria. If deficiencies are already identified, the service auditor is not required to test the effectiveness of those controls.

The service auditor is responsible for designing and performing the tests of controls, which may involve making inquiries, reperforming controls, observing service organization personnel performing the controls, and reviewing documentation. This allows the service auditor to obtain evidence of how the control was applied, the consistency with which it was applied, and the person applying it. This also aids the auditor in ascertaining whether controls are dependent on other controls.

Timing is a critical factor that the service auditor should consider when designing tests of controls. Relevant factors include understanding the period in which the data will be available and the potential for data to be overwritten if not obtained timely. Testing can be performed at interim dates, at the end of an examination period, or after the examination period if controls in operation do not leave evidence until after the end of the period.

The size and frequency of sampling when testing controls also must be considered. Variables that influence this include how often a control is performed, the expectation that a control will actually deviate, the testing period length, and the reliability of the evidence.

3.3.2   Controls That Did Not Need to Operate

Some controls, due to the nature of their operation or circumstance, either can't operate during the testing period or are not prudent to operate. For instance, controls that relate to authenticating a new employee's identity may not be able to be performed because there was no new employee to onboard. In these instances, the service auditor does not need to modify the opinion on operating effectiveness of controls.

3.3.3   Identifying Deviations in Operating Effectiveness of Controls

As deviations in the operating effectiveness of controls are discovered, the service auditor should accumulate documentation of those occurrences. If a service auditor cannot obtain reasonable assurance that system requirements or service commitments are being met, then the deficiency should be considered material.

If the deviations are the result of fraud, the service auditor should assess the risk that the system description does not accurately reflect the system that was designed, and the operating controls are not operating effectively. The service auditor should also consider applicable noncompliance with regulations, and it may be appropriate for the auditor to do the following:

■   Hold discussions with the appropriate parties.

■   Request that the appropriate party consult legal counsel, a regulator, or a qualified third party.

■   Consider implications related to other aspects of the engagement.

■   Obtain legal advice about different courses of action that could be taken and their consequences.

■   Communicate directly with regulators or appropriate third parties.

■   Withdraw from the engagement.

If the service auditor identifies other systems not within the scope of the audit that are affected by a system incident, the auditor should understand the nature and cause of the incident as it could be the result of ineffective controls of the system being audited.

If the incident is the result of a security breach, then the auditor should determine whether the inherent risks of the system environment are different than originally assessed, or whether the system was compromised. This reassessment of risk may require that additional procedures be performed or new evidence obtained of additional controls that are suitably designed that do provide reasonable assurance that service requirements and commitments were met based on trust services criteria.

Ultimately, the service auditor decides whether the identified deviations, either individually or combined, are material. If they are considered material, then the auditor must modify the opinion on operating effectiveness.

4 COSO Internal Control Framework and Blockchain

4.1 COSO Internal Control Framework for IT systems

The Committee of Sponsoring Organizations (COSO) has developed guidance and frameworks covering the areas of internal control, risk management, and fraud deterrence. Within its five-point *Internal Control—Integrated Framework* ("the framework"), there are two categories with principles that pertain specifically to internal control over information technology.

Within the Control Activities category, principle 11 states that there should be general controls over technology in order to achieve organizational objectives. To establish these controls, the company must understand the dependency between general controls over technology and the use of technology in business processes. The company must also establish controls over relevant technology infrastructure, security management, technology, acquisition, and maintenance processes.

Within the Information and Communication category, principle 13 states that organizations should acquire, create, and use quality information in order to support internal controls. This includes:

- identifying the company's information needs;
- capturing both external and internal sources of data;
- processing relevant data into useful information; and
- maintaining quality when processing that data.

Principle 14 states that effective communication of information is necessary to support internal controls. This means communicating internal information to the proper stakeholders, including the board of directors; providing communication lines that are separate from those directly to management; and selecting relevant methods of communication.

Illustration 4 COSO Principles

Spinal Surgery Clinic (SSC) P.A., a large group of physicians focusing on spinal surgery, recently had an outside firm perform an IT audit as recommended by SSC's board of directors. The findings resulted in recommendations that followed the COSO *Internal Control—Integrated Framework* principles 11, 13, and 14. As such, SSC invested in new technology that required user identities to be verified by multiple points of validation other than just a password in order to access patient accounts (in line with principle 11). Additionally, SSC adopted a state-of-the-art data cleansing system in an effort to acquire and use error-free data to enhance patient outcomes, which aligned with principle 13. Lastly, to address principle 14, SSC began performing regular reviews of key IT functions and started issuing monthly reports of internal control to the board of directors.

4.1.1 Blockchain Overview

Blockchain is a control system originally designed to govern the creation and distribution of Bitcoin. Bitcoin is a digital currency that exists only in electronic form, called a cryptocurrency. Bitcoin must be "mined" in order to confirm transactions. Mining cryptocurrencies involves a person or group of people performing cryptography, which is the solving of complex mathematical equations.

Through cryptography, blocks of a fixed number of transactions are confirmed at a time. The reward for solving (validating) the equation is both:

- the receipt of bitcoin; and

- the validation of a new block of transactions.

Because electronic data can be easily copied and altered, the accounting system governing it must prevent the copying or alteration of the cryptocurrency; otherwise, the currency may become instantly worthless through counterfeiting. Blockchain technology was developed to prevent bitcoin from being replicated and to limit its initial creation so that there is only a finite number of bitcoins.

The value of blockchain is its resistance to alteration, multiparty transaction validation, and decentralized nature. Alteration is difficult because each block adds to all prior blocks, enabling everyone to view all blocks in the chain to the beginning of the entire chain. This serves as a form of audit trail for blockchain users and service auditors performing SOC 2® engagements:

- An auditor can use the chain to verify transactions by validating cryptographic signatures, time stamps, and tracing wallet addresses.

- A service auditor could verify the security of nodes on the network and supporting infrastructure to enhance the physical or virtual integrity of the blockchain.

  - Not all data needed to validate transactions is on the blockchain, so service auditors may need to consider the potential for off-chain data.

  - Off-chain data may include personal information tied to an address, or business data such as a supply chain using blockchain technology to document production updates.

Another key value of blockchain technology, specifically decentralized blockchains like Bitcoin, is its ability to be partially detached from government control, although many nations regulate both the trading of certain types of cryptocurrencies and the exchanges on which those currencies trade. In some cases, cryptocurrencies are banned entirely, while others require the registration of those currencies as securities and require the exchanges to meet the same standards as stock exchanges such as the NASDAQ or the London Stock Exchange.

4.1.2 Applying COSO to Blockchain

COSO provides guidance on how the internal control framework should be leveraged to implement controls to address the risks associated with blockchain technology. Blockchain creates implications in each of the components of the COSO framework. With blockchain, record keeping is completely transformed by recording transactions with minimal human intervention. Transactions are immutable and irreversible, creating record integrity. While certain risks are eliminated with blockchain, new risks arise.

An organization must manage the control environment where its entity is intertwined with other entities or people participating in the blockchain. An organization will not have complete control.

Likewise, blockchain has no centralized management overseeing its activity. That means no particular entity can be held accountable or responsible if things go wrong. An organization cannot simply engage a SOC auditor to assess controls. This decentralization is a unique challenge with blockchain. Organizations must find alternative ways to gain assurance over blockchain controls.

For financial reporting, blockchain's attributes increase the visibility of transactions and the availability of data:

- Blockchain's attributes allow management to support its financial records.
- Blockchain's attributes make audits of blockchain transactions easier because of automatic audit trails.
- Management can provide financial information to stakeholders faster and more effectively.

In the event of a SOC 2® engagement, a service auditor should consider the trust services criteria (security, availability, processing integrity, confidentiality, and privacy) as it relates to each of the COSO's five control components.

For example, the engagement team should determine whether the processing integrity of transactions processed on the blockchain's ledger meets standards required in the COSO's control environment, such as principle 4's requirement to demonstrate commitment to competence.

However, it should be noted that due to the nature of most decentralized blockchains, certain control components might not be met in the traditional sense, including component 2 concerning oversight responsibility or component 5 covering accountability. This is because decentralization distributes accountability and oversight so that there is not one individual or a small group that dictates policies and procedures for the entire blockchain. Service auditors may need to adjust their perspective on how a control is met or restrict SOC 2® engagements to organizations with a centralized blockchain.

The following table shows how the COSO's five control components and 17 principles help evaluate risks related to blockchain.

Components	Principles	How COSO Helps Evaluate Blockchain Risks
Control Environment	1. Demonstrates commitment to integrity and ethical values	Outlines actions for a board to make regarding a code of conduct to validate integrity, ethical values, and compliance.
	2. Exercises oversight responsibility	Recommends enhancing the board and audit committee's understanding of blockchain potential uses and how to effectively manage it.
	3. Establishes structure, authority, and responsibility	Gives recommendations on establishing cross-disciplinary teams for implementing blockchain, and defining responsibility and authority for blockchain solutions.
	4. Demonstrates commitment to competence	Recommends reevaluating competencies and continuously monitoring the blockchain ecosystem for new developments in its construct or application.

Control Environment (continued)	5. Enforces accountability	Gives guidance on identifying who is responsible and who has authority in the blockchain, including segregation of duties and who has access to private keys to authorize transactions.
Risk Assessment	6. Specifies suitable objectives	Advocates for the establishment of objectives so that the implementation of a blockchain supports verifiable and reliable financial records and reports.
	7. Identifies and analyzes risk	Proposes developing robust risk assessment processes prior to implementing a blockchain solution.
	8. Assesses fraud risk	Recommends engaging IT and blockchain specialists to identify areas of risk and potential fraud schemes.
	9. Identifies and analyzes significant change	Endorses using strong change-control processes when deploying or amending a blockchain.
Control Activities	10. Selects and develops control activities	Outlines general and specific control activities for critical aspects of a blockchain such as nodes, consensus protocols, private keys, and smart contracts.
	11. Selects and develops general controls over technology	
	12. Deploys control activities through policies and procedures	Lists considerations for policies and procedures addressing internal controls, new risks, and accounting related to blockchain applications.
Information and Communication	13. Uses relevant, quality information	Proposes the use of data analytics procedures to get relevant and quality data from the blockchain to be used to support management objectives.
	14. Communicates internally	Recommends educating internal stakeholders on how blockchain will be used by the business; also endorses developing communication methods to ensure operational changes are communicated appropriately.
	15. Communicates externally	Suggests engaging external auditors during development of blockchain applications in a company's processes.
Monitoring Activities	16. Conducts ongoing and/ or separate evaluations	Encourages the use of computerized continuous monitoring techniques due to the volume of transactions being processed; also recommends ongoing evaluations to detect changes or updates to technology to ensure controls exist and are still working.
	17. Evaluates and communicates deficiencies	Recommends identifying talent that can identify changes from a company's baseline, correct deficiencies, and then communicate those deficiencies.

When implementing the COSO's controls to a blockchain setting, organizations should consider the following:

- Focus on preventative controls due to volume and speed of transactions being processed.

- Increase the frequency of detective controls, also due to the volume of transactions.

- Develop controls that use other analytic technology like artificial intelligence tools, such as large language models (LLM), which are good at quickly identifying bugs in code.

- Develop a code of conduct and establish policies that comply with KYC (Know-Your-Customer) regulations and AML (Anti-Money Laundering) policies.

- Create cross-disciplinary teams with segregation of duties in mind and with clear reporting lines that identify all users participating in the blockchain's creation and maintenance.

3 Availability, Resiliency, and Disaster Recovery

1 System Availability

1.1 Availability Scope

Availability, or being able to perform business functions or meet business objectives, is critical to a business's success. The concept of availability has various components. It includes system availability, which is when business data is accessible and IT systems are operating normally. Availability also includes availability of an organization's human capital and personnel being ready and able to perform in normal operations.

The risk of normal operations failing in part, or as a whole, must be evaluated and mitigated through business resiliency programs. Even minor periods of paused operations or system downtime can cause organizations major problems, including loss of revenue, data, trust, and customers. There are a few key considerations when planning how to maintain availability. The following graphic depicts the integration of such key considerations:

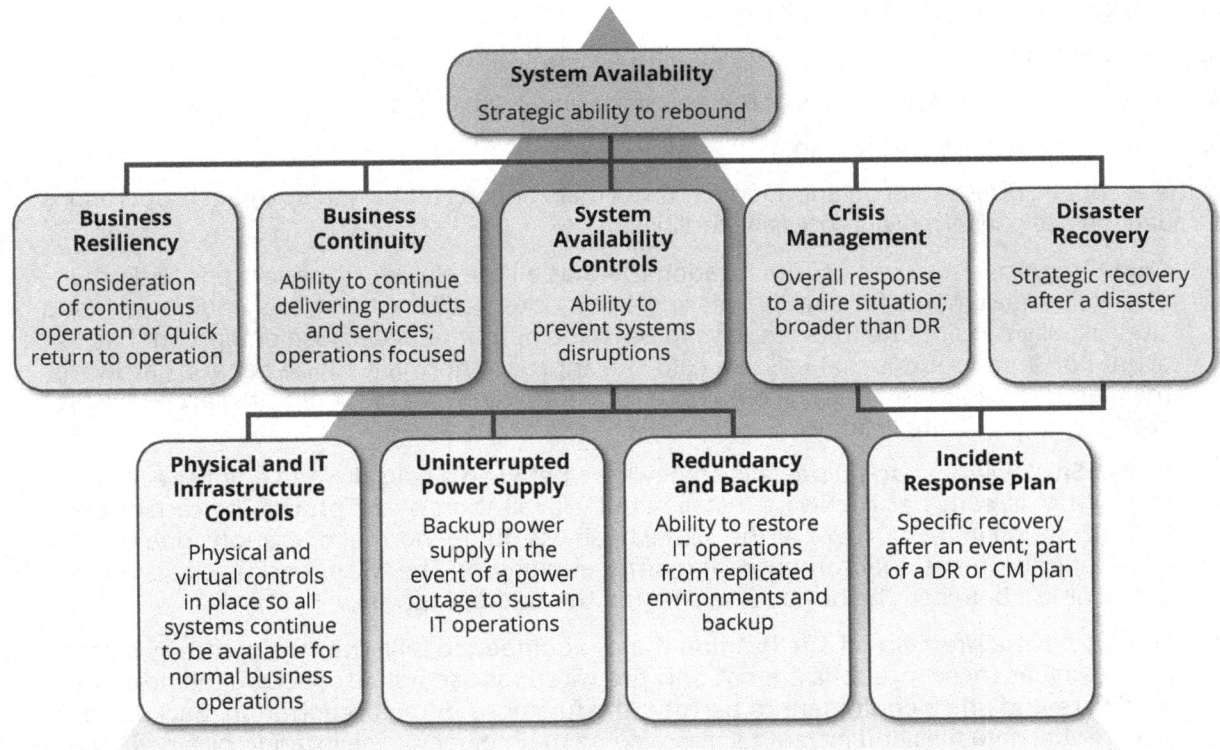

1.1.1 Business Resiliency

Business resiliency is the integration of system availability controls, disaster recovery plans, business continuity plans, and crisis management plans into a central set of procedures to consider whether a business can continue to operate or quickly return to operations without irreparable harm to its people, information, or assets.

Organizations must identify what activities are necessary to the core operations of their organization and assess existing threats to those activities. Once critical systems and processes are identified, management can begin building a business resiliency program to determine whether these vital functions can quickly be repaired and put back into operation given a business crisis or disruption.

1.1.2 Disaster Recovery

A major component of a business resiliency program is disaster recovery. Disaster recovery consists of an entity's plans for restoring and continuing its information technology function in the event of the destruction of not only program and data files, but also computer processing capability.

Short-term problems or outages do not normally constitute disasters. If processing cannot be quickly reestablished at the original processing site (possibly because the original processing site no longer exists), then disaster recovery is necessary.

The steps in a disaster recovery plan are to:

1. assess the risks;

2. identify mission-critical applications and data;

3. develop a plan for handling the mission-critical applications;

4. determine the responsibilities of the personnel involved in disaster recovery; and

5. test the disaster recovery plan.

In the event of a disaster, an organization has three main options for how to maintain IT operations through the use of alternative processing facilities:

1. **Cold Site:** A *cold site* is an off-site location that has all the electrical connections and other physical requirements for data processing, but it does not have the actual equipment. Cold sites usually require one to three days to be made operational because equipment has to be acquired. Organizations that utilize a cold-site approach normally utilize generic hardware that can be readily (and quickly) obtained from hardware vendors. Cold sites are the least costly form of off-site location.

2. **Warm Site:** A *warm backup site* falls somewhere between a cold site and a hot site. It is a facility that already has hardware installed but will fall short of the processing capabilities typically found in a hot site or at the actual business during normal operations due to a lack of fully operational computer and office equipment. The warm backup site is the compromise between the hot backup site and the cold backup site.

3. **Hot Site:** A *hot site* is an off-site location that is equipped to take over the company's data processing as these locations are not only pre-wired for use but also include the necessary hardware and office equipment to perform the functions of the organization. Backup copies of essential data files and programs may also be maintained at the location or a nearby data storage facility. Hot sites are more expensive than cold sites.

The following matrix depicts key characteristics of each of these sites:

	Location	Connections in Place?	Equipment in Place?	Days to Be Operational	Cost
Cold Site	Off-site	Yes	No	1–3 days	Cheapest
Warm Site	Off-site	Yes/No	Yes/No	0–3 days	Moderately expensive
Hot Site	Off-site	Yes	Yes	Immediately	Most expensive

1.1.3 Business Continuity Plans

Disaster recovery plans are focused on restoring the IT infrastructure during a disaster while business continuity plans are focused on keeping the business operational. Business continuity plans are more comprehensive than disaster recovery plans and contain contingency and mitigation procedures around all business processes, including relocating facilities, human resource tasks, and managing relationships with customers and suppliers. The overall goal of the business continuity plan will be how to continue operations or restore operations in the most efficient and effective manner possible with consideration given to all aspects of the organization. Business continuity plans must consider the following:

- Identify the organization's key business processes.
- Identify the risks that exist in key business processes.
- Determine the acceptable downtime for key business processes.
- Implement mitigation and contingency plans to address risks and downtimes.

1.1.4 SOC 2® Engagement Consideration of Business Continuity Plan Testing

During the performance of a SOC 2® engagement, service auditors may verify that an organization's business continuity plan testing is performed on a periodic basis. The engagement auditor's point of focus during the engagement would be to determine whether the organization's business continuity plan:

- was based on relevant and likely scenarios;
- was focused on components that can significantly impair the company;
- considered scenarios in which key personnel are lacking; and
- was periodically revised based on test results.

Illustration 1	Business Continuity Plan

Health One Inc., a health insurance company serving members nationwide, reviews its business continuity plan annually. The company's main office is located in a region where hurricanes threaten business operations each year. Although most of the company's employees work remotely, many lose internet access during natural disasters, making them unable to work from their homes.

As part of Health One's business continuity plan, the company relocates a core team of employees to a safe, operational facility. The facility is secure and has internet access and telephone services. Additionally, the company moved all critical applications and systems to the cloud several years ago as part of its business continuity plan. By using the cloud, the company can determine whether, in the event of a disaster, the relocated core team can resume necessary business operations on behalf of the company.

1.1.5 Business Impact Analysis

Identifying and assessing risks is a key component in building a business resiliency program. This assessment can be done by performing a business impact analysis (BIA). This analysis identifies the business units, departments, and processes that are essential to the survival of an entity as well as the organizational impact in the event of failure or disruption.

The BIA will identify how quickly essential business units and/or processes can return to full operation following a disaster. The BIA will also identify the resources required to resume business operations. For example, a specific department may utilize custom hardware/software, operate in locations with challenging geographic or weather conditions, or depend on third-party vendors.

- Under a **high-impact (H)** category, the department:
    - cannot operate without this resource;
    - may experience a high recovery cost; or
    - may fail to meet the organization's objectives or maintain its reputation.
- Under a **moderate- or medium-impact (M)** category, the department:
    - could partially function temporarily for a period of days or a week;
    - may experience some cost of recovery; or
    - may fail to meet the organization's objectives or maintain its reputation.
- Under a **low-impact (L)** category, the department:
    - could operate for an extended period of time; or
    - may notice an effect on achieving the organization's objectives or maintaining its reputation.

The BIA is made up of the following steps:

1. **Establish the BIA Approach:** Agreement on the necessary approach to performing the BIA is critical and must first be clearly outlined by the organization. During this phase, executives and relevant managers define the impact types and criteria, as well as the time frames to observe and the methodology to use.

2. **Identify Critical Resources:** Management must clearly define critical functions in the organization and delineate which IT resources are required to perform them. This will highlight organizational processes that are the most vulnerable to disruption. This step involves a combination of interviews with key personnel and documentation review.

3. **Define Disruption Impacts:** In this phase, the organization must identify and evaluate the impact of a service disruption by understanding its effects over time and the resources negatively affected or required to deal with the disruption. Risks can include quantitative or qualitative effects and may be natural or human-inflicted threats.

4. **Estimate Losses:** This step involves the management team outlining an exhaustive list of potential risks and events that could occur that would disrupt operations and assigning each of those threats a probability of likelihood. This probability is referred to as the annualized rate of occurrence. Potential losses can be quantified by using the ARO and the variables in the illustration below to calculate the annualized loss expectancy.

5. **Establish Recovery Priorities:** Management must prioritize recovery strategies to decide which tasks personnel should address first. This will vary depending on the maximum outage time that a particular resource can handle, with those resources that have a lower tolerance threshold targeted first. For example, resources that can only be down four hours before a significant impact to the business occurs will be addressed before a resource that can be down 24 hours.

6. **Create the BIA Report:** These reports may be completed at the department level, business unit level, product level, or by any other appropriate means of segregating a business to evaluate risk, as long as all known risks have been addressed. These individual reports can then be combined to form a company-wide BIA.

7. **Implement BIA Recommendations:** This phase involves senior management evaluating the comprehensive BIA report, determining which risks pose the greatest threat, and implementing preventative or corrective actions to remediate those threats.

Illustration 2　BIA Estimation of Losses

BuildTech Inc., a manufacturing company specializing in construction equipment, is conducting its business impact analysis and is estimating its losses from potential risks and events that may disrupt operations. The organization determined that a key risk area would be the partial flooding of the southern portion of BuildTech's $5 million data center, which processes the analytic workflows pertaining to the company's proprietary software embedded in its construction equipment, which makes up 40 percent of the data center, due to excessive rain or severe weather systems. Based on research and prior knowledge, it was determined that flooding would occur every 20 years. BuildTech Inc. wishes to annualize the cost of this risk.

To gain an understanding of the annualized loss expectancy of a flood, BuildTech Inc. would utilize the following formulas:

1. **Annualized Rate of Occurrence (ARO)** is the expected frequency of occurrences in a year.

    - Research and historical data of the area show that the occurrence would happen roughly once every 20 years.

    - ARO is calculated by taking the number of occurrences and dividing it by the relevant year(s):

        $1 / 20 = 0.05$

2. **Exposure Factor (EF)** is the damage in terms of dollars, expressed as a percentage of an asset's value.

    - Based on assessments of the areas of the data center subject to damage from flooding, it was determined that 40 percent of the data center is at risk of damage if a flood was to occur.

    - The EF for this flooding risk to the data center would be 40 percent.

3. **Single Loss Expectancy (SLE)** is the cost of an individual loss.

    - SLE is calculated as the exposure factor multiplied by value of the asset.

    - BuildTech's SLE would be the EF (40%) multiplied by the data center's value ($5,000,000) = $2,000,000.

4. **Annualized Loss Expectancy (ALE)** is the cost of a specific loss in a given year.

    - ALE is calculated by taking the single loss expectancy and multiplying it by the annualized rate of occurrence.

    - BuildTech's ALE would be the SLE ($2,000,000) multiplied by the ARO (0.05) = $100,000.

1.1.6   Crisis Management Plans

In terms of business operations, a crisis is an unexpected, large-scale incident that can cause major negative effects on an organization and its stakeholders. Crisis management policies are vital, as a crisis presents stressful situations that involve important decisions that must be made quickly. These decisions can be difficult if an organization does not have clearly defined roles, responsibilities, and procedures. The goals of a crisis management plan should be to lessen the impact of the crisis, protect people, protect organizational reputation, and return to normal operations as soon as possible.

Crisis management policies should address the following:

- Risk assessment of what potential crises the organization could face and how to properly respond.

- Procedures for implementation include the steps management and employees must perform to put the plan into operation.

- The crisis response command center is where the directives originate during a crisis. This may be a physical or virtual location.

- Crisis management roles and responsibilities must be set so the organization understands who oversees all final decisions and the roles and responsibilities of each individual.

- Internal and external communication lines must be established so parties can communicate during a crisis.

- Employees must be properly trained on the crisis management policies and procedures so they understand all necessary courses of action during a crisis.

Pass Key

Business resiliency is the overall integration of procedures implemented to keep operations running smoothly, while disaster recovery, business continuity, and crisis management plans are different potential components of a business resiliency program. Disaster recovery focuses on IT functions; business continuity focuses on non-IT, operational, and personnel functions; and crisis management focuses on large-scale incidents considered a crisis.

1.2   System Availability Risks

Because technology is critical to the operations of most modern businesses, system availability may be the largest risk an organization faces. There are many risks that can occur and cause a loss of data or business operations. Those risks and accompanying threats include the following:

- **Failure of IT Infrastructure:** Availability of systems may directly be affected by failures in hardware, software, and network applications. These failures can result from:

    - Use of outdated infrastructure

    - Lack of system maintenance

    - System infected with malware

    - Physical damage occurring to systems from:

        — Natural disasters such as fires, floods, tornadoes, hurricanes, and earthquakes

        — Political threats such as terrorist attacks and war

        — Accidental or malicious damage from individuals

    - Cyberattacks that purposely overload and cause damage to the systems, such as the use of a denial-of-service attack

- **Insufficient Capacity and Resources:** System availability may be slowed down or disrupted if an organization's IT infrastructure is unable to meet the processing or storage needs of current operational demands. This concept also applies to not having appropriate resources in the form of staff to operate and maintain the IT infrastructure.

- **Lack of Business Resiliency:** Organizations must have a comprehensive business resiliency program to recover from system disruptions. If a business resiliency program is insufficient or nonexistent, organizations may lose critical, confidential, or private data; recover slowly from a disruption; or potentially never recover.

Specific IT processes exist to mitigate against these risks and provide access to data and IT systems in the event of a threat.

1.2.1   Mirroring

Data backups, for example, help avoid complete data loss. Mirroring, a process that applies to data storage and backup, entails copying a database onto a different machine for the purpose of data redundancy in the event the primary database fails.

1.2.2   Replication

Replication involves copying and transferring data between different databases located in different sites, such as a geographically different data center or the cloud. Replication allows operations to resume quickly using data in the secondary site after a system failure.

1.2.3 Secondary Internet Sources

If an organization experiences an internet outage without a power failure, secondary internet connections can be used to sustain normal business operations. Having two internet connections at critical locations helps mitigate this issue. Another mitigation technique would be internet provided via cellular connection using devices such as smartphone hot spots or stand-alone wireless hot spots; hot spots can be used temporarily to replace primary internet sources if only one main connection exists. Alternatively, wireless hot spot adapters can be attached to existing networking infrastructure and source internet from a cell tower to power the existing switches and cables.

1.2.4 Metrics for System Availability

Organizations use specific metrics when assessing system availability and risks. When companies use third-party service organizations to manage IT operations, the service organization generally must adhere to an agreed service time (AST) and a minimal amount of downtime (DT) specified in a service level agreement (SLA). The agreed service time refers to the amount of time that services are operational, expressed in hours or days. Downtime refers to the amount of time a system or application is not functional. These terms are often used to calculate a system's overall availability, to determine whether a service organization is meeting performance standards outlined in an SLA.

Other key metrics used for measuring system availability include the following:

- **Maximum Tolerable Downtime (MTD):** The amount of time a business can tolerate an outage without causing long-term significant damage. Typically, managed service providers have a contractual amount of downtime that cannot be surpassed within a given period of time, usually monthly.

- **Recovery Point Objective (RPO):** The maximum threshold for acceptable data lost after an unplanned negative event. It defines the "age" of the data that must be recovered to resume normal operations (e.g., recover the data up to five minutes prior to the incident, allowing a maximum loss of five minutes of trading data). Applications or processes that are considered to be less critical may have a higher RPO.

- **Recovery Time Objective (RTO):** The maximum amount of time it should take to restore business operations to a target state following a system failure. For example, a company may say that it must take no longer than 12 hours to restore IT operations.

- **Mean Time to Repair (MTTR):** Average length of time it takes to repair a damaged or inoperable device. This is similar to RTO, but MTTR is the average taken over a period of time instead of a target or goal.

- **Recovery Time Actual (RTA):** The actual time it takes to restore business operations to its target state after a system failure.

- **Recovery Point Actual (RPA):** The actual point in time to which data can be recovered (e.g., recover all trading data up to two minutes prior to the incident).

2   System Availability Controls

System availability controls include activities to prevent system disruptions and loss of information as well as procedures to continue operations or provide quick recovery from an incident. Crisis management, disaster recovery, and business continuity plans are all components of system availability controls. In addition to these plans, system availability controls include the following.

2.1   Physical Controls

A major threat to system availability is damage caused to physical hardware components. As a result, controls must be put in place to deter damage to the IT infrastructure, including:

- Physical access controls (i.e., door locks, security guards, cameras, etc.)
- Fire alarms and sprinklers
- Facility design to protect against flooding and overheating, such as raised floors and air-conditioning systems

2.2   IT Infrastructure Controls

Controls around the IT infrastructure, including hardware, software, and network components, can provide mitigation of malicious attacks and other actions that can compromise systems. These controls include:

- Continuously using anti-malware software and patch management to fix vulnerabilities
- Periodic reviews of IT infrastructure components to ensure they are not outdated
- Network security controls
- Access and authorization logical controls

2.3   Uninterrupted Power Supply

An *uninterrupted power supply* (UPS) is a device that maintains a continuous supply of electrical power to connected equipment. A UPS, also called battery backup, is used to prevent a system from shutting down improperly during an outage. A UPS can prevent data loss and can protect the integrity of a backup while it is being performed. When a power failure occurs, the UPS switches to its own power source instantaneously so that there is no interruption in power to the system. A UPS is not a backup standby generator; the battery will run out eventually.

2.4   Redundancy

Organizations may choose to have redundant hardware, software, and storage as a normal part of their operations. This allows them to easily switch from a failed unit, such as a malfunctioning router or switch, to another unit already in operation. Having redundant IT assets can also apply to data storage and backup. Redundant arrays of independent drives (RAID) allow organizations to record data on multiple disk drives at one time for the purpose of data redundancy in the event one disk drive fails.

2.5   System Backup

When planning a business resiliency program or evaluating system availability risks, organizations must decide what types of backups to perform to recover lost data.

- **Full:** Exact copy of the entire database. Full backups are time-consuming, so most organizations only do full backups weekly and supplement them with daily partial backups. Recovering from an incident using a full backup is generally the least time-consuming recovery process compared to other backups due to the fact that there is only one copy of all systems and data that needs to be restored, rather than a full backup plus partial backups. While time-consuming to create, full backups are the least time-consuming to restore.

- **Incremental:** Involves copying only the data items that have changed since the last backup. This produces a set of incremental backup files, each containing the results of one day's transactions. Restoration involves first loading the last full backup and then installing each subsequent incremental backup in the proper sequence. Recovery is generally the slowest of the three because a full backup copy must be restored as well as each incremental backup. However, initial creation of the backup file for each incremental load is fast. So, companies must decide if they prefer a faster time to create a backup and slower time to recovery, or a slower time to create a backup and faster time to recovery.

- **Differential:** Copies all changes made since the last full backup. Thus, each new differential backup file contains the cumulative effects of all activity since the last full backup. Consequently, except for the first day following a full backup, daily differential backups take longer than incremental backups. Restoration is simpler, however, because the last full backup needs to be supplemented with only the most recent differential backup, instead of a set of daily incremental backup files. Recovery using a differential backup is slower than a full backup but faster than an incremental one because only two copies are needed for restoration—the most recent full backup and the single differential backup.

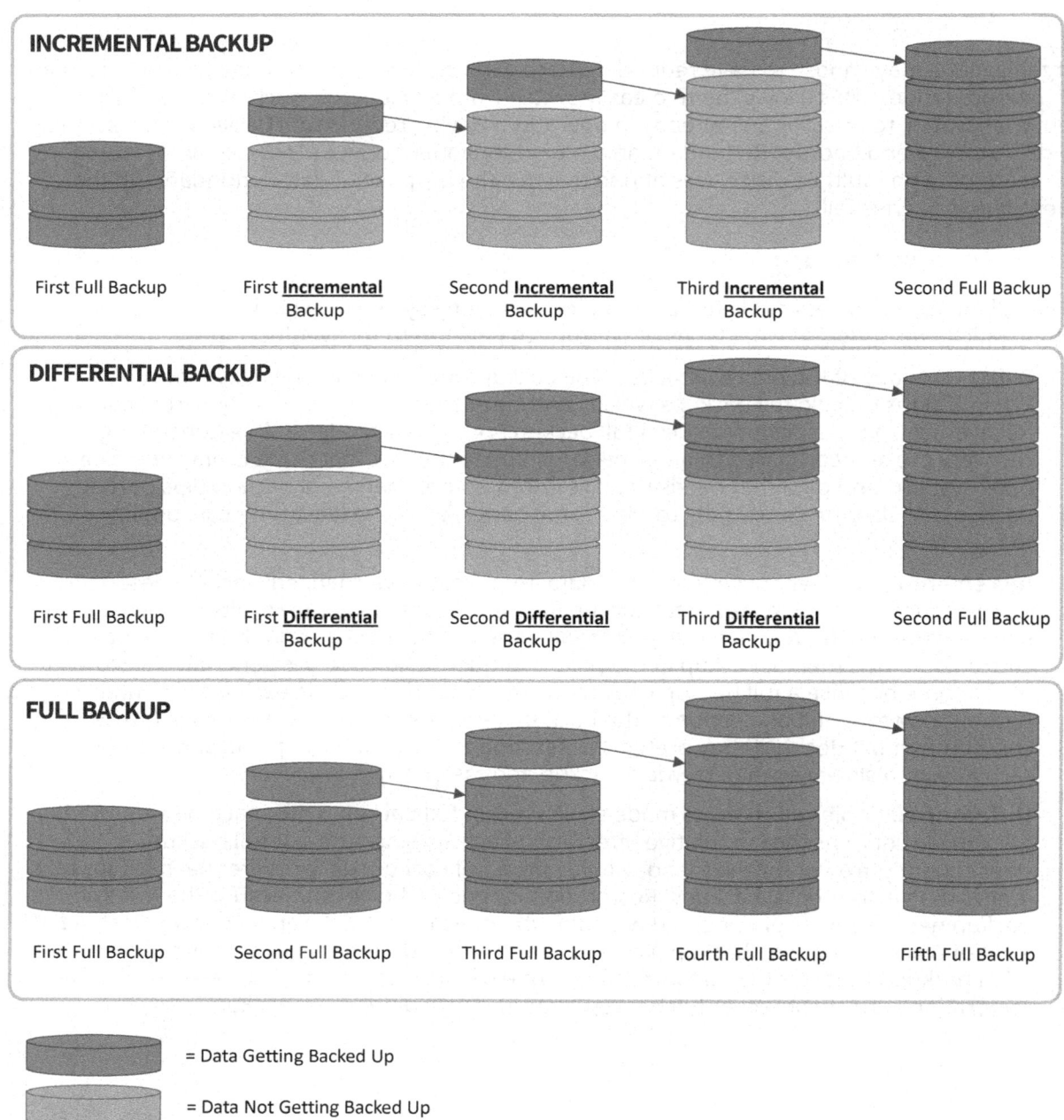

INCREMENTAL BACKUP

First Full Backup   First **Incremental**   Second **Incremental**   Third **Incremental**   Second Full Backup
Backup   Backup   Backup

DIFFERENTIAL BACKUP

First Full Backup   First **Differential**   Second **Differential**   Third **Differential**   Second Full Backup
Backup   Backup   Backup

FULL BACKUP

First Full Backup   Second Full Backup   Third Full Backup   Fourth Full Backup   Fifth Full Backup

= Data Getting Backed Up

= Data Not Getting Backed Up

> **Illustration 3   System Backups**
>
> The IT director at a university manages the organization's system backups to help avoid complete data loss. The university has a significant amount of data requiring backup, so the IT director, with management approval, decided to implement full backups twice a month. These backups take several hours to complete. On a daily basis, the IT department performs incremental backups. In the event of a system failure, the university will have access to all data through both its full backup files and incremental files.

2.6   Detecting Deficiencies in Control Design

One of the SOC 2® trust services criteria is availability, which covers controls regarding an organization's system operation and performance. If an organization's service commitments or business objectives necessitate system availability, this trust service criteria should be included in a SOC 2® audit.

The specific criteria for availability include infrastructure capacity and monitoring, backups and recovery infrastructure, and testing recovery plans. To detect deficiencies in availability controls, SOC 2® auditors should consider the following:

- **Infrastructure Capacity and Monitoring:** Observe an organization's monitoring tool showing capacity metrics being monitored (e.g., CPU utilization and disk I/O). If proper monitoring is not in place, an organization risks maxing out infrastructure capacity. If proper recovery infrastructure is not in place, an organization risks significant downtime and data loss in the event of a system failure.

- **Recovery Plans:** Request and review an organization's disaster recovery and business continuity plans and request evidence showing when the plans were last tested and the results. If recovery plans are not in place or not properly tested, a disaster could occur, and the organization would not have a clear procedure to follow to recover efficiently and effectively.

NOTES

1 Change Management Overview

1.1 Defining Change Management

Change management is a term used to describe the policies, procedures, and resources employed to govern change in an organization. These changes may be initiated from within the organization or imposed from sources outside the organization, but they will usually have an impact on IT infrastructure such as internal hardware, software applications, and governance no matter the source.

The scope of change to be managed can range from something as routine as implementing a new software update to an initiative more complex and as infrequent as overhauling an organization's core switching architecture. Regardless of the scope or size of a change management project, potential risks need to be mitigated to minimize disruption to core business functions and operations.

1.2 The Change Management Process

A robust change management process is a key component for successfully ensuring that an organization can keep up with changing application and hardware needs without losing the ability to operate or achieve its strategic objectives. The following steps can help a company chart its path from change inception to implementation:

1. Identify and define the need for system changes.

2. Design a high-level plan including goals to be achieved because of the system change.

3. Obtain approval from management for the change.

4. Develop an appropriate budget and time line.

5. Assign personnel responsible for managing the system change.

6. Identify and address potential risks that could occur during the change or post implementation.

7. Provide an implementation road map.

8. Procure necessary resources and train the appropriate personnel.

9. Test the system change.

10. Execute the implementation plan.

11. Review and monitor change implementation and test as needed to verify effective implementation.

1.3 Types of Environments

Changes should be implemented in segregated environments within an organization so that normal business operations are not disrupted. The different forms of computing environments include the following:

- **Development:** In a development environment, software programmers write code to create application prototypes. There is typically a source code editing tool which is used to create and modify code syntax, automation tools that have preconfigured code, and a debugging tool to help fix errors.

- **Testing:** In a test environment, developers test and debug code to identify errors that need to be corrected. This may be considered the same as the development environment, but some organizations may keep it intentionally separate so that the focus is solely on debugging errors in an application that is mostly complete.

- **Staging:** In a staging environment, organizations can test programs that are in their final phases of development in a production-like environment. This is intended to test functionality, compatibility, security, and performance prior to deployment.

- **Production:** This is the environment in which an application is deployed and made available to end users.

- **Disaster Recovery:** Organizations set up a disaster recovery environment to ensure that applications can be restored quickly, save critical data and systems, notify management, and recover in the event of an outage or attack.

2 Change Management Risks

A key component of change management is to identify the potential risks that could occur as a result of the change. These risks are present in all steps of change from acquisition to implementation and can affect existing systems, processes, and employees. When assessing change management risks in a SOC 2® engagement, service auditors should refer to the AICPA's trust services criterion CC8.1. This criterion recommends service organizations have policies and practices in place that properly authorize, design, develop or purchase, configure, document, test, approve, and implement changes to the company's infrastructure, data, and applications to meet corporate objectives.

2.1 Selection and Acquisition Risks

Selecting and acquiring new IT resources is a fundamental area in which risks exist in the change management process. Examples include:

- **Lack of Expertise:** When selecting and acquiring software, there is a risk that the purchasing agent does not have the expertise or organizational perspective to purchase software that meets the needs of an organization.

- **Lack of a Formal Selection and Acquisition Process:** There is a risk that an organization either does not have or does not follow a formal selection and acquisition process as it pertains to software. This could result in overspending, inappropriate related party transactions or kickbacks, or software that does not align with the IT governance strategy.

- **Software/Hardware Vulnerability and Incompatibility:** When selecting and acquiring software and hardware packages, there is the risk that proper safeguards and security features that are needed to adequately protect an organization from unauthorized use do not exist. There is also the risk that newly acquired hardware and software are incompatible with each other or with existing resources that will remain in production.

To help combat selection and acquisition risks, the AICPA's trust services criterion CC5.1 can be applied, which recommends that companies select and develop controls that help mitigate risks to meet business objectives. The AICPA also provides the following illustration in its SOC 2® guidance to help provide context to the ways in which this control can be met, from both the service organization's perspective and the service auditor's:

- **Service Organization's Perspective:** Perform annual risk assessments to determine whether identified risks and the controls linked to those risks are adequate. If new controls are needed due to new processes, the organization can use the proper change management process to implement them.

- **Service Auditor's Perspective:** Obtain and inspect the annual risk assessment performed by the service organization to determine that new controls were implemented to address risks not sufficiently addressed by existing controls. The service auditor should inspect a sample of the system change requests to determine whether the proper change management process was used.

2.2   Integration Risks

Once the software has been selected and acquired, it must be integrated into existing systems and processes. This may prove to be one of the most difficult risks to manage, because there are many nuances that are further complicated by employee perceptions and attitudes toward accepting change. Examples of integration risks include:

- **User Resistance:** When change occurs (especially technology-related changes), there is often resistance to adoption of the change by employees. As a result, there is a risk that employees do not adapt to the change, ignore training, and ultimately do not follow through with change appropriately.

- **Lack of Management Support:** If management does not provide both resources and adequate support, this could magnify existing employee resistance.

- **Lack of Stakeholder Support:** The stakeholders involved in the change may range from employees to suppliers to customers, any of which may have an adverse reaction or disposition toward change.

- **Resource Concerns:** Frequently, change can be resource-intensive from both financial and labor perspectives. As a result, appropriate resources may not be made available for the change, which may lead to ineffective implementation.

- **Business Disruption:** When making major changes to IT infrastructure, there is the potential for brief or even prolonged information system failures. This could cause significant disruptions to core functions and could have long-term negative consequences for the organization.

- **Lack of System Integration:** Due to the ever-changing technological landscape, organizations may operate many different systems, some of which may be legacy systems (original or older software programs) that do not effectively adapt or integrate with more modern systems.

2.3   Outsourcing Risks

When planning a significant IT change or system upgrade, some organizations choose to outsource the change management process. This may be pursued as a cost-saving approach or to leverage the expertise of an external agency. Along with the benefits of outsourcing change management come risks. These risks include:

- **Lack of Organizational Knowledge:** Outsourcing the change management process could leave the organization vulnerable, because it must rely on the third party to fully comprehend the organization's business model and needs so the third party can integrate that change into the organization without causing disruption.

- **Uncertainty of the Third Party's Knowledge and Management:** When outsourcing change management or any IT function, there is a risk that the external party has ineffective or weak management, inexperienced or underqualified staff, and a lack of technology expertise. These risks can cause the outsourcing of IT to fail.

- **Lack of Security:** Outsourcing IT functions can lead to transmission of sensitive and confidential data. As a result, there is a risk that an external organization does not have sufficient or effective safeguards to make sure that client, customer, employee, or operational information is kept secure.

3   Change Management Controls

3.1   Change Management and New System Controls

Once all risks in the change management process have been identified, controls are designed to minimize the possibility that the inherent risks will cause business disruptions or negatively impact IT systems. Change management controls include the following:

- **Policies and Procedures:** Clear change management guidelines are needed to outline how the change management process should be executed, from selection to integration and maintenance.

- **Emergency Change Policies:** Separate contingency policies and procedures provide direction for emergency change situations that allow for an expedited process that still maintains an audit trail and appropriate controls. Emergency changes arise when a crisis or time-sensitive threat requires a quick response, such as an operating system patch that exposes a company to severe security threats.

- **Standardized Change Requests:** Standardizing change requests by using consistent forms and request protocols helps complete all required changes in a timely fashion.

- **Impact Assessment:** Analysis documenting the effect a change will have on the organization's business activities as well as any potential disruptions will help prepare an organization for successful change implementation.

- **Authorization:** Requiring designated levels of authorization for changes, including material modifications to the initial change plan, is necessary to protect against unauthorized modification to a project's scope.

- **Separation of Duties:** Properly separating job roles will help protect assets or information from being utilized improperly. This would include, for example, distinguishing team members who develop and design specific components from employees responsible for placing those components into production.

- **Conversion Controls:** When migrating from an existing system or process to the new ones, conversion controls help minimize data conversion errors related to the impacted IT assets and resources.

- **Reversion Access:** Some changes may cause unexpected complications; therefore, it is important to have the ability to revert to the prior system or process that existed before the change.

  This can be accomplished through parallel implementation in which the organization maintains two environments at the initial onset of the change, one with the change implemented (development environment) and one without the change implemented (production environment).

- **Pre-implementation Testing:** Before moving the change into production, testing will help determine if the change is functioning properly and there are no irregularities.

- **Post-implementation Testing:** After the change is moved into production, reconciling transactions processed in the new environment against the same transactions that were processed in the previous environment will validate whether the change was implemented properly.

- **Ongoing Monitoring:** Continuous periodic reviews after implementation will promote long-term success. This may commence at shorter intervals (weekly) but can move to greater intervals (monthly/quarterly/annually) as the change proves successful over time.

3.1.1 Evaluating the Impact of System Changes on Internal Controls

Trust services criteria for SOC 2® engagements require service organizations to identify and assess the potential impact that changes could have on a system of internal control. To accomplish that, organizations should perform an annual risk assessment process that evaluates the following:

- The economic, regulatory, and physical environment in which the company operates.

- The business environment, industry, competition, and consumer dynamics.

- The effect of how new lines of business, modified lines of business, expanding through acquisition, or downsizing through divesting can affect internal control.

- Management's attitude toward internal controls.

- Changes in the technology environment.

- Partnerships with vendors and other businesses.

Service auditors performing SOC 2® engagements should also consider the trust services criteria when testing controls. This may involve inspecting management's annual risk assessment to enhance the likelihood that management identified the need to implement new controls to mitigate risks that were not sufficiently addressed. The auditor should sample system change requests to verify that management followed the change management process for new controls that were identified.

3.2   Documenting System Controls

Documentation can be a form of change management control in that it provides a log of changes made to a system or process. Good documentation practices can help organizations track and manage changes in a way that is efficient, effective, and compliant with relevant regulations and policies.

Documenting system changes allows organizations to better understand how a system functions and evolves over time, which can be useful for a variety of reasons such as:

- troubleshooting;
- staff training and education; and
- improving system performance.

3.2.1   Baseline Configuration

Documenting changes to a system should start with a baseline configuration, which is establishing a starting point for reconfigurations so that changes are deployed in a consistent and secure environment. Baselines can be used as a benchmark to compare current progress or performance of a system. This is useful when searching for patterns or trends, as it allows IT teams to better understand the root cause of issues and evaluate the effectiveness of changes implemented.

The use of checklists is often employed when launching from a baseline. The starting point is the baseline, and then items on the checklist are marked with time stamps as they are completed. This provides a linear path so managers can trace preceding steps to understand the changes implemented.

Creating baseline images is also commonly used. This involves creating an image with a graphical depiction of a system, which outlines important devices, personnel, and their interconnectivity. As changes are made to the system and the image is updated, managers can compare the two for an understanding of the changes.

Baseline configuration metrics used may include system uptime, resource utilization, and failover time. If system uptime, or the amount of time a system is available for use, decreases after the implementation, then management would know that the system updates were detrimental. Similarly, if resource utilization increased so that more computing resources were required or if failover time increased, which resulted in a delay of backup resources coming online in a system outage, then the system update may also be considered unsuccessful.

3.2.2   System Component Inventory

A system component inventory is a list of items that comprise a system including hardware, software, peripherals, and other IT assets. The inventory should include the purpose of the component, its location, the current status, and whether it is functioning properly. This information can be used to track the following:

- Components that are nearing end of life
- Repairs and maintenance that have been made
- Component owners
- Upgrades and replacements that need to be made
- Guidance related to troubleshooting
- Specs such as model types and serial numbers

3.3   Testing and Implementing Change Control Policies

Depending on which change management controls an organization implements, there are different procedures for testing the controls to enhance the likelihood that they are operating as intended. The procedures will vary based on the types of applications, infrastructure components, or system configurations to which the control is being applied. One of the widely used procedures is the closed loop verification. Closed loop verification is a critical change management step that involves continuously monitoring the output from the changes, comparing it with the desired outcome, and calibrating the changes to minimize discrepancies from the acceptance criteria. Procedures for testing change management controls for IT resources include multiple components.

3.3.1   Acceptance Criteria

When evaluating change control policies, management should establish acceptance criteria that are measurable and specific so that change can be objectively evaluated. Adequately structured acceptance criteria help enhance the likelihood that changes to systems or processes are clear and concise, properly tested prior to implementation, adequately documented, approved by stakeholders, evaluated so that the impact is understood, and reviewed and monitored after implementation, consistent with the close.

Acceptance criteria metrics may be either qualitative or quantitative. Examples include the following:

- **Performance:** Quantitatively, this may be measured using metrics such as a newly configured system's uptime, downtime, or speed in terms of seconds or minutes. If assessed qualitatively, this could simply be a rating by a testing panel of perceived performance.

- **Functionality:** This metric would be qualitative and assess whether an application or infrastructure component performs a target function and how efficient or practical it is to use the system in its intended environment.

- **Scalability:** The ease of the system's ability to scale up or down would be quantitatively measured by using such metrics as the maximum number of transactions that can be processed, users that can be logged on, or customers that a system can handle.

- **Compliance:** This may be measured by an objective qualitative assessment that renders a yes or no verdict of compliance. Either an application or infrastructure component complies, or it does not. This would typically be evaluated by an expert in a particular regulation or standard who would compare aspects of the system to the applicable standard.

3.3.2   Logging

Analyzing logs is also a critical part of testing and implementing change control policies. Logging is the process of recording events into logs or databases so that an organization can track activities that occur on a system. By capturing communications and changes, companies can determine whether change control policies are being followed and investigate known violations of policy. Frequently used log types include the following:

- **Application Logs:** These logs record application data such as when an employee accesses or views a table or executes a certain function, or when an error occurs that causes the program to stop functioning.

- **Change Logs:** This type of log tracks changes that were requested, approved, and implemented and may be a part of a disaster recovery program. Having a snapshot of these changes will allow IT administrators to restore a system back to a given point in time prior to a change.

- **Event Logs:** This broad category of logs records various events that occur on a system including directory logs, DNS (domain name system) server logs, endpoint logs, security event logs, and basic system logs.

  - Directory logs provide data on events involving Active Directory (AD), which is related to authenticating users, governing privileges for users and groups, and the devices that access AD.

  - DNS server logs contain information on source and destination IP addresses, query and response details, time stamps, and errors.

  - Endpoint logs record events at the device level such as what devices connect to a laptop, the files or programs installed on that device, and the networks to which it connects.

  - Security event logs track access to system resources such as shared folders, printers, and files.

  - System logs record events like when a system is started, rebooted, or updated.

- **Firewall Logs:** These logs record all traffic that flows through a firewall such as packet information containing ports used, IP addresses, protocol used, action taken by the firewall, the reason for the action, and the time and date the packet was transmitted.

- **Network Logs:** Also referred to as perimeter logs, these provide intelligence from devices that guard a network's perimeter such as virtual private networks, firewalls, and intrusion detection systems. By monitoring this activity, organizations can detect attacks, identify misconfigured devices, and find other potentially threatening behavior.

- **Proxy Logs:** Proxy servers can control internet access and enhance performance for users. The logs for proxy servers show details such as which sites a user visits, the time, and how long the user viewed certain pages.

Illustration 1   Proxy Log Data

The following proxy log shows that a user, John Doe, visited cnn.com at 4:35 p.m. on October 11, 2026, and stayed on that page for approximately two minutes before visiting the business news section. John's IP address is also given, as is shown below.

10/11/2026 4:35:55 PM User-JDoe 192.178.10.10 GET https://cnn.com/

10/11/2026 4:37:32 PM User-JDoe 192.178.10.10 GET https://www.cnn.com/business

---

3.3.3 Test Results

System administrators should evaluate the results of testing the design and implementation of change control policies. Such evaluations include the following:

- Review written change management policies, confirm policies are kept up to date, and determine whether the proper acceptance criteria are documented in those policies.

- Review documentation for implemented changes and request evidence showing that the company's change management policy was followed when implementing the changes.

- Confirm that all necessary authorizations were obtained throughout the project.

- Review the change requests made and determine whether the requests were made using a company's standardized form.

- Request evidence showing which employees or teams performed which duties during the project to determine whether there was proper separation of duties.

- Execute testing of change controls and evaluate the results of those tests.

- Perform monitoring activities to review results of all testing performed throughout the project and post-implementation and confirm that all necessary changes or updates were made.

3.3.4 Monitoring

Monitoring in the context of testing and implementing change control policies provides accountability, the ability to troubleshoot, and tools for identifying and solving problems. Regarding accountability, employees are held responsible for their actions through authenticating a unique user ID, audit trails, and other methods of surveillance. These are monitored and reviewed for any violation of policy or breach, with unacceptable occurrences resulting in disciplinary action or termination.

Monitoring techniques, such as reviewing audit trails and performing log analyses, help administrators evaluate system events so they can identify, diagnose, and troubleshoot problems. Log analysis is a form of monitoring that involves analyzing logs to search for anomalies, patterns, trends, or unauthorized behavior. One difficulty in performing log analysis is that the volume of data an analyst must sort through is immense. This makes automated tools critical for this type of analysis.

3.3.5 Testing Using Continuous Adoption

Companies often use continuous software development practices such as continuous integration and continuous deployment, which are designed to streamline the testing process and providing a feedback loop that is more timely than the traditional "build-test-deploy" model. With continuous integration, developers regularly merge changes to their code in a central repository in which they automate building and testing code. This approach of integrating code more frequently helps identify bugs faster, enhances application quality, and shortens the time needed to release software updates.

In continuous deployment, software is automatically created, tested, and then deployed to a production environment. This minimizes the cycle time for writing code and releasing new software versions while still maintaining some form of testing so application and system operations will not be interrupted.

However, continuous software development methods do create some risk in that not all code is proven, and bugs will occasionally be released to a live environment. Implementing a continuous mentality can be challenging for coding that is complex or has a high level of interdependencies between applications. Controls such as automated testing, static code analysis, and code reviews can help reduce the risks and be more in line with the closed loop verification concept.

Additionally, the cultural shift within an organization from a "build-test-deploy" environment to a continuous one may be difficult. More work is required up front to determine whether sufficient standardized testing processes are in place, rather than applying customized testing as products are developed.

4   Managing Change in Systems

Two of the most common IT change management methodologies are the waterfall model and the Agile model. While both of these models have historically been used to manage software development and other technical IT projects, their principles are flexible enough to be applied more generally to modern change management practices across different organizational functions. This means the waterfall and Agile methodologies can be implemented in disciplines such as finance or logistics to optimize managing change. Since the primary difference between the models is flexibility, some cross-disciplinary change management projects may gravitate toward one or the other.

4.1   The Waterfall Model

The waterfall model is characterized by different teams of employees performing separate tasks in sequence, with each team beginning work from the pre-written authoritative agreement of the preceding team and then ending work when the business requirements for the team have been met. The project then passes to the next team. Examples of challenges associated with the waterfall model include:

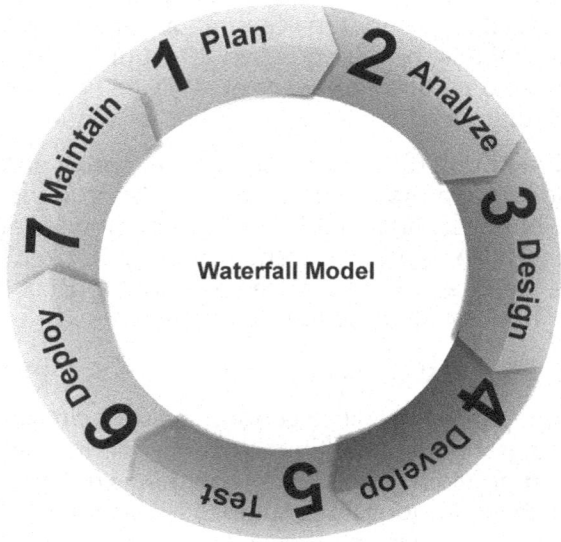

- It requires a great deal of time to complete.

- The benefits of the new system are not realized until completion.

- There is no customer input and change can be difficult to manage.

- Some employees may be idle before beginning or after completing their step in the process.

4.2   The Agile Method

The Agile framework was created to address issues with the waterfall model. Agile offers a more flexible approach to change management and is characterized by cross-functional teams, each dedicated to particular functions or improvements of a system drawn from a prioritized list of the customer's remaining needs for the system.

Unlike the waterfall model where teams work linearly, the agile model is characterized by different teams working on different phases or tasks simultaneously. Teams work with shorter deadlines to encourage efficiency, which makes communication critical. The Agile model also allows changes of direction throughout the project, accounting for stakeholder feedback through consistent communication and any changes in the technology landscape that can occur over the course of an extensive project. The final outcome of the project can evolve throughout the project's life cycle.

The Agile process can be characterized using the following steps:

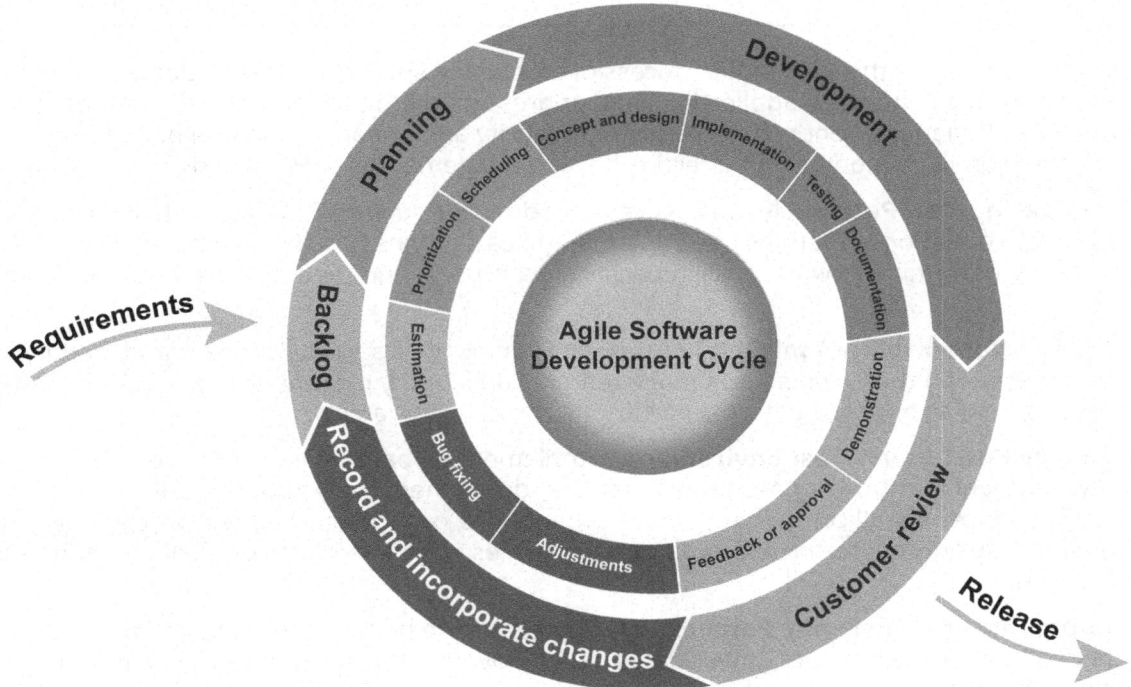

The Agile principles are as follows:

1. Satisfy the customer with early and continuous delivery of the highest-priority features.

2. Welcome change; a change request is an opportunity to be closer to customer needs.

3. Deliver working software frequently; working software is the primary measure of progress.

4. Complete only the work requested by the customer.

5. Conduct short, frequent, and regular meetings to maintain focus and make adjustments.

Illustration 2   Implementing Agile in Software Development

Refraction Realty (RR) contracted with a software development company to develop an online client portal. The portal will allow RR's clients to interact with agents, review documents, and schedule closing appointments. When planning the portal project, RR and the developers discussed which project management model would serve them best. RR had a clear vision for the portal and wanted to be heavily involved in the project. The team ultimately decided to apply the Agile model. Throughout the project, the software group worked quickly and simultaneously on multiple modules of the portal, giving RR time to review and test modules as they were completed. Upon each review, RR provided feedback on functionality and user interface. These reviews helped RR realize they wanted two additional modules.

The developers applied the feedback and completed the new modules. Because of RR's involvement, the teams minimized major changes at the very end of the project. Once RR was pleased with the portal in developer mode, RR launched the portal to its clients.

5   Patch Management

Patch management is the systematic process of identifying specific vulnerabilities or software bugs in operating systems or applications and addressing them with patches, or fixes, between releases. Patch management promotes system security and enhances the likelihood that systems are running smoothly. An effective patch management process includes:

- **Evaluating New Patch Releases:** As vendors discover new vulnerabilities, they release patches so that organizations can implement fixes. IT managers must evaluate those patches, determine how they will impact their company, and then devise plans to implement them.

- **Using a Vulnerability Tool:** This helps organizations track security controls and identify weaknesses on their own so that management can identify patches needed, as opposed to waiting until a vendor or external parties discover a vulnerability.

- **Testing Patches in a Test Environment:** Implementing patches in a nonproduction environment is critical, if possible, so that they do not negatively impact system performance. Not all companies have the manpower or technical knowhow to test patches, so this may only be performed by larger companies in an attempt to prevent company-wide outages.

- **Approving and Deploying Patches:** After patches have been successfully reviewed and tested by IT administrators, the updates are deployed to the appropriate system during a scheduled downtime to minimize disruptions.

- **Verifying Patches Deployed:** Verification of successful patching should be performed after testing and deployment, which should then be followed by monitoring so that any system issues can be identified and resolved after deployment.

Many organizations have regular schedules for announcing patches for their clients, such as a particular day each month or year. This allows companies time to anticipate and prepare for updates, but it also may be exploited by bad actors. For example, a fraudster may plan an attack that launches the same day a patch is announced because he or she knows that it will be days or weeks before that patch is disseminated and implemented by all organizations.

For service organizations subject to SOC 2® audits, the AICPA recommends maintaining a documented patch management process to meet its trust services criteria regarding properly authorizing and implementing changes to meet company objectives. For service auditors testing related controls in SOC 2® engagements, they should inspect the service organization's policies and procedures to determine whether they include rules on patch management and change management.

6   System Conversion Methods

Organizations have various options when converting their computer systems, such as software, hardware, and data, from one information system to another. The choice will vary for each company depending on its own unique needs, with smaller companies more likely to select a more aggressive approach such as the direct changeover method, and larger companies more likely to take a more cautious path, choosing a parallel or phased approach.

The different conversion methods are as follows:

- **Direct:** This conversion method involves the organization ceasing the use of the old system and starting the new one immediately. The risk with the direct changeover method is that if the new system does not work, business operations could be severely hindered or cease to function altogether depending on what the system is supporting (such as an online retailer that relies solely on sales from its platform).

- **Parallel:** The new system is implemented while the old system is still in use for an extended period of time with this conversion method. The downside with this approach is that it requires a significant amount of effort from personnel because they must operate two systems simultaneously.

- **Pilot:** In this method, an organization performs a conversion on a small scale within a test environment while continuing to use the older system. It allows for validation and testing before rolling it out to the entire organization so that adjustments can be made prior to full implementation.

- **Phased:** Also referred to as gradual or modular conversion, this transition plan gradually adds volume to the new system while still operating the old system. This approach is useful for businesses with distributed locations as it allows them to implement one site at a time.

- **Hybrid:** These are custom combinations of the above approaches, tailored to the unique needs of an organization.

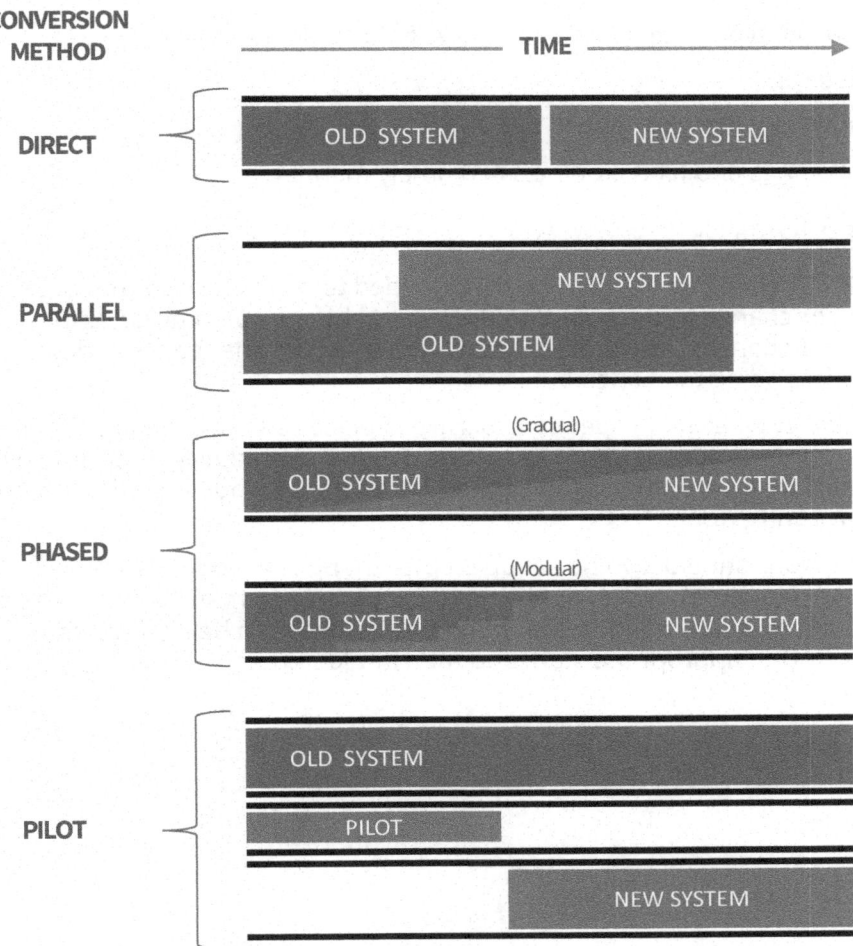

7   Change Management Testing Strategies

Every system within an organization should be subject to ongoing change management testing to determine whether newly installed systems and updates to existing systems do not lead to functional issues or security vulnerabilities. This testing should be subject to review and have mechanisms in place to reverse change, should it be necessary.

7.1   Purpose of Testing

Testing software accomplishes the following:

- Testing determines whether the software is operating as expected.
- Testing discovers errors, defects, missing components, and gaps in the software.
- Testing verifies that the end product meets the business and user requirements.

7.2   Software Testing Process

The software testing process for change management generally follows these steps:

1. Establish a testing plan including roles, responsibilities, and a time line.
2. Identify and prioritize the key areas of the software to test.
3. Determine which type of test to run and specify the test objectives.
4. Execute the tests.
5. Log the results and identify defects.
6. Report the findings and fix the defects in a timely manner.

7.3   Change Review

A formal change advisory board (CAB) is recommended to be in place so that organizations can adequately plan for change and respond to unwanted change outcomes. A CAB can approve changes, document changes, notify users of upcoming or past changes, and deploy resources for testing and responding to change.

CABs should consider whether proper controls are in place so that there are separate environments for testing, staging, and production. For instance, developers should not have access to a production environment and application operators should not have access to a development environment.

Automatic notifications should also be set up so that changes to code are immediately sent to the appropriate personnel, removing the need to rely on a human for such changes. Code repository tools can be established so that potential changes can be aggregated, reviewed, approved by the CAB or appropriate staff, and then implemented.

Illustration 3   Change Advisory Board

A large electronic health care billing software provider, Lasso Co., develops, sells, and supports applications that allow health care companies to bill insurance payors directly using electronic data interchange (EDI). Health care companies perform services, document those services in the electronic health record (EHR) system, and then submit those claims for reimbursement.

Lasso has a separate development environment of its software with a replica of customer data for its largest clients. This allows Lasso to troubleshoot issues with data that mirrors its clients' data so that solutions are quick and client specific. After hiring a new developer, Lasso temporarily turns off the control that prevents test data from actually being submitted to insurance companies for payment. As a result, actual claims that were already sent by the client were unintentionally resubmitted for payment by the new Lasso developer using the mirrored test claims. Many claims were paid twice, which required the client to spend hours identifying duplicate claims and it triggered an audit by several of its payors. Most importantly, this change was not caught by Lasso. Rather, it was identified by the client after an extended period of time.

If a CAB was established, controls would have been in place so that this would not have been possible, or at the least a CAB would have alerted Lasso managers of the change. A CAB would have also alerted users of the change immediately so that productivity could be saved and then efforts could begin to restore the organization to a pre-event state.

7.4   Rollback

Upon discovery of unwanted changes, an organization's CAB or IT team should notify users prior to reversing or rolling back those changes to prevent loss of productivity. Rollbacks require a complete inventory of system configurations for applications and operating systems so that systems can be restored to a state that existed prior to the change.

There should also be post-implementation reviews to determine whether a change or rollback was correctly installed or uninstalled. Depending on the extent of the implementation, this can either be done through testing each change on all devices or applications, or through validation sampling in which only a small subset is tested.

7.5   Types of Testing Performed

There are various types of system tests that can be performed to evaluate systems in development to determine whether they are working as intended. The following are examples of some of the most common tests:

- **Unit Testing:** This refers to the process of examining the smallest increment, or unit, of an application. Unit testing can be broken down by function so that developers evaluate units of code that perform specific tasks as the application is being developed. By focusing on a single unit, software developers do not have to consider broader system issues like how one unit may interact with another.

- **Integration Testing:** Also referred to as thread testing or string testing, this assessment is usually performed after unit testing to enhance the likelihood that different components or modules within an application will work cohesively once all units are integrated. Integration testing also helps plan for future system maintenance and updates, allowing managers the opportunity to identify weaknesses or security vulnerabilities that may require future patching.

- **System Testing:** This verifies that all combined modules of a completed application work as designed in totality. System testing focuses on the overall functionality of the program and may be evaluated by a quality assurance team to discover any material defects prior to releasing the final product.

- **Acceptance Testing:** In this quality assurance phase, developers assess an application to determine whether it meets end-user requirements. Acceptance testing may involve beta testing in which a sample of the target customers tries the application, or it could involve end-user testing in which employees test the unfinished product.

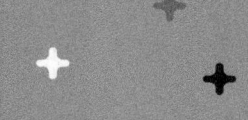
Data is an essential element for decision making, auditing, and analysis. Data is constantly being created through transactional systems, artificial intelligence, the Internet of Things, and even manually. It is critical for companies to understand what data they have access to and how to use it responsibly to make business decisions. The data life cycle aids in that process.

1 Data Life Cycle

The data life cycle describes the sequential steps all business data must go through from creation, through its use, storage, and final disposal. This process can be summarized in eight steps:

1. Definition
2. Capture
3. Preparation
4. Synthesis
5. Analytics and usage
6. Publication
7. Archival
8. Purging

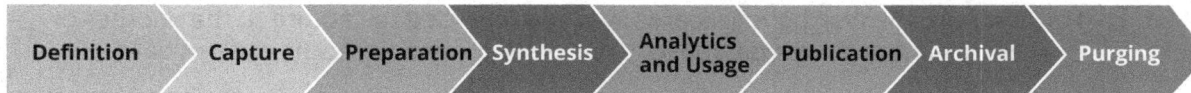

1.1 Definition

The first step in the data life cycle is defining what data a business needs and where to capture or retrieve such data. Determining what data a business needs and where such data would be retrieved from helps enhance the likelihood that selected data is relevant to the goals of data collection for the business.

1.2 Capture/Creation

Following the definition stage of the data life cycle, the next step is to obtain the data, either by creating data internally or capturing data from where it has been created externally.

- Internal data is a type of digital asset created by the company manually (e.g., keying in a sales order), automatically (e.g., system logs, electronic data interchange, etc.), or semiautomatically (e.g., an employee-reviewed sales order record created through optical character recognition of a customer's purchase-order PDF, etc.).

- When data is obtained from an external source, there is added complexity such as integrity, safety, and copyrights. Companies may need to sign contracts regarding usage and privacy to obtain external data, and/or there may be a cost associated with obtaining external data.

When internal data is generated manually or semiautomatically, a few input checks are typically employed to maintain the integrity and accuracy of the data. These input checks include:

- **Field Check:** Checks the input type to ensure the input is consistent with the field requirement (text/string, date, time, numeric/integer/float).

- **Reasonableness Check:** Compares inputs against the expected norm based on the context of the data. For instance, when a purchase order is initiated to purchase ten times the ordinary quantity when compared to the past 12 months, the system will prompt a warning message to ask the user to check the quantity inputted.

- **Completeness Check:** Checks for missing mandatory fields.

- **Validity Check:** Verifies data against predefined rules or reference data (e.g., zip code, phone number, etc.).

- **Limit Check:** Checks the data values against predefined upper/lower limits.

- **Size Check:** Checks if the number of characters exceeds the max allowed for the field.

1.3 Preparation

Once the data has been obtained, there are two steps in the life cycle that must be completed before the data is ready for analysis or use: preparation and synthesis. The purpose of the preparation step is to determine whether the data is complete, clean, current, encrypted, and user-friendly.

- **Enhancing Completeness and Integrity of Data:** Any time data is moved from one location to another (whether that's from an internal database to a different internal database or obtaining external data), it is possible that some of the required data could have been lost during the capture process.

  - It is critical to determine whether the data is complete and that the integrity of the data remains (that none of the data have been manipulated, tampered with, or duplicated during the extraction).

  - The following four steps should be completed to validate captured data:

    1. Compare the number of records that you intended to capture to the number of records in the source database to check for potential missing rows of data.

    2. Compare descriptive statistics for numeric fields if you are privy to checksums from the original data source. Comparing those statistics helps to check for potential missing data or incorrectly formatted fields.

    3. Validate that field formats (e.g., string/text, date, time, double/numbers) are consistent with the source to ensure that the formatting transferred appropriately.

    4. Compare character limits for the attributes in the source file to the new file to ensure data was not lost due to mismatched character limits.

- **Data Integration:** When data is sourced externally (e.g., foreign exchange rates), it is critical to design the data architecture to ensure that the data pipeline is integrated with the target location/database and ensure any ongoing updates of the external source are timely and accurately loaded in the target location/database.

- **Cleaning Data:** After validating the completeness and integrity of captured data, the data need to be assessed for quality in preparation for analysis. The following five steps should be completed to clean captured data:

  1. Remove unnecessary headings or subtotals that would otherwise obstruct data synthesis or analysis.

  2. Clean leading zeroes and nonprintable characters to ensure consistency across data values.

3. Format negative numbers to ensure consistency across numerical values.

4. Identify and correct inconsistencies across data in general. These inconsistencies will need to be replaced with a common value before analysis if the analysis will require grouping data based on that attribute.

   —For example, if there is a state field, California could be formatted as "CA," "Cal," "Ca.," and so on.

5. Address inconsistent data types (e.g., datetime, doubles, string, integer, etc.).

- **Data Encryption:** The sensitivity of data and the consideration of integrity would generally require encryptions both in data transit and data storage.

1.4   Synthesis

The synthesis step is a bridge between preparation and usage—once you have determined how you intend to use the captured data, you can create calculated fields to prepare that data for quicker usage and analysis. While synthesis is not always a necessary stage, if there is data that can be synthesized, this is the step in which such field creation would occur.

An example of data that can be synthesized would include the creation of a calculation for net sales based on existing gross sales and sales returns, allowances, and discounts fields.

1.5   Analytics and Usage

Once the data has been prepared for use through capture, preparation, and synthesis, the data is ready for practical use in the organization to create reports and inform decisions. The stage of analytics and usage lasts for as long as the data is useful to analysts in the company.

The stage of analytics and usage focuses on the data being useful to the internal company—not being shared with external users or stakeholders. If the data will be shared externally, that is addressed in the next step of the data life cycle, publication.

1.6   Publication

After data is prepared for internal use, the data may also be shared with external users. Examples of sharing data externally are sending monthly statements to clients, publishing financial statements, and sending quotes to customers. When data is shared externally, the data is considered published and the internal company no longer has sole control of how that data will be used, further shared, archived, or purged. For those reasons, it is critical for companies to take care regarding what data they share with external users.

1.7   Archival

Following the decline in need of specific data sets (e.g., financial data past the relevant analytical period set by the company or data sets not accessed/utilized for an extended period of time), data sets are moved from active systems to passive systems for archiving to free up storage resources for the active systems, enhance active system performance, and reduce security risks. Optimally, archived data will be tested for accuracy and completeness prior to removal from active systems.

1.8   Purging

The end of the data life cycle occurs when the data is completely removed (purged) from the company's storage systems (archived and otherwise). It is critical to ensure that the data has truly reached the end of its use and there is no requirement (legal or otherwise) to maintain the archived data, and once it is time to purge the data, it is critical to ensure the data is completely purged.

2 Types of Data Collection

Creating or capturing data is the first step in the data life cycle, and data can be collected through a variety of methods. Three such methods are:

- Extract, transform, and load (ETL)
- Active data collection
- Passive data collection

2.1 Extract, Transform, and Load (ETL)

When data already exists, whether that data is internal or external, the data must be extracted from its original source, transformed into useful information, and loaded into the tool you choose to use for analysis. The steps of ETL are similar to the steps discussed in the data life cycle section (capture, preparation, and synthesis), but ETL is a more specific method for collecting existing data in order to answer a specific data analysis question.

2.2 Active Data Collection

On the other hand, when you need to collect new data from your employees, customers, users, etc., you need to actively collect that data. When you directly ask your users for data, you are participating in active data collection. This can occur from survey or interview results as well as forms gathering personal information such as users' emails, phone numbers, or addresses.

2.3 Passive Data Collection

As our employees, customers, users, etc. become increasingly connected to each other and to the companies they interact with through the Internet of Things and artificial intelligence, it is possible for companies to gather information without direct permission from their users through tracking web usage via cookies or gathering time stamps of when users interact with your website or online store.

6 Data Storage and Database Design

1 Storage Processing and Repositories

Data storage is a type of technology specifically designed for retention of information and help with accessibility for authorized users to perform business activities effectively and efficiently. Common types of data storage include the following:

- **Operational Data Store (ODS):** An ODS is a repository of transactional data from multiple sources and is often an interim area between a data source and data warehouses.

    - Captured transactional data could be related to operational activities such as customer orders, sales, or vendor payments. It could also be system-related, measuring available storage, system latency, or the number of records processed by a given system.

    - ODS data sets are smaller and are frequently overwritten as transactions are modified, processed, and reported.

- **Data Warehouse:** Data warehouses are very large data repositories that are centralized and used for reporting and analysis rather than for transactional purposes.

    - A data warehouse pulls data either directly from enterprise systems with transactional data or from an ODS.

    - This data is then combined into a single repository that can be used for reporting, to create data marts, or for a variety of other purposes.

- **Data Mart:** A data mart is much like a data warehouse but is more focused on a specific purpose such as marketing or logistics and is often a subset of a data warehouse.

    - Different departments within a company may need tailored data marts to operate more effectively, so they select highly relevant data points from a data warehouse to create their own data mart.

- **Data Lake:** A data lake is a repository similar to a data warehouse, but it contains both structured and unstructured data, with data mostly being in its natural or raw format.

    - A data lake is different from data warehouses because it does not have a predefined data structure or schema. Alternatively, the data stored in the data lake is not indexed or prepped and can be access by a user in its original form.

    - This contrasts with a data warehouse, which has a predefined schema that is in place to enable quick processing and analysis.

1.1   On-Premises Storage vs. Cloud-based Storage

Traditionally, all data that a company created or captured has been stored in physical drives or servers in the company's data centers. These on-site data repositories (ODS, data warehouse, data mart, and data lake) are referred to as "on-premises storage." However, with improving cloud computing technology and the exponential growth in data volume, maintaining the repository infrastructure on-premises becomes costly and cumbersome.

- Cloud technologies allow data to be securely stored in (or migrated to) the cloud.

- Cloud-based storage is highly scalable, allowing companies to store as much or as little data as they need and consume the data with agility.

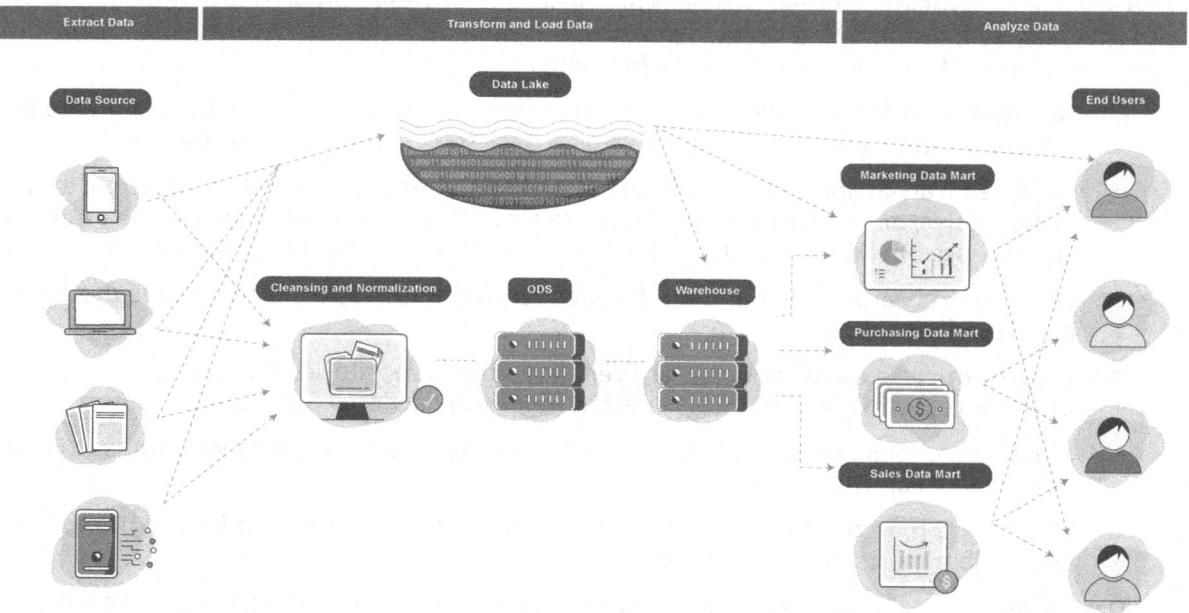

2   Relational Database Design

2.1   Relational Databases

Within an organization, data can be stored in a variety of ways; however, one of the most efficient and effective methods is to store data in a relational database.

Repositories such as data warehouses and operational data stores are often designed and built according to a relational database design. Relational databases are the most common method for storing structured data because of the benefits the data model provides.

Storing data in a normalized, relational database helps to reasonably assure that data are complete, not redundant, and that business rules and internal controls are enforced; it also aids communication and integration across business processes. This differs from less complex methods of storage such as "flat files," which are files that contain plain text with no structural interrelationships within that file (such as an Excel or CSV file).

The benefits associated with relational databases are detailed here:

- **Completeness:** Relational databases assist with the goal that all data required for a business process are included in the data set.

- **No Redundancy:** Storing redundant data is to be avoided for several reasons:

  - it takes up unnecessary resources (which can be expensive);

  - it takes up unnecessary processing to run reports to check whether there are not multiple versions of the truth; and

  - it increases the risk of data-entry errors.

It should be noted that normalized relational databases require there to be one version of the truth and for each element of data to be stored in only one place.

- **Business Rules Enforcement:** Relational databases can be designed and used to aid in the placement and enforcement of internal controls and business rules.

- **Communication and Integration of Business Processes:** Relational databases should be designed to support business processes across the organization, which results in improved communication across functional areas and more integrated business processes.

Relational databases store data across a series of related tables. Each table contains columns (attributes) and rows (records) that are made of data. Each column in a table must be both unique and relevant to the purpose of the table. There are three types of columns:

- primary keys;

- foreign keys; and

- descriptive attributes.

Each column must be designated a specific data type. These data elements are described in the sections below.

2.1.1 Tables

The existence of more than one table in a relational database is the first differentiator between flat files and relational databases; relational databases are made up of at least two tables that are related. Tables are organizational structures that establish columns and rows to store specific types of data records. Tables in relational databases are also referred to as entities, particularly while the database is being designed.

Each table represents an object in the database; for instance, a database that contains data relevant to a sales process would contain a table dedicated to the customers, the employees, the sales orders, and the inventory. The customers table would store the data relevant to each customer in the company's customer list, along with their descriptive information such as their names, addresses, and phone numbers.

2.1.2 Attributes

Columns in relational database tables are also referred to as attributes. Attributes describe the characteristics or properties desired to be known about each entity. For example, an attribute (column) in the customers table may be "Last Name."

Attributes in a table must be unique to that table and relevant to the purpose of the table. There are three types of columns: primary keys, foreign keys, and descriptive attributes.

2.1.3 Records

Rows in relational database tables are also referred to as records. Each record contains information about one entity within the table. For example, a record in the customers table would provide certain information about a single customer.

2.1.4 Fields

A field is space created at the intersection of a column and row in a table in which data is entered. The information placed inside the field is a "data value."

2.1.5 Data Types

Each attribute (column) in a table has a designated data type. Data types specify how the data is stored and indicate how the data in a given attribute can be analyzed. Examples of data types are numerical, text, or date/time. Attributes that have meaningful numerical value, such as cost or quantity, should be classified as numerical data types to ensure that the data in those fields can function in mathematical equations such as sums or averages.

2.1.6 Database Keys

As mentioned above, attributes are either primary keys, foreign keys, or descriptive attributes. While each attribute in a table must be uniquely named, each row is not inherently uniquely named without a database key. Database keys help to uniquely identify each record in a table (and thus, uniquely identify each field at a cross section of attribute and record) and facilitate the relationships between related tables.

- **Primary Key:** A primary key attribute is required in every table. The primary key is typically made up of one column. The purpose of the primary key is to help solidify that each row in the table is unique, so it is often referred as a "unique identifier."

  - The primary key is rarely truly descriptive; instead, a collection of letters or simply sequential numbers are often used.

  - Students may already be familiar with a unique identifier—a student ID at the university is the way student information is stored as a unique record in the university's data model.

  - Other examples of unique identifiers may include online order numbers, invoice numbers, account numbers, social security numbers, and driver's license numbers.

- **Composite Primary Key:** Sometimes a table does not have one single attribute that can uniquely identify each record in a table, so more than one attribute can combine to uniquely identify each record in the table. When more than one attribute is necessary to function as a unique identifier, that is referred to as a composite primary key.

- **Foreign Key:** Foreign keys are attributes in one table that are also primary keys in another table. For example, "Customer ID" may be the primary key in the customers table; however, it is a foreign key in the sales orders table.

  - The same customer ID may appear multiple times in the sales orders table because a single customer can place more than one order.

  - The link between a primary key in one table and a foreign key in another table is what creates a relationship between tables. In other words, foreign keys exist to implement relationships between tables. Whenever two tables are related, one of those tables must contain a foreign key to create the relationship.

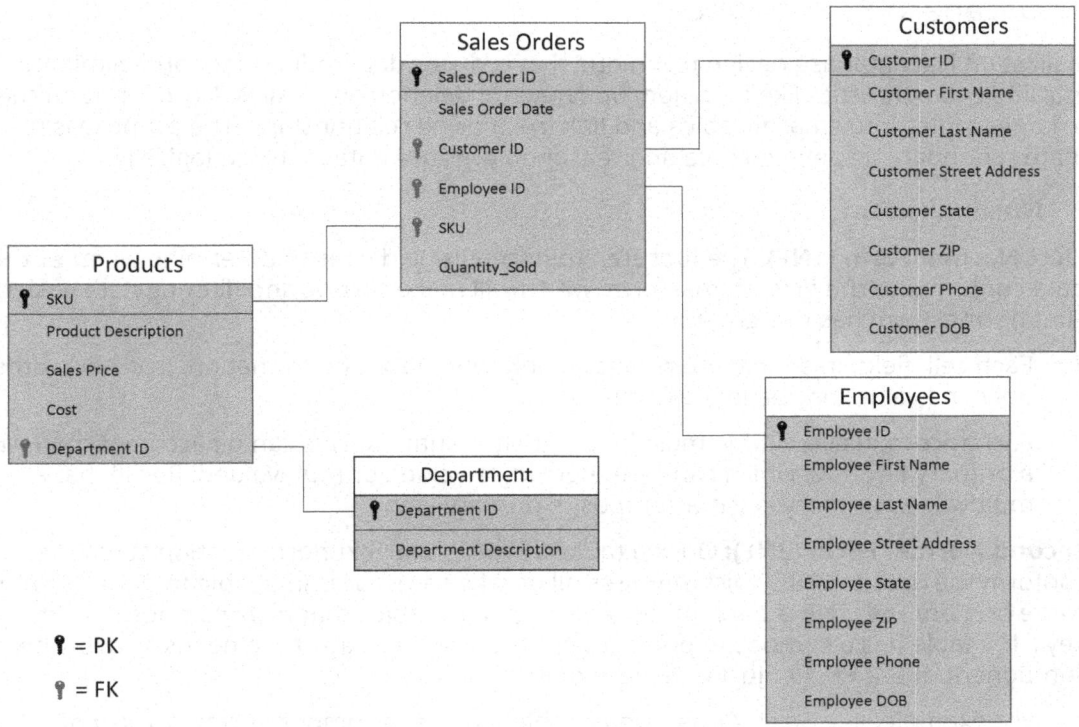

$\mathbf{9}$ = PK

$\mathbf{9}$ = FK

2.2   Data Dictionary

Once processes come together to be supported in one database, the amount of data can be massive. Understanding the processes and the basics of how data are stored is critical, but even with a sound foundation, it would be nearly impossible for an individual to remember where each piece of data is stored, or what each piece of data represents.

Creating and using a data dictionary is paramount in helping database administrators maintain databases and analysts identify the data they need to use.

- Data dictionaries are a type of metadata—data about data.

- Data dictionaries provide and summarize information about the data in a database to make it easier to work with the data and understand how it can be used to inform decisions and build meaningful reports.

Depending on the structure of how data is stored, a data dictionary can be as simple as detailing the attribute names and a description of each attribute. The description helps solidify that the data in each attribute are used and analyzed in the appropriate way—it's always important to remember that technology will do exactly what it is told to do, so the user must be intentional!

- For example: If a user runs analysis on an attribute thinking it means one thing when it actually means another, the user could make some material mistakes and inaccurate decisions even when the user is working with data validated for completeness and integrity.

- It is critical to get to know the data through database schemas and data dictionaries thoroughly before attempting to perform any data analysis or reporting.

When working with data stored in a relational database, more attributes are available to keep track of in the data dictionary, such as whether the attribute is a database key (primary or foreign), whether the field is required, the data type, if there is a default value (and if so, what the default value is), the field size, and any notes necessary to further understand each field.

2.3 Database Redundancy

Normalization is a database design technique that reduces data redundancy and eliminates undesirable characteristics like insertion, update, and deletion anomalies. Normalization rules divide larger tables into smaller tables and link them using relationships. The purpose is to eliminate redundant (repetitive) data and reasonably assure data is stored logically.

2.3.1 Normalization

▨ **First Normal Form (1NF):** The first step to normalizing data is to determine whether the data conforms to the first normal form, which will make sorting and filtering data easier. First normal form has two criteria:

1. Each cell (field) in a table must contain only one piece of information. In other words, only one value may be in a column.

2. Each record in every table must be uniquely identified. This can be accomplished with a primary key (PK), which can be either single-valued or multivalued. Recall that a multivalued primary key is a composite primary key.

▨ **Second Normal Form (2NF):** Once a table is in 1NF, the next normalization step is to conform the data to 2NF, which requires all non-key attributes in a table to depend on the *entire* primary key. 2NF is particularly meaningful for tables that have composite primary keys. If a table has a composite primary key, every non-key attribute needs to describe each component of the PK, not just one piece of it.

   • For example: in a Sales_Order_Detail table that has a composite primary key of SO_ID and Inventory_ID, every additional (non-key) attribute must depend on both the sales order and the inventory item.

   • An attribute such as Quantity_Ordered would pass the 2NF test. However, an attribute such as Inventory_Name would not pass the 2NF test, because Inventory_Name only describes Inventory_ID—it is unnecessary to understand anything about the SO_ID to gather what the Inventory_Name is based on Inventory_ID.

▨ **Third Normal Form (3NF):** Finally, once a table is in both 1NF and 2NF, the next normalization step is to ascertain that each column in a table describes *only* the PK. This is subtly different from 2NF, which requires every attribute to depend on the *entire* PK. In this instance, 3NF wants to establish that none of the non-key attributes depend on other non-key attributes (also known as transitive attributes).

   • For example: a SalesOrder table that has a primary key of SO_ID and a foreign key of EmployeeID is permissible—the EmployeeID fields indicate which employee was responsible for each sale.

   • If the Sales Order table also had an attribute labeled EmployeeName, that would violate 3NF, because EmployeeName depends on the foreign key of EmployeeID, but not on the primary key of SO_ID.

   • Attributes that violate 3NF are referred to as transitively dependent columns, which means that the attribute depends on not just the PK but on another non-key attribute, as well.

A common way to describe normalization is to take the quote from A Few Good Men, "the truth, the whole truth, and nothing but the truth," and adjust it to describe tables in a relational database and the attributes within a given table—"the key, the whole key, and nothing but the key."

▪ The first part of that phrase—"the key"—refers to having a primary key in the first place, which is established by 1NF.

▪ The second part of the phrase, "the whole key" refers to the necessity of every attribute relying on the entire composite primary key (2NF).

▪ The third part of the phrase, "nothing but the key," refers to the necessity for every attribute to rely only on the primary key, not any other non-key (transitive) attributes.

Pass Key

Remember, the forms are progressive, meaning that to qualify for 3NF, a table must first satisfy the rules for 2NF, and the 2NF form must adhere to those for 1NF.

3   Database Models and Schemas

Relational databases must be designed with normalization in mind, and databases are supported by data models and database schemas. Data models are conceptual representations of the data structures in an information system and are not restricted to relational databases only.

A database schema is a set of instructions to tell the database engine how to organize data to be in compliance with the data models. It defines the actual structure of the database, including the tables, columns, and relationships between the data entities. A database schema specifies how the data will be stored and ultimately accessed in the database.

While a data model and a database schema may be related, they are not the same thing. A data model is a high-level design of the data structures in an information system, while a database schema is the actual implementation and execution of that design in a specific relational database.

3.1   Data Models

Data models describe the high-level design of data structures in an information system. There are different aspects to data models, including conceptual, logical, and physical. These models are created in stages. They start with conceptual (least complex), moving through logical and into physical (the most complex). These models are appropriate for different audiences.

The vast amount of detail provided in the physical data model is not necessary for someone only seeking a high or abstract level of understanding of the system. However, a database administrator needing to fine-tune performance issues would require the details of the physical data model. The physical data model will contain many of the items that are included in the data dictionary, such as attribute names and their data types.

3.1.1 Conceptual

A conceptual data model is a high-level, big-picture representation of the data structures in an information system. It defines the main entities and relationships of the data, without going into the details of the attributes or the physical implementation of the database. A conceptual data model is used to understand the overall structure and meaning of the data in an information system, and it is useful for communicating the design of a data model to stakeholders.

It is possible for conceptual data models to have additional detail, up to and including attribute values, but conceptual data models are typically kept to a minimal level of detail. The simplest version of what a conceptual data model could be is showcased in the below graph. This model contains five entities. The sales orders entity is related to four tables—customers, employees, and products—and the products table has one additional relationship to the department entity. This model provides a high-level overview of how five entities may be stored in a relational database to support a sales process.

A conceptual data model is an excellent place for discussion to begin with stakeholders and potential system users to determine that what needs to be stored in the system has been captured without providing overwhelming or unnecessary details.

- Conceptual models are relatively easy to create without requiring advanced software—or any software at all, for that matter. Simple paper and pencil can be used to create conceptual models, which can then be easily modified.

- Once the conceptual model has been approved, additional details can be added in through the logical and physical models.

3.1.2 Logical

A logical data model is a more detailed representation of the data structures in an information system at the level of the data itself, thus providing more detail than a conceptual data model. It defines not only the entities and relationships for the data that will ultimately be built into an information system, but also the attributes of each entity. Logical data models are useful for data-oriented projects, such as designing a data warehouse or system development.

If the initial conceptual data model is more detailed to include attributes (as mentioned above), then the two key differences between the logical and the conceptual models will include:

* the logical model will identify the primary and foreign keys in each entity; and

* the logical model adjusts any entity-relationship issues related to first normal form or second normal form.

In this model, the difference is showcased between the conceptual model of entities and relationships and the logical model adjustment to include attributes, including primary key and foreign key designations (similar to the database keys model). In the graph below, the same five entities and relationships from the conceptual model are showcased. However, each entity has not only attributes but also a primary key designated in the logical model.

The relationships between the entities also exhibit more details to show the connection between related foreign keys and primary keys. This provides more detail about how normalization works—for example, in the sales orders table, the product description is not included (even though it may be meaningful in data analysis to know the names of the products that have sold the most or least, etc.).

It is not necessary to list the descriptive attribute of product description in the sales orders table based on the relationship between Products.SKU → Sales_Orders.SKU. A user of the system could look up the corresponding SKU from the sales orders table in the products table to identify the descriptive attribute of product description (also, the sales price, cost, and department ID).

While a logical data model provides additional information as compared to a conceptual data model, it is still not detailed enough to inform how to build a complete, normalized database.

3.1.3 Physical

A physical data model is the most detailed representation of data structures compared to conceptual or logical data models. Physical data models specify how the data will be stored in the database. In a physical data model, entities can be referred to as tables and attributes can be referred to as columns because this model should be complete enough that the database can be built based on the description in this model.

In addition to including entities (tables), relationships, and attributes (columns—including primary and foreign key identification), the details often included in a data dictionary for each attribute can be included in this data model—most specifically the data type of each attribute.

The character limit (if applicable) can be included, as well as if the field is required and any default values for fields.

The increased level of detail provided in physical data models makes these models useful as a guide for database implementation and system performance improvements once the database is implemented.

The relationships and five entities from the conceptual and logical data models are exhibited in this model, along with the attributes and the primary and foreign key designations where applicable, but in this physical model the data type can also be seen. The character limit can be seen in this physical model in places where it is meaningful.

There are many data types, but the data types represented in the model below are detailed in the following table:

Data Type	Description
Int	Whole number values—these allow the system to perform mathematical calculations on the figures, although that is not always a required component of integers (for instance in primary key values, it would not be meaningful to sum or average those values. If the fields are represented as whole numbers, they can be stored as data type "int" or text).
Char(#)	String or number values; the number in parentheses in the character limit.
Date/time	Date/time values are special versions of numerical values that allow the system to perform mathematical calculations based on the calendar year and 24:00:00 time.
Decimal	Decimal values—different from integers because decimal values are not limited to whole numbers. Decimal values are also numerical and allow the system to perform mathematical calculations.
Text	Sometimes also referred to as "string" values, text or string values represent any value that is non-numeric (this can include strings of numbers that appear numeric to the human eye but are not interpreted as numerically or mathematically meaningful).

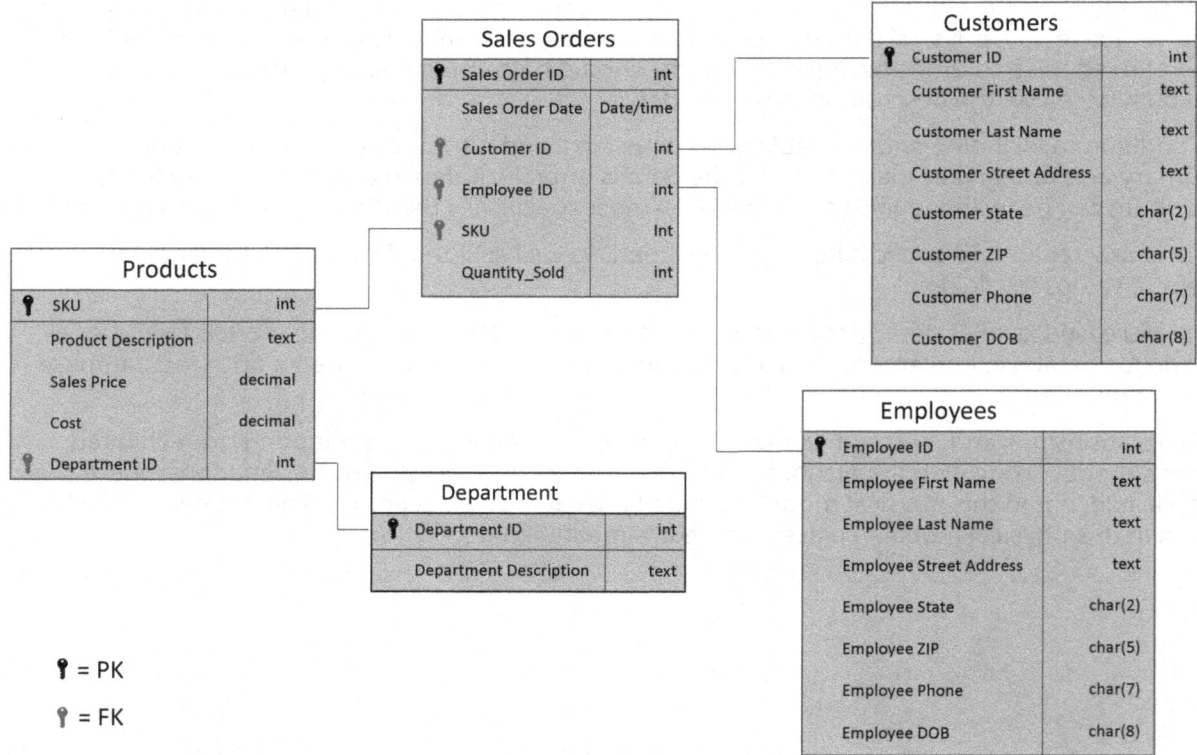

The following table provides a summary of how conceptual, logical, and physical models differ. It is worth noting how each data model builds on the previous model—so an effective logical model that lacks any characteristics of the conceptual model will not be seen, and an effective physical model that lacks any characteristics of the logical model will also not be seen.

Feature	Conceptual	Logical	Physical
Table name	✓	✓	✓
Table relationships	✓	✓	✓
Primary keys		✓	✓
Foreign keys		✓	✓
Column data types			✓

3.2   Database Schemas

Once the data model is set and the database is prepared to be implemented, the actual implementation of the data model will follow a schema. Prior discussions included modeling databases using the first, second, and third normal forms, which is typically used for transactional, relational databases. For data warehouses and data marts, there are two additional popular schemas, star schema and snowflake schema. Star and snowflake schemas have two types of tables: fact tables and dimension tables.

- **Fact Table:** Fact tables contain measures or metrics, which are referred to as facts. These facts measure the business, such as sales, cost of goods, or profit. Fact tables do not contain descriptive elements about the business, but they do contain foreign keys to the dimension tables. These foreign keys relate each row of data in the fact table to its corresponding dimensions to provide context.

- **Dimension Table:** Dimension tables contain descriptive or contextual data for measures such as dates, product names, and customer names. These descriptive attributes describe a dimension; for example, a time table stores the various aspects of time such as year, quarter, month, and day.

3.2.1   Star Schema

The Star schema is the most common schema for dimensional modeling, and it is also the simplest schema for dimensional modeling.

Data in a star schema is organized into a central fact table with associated dimension tables surrounding it, hence why the schema is called a "star," because the diagram of the schema looks like a star, with the fact table in the center and the dimension tables arranged around it.

3.2.2 Snowflake Schema

A snowflake schema is similar to a star schema, but with the dimension tables further normalized. In a snowflake schema, the dimension tables are broken down into multiple related tables, rather than a single table.

- The snowflake schema can be more complex than the star schema, as it requires more tables and more foreign keys to link the tables together. However, it can also be more flexible, as it allows for more detailed information to be stored about the dimensions.

- A snowflake schema strikes a balance between the benefits of a normalized schema and a star schema.

Dimensional modeling using star or snowflake schemas is typically easier for business users to understand, which results in easier reporting. Most business intelligence tools, such as Tableau or Power BI, work very well with star and snowflake schemas.

However, since dimensional modeling does not result in normalized databases, the advantage of having "one version of the truth" across the tables in a system is lost. Data will be redundant in a denormalized data model, so whenever a change is necessary in the system, that change will need to be updated in every area where it has been duplicated.

1 Data Extraction With SQL Queries

Structured query language (SQL) is a computer language to interact with data (tables, records, and attributes) in a relational database. Through SQL statements, records and entire tables can be created, updated, deleted, and viewed (and ultimately extracted). For data analytics, the focus should be on viewing and extracting data that match the criteria of our analysis goals. SQL statements used to view and extract data are called SQL queries, which can be thought of as asking the database a question and receiving an answer based on the criteria placed in the SQL query.

Using SQL, data can be retrieved from one or more tables and organized in a way that is more intuitive and useful for data analysis and reporting than the way the data are stored in a relational database. It is critical to understand the data the user has access to in a database—the tables, how they are related, and their respective primary and foreign keys—in order to write SQL queries. This is why understanding data dictionaries and data models is integral to data analysis.

SQL queries are written to indicate which subset of data is intended for extraction—including the intention to filter results based on any criteria (such as filtering by a particular date, customer, or location) or aggregate existing data (such as sum total sales or sum quantity sold). SQL queries are made up of SQL commands and database elements, which make up SQL clauses.

- **SQL Commands:** SQL commands are language-specific words, such as SELECT, FROM, JOIN, GROUP BY, HAVING, WHERE, and ORDER BY. Case does not matter for SQL commands; however, uppercase is commonly used for SQL commands to differentiate them from database elements.

- **Database Elements:** Database elements are references to table names, attribute names, or criteria. Database elements must be spelled exactly the same as the table names or record names in the database, however case does not matter. It is common to use proper case for database elements to improve readability and to differentiate the database elements from the SQL commands.

1.1 SQL Clauses

SQL clauses are phrases that begin with SQL commands and include database elements (such as attribute names or table names). There is a required order for SQL clauses, and SQL queries typically begin with two clauses: SELECT and FROM.

1.1.1 Introduction to SELECT

- SELECT indicates which attributes the user wishes to view. For example, the Customers table contains a complete customer list with several descriptive attributes for each of the company's customers. If a user would like to see a full customer list, but only the three columns of FirstName, LastName, and State, the user can just select those three attributes in the first line of the query:

  SELECT FirstName, LastName, State

- SQL string functions are used in the SELECT clause to adjust string (categorical or text) values to combine or remove characters from a set of attributes.

1.1.2 Introduction to FROM

▨ FROM lets the database management system know which table(s) contain(s) the attributes that the user is selecting. For instance, in the previous query, the three attributes in the SELECT clause come from the Customers table. So that query can be completed with the following FROM clause:

FROM Customers

1.1.3 Using SELECT and FROM together

▨ Placing the two clauses from the Introduction to SELECT and Introduction to FROM sections together, a query is ready to run:

SELECT FirstName, LastName, State

FROM Customers

▨ If the same three columns are to be reviewed, but the LastName column needs to be seen as the first column so that the results more closely resemble a phone book, the order of the attributes listed can be changed in the SELECT statement. This query will return the same number of records but with a different order of attributes (columns).

▨ If the need arises to select every attribute in the same order as they exist in the table, a shortcut can be used to select all:

SELECT *

FROM Customers

1.1.4 Introduction to WHERE

▨ A simple SELECT FROM query is not complex on its own, but when additional clauses are added, the focus can expand on the particular data necessary for the questions needing an answer or analysis requested to run.

▨ WHERE behaves like a filter in Excel. The syntax of a simple WHERE clause is the following:

- WHERE [attribute_name] = [criteria]

- The attribute_name needs to be spelled exactly the way it is in the database without any formatting (for example, do not place the attribute name in quotations).

▨ More information on formatting the WHERE clause:

- Each attribute in a database table is stored as a specific data type. These data types can be generally categorized into three groups: text, number, and date. The WHERE criteria will be formatted differently depending on the data type of the attribute being filtered.

- Most text data types are descriptive or categorical elements in the database. When filtering for criteria from a text attribute, the criteria must be surrounded in quotes.

- Attributes that contain meaningful numerical data that could be summed or averaged are number data types. When filtering for criteria from a number attribute, there is no need to format the criteria at all.

- Attributes that describe the day a transaction was created (or shipped, returned, or any other meaningful date) are date data types.

1.1.5 Expanding the Usage of SELECT: Aggregates

▪ SQL aggregate functions are used in the SELECT clause of an SQL query to create grand total or subtotal values in a query output. Common SQL aggregate functions are SUM(), COUNT(), AVG(), MIN(), and MAX().

▪ To aggregate means to form a group or a cluster. In SQL, aggregated data represents grand totals or subtotals of data. For example, if the intent is to not simply view all of the individual orders in a Sales Orders table, but rather to see a total count of how many orders were in a table, or to see the grand total quantity of products ever sold, the data would need to be aggregated.

▪ The following functions are commonly used in the SELECT clause to aggregate data:

- SUM(attribute)

- COUNT(attribute)

- AVG(attribute)

▪ The following query uses an aggregate function that would result in a total count of orders in the Sales_Orders table:

SELECT COUNT(Sales_Order_ID)

FROM Sales_Orders

1.1.6 Introduction to GROUP BY

▪ Aggregates are extremely useful to return grand totals of the data that are stored in a database. But sometimes it is preferable to view those data by subtotals instead. When that is the case, two modifications must be made to the SELECT FROM query that returns a grand total.

- Step 1: Determine which field to aggregate.

- Step 2: Determine which field is preferred to group the aggregate by.

- Step 3: Place the descriptive attribute and the aggregate function in SELECT.

- Step 4: Indicate which table contains the attributes and place that table in FROM.

- Step 5: Add a third clause, GROUP BY, which will also contain the descriptive attribute that is preferred to group the aggregate by.

▪ Example:

SELECT CustomerID, COUNT(Sales_Order_ID)

FROM Sales_Orders

GROUP BY CustomerID

1.1.7 Introduction to HAVING

▪ When running a query to gather subtotals using a GROUP BY clause, the results can be filtered in a similar way to using WHERE. SQL cannot filter aggregate measures in the WHERE clause, though, so the appropriate filter clause for aggregate measures is HAVING.

▪ The format of the HAVING clause is similar to WHERE:

HAVING aggregate(attribute) = Criteria

- The aggregate can be any aggregate value, SUM(), AVG(), or COUNT()

- The attribute is the field being aggregated, COUNT(Sales_Order_ID) or SUM(Quantity)

- The = can be replaced with any operator, =, <, >, =<, =>, <>

- In SQL filtering clauses (WHERE and HAVING), SQL operators are required to describe the type of filtering that is necessary

- Common SQL operators are =, <, >, =<, =>, <>

- The criteria are the number values that the results are being filtered on

1.1.8 INTRODUCTION to JOINs and ON

▪ The power of SQL extends beyond relatively simple SELECT FROM WHERE clauses. Since relational databases are focused on reducing redundancy, there are often important details that may be used for analysis stored across two or three different tables.

▪ For example, there may be an interest to know the phone number of each customer associated with their different sales orders. Each order is stored in the Sales Orders table, but the details about the customers (including their phone numbers) are stored in the Customers table. To retrieve data from both tables, it is important to first make sure that the tables are related. This is accomplished by looking at the database schema and identifying the matching primary and foreign keys.

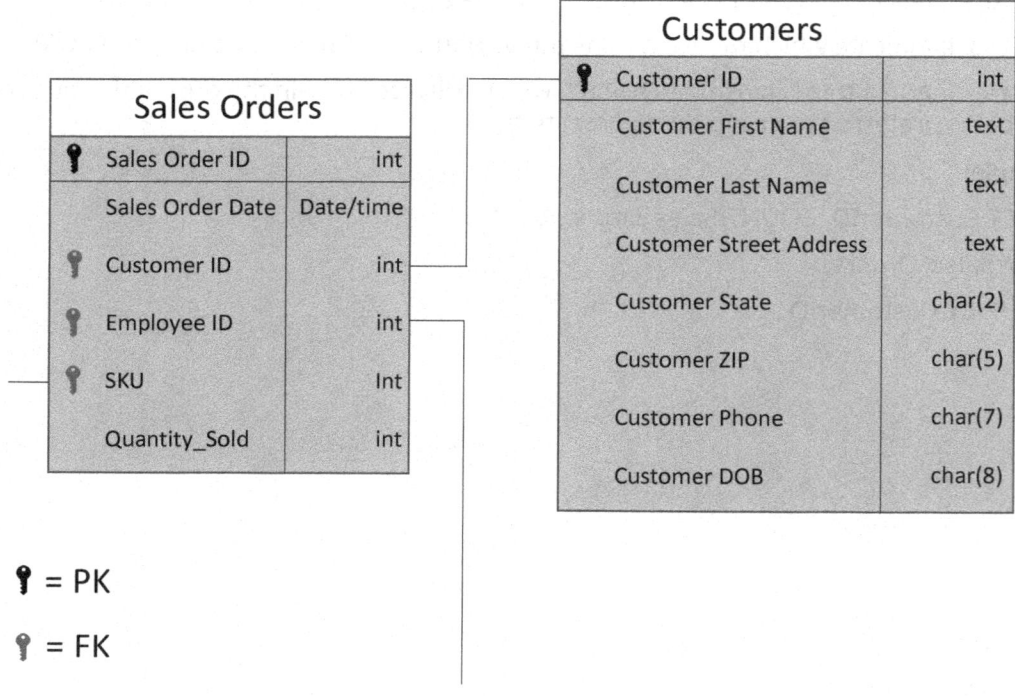

- By reviewing an excerpt of the above database schema, the Sales Orders and Customers tables are related by the common keys of Customer ID. In order to retrieve data from more than one table, use SQL JOINs. The two most common join types are INNER JOINs and LEFT JOINs.

- The template for using an INNER JOIN is:

  FROM table1

  INNER JOIN table2

  ON table1.matching_key = table2.matching_key

  - In an INNER JOIN, the order of the tables does not matter; the user could place the Customers table in either the FROM or the INNER JOIN clause, and the order of the tables does not matter in the ON clause. What matters is that both tables are indicated when intending to retrieve data, and that the two different tables are indicated with their matching keys in the ON clause.

  - To select all of the matching data from the Customers table and the Sales_Orders table, the following query can be run:

    SELECT *

    FROM Customers

    INNER JOIN Sales_Orders

    ON Customers.CustomerID = Sales_Orders.CustomerID

  - INNER JOINs not only work to retrieve data from two tables but, more specifically, an INNER JOIN will retrieve only the data for which there is a match in both tables. That is, if there is a Sales_Order recorded without CustomerID information, the INNER JOIN query would not return that sales order—it would only return sales orders that have verified customers recorded. The same goes for the other table in an INNER JOIN; if there are any customers in the Customers table that have not yet participated on a Sales Order, the INNER JOIN query would not provide any data on those customers. It will only provide data on customers who have a CustomerID listed in the Sales Order table.

- Unlike INNER JOINs, a LEFT JOIN will provide data for which there is not a match. If it is important to see all of the data from the Customers table, even if there isn't a match in the Sales_Orders table, then instead of running an INNER JOIN, replace the word INNER with the word LEFT. The template for a LEFT JOIN is:

  FROM table1

  LEFT JOIN table2

  ON table1.matching_key = table2.matching_key

  - In a LEFT JOIN, the order of tables listed in the FROM and LEFT JOIN clauses does matter. The table listed in the FROM clause is the "left" table; data that does not have a match will be returned from this table.

1.1.9 Summary of SQL Commands

▪ Common SQL commands are SELECT, FROM, WHERE, GROUP BY, HAVING, and JOIN, ON. A summary of each of these commands is in the following table:

SQL Command	Purpose	Example
SELECT	Required as the first clause in most SQL queries. SELECT indicates which attributes are requested to view.	Ex. 1: SELECT Product_Description, Sales_Price Ex. 2: SELECT * Ex. 3: SELECT Customer_ID, SUM(Quantity_Sold)
FROM	Required as the second clause in most SQL queries. FROM indicates which table the attribute(s) requested to SELECT are located in.	FROM Products
WHERE	The WHERE clause is used to filter results. The syntax of a simpler WHERE clause is: WHERE [*attribute name*] = [*criteria*].	Ex. 1: WHERE Sales_Price > 10 Ex. 2: WHERE State = 'AR'
GROUP BY	When needing to aggregate data into subtotals based on categories (such as state, customer, or product), the GROUP BY clause is necessary to create subtotals.	GROUP BY Customer_ID
HAVING	Similar to the WHERE clause, the HAVING clause is used to filter data, but instead of filtering attributes, the HAVING clause is used to filter aggregated data.	HAVING SUM(Quantity_Sold) > 200
JOIN, ON	When needing to retrieve data from more than one table, the JOIN and ON clauses are required to indicate the second table and how the tables are related (via the related primary key and foreign key)	FROM Customers JOIN Sales_Orders ON Customers.Customer_ID = Sales_Orders.Customer_ID

2 Data Integration

Data stored in relational databases are stored across many different tables, but often reports and decisions need to be made based on data stored across several different tables; and sometimes reports and decisions require data not just across different tables in the same database but even from different data sources altogether.

Most popular data analysis and data visualization tools such as Excel, Microsoft Power BI, Tableau Desktop, and Alteryx have built-in integrations with an abundance of common applications, data warehouse tools, and databases. When retrieving data from a large data source such as a database or data warehouse, it can be useful to couple SQL with the built-in integrations in order to limit the data required to only the data that is necessary.

2.1 Application of Data Integration

For financial analysis, it is common to combine an internal company's financial statements with external market data from an online financial database such as Bloomberg or Yahoo Finance. More specifically, an analyst may collect external data to compare the company's financial performance relative to its industry peers, including other companies' financial statements and generally interest rates, inflation rates, and gross domestic product to help place their own company's financial performance into context.

For operational analysis, it is common for relevant data to be stored across different databases or spreadsheets that need to be integrated to make operational decisions or assess performance. For example, combining data from a production database or the production plans with supply chain data can help analysts identify areas of inefficiency such as over- or underproduction so that production schedules can be optimized.

3 Visualizing the Flow of Processes and Data

Organizations are made up of many complex processes, and those complex processes are supported by an abundance of data. Visualizing the steps of processes across roles in an organization and the flow of data that supports processes can explain how a business works and help users understand when data is created and how it is used.

Flowcharts are common tools for depicting process or data flows that help analysts understand processes and analyze those processes for improvement—whether that improvement is based on effectiveness, efficiency, or improved internal controls. There are a variety of templates for flowcharts, including the Business Process Modeling Notation (BPMN), which is used to create flowcharts referred to as activity models and data flow diagrams (DFD), which are used to describe the flow of the data through a process.

3.1   BPMN Activity Models

BPMN is a standardized tool for creating diagrams, with set symbols and rules to depict business processes. This tool enables users to use a common set of concepts and principles to communicate business processes so that they can be documented, improved, and managed.

BPMN activity models can not only be used to improve effectiveness and efficiency of processes among human participants in a process—they can also be examined to identify process areas that could be automated. A rule of automation is that the more rule-bound a process is, the easier it is to automate. Once BPMN activity models are created, they can be analyzed for how rule-bound the steps and decisions associated with the process are. There are significant cost savings associated with automating repetitive processes.

While there are numerous notations within different categories, the following describe the most common symbols and rules.

3.1.1   Flow Activities

A primary purpose of a BPMN activity model is to describe which organizations are involved in a process, and within those organizations to describe how the process is separated across roles/duties. The metaphor of "swim pools" and "swim lanes" is used to visualize the different organizations and roles.

- **Pools:** Pools are used to quickly showcase how many organizations are involved in a given process. Every BPMN model should include one pool at a minimum—that pool will indicate the *internal* organization involved in a process. For instance, in a sales process, the internal organization will be the selling organization, and a separate *external* organization will be the customer. However, there are occasionally processes that are fully internal, such as payroll. In this case, a BPMN activity model may have only one pool.

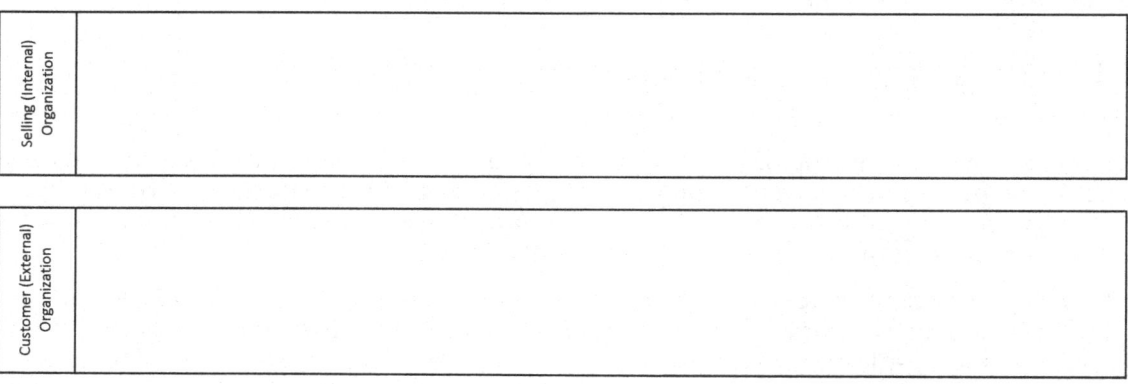

- **Swim Lanes:** Swim lanes are more granular than pools. Swim lanes indicate the segregation of duties within an organization. If there are different roles within one organization involved in a process, then the pool will be separated into separate pools to indicate which role is responsible for which step in the process. For example, in the selling (internal) organization, there might be a sales representative role that is separate from a cashier role. In the following model, the pool for the internal organization has now been split into two lanes— one for the sales representative and another for the cashier, while the pool for the customer remains one pool (without separate lanes).

| Selling (Internal) Organization | Sales Representative | |
| | Cashier | |

| Customer (External) Organization | |

3.1.2 Events

Events describe how a process begins or ends. Events are not actions; they simply indicate when a process kicks off (think of it as a trigger) and when a process is complete. Events are circles. The thickness of the circle depends on whether the event is a start, intermediate, or end event.

- **Start Events:** Every pool within a BPMN model must begin with one and only one start event. Remember: start events are based on *pools*, not *swim lanes*—regardless of how many swim lanes there are in a pool, there should only be one start event per pool. Start events are smooth circles:

- **End Events:** Every pool must end with at least one end event. However: end events are not based on *swim lanes*—regardless of how many swim lanes there are in a pool, a process may still end with only one end event. Additional end events only indicate the potential that a process is cut short early or has multiple ways to end. End events are bold circles:

- **Intermediate Events:** Intermediate events are not a required element of every BPMN diagram, but they exist to indicate when something changes the course of a process, such as a time delay or an error. Intermediate events are two-lined circles.

3.1.3 Tasks

Every action in a process is documented as a task, which is a rectangle with rounded edges. Consider every step a person or a system must take to complete a task, and each of those steps must exist as its own task. For example, in a sales process, the first task might be "Input Customer Name," followed by "Select Product," then "Select Quantity."

It is worth revisiting the model shared previously with the two separate pools for the selling and customer organizations. To simplify the new objects, the tasks will be kept in the selling organization to three tasks, all of which are completed by only one role (so there are not separate swim lanes). At this point, the BPMN activity model (including only the internal organization) would appear as follows:

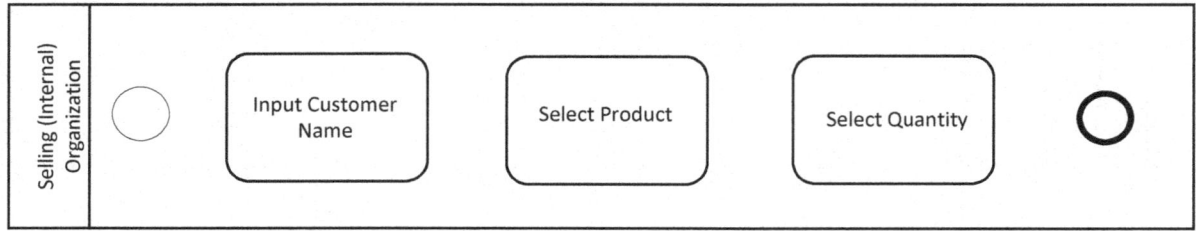

Other than recognizing that the sales process is not complete (and lacking segregation of duties or separate organizations marked by lanes or pools), it can be noted that the BPMN objects are not yet connected to one another. The next step is to connect them.

3.1.4 Connecting Objects

▪ **Sequence Flows:** Every object within one pool must be connected with sequence flows. BPMN activity models are traditionally read from left to right, with the start event as the left-most object and the end event(s) as the right-most object(s) in a pool. Start events kick off the process, with a sequence flow extending to the right from the start event to the first task, then each object continues receiving sequence flows and extending sequence flows to the next object until the process culminates in the end event(s) that receives a sequence flow, then the process ends. Sequence flows are smooth-lined arrows.

Adding the sequence flows to the above model (still only considering the internal organization with three simple tasks) will enhance the model:

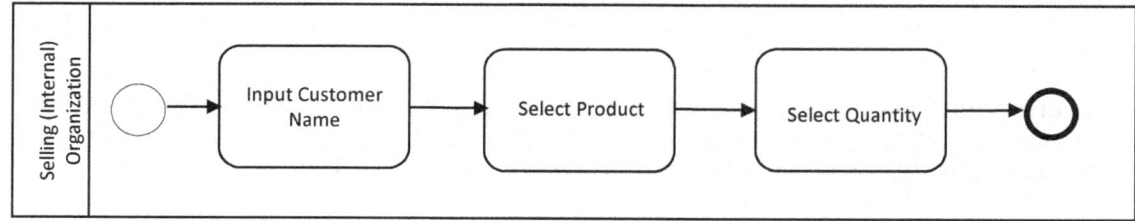

- **Message Flows:** When a BPMN model requires more than one pool (for instance, in the previously examined sales process in which there is also a customer, or when there is a purchasing process where there is also a supplier/vendor/manufacturer), there will be occasional required communication between the internal and external organizations. In this case, the communication will not be indicated by a sequence flow but by a message flow.

  Message flows look similar to sequence flows, shown as dashed arrows, but they only function to indicate communication between two separate pools—they should never be used within one pool to indicate communication between lanes in the same pool. The direction of the message flow should indicate the direction of communication; whoever is answering a question and/or providing information should "send" information to the other pool.

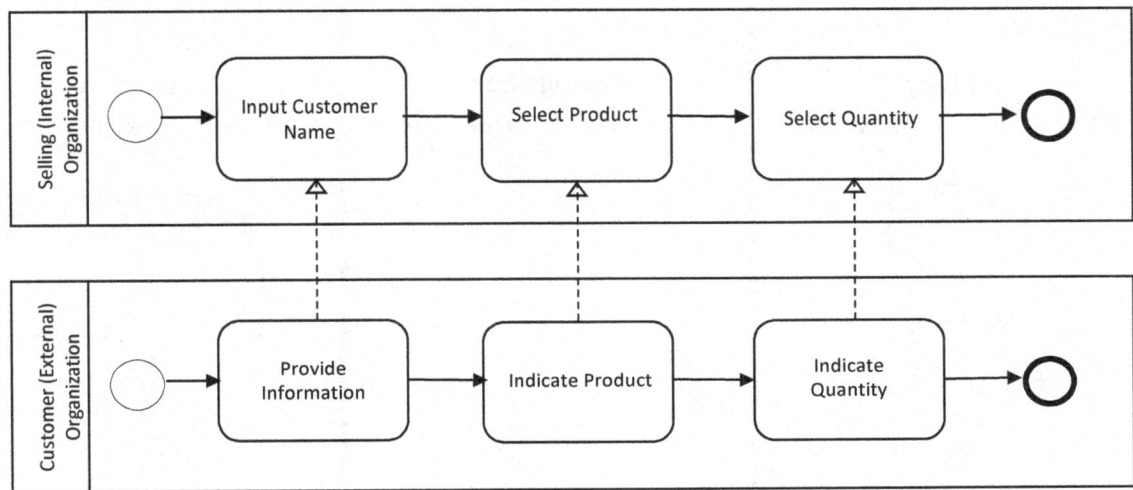

3.1.5 Gateways

So far, the models have been simple and have easily flowed from the start event—through tasks—and ultimately to an end event. An important step in process analysis is to question the drafts continuously during the analysis phase of a project to determine that all of the requirements have been documented and expectations have been discussed.

- For this example, each task should be questioned and analyzed to determine if the tasks can move from start event to end event effectively, and that nothing could go wrong in any of the steps (be it error, fraud, etc.). Gateways help provide analysis opportunities for when a task shouldn't result in only one possible sequence flow but rather more than one—be it two, three, or more.

- A task (such as "indicate product" and "indicate quantity") can occur mundanely enough, but then as soon as the system recognizes that it is possible that there is not sufficient inventory for the product and quantity mix that the customer ordered, there needs to be a gateway to provide all of the possible directions a sales representative might go in.

- The gateway (shaped like a diamond) is a question, not a task. There should not be any active verbs in the annotation of the text of a gateway, only a question. In this instance, the gateway label could read, "Is there sufficient quantity of this product?" (or, if that is too wordy, simply "Sufficient quantity?").

■ There is an abundance of rules that relate to gateways, but the most important regard sequence flows exiting a task object. Task objects should always have one and only one sequence flow "exiting" the task, so if there are two potential exits or flows away from a sequence flow, then an opportunity is identified to use a gateway.

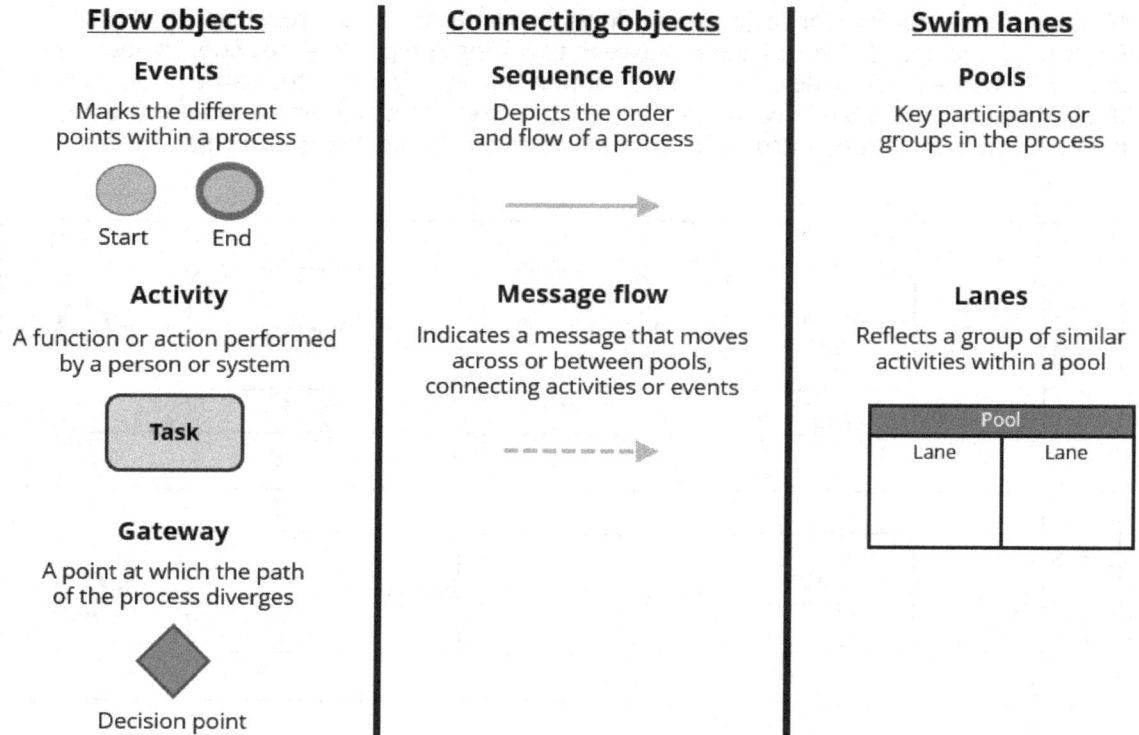

3.2 Data Flow Diagrams

A data flow diagram is a standardized tool for creating diagrams that describe the way data moves through an organization. While there are BPMN objects that can be used in BPMN activity models to indicate data stores, data flow diagrams offer a more granular level of detail about how data moves through a process or system that BPMN activity models alone do not provide. While data flow diagrams are more granular than BPMN activity models, there are fewer objects used in data flow diagrams. The four objects in a data flow diagram are similar in shape to the objects in a BPMN activity model.

3.2.1 Process

A process indicates any action that results in data changing and producing a new output. The labels for processes are similar to the labels in BPMN activity model tasks; they are formatted as a short sentence such as "Input Customer Information." The shape of a process object is depicted as either a rectangle with rounded corners or a circle.

3.2.2   Data Flow

A data flow indicates the direction that data flows through processes. Data flows are labeled to indicate the data that is flowing between processes—for example, "Customer Contact Details." The shape of a data flow object is an arrow, either curved or straight.

3.2.3   Data Store or Warehouse

A data store object indicates where data is stored for later use—for example, a database, a SharePoint folder, or even a physical filing cabinet. The shape of a data store object is an open-ended rectangle.

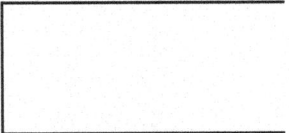

3.2.4   External Entity or Terminator

An entity object indicates the external entity (organization, group of people, or different department) that receives the data at the end of a set of processes represented in a data flow diagram. The shape of an entity object is square.

Example: Simple Data Flow Diagram

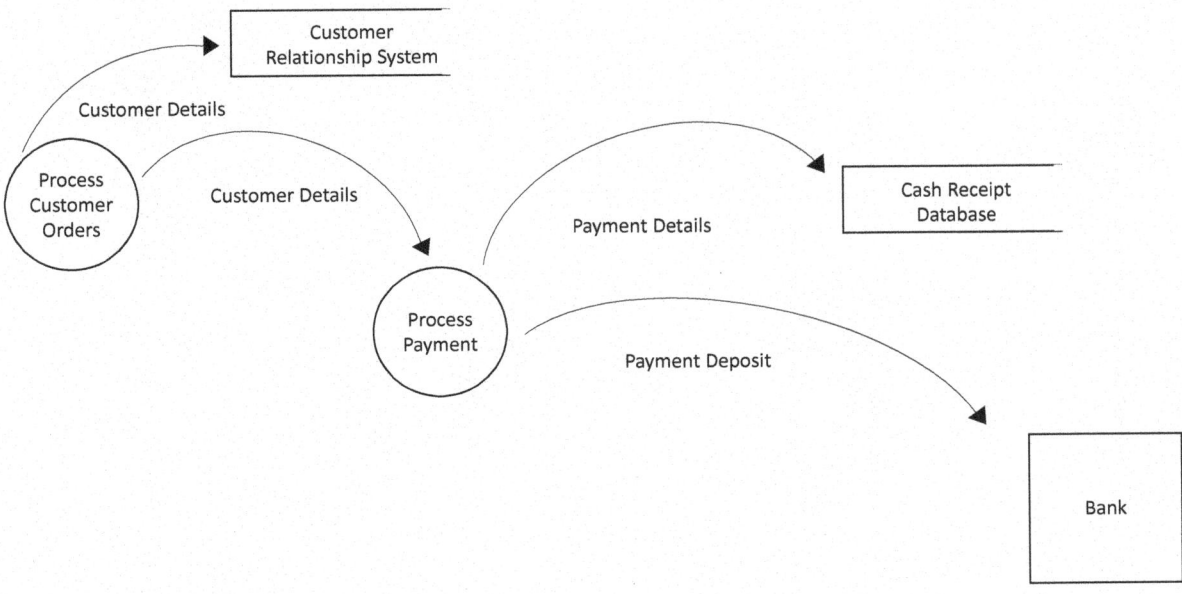

NOTES

ISC
3

Security and Confidentiality

Module

1 Cybersecurity Risk Management Overview

Cybersecurity is the practice of protecting an organization's IT infrastructure and critical data from bad actors by deploying a variety of technologies, internal control processes, and best practices to mitigate the business impact of these attacks. The goal of a cybersecurity program is to manage the cybersecurity risks by securing and enhancing confidentiality, data integrity, and availability.

Successful cyberattacks can cost an organization monetary and nonmonetary losses to restore its ability to work with customers, vendors, and partner organizations. These attacks are threats to both individuals and organizations. Breaches of data, theft, service interruptions, and regulatory noncompliance are the highest of security concerns for senior executives and others who are charged with IT governance.

- **Data Breaches:** Data breaches occur when information is compromised and utilized without the authorization of the owner. Examples of attacks that can result in data breaches include ransomware, phishing, malware, and compromised passwords.

- **Service Disruptions:** Service disruptions are unplanned events that cause a general system or major application to be inoperable for an unacceptable length of time. Some examples of the causes of service disruptions include malware, distributed denial-of-service (DDoS) attacks, SQL injections, and password attacks.

- **Compliance Risk:** Regulators can require organizations to comply with cybersecurity regulations. The failure to comply with these regulations can result in fines and financial penalties. Examples of areas involving compliance risk include HIPPA, GDPR, PCI-DSS, and ISO/IEC 27001.

To combat these threats, organizations should develop a program to mitigate cybersecurity risks and constantly develop innovative security measures that keep up with the ever-changing technology landscape.

2   Cyberattacks

A cyberattack is any kind of malicious activity that targets computer information systems, infrastructures, computer networks, or personal computer devices, and attempts to collect, disrupt, deny, degrade, or destroy information system resources or the information itself. The impacts of such attacks can directly or indirectly affect the organization, its customers, its vendors, or potentially its partner organizations. The method of execution of an attack can be grouped into one of the following categories: network-based attacks, host-based attacks, social engineering attacks, application-based attacks, physical attacks, and supply chain attacks.

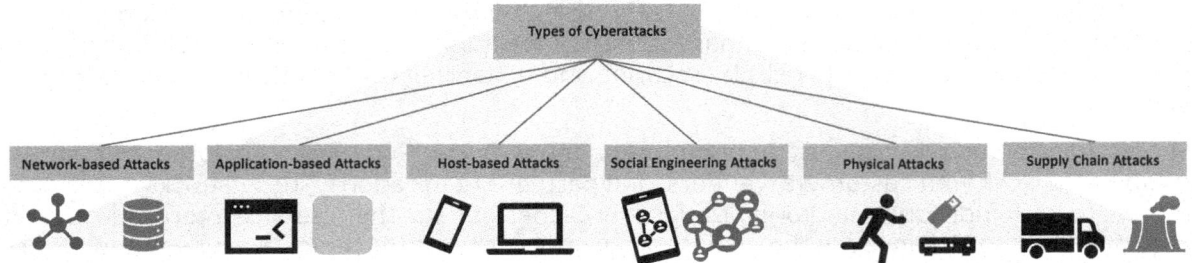

2.1   Types of Threat Agents

A threat agent is an internal or external attacker that could negatively impact data security through theft, manipulation, or control of sensitive information or systems.

There are several types of threat agents (i.e., people who build malware and perform attacks on infrastructure and applications). There is usually a particular goal, such as financial gain or the destruction of data.

Examples of the types of different threat agents include:

- **Attacker, Threat Actor, or Hacker:** These are individuals, or groups of individuals known as hacking rings or advanced persistent threats (APTs), that target people or organizations to gain access to systems, networks, and data. This classification of threat agents is broad and has a wide range of objectives which include stealing property, destabilizing businesses, spying on governments, disseminating true or false information, or attempting to achieve some form of financial gain.

- **Adversary:** These are actors with interests in conflict with the organization. They are incentivized to perform malicious actions against the organization's cyber resources such as intercepting purchases, theft of data, tampering with hardware prior to installation, social engineering attacks, and more.

- **Government-sponsored/State-sponsored Actors:** These threat actors are funded, directed, or sponsored by nations. They've been known to steal and exfiltrate intellectual property, sensitive information, and even funds to further their nations' espionage causes.

- **Hacktivists:** These are usually groups of hackers that operate to promote certain social causes or political agendas. Likewise, there are also groups of hackers that operate on a self-proclaimed relatively moral basis by staying away from certain targets, such as hospitals, churches, and other organizations that have altruistic purposes or missions.

- **Insiders:** Insiders are employees that either organically developed into a person with malicious intentions or intentionally infiltrated an organization to achieve nefarious objectives. These individuals represent a significant internal threat to any organization's cybersecurity because of the amount of access they have working from within a company's safeguards.

- **External Threats:** Threats that occur from outside of the organization, entity, or individual that is the target of the cyberattack.

2.2   Types of Cyberattacks

- **Network-Based Attacks:** These attacks target the infrastructure of a network, including switches, routers, servers, and cabling, with the intent to gain unauthorized access or disrupt operations for users.

  - **Backdoors and Trapdoors:** These are methods to bypass security access procedures by creating an entry and exit point to a network that is undocumented. Trapdoors are often installed by system owners so they can bypass security measures to gain quick access, whereas backdoors may be intentionally installed or unintentionally left available due to product defects. While neither of these are an attack on a network, they facilitate entry into the network that can be used to execute attacks.

  - **Covert Channels:** These are mechanisms used to transmit data using methods not originally intended for data transmission by the system designers. These channels violate the entity's security policy but do not exceed the entity's access authorization, so they can communicate data in small parts. Based on the method of hiding the information, there are two types of covert channels:

    - **Storage Channels:** Data is transmitted by modifying a storage location, allowing another party with lower security permission to access the data.

    - **Timing Channels:** The delay (or gap) in transmitting data packets is used to hide a transmission.

  - **Buffer Overflows:** Attackers overload a program's buffer, the temporary storage, with more input than it is designed to hold. This may cause the program to overwrite the memory of an application or crash. The attacker can then inject malicious code or take control of a system.

  - **Denial-of-Service (DoS):** An attacker floods a system's network by congesting it with large volumes of traffic that are greater than the bandwidth it was designed to handle. This excess volume consumes the network's resources so that it cannot respond to service requests, leaving it vulnerable to network protocol or application exploitation.

  - **Distributed Denial-of-Service (DDoS) Attacks:** These occur when multiple attackers or compromised devices are working in unison to flood an organization's network with traffic. These attacks manipulate the operation of network equipment and services in such a way that they may be more powerful than a traditional DoS attack.

  - **Man-in-the-Middle (MITM) Attacks:** The attacker acts as an intermediary between two parties intercepting communications, acting as a legitimate entity within a typical secure session. As information is passed between the two parties, the attacker can read or redirect traffic.

- **Port Scanning Attacks:** Scanning networks for open ports is frequently done by attackers to find vulnerabilities that can be exploited so that they can gain unauthorized access to a company's network.

  —While ports can be physical (e.g., HDMI, USB, Ethernet ports), this attack focuses on logical ports that are used for protocols such as TCP (Transmission Control Protocol) port 80, which is one of the most common ports used on the internet.

  —It is normal for companies to have open ports, but misconfigured open ports with vulnerabilities create weaknesses that allow unauthorized access.

  —Common vulnerabilities include unsecured protocols, unpatched protocols, poor login credentials, and poorly configured firewalls.

- **Ransomware Attacks:** These are attacks that typically come in the form of malware that locks a user or a company's operating systems, applications, and the ability to access data unless a ransom is paid.

- **Reverse Shell Attacks:** Also referred to as "connect-back shells." A victim initiates communication with an attacker from behind a company's firewall so that the attacker can bypass the firewall and any other network safeguards and remotely control the victim's machine. Since the original contact is not established from outside of the company's network, normal filtering and firewall protection are bypassed.

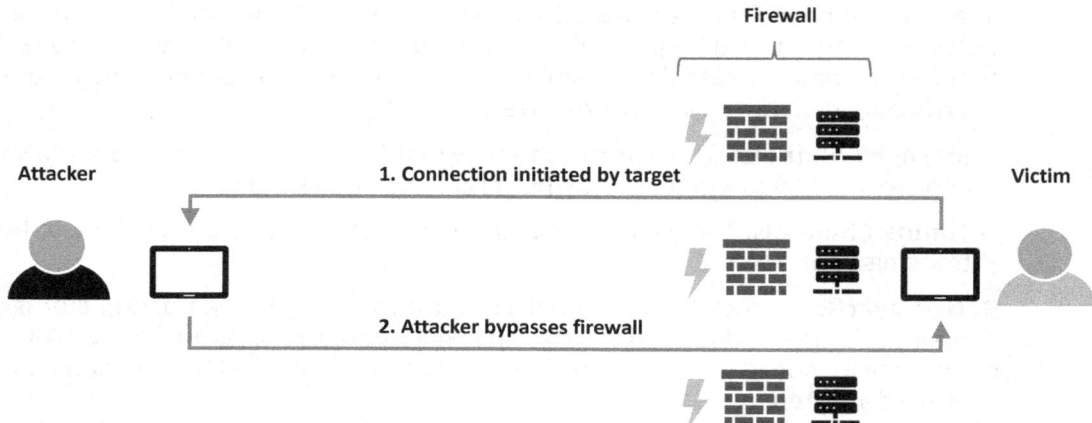

- **Replay Attacks (Eavesdropping):** These are a type of MITM attack in which a cybercriminal eavesdrops on a secure network communication, intercepts it, and then "replays" the message at a later time to the intended target to gain access to the network and the data that is behind the firewall. Hackers don't need the added skill of decrypting a message because they have already tapped into the company's network.

- **Return-Oriented Attacks:** Also known as "return-oriented programming attacks," these use a sophisticated technique that utilizes pieces of legitimate original system code (each a gadget) in a sequence to perform operations useful to the attacker. Each gadget ends with a "return" instruction, causing the next gadget to execute and carry out complex operations.

- **Spoofing:** The act of impersonating someone or something to obtain unauthorized system access by using falsified credentials or imitating a legitimate person or entity by using fake IP addresses, domains, or email addresses.

  —**Address Resolution Spoofing (ARS):** This spoofing attack involves a fraudulent act of falsifying the mapping of media access control (MAC) addresses on a network to IP addresses. All devices on a network have MAC addresses that map to IP addresses. By using ARS, the attacker links its MAC address with the target's IP addresses so that devices can communicate with each other point to point (IP address to IP address). Manipulating the mapping of the ARS means fraudsters can channel messages to alternate destinations.

  —**DNS Spoofing:** A spoofing attack that involves a perpetrator modifying the domain-name-to-IP-address mapping known as the domain name system (DNS). A company's DNS server translates domain names to IP addresses. For instance, www.MyCompany.com might be converted to 111.100.1.10. If this mapping is tweaked by an attacker to redirect someone to another IP address that leads to a mimicked website, the victim could potentially enter usernames, passwords, or sensitive information, or download a malicious application from the fake site.

  —**Hyperlink Spoofing:** The alteration of hyperlink URLs that redirect the victim away from their intended destination and send them to a nefarious location.

- **Application-Based Attacks:** These forms of attacks target specific software or applications (desktop or web) such as databases or websites to gain unauthorized access or disrupt functionality.

  - **Structured Query Language (SQL) Injection:** An application attack in which an attacker injects malicious SQL code into existing SQL code on a company's website to gain unauthorized access to a company's data.

    —Attackers may not have direct access to a company's database server that contains company data, but it can gain access through the company's web server, which may connect directly to a company's database server.

    —By injecting malicious SQL code into the web server directly from the internet, the attacker is able to access the database server by manipulating the web server.

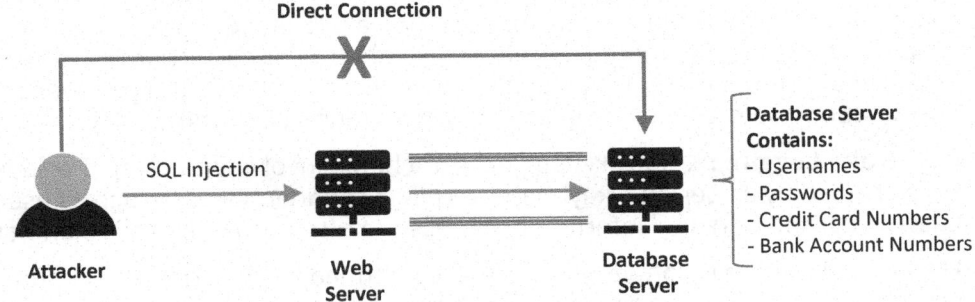

  - **Cross-Site Scripting (XSS):** Similar to an SQL injection, but these attacks inject code to a company's website that attacks users visiting the company's website. When a user visits the site, the user's browser executes the malicious code and performs the attack, which may compromise the user's data, such as usernames, passwords, and other sensitive information.

Pass Key

The main difference between SQL injection and XSS is the main target of the attack. SQL injection targets the database, whereas the XSS targets the company's website to compromise website user's data. They are commonly the result of poor input controls of a company's website.

- **Race Condition:** An attacker exploits a system or application that relies on a specific sequence of operations. By forcing the application to perform two or more operations out of order or simultaneously, an attacker may gain unauthorized access or execute a fraudulent act.

- **Mobile Code:** Any software program designed to move from computer to computer to "infect" other applications by altering them in some way to include a version of the code. Malicious mobile code is commonly referred to as a "virus." Viruses can come in many forms, including the following:

  - **Overwrite Virus:** These viruses delete or overwrite information in the infected file. Typically, removal of the virus requires deletion of the file.

  - **Multi-Partite Virus:** This type of virus uses a mixture of infection methods to infect files, trying different ways to infect a file if others fail.

  - **Parasitic Virus:** These viruses launch when an application that has the virus launches and the same rights held by the program being launched are given to the virus.

  - **Polymorphic Virus:** This form of virus mutates by changing its structure so that it can avoid detection.

  - **Resident Virus:** These viruses install a copy of themselves on a computer's memory.

- **Host-Based Attacks:** These attacks target a single host such as a laptop, mobile device, or a server to disrupt functionality or obtain unauthorized access.

  - **Brute Force Attacks:** These are password-cracking schemes in which attackers use an automated program that attempts to guess a password. The program tries all possible combinations of potential passwords based on a preset algorithm, which can be as simple as starting with the first letter of the alphabet for each character and trying all possible combinations, or it may first try common phrases and password/number combinations before advancing to other permutation algorithms.

  - **Keystroke Logging:** Keystroke logging is a scheme involving tracking the sequence of keys pressed by a user on a keyboard to collect confidential data such as usernames, passwords, and personal information. These are often delivered as Trojan horses.

  - **Malware:** Malware is software or firmware intended to perform an unauthorized process that has an adverse impact on the confidentiality, integrity, or availability of an information system. Common examples are viruses, worms, Trojan horses, adware, spyware, and other code-based programs that infect a host.

  - **Rogue Mobile Apps:** These attacks involve the use of a malicious app that appears legitimate. A fraudulent party creates a mobile application that is installed by a victim unsuspectingly and that app then steals information, gives the attacker unauthorized access, or executes some other malicious act.

▨ **Social Engineering Attacks:** These attacks involve the use of psychological manipulation or deception to get employees to divulge sensitive information, provide unauthorized access, or assist an attacker in committing fraud. Human interaction through email, text, direct messaging, or social media is the primary medium through which perpetrators gain confidence and trust.

- **Phishing:** Phishing is a form of digital social engineering that uses authentic looking—but bogus—emails that request information from users or direct them to a fake website that requests information.

- **Spear Phishing:** This form of phishing targets employees in a corporate entity by posing as a legitimate department or employee, such as human resources or the IT director. The goal is to obtain confidential information such as usernames, passwords, or personal data that can be used for exploitation.

- **Business Email Compromise (BEC):** This is a form of phishing that targets executives and other high-ranking individuals. It typically involves schemes to get the executive to transfer money through a wire, pay fake foreign suppliers, or send sensitive data to someone impersonating an attorney or other employee. This scheme has also been called *whaling*.

- **Pretexting:** This attack is similar to BEC and spear phishing, but it involves creating a fake identity or scenario so that the employee has a sense of urgency to act. By using this form of pretext, or false reason, the attacker is able to obtain sensitive information or manipulate the victim into performing some other fraudulent act.

- **Catfishing:** This scheme involves the creation of a fake online persona that is used to lure a victim into a personal relationship with a fraudster. The person conducting the scheme then appeals to the emotional nature of the victim and requests money, gifts, or other items of value.

- **Pharming:** This attack is often used in combination with phishing as it involves a victim entering personal information into a website or portal that imitates a legitimate website. The link to the fraudulent site may be in a phishing email. The scheme may even involve the manipulation of Domain Name System (DNS) servers so that the website's URL replicates the correct address.

- **Vishing:** This technique involves fraudulent schemes using the telephonic system Voice over Internet Protocol (VoIP). Schemes normally involve a spoofed or fraudulent caller ID that is tied to a legitimate business or person. Attackers often use incoming recorded messages that may be interactive and use key tones or voice recognition to convert information input by the victim into numbers or letters.

▨ **Physical (On-Premises) Attacks:** This is a security breach carried out on an organization's premises or performed in some way that physically involves a bad actor gaining control of sensitive data, hardware, and/or software.

- **Intercepting Discarded Equipment:** By obtaining access to outdated or discarded equipment in the trash or through companies that accept discarded equipment, fraudsters can steal sensitive data stored on such devices.

- **Piggybacking:** This method of attack involves an attacker using an authorized person's access to gain entrance to a physical location or electronic access.

- **Targeted by Attackers:** On-premises infrastructures are often targets of hacking groups or attackers because they know that many organizations lack sophisticated cybersecurity defenses. This lack of protection may be due to the cost of implementation or a lack of awareness of potential cyber threats.

- **Tampering:** This involves gaining physical access to a company's IT infrastructure and modifying the way its network collects, stores, processes, or transmits data. This can be done by physically rewiring cabling, plugging in directly to network equipment, or adding an unauthorized device to the existing network.

- **Theft:** This refers to the act of physically stealing data, hardware, or software.

- **Supply Chain Attacks:** These attacks use cyber tactics to target the production and distribution of goods within a supply chain so that there are larger disruptions in the normal operations of a company, government, or other entity.

  - **Embedded Software Code:** This form of attack involves inserting code into prepackaged software or firmware being sold to a company that later installs the software after purchase.

  - **Foreign-Sourced Attacks:** In many countries, governments have deep and widespread control of companies in the private sector. Those governments may use products sold to other countries to conduct surveillance or deliver malicious code.

  - **Preinstalled Malware on Hardware:** This method of attack involves installing malware on devices that will be used by companies in a supply chain, such as USB drives, cameras, or phones. Once the company acquiring the devices connects them to the company's network, the malware executes.

  - **Vendor Attacks:** This attack is perpetrated upon key vendors of a target company so that the normal production of goods or business operations is disrupted.

  - **Watering Hole Attacks:** In this method of attack, fraudsters identify websites of suppliers, customers, or regulatory entities that are known to be used by several companies or even entire industries. The attackers then look for weaknesses at that third party that can be used to deliver malware, steal data, or obtain unauthorized access.

Illustration 1   The Invasive Impact of Cyberattacks

Given the interconnections of organizations with their customers, vendors, and partner organizations, the impact of a cyberattack upon one organization could have a profound impact on other organizations. Below are examples of how these attacks could impact stakeholders outside the organization.

Example Attack	Customer Impact	Vendor Impact	Partner Organization's Impact
Ransomware Attack: The attacker encrypted the company's servers and databases, preventing the company from accessing customer data and processing orders	Unable to deliver products to customers, causing interruption of the company's customers' fulfillments	Vendors are unable to communicate with the company through electronic data interchange channels to fulfill purchase orders	Financial losses due to ransom payment to support the victim of the attack
Mobile Code: The attacker infected the company with a virus that deletes critical contact data and spreads the virus through the business network	The customer's ordering systems are infected by the virus causing data loss	The vendor's systems were infected, causing the vendor to lose critical production data	The partner must reallocate resources to support the company under attack, causing disruptions in its main operations
Malware: The attacker infected the company's servers and exposed confidential customer data	Confidential customer data is exposed to the attacker	Vendor banking information is exposed to the attacker	Reputation loss and potential class-action lawsuit

2.3   Stages in a Cyberattack

While there are a variety of cyberattacks, they all share some of the following steps or phases:

- **Reconnaissance:** In this first stage, attackers discover and collect as much information about the target IT system as possible. Information obtained may include the location of facilities, the type of network and infrastructure deployed, security measures in place, and the names of employees as well as the management hierarchy. During this phase, attackers may also search for specific vulnerabilities, such as open ports that are not adequately protected or known software applications that have not been sufficiently patched.

- **Gaining Access:** This is the step in a cyberattack when the information collected in the previous steps is used to gain access to the target of an attack using a variety of techniques.

- **Escalation of Privileges:** Once unauthorized access into a system is obtained, attackers attempt to gain higher levels of access in this stage. This may be done by obtaining the credentials of a user with higher privileges.

- **Maintaining Access:** In this stage, the attacker remains in the system for a sustained period of time until the attack is completed and looks for alternative ways to prolong access or return later.

- **Network Exploitation and Exfiltration:** In this stage, attackers proceed with the objective of disrupting system operations by stealing sensitive data, modifying data, disabling access to systems or data, or performing other malicious activities.

▪ **Covering Tracks:** This step occurs while the attack is in progress or after the attack is completed and involves the attacker concealing the entry or exit points in which access was breached. This can be done by:

- Disabling audit functionality
- Clearing logs
- Modifying logs and registry files
- Removing all files and/or folders created

3   Risks Related to Cloud Computing

Cloud computing is a way for organizations to store, use, process, and share data, software, and applications without the need to own or manage the resources required to perform those functions on company premises. Companies access the needed computing power using the internet. The data and software applications used in a cloud computing environment are often stored and managed by third-party providers, which causes a significant amount of sensitive information and user applications to be at risk.

Despite this risk, most cloud providers are seen as being more secure than a company managing its own IT infrastructure on its own premises (referred to as on-premises). This is because most cloud providers are required to maintain high levels of security protocols and procedures, and upgrade to the latest versions with security patches and internal controls due to regulations such as GDPR and HIPAA.

It is also common for third-party cloud providers to have SOC 2® engagements, which are independent audits of management's attestation regarding the cloud service provider's controls and other claims made by management regarding security over their customer's data, privacy, and confidentiality. Information to be included within the SOC 2® engagement report may include how controls at the service organization address the Cloud Security Alliance's Cloud Controls Matrix, whereas the engagement team would consider relevant established criteria related to the security of a system.

Below are some risks specific to cloud computing for which a firm should be aware:

▪ **Additional Industry Exposure:** By nature of design, organizations subscribing to a cloud provider may be exposed to other subscribing organizations and their unique industry risks. Cyber threats that one company might not be exposed to become a risk to the other companies that share the same cloud computing provider.

▪ **Cloud Malware Injection Attacks:** An attack specific to cloud computing-based systems in which an attacker gains access to the cloud environment and then injects malware so that data can be stolen, services disrupted, or further access gained.

▪ **Compliance Violations:** Cloud computing relies on third-party hosts, and there is the compliance risk that these hosts or service providers do not have the security protocols and procedures in place to meet regulations on privacy and confidentiality (i.e., HIPPA and GDPR regulations).

▪ **Loss of Control:** Not having physical or logical access to computing equipment means an organization using cloud computing services will relinquish some control over its infrastructure. As a result, changes or upgrades to the cybersecurity measures may not be timely or up to the standard that the subscribing company prefers.

▪ **Loss of Data:** The third-party cloud computing services provider is susceptible, albeit less likely than most businesses, to data breaches, losing data, or exposing data.

■ **Loss of Visibility**: Loss of full visibility of the company's IT infrastructure comes with a loss of control. The only entity that has full visibility is the cloud provider, which means the subscribing organization does not know all of its risks.

■ **Multi-Cloud and Hybrid Management Issues:** A company subscribes to various cloud-based solutions and/or maintains some on-premises IT infrastructure. While having a hybrid or multi-cloud setup can be part of a good cybersecurity diversification plan, it may prove challenging to integrate and monitor multiple environments, which could make detecting a cyberattack difficult.

■ **Theft or Loss of Intellectual Property:** Cloud applications store various types of data for companies, including proprietary information, and there is the risk that the service provider lacks sufficient controls over the data, which results in theft or loss of intellectual property (IP).

4   Risks Related to Mobile Technologies

Mobile devices such as smartphones, tablets, and wearables that can access the internet all have risks for both users and their employers. While these devices have evolved to become a regular part of corporate life and enhance productivity, their mobility and lack of oversight introduce cybersecurity risks that should be addressed.

Most mobile devices are similar to computers in terms of functionality and the type of information they access. As such, they face similar security threats as an organization. However, some of their differences are at the root of mobile device cybersecurity issues, such as the fact that mobile device operating systems are different than their computer counterparts.

A separate set of patches and updates must be maintained so that operating systems can be updated. Another difference is that immobile desktop computers are not constantly exposed to public networks like mobile devices are. As a result, companies must install software on every mobile device to monitor and protect users from potential attacks. If protective software is not used, policies should be in place that provide guidelines for safe usage.

Other risks and cybersecurity threats specific to mobile devices include the following:

■ **Application Malware:** This threat occurs when a user downloads an application that appears to be legitimate but gives an unauthorized user access to the device. For example, when a user visits a site, malware could be installed that steals private information without the user's knowledge.

■ **Lack of Updates:** There could be uninstalled patches and security fixes that have yet to be installed at a given point in time that leave the device vulnerable. Devices that go long periods of time without updates are at risk.

■ **Lack of Encryption:** Many mobile devices are not encrypted and only rely on a passcode for secure access. Once access is gained, passwords can be reset on the web by using the victim's email on the mobile device.

■ **Physical Threats:** Examples of physical threats include loss or theft of a mobile device. If the device does not have sufficient access controls, theft could lead to an unauthorized user gaining the ability to access sensitive information and applications.

■ **Unsecured Wi-Fi Networks:** Users of mobile devices often connect to public unsecured networks which means anyone on the same network could potentially access that device, steal sensitive information, or infect the device with malware.

- **Location Tracking:** Unauthorized tracking is a risk that involves a threat actor using Global Positioning System (GPS) technology to locate people, devices, or other assets. With this knowledge, attackers can devise plans that use the victim's location to perpetrate an attack.

Threat actors can also use mobile storage devices such as USB drives, memory cards, or optical discs to infect other devices. For instance, USB drives can be easily plugged into a laptop or desktop and quickly install software that can compromise the device.

Mobile devices can also be monitored or surveilled for the purpose of eavesdropping. Equipment such as cell-site simulators, Bluetooth scanners, and international mobile subscriber identity (IMSI) catchers can be used to intercept calls or text messages within a specific radius.

5   Risks Related to the Internet of Things

The Internet of Things (IoT) is a class of smart devices connected to the internet that provide automation and remote control for other devices in a home or office setting such as cameras, tablets, wearable devices, phones, and alarm systems. Organizations continue to integrate IoT devices into normal business operations. As such, companies must consider cybersecurity implications that this technology introduces.

Relevant cyber threats specific to IoT technology include:

- **Device Mismanagement:** Insufficient password controls and device mismanagement can increase the risk of a cyberattack. This can lead to the loss of critical information or access to the devices on the IoT network.

- **Device Spoofing:** This is when an attacker connects illegitimate devices to a company network to gain information or perform unauthorized activities. Illegitimate devices may include phony devices or standard devices being modified for malicious attack.

- **Escalated Cyberattacks:** IoT devices can be used as an attack base to infect more machines, or as an entry point for access into a connected network.

- **Expanded Footprint:** IoT devices paired with other devices that are directly connected to a company's core network expand the footprint of total devices under a company's purview, thus increasing the number of points subjected to attack.

- **Information Theft:** Since IoT devices are connected to the internet, they have the potential for sensitive data to be stolen or exploited because that data is either stored in the cloud or on other devices that can be accessed

- **Outdated Firmware:** Firmware is software that is preinstalled on a device that controls its local functions, much like the software that comes installed on a printer or scanner. When firmware is not updated to the latest version, attackers can exploit the vulnerability of outdated firmware to gain access and control a device. Since employees often wear IoT devices or bring their own into a company's office without alerting IT personnel, they are often missed as a part of the organization's cybersecurity defenses.

- **Malware:** IoT networks and devices are susceptible to cyberattacks due to the often-limited computing power among the individual devices connected to the network. A common example of malware attacks for IoT technology is ransomware, where the malware code denies access to the devices without a financial consideration paid by the user.

- **Network Attacks:** Threat actors can launch DoS attacks on IoT networks and devices just as they can with traditional networks. These types of attacks overburden a network with traffic via IoT devices and render it useless.

6   Threat Modeling and the Overall Threat Landscape

Threat modeling is the process of identifying, analyzing, and mitigating threats to a network, system, or application. The goal is to understand all risks a system could face and develop controls and countermeasures to minimize the impact of a risk or to try and prevent it from happening. Developing a threat model forces companies to identify weaknesses and vulnerabilities that need to be addressed. The first step of threat modeling is to use the confidentiality, integrity, and availability (CIA or CIA triad) method to define what needs to be protected in the organization. For instance, an organization could identify sensitive customer information (confidentiality), company proprietary data or processes (integrity), and/or reliability of its customer portal (availability) to be the main target for protection.

Part of threat modeling involves evaluating the threat landscape, which is the total range of potential threats that an organization and its IT infrastructure may face. Organizations should regularly assess the threat landscape because new threats are continuously evolving. One way to do this is by using threat intelligence platforms, which help organizations get information on the latest threats and vulnerabilities so companies can prioritize their cybersecurity efforts.

Elements that should be considered when evaluating the threat landscape include different attack vectors or methods, the magnitude of impact of a threat, existing vulnerabilities, and the types of threats (social engineering attacks, insider threats, network attacks, etc.).

6.1   Phases of Threat Modeling

Threat modeling typically involves the following phases:

- **Identify Assets:** This involves inventorying all assets that need to be protected against threats using the CIA triad.

- **Identify Threats:** This includes identifying the threat types and characteristics, such as intent, targeting, and potential method of attack. Realistic threat scenarios should also be discussed and used for planning.

- **Perform Reduction Analysis:** This phase involves decomposing the asset being protected from the threat. The intent is to gain a greater understanding of how the asset interacts with potential threats whether they are systems, applications, or networks. The decomposition process involves understanding trust and security changes, the flow of data, where input can be received, security clearances, and any related policies and procedures.

- **Analyze Impact of an Attack:** Quantifying the impact of an attack in terms of dollars will help prioritize solutions. Understanding other qualitative effects should also be considered.

- **Develop Countermeasures and Controls:** This may include implementing security controls like intrusion detection systems, contingency plans, and security protocols in the event of a successful attack. Responses should be prioritized based on the threat with the greatest risk.

- **Review and Evaluate:** Periodically evaluating the threat model should be done so that updates can be made based on new risks in the threat landscape.

6.2   Threat Methodologies

There are three commonly used methodologies for threat models known as the Process for Attack Simulation and Threat Analysis (PASTA) threat model; the Visual, Agile, and Simple Threat (VAST) threat model; and Spoofing, Tampering, Repudiation, Information Disclosure, Denial-of-service attack, and Elevation of privilege (STRIDE) threat model.

6.2.1   PASTA Threat Model

The PASTA threat model has seven stages that focus on risks and countermeasures that are prioritized by the value of the assets being protected. The seven stages are:

1.   definition of the objectives (DO) for the analysis of risks;

2.   definition of the technical scope (DTS);

3.   application decomposition and analysis (ADA);

4.   threat analysis (TA);

5.   weakness and vulnerability analysis (WVA);

6.   attack modeling and simulation (AMS); and

7.   risk analysis and management (RAM).

6.2.2   VAST Threat Model

The VAST threat model is based on the Agile project management methodology. Its goal is to integrate threat management into a programming environment on a scalable basis.

6.2.3   STRIDE Threat Model

STRIDE is a threat model developed by Microsoft that is used for assessing threats related to applications and operating systems. Its six threat concepts listed in its name are broad enough to cover threat concerns other than applications, such as network threats or social engineering.

1 The COSO Framework and Its Relationship With Cyber Risks and Controls

COSO is the Committee of Sponsoring Organizations, an advisory group that provides guidance on internal controls, fraud deterrence, and risk management. The organization is known for the COSO internal control framework that was created in 1992 and became an industry-wide benchmark for internal control practices. The most recent version of the framework, titled COSO 2013, often refers to the COSO cube, a three-dimensional diagram showing how the various elements of an internal control system work together.

COSO has also published a companion framework to COSO 2013 for enterprise risk management. This framework, titled COSO 2017 Enterprise Risk Management, can be used as a reference for organizations to assess risks and to develop strategies around risk and business performance.

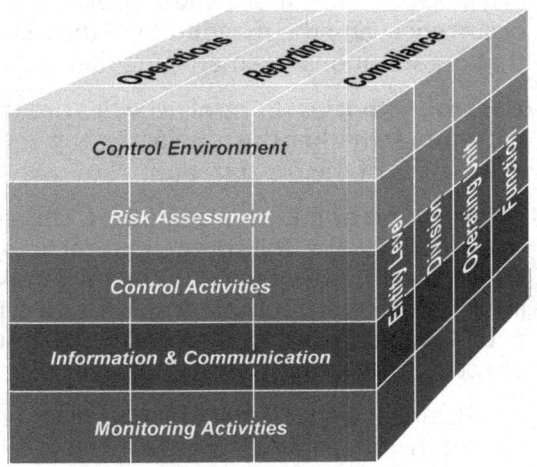

Internal Control—Integrated Framework, © 2013 Committee of Sponsoring Organizations of the Treadway Commission (COSO). Used with permission.

The COSO framework classifies internal control objectives into three groups: operations, reporting, and compliance. These groups are applicable to cybersecurity as follows:

- **Operational Objectives:** These include performance measures and safeguards that can help increase the likelihood that an organization's IT assets are protected against cybersecurity threats and fraud. They focus on the effectiveness and efficiency of business operations.

- **Reporting Objectives:** These objectives are related to increasing the likelihood that cybersecurity controls are in place so that they do not affect internal and external financial and nonfinancial reporting. The objectives have a focus on transparency, reliability, timeliness, and trustworthiness as determined by standard-setting bodies, regulators, and an organization's own policies.

- **Compliance Objectives:** These are based on adherence to governmental laws and compliance regulations. As it relates to cybersecurity, this includes compliance with industry standards such as those issued by NIST, U.S. regulations like the Health Insurance Portability and Accountability Act (HIPAA), and international laws like the General Data Protection Regulation (GDPR).

There are also five components of the COSO internal control framework. These can be applied to cybersecurity efforts to prevent, detect, and respond to cyber threats as follows:

- **Control Environment:** The control environment is often referred to as the tone at the top and sets ethical values for an organization by creating a top-down approach to push forward the COSO framework throughout the organization.

  - Senior management and those charged with governance should act as champions to raise awareness of cyber threats; guide the development of key IT policies, processes, and procedures; provide guidance on incident response management; and educate the workforce regarding the roles of safeguarding a company's digital assets and resources.

- **Risk Assessment:** This component involves performing risk assessments to evaluate internal and external factors. It can be applied to cyber threats by tailoring the organization's risk assessment procedures to analyze cyber risks, their likelihood of occurrence, and the magnitude of their impact. Assessments provide reasonable assurance that organizations are managing their cyber risks to an acceptable risk tolerance.

- **Control Activities:** Control activities are the policies and procedures put in place to help determine whether the tone at the top set by the control environment is being implemented at all levels of the organization.

- **Information and Communication:** This component focuses on using consistent and relevant language, following best practices for sharing information, and communicating internally and externally with the right stakeholders all to support internal controls. Sharing information about company policies on cyber threats, how to detect potential cyber threats, and how to respond to cybersecurity events is critical for any organization. Examples of effective communication include:

  - Business impact analysis reports reviewed by management that outline the impact of interrupting key business functions

  - Employee meetings on policies regarding cybersecurity

  - Periodic emails addressing cybersecurity internal controls to the entire company

  - Mandatory annual training of cyber threats and company policies

- **Monitoring Activities:** Monitoring internal controls is the component that should be practiced on an ongoing basis to identify areas of risk vulnerability and to determine effectiveness and efficiencies. This is especially important for cybersecurity threats because attacks are always evolving. Examples of monitoring practices and controls that should be in place, evaluated, and adjusted include:

  - Penetration testing

  - Vulnerability scanning and assessments

  - Periodic phishing reports

Looking at cyber risk through a COSO lens can allow management to better communicate their risk tolerance levels and objectives for the business. If clear priorities are established by management, then the employees tasked with cybersecurity can focus on assessing the risk associated with systems most likely to be attacked, and the points of potential vulnerability in the IT system.

2 Security Policies, Standards, and Procedures

To enhance cybersecurity defenses and enhance IT infrastructure resiliency, security rules must be carefully coupled with technology at multiple levels of an organization. At the uppermost level is a collection of security policies, which serves as an overview of an organization's security needs and strategic plan for what should be implemented.

At the next level is a set of standards that organizations use as a benchmark to accomplish the goals defined by the security policies. At the bottom level, there are standard operating procedures that are typically detailed documents that specifically outline how to perform business processes. Security policies, standards, and procedures are subject to review by service auditors in a SOC 2® engagement when the organization is a service organization.

2.1 Security Policies

Security policies are the foundation of an organization's security framework, which serves as a comprehensive guide for its implementation. This document outlines the extent to which security measures are applied to various company resources. It provides clear terms, definitive roles and responsibilities, and acceptable levels of risk. Security policies are also evidence of due care by senior management against intrusions, attacks, and natural disasters.

Organizations often have domain-specific policies that help partition different organizational focus points. For instance, policies may be divided into user policies that govern employee behavior relative to IT, regulatory policies to comply with applicable laws, and system-based policies that cover network or software. Organizations often create acceptable use policies to govern these domains and carry out security policies.

Further examples of security policies and related processes in place by a service organization may include the following:

- Data classification and business impact assessment
- Selection, documentation, and implementation of security controls
- Assessment of security controls
- User access authorization and provisioning
- Monitoring of security controls

2.1.1 Acceptable Use Policy

An *acceptable use policy (AUP)* is a control document that is created by an organization to regulate and protect technology resources by assigning varying levels of responsibilities to job roles, listing acceptable behaviors by employees and vendors, and specifying consequences of those who violate the AUP. Users are often asked to sign and agree to the terms of an AUP prior to being granted access to systems, applications, and devices issued by the organization. An AUP will generally cover the following:

- Definition, scope, and purpose of the policy
- Acceptable use of personal devices for business activities
- Acceptable mobile devices approved for use
- Device maintenance
- Confidentiality

- Monitoring and enforcement of actions on company devices
- Restricted activities and software downloads on company devices
- Software that must be installed for security purposes
- Security requirements
- Terms about termination if policy is violated

2.1.2 Mobile Device Security Policies

One of the greatest threats to an organization is poor management of the way mobile devices are used by employees. As such, strict policies should be developed along with the proper technological safeguards to channel mobile device use and interaction with a company's network. Having AUPs specific to mobile devices helps accomplish this.

An AUP for a mobile device is a subset of a company-wide AUP that defines policies for tablets, smartphones, smart watches, and other similar mobile devices. Using these devices gives users access to the same data, systems, and applications as traditional hardware such as laptops and desktops. Mobile device AUPs usually stipulate password protection rules, multifactor authentication requirements, any required encryption, web browsing rules, parameters for connecting to public networks, and policies regarding other applications or file downloads on the devices.

2.1.3 Bring-Your-Own-Device Policies

Another common mobile device policy is a *bring-your-own-device (BYOD)* policy, which allows employees to use their personally owned devices for work-related activities and for connecting directly to a company's network. BYOD policies may include some of the same elements as an AUP but will address the following items that are only relevant to personal devices used for work:

- **Monitoring and Enforcement of Actions on Personal Devices:** The extent of an organization's purview over an employee's activity on personal devices will vary by company, along with the balance of privacy and surveillance. Companies must enforce an appropriate level of monitoring to prevent intrusion from malicious actors but also set standards for respecting employee privacy.

- **Ownership of the Data on the Device:** Companies will have varying stances on this but generally they will assume that all information pertaining to company records, clients, vendors, and contacts are property of the organization, not the employee. Rare instances may exist in which the employee has more ownership than the company.

- **Personal Liability and Indemnification:** BYOD policies may stipulate when an employee is personally liable versus when liability is placed on the company. The policy may also cover indemnification, defining who is responsible for compensating someone for losses in the event the employee or company is assigned blame.

- **Restricted Activities and Application Downloads on Personal Devices:** While personal devices are property of the employee, company policies may be written so that certain applications are disallowed to prevent data breaches, data leakage, or access to a company's network.

BYOD policies also apply to nonmobile devices. By allowing these in addition to mobile devices, various risks to the organization are created. These risks include the possibility of leaking sensitive data, breaking compliance with regulations, and providing another inlet for bad actors to access company data.

2.2   Security Standards

Security standards are organizational requirements that are either mandatory by law or adopted by companies as guidelines for best practices. Standards are the next level of security rules beneath policies that serve as a course of action to achieve security policies. Standards also might define a minimum level of performance and may provide recommendations on how to implement policies.

Examples of common standards include:

▪ frameworks issued by the National Institute of Standards and Technology (NIST);

▪ privacy laws like the General Data Protection Regulation (GDPR) issued by the European Union; and

▪ industry standards like the Payment Card Industry Data Security Standard (PCI DSS) issued by the PCI Security Standards Council.

2.3   Security Standard Operating Procedures

Standard operating procedures (SOPs) are the lowest level of documentation that provide detailed instructions on how to perform specific security tasks or controls. These SOPs usually involve a combination of systems, software, and physical actions so that the goals of the security policy and standards are achieved.

It is recommended to segment SOPs so that they are not all in a single document. This prevents one person from having access to instructions for every security practice in the company. Rather, policy owners in separate departments can own SOPs relevant to their job roles and company functions. When policies are adjusted or need updating, policy owners can make adjustments accordingly.

3   Network Protection Methods

3.1   Network Components

A network is a system of physical and virtual devices that are connected using wired cables or wireless technology that communicate using a mixture of different protocols so that users can send, receive, and store data. Protocols are sets of rules that govern how a device communicates with other devices in a network. Some of the hardware used in a network includes:

▪ **Access Point (AP):** A wireless connection point for users to directly connect to a wired network using wireless-enabled devices.

▪ **Bridges:** A bridge connects separate networks that use the same protocol, even if those networks have different topologies or transmission speeds. Bridges operate at the data link layer of a network.

▪ **Computers:** Desktop and laptop computers are user endpoint devices that are the primary means of user interaction with a network.

▪ **Gateway:** Gateways connect multiple networks that use different protocols, translating one protocol to another so that the two networks can interact. Gateways can operate in all layers of a network but frequently operate in the application layer.

▪ **Hubs:** Hubs are connection points that link multiple systems and devices using the same protocol within a single network. Hubs receive data packets and forward them to all other devices.

- **Mobile Phones and Tablets:** Devices that are another primary means through which users connect to a network.

- **Modems:** Devices that modulate between digital information and an analog signal to support networks. They are most commonly used to connect computers to the internet.

- **Proxies:** A form of gateway that does not translate protocols but rather acts as a mediator that performs functions on behalf of another network using the same protocol instead of just connecting the networks.

- **Routers:** Devices that control data flow on a network using the same protocol by receiving incoming data packets and forwarding those to the correct destination based on IP addresses.

- **Servers:** Devices that support computers and networks by performing different core functions such as running applications with application servers, storing files with a file server, or storing data using a database server.

- **Signal Modifiers:** Devices such as amplifiers, concentrators, and repeaters receive signals and then modify them by increasing the signal strength, combining multiple signals, or simply regenerating the signal. The types of signals could be electrical, radio frequency, audio, or optical.

- **Switches:** Similar to hubs, but instead of broadcasting received signals to every other networked device, switches only route traffic to target destinations, connecting various devices within a network for most modern organizations.

3.2 Network Security

There are a variety of security methods available to companies that focus specifically on network security to defend against cyberattacks, including the following:

- **Network Segmentation or Isolation:** The process of controlling network traffic so that it is either inaccessible or separated from outside communications or other segments within an organization's own network. This form of pocketed isolation improves overall network security.

- **Firewall:** Firewalls are physical devices, software, or both that filter and monitor incoming and outgoing network traffic to a public network to block malicious activity from attackers.

- **Service Set Identifier (SSID):** The name assigned to a wireless network is known as an SSID and is broadcast by a wireless access point within a certain range so that wireless-enabled devices can connect. One way to improve wireless network security is to make networks less visible by disabling SSID broadcasting so that the broadcasting device, usually a router, stops acting as a beacon that transmits a signal to nearby devices giving the SSID name, reducing visibility.

- **Virtual Private Network (VPN):** A virtual network built on top of existing physical networks that provides a means of secure communications using encryption protocols such as tunneling or Internet Protocol Security (IPsec).

  - Tunneling is a process in which the data, or packets, in one protocol are encapsulated in packets within a different protocol, which creates a tunnel of protection.

  - IPsec uses cryptography to encrypt communications, provide access control, and authenticate using IP protocols. IPsec operates similarly to tunneling, but it can also be used to only encrypt certain pieces of data, the payload, rather than an entire IP packet. This level of protection gives VPN users secure remote access to company applications, data, and systems.

▨ **Wi-Fi Protected Access (WPA):** A security protocol that encrypts traffic between a wireless access point, such as a switch, and a mobile device. However, it does not encrypt traffic that travels through a wired connection once it is out of the wireless access point.

- WPA's first successor, WPA2, is a similar protocol that provides an additional layer of data encryption using the Advanced Encryption Standard (AES) to provide even more security for a network.

- WPA3 provides even stronger security through more sophisticated encryption, secure handshakes (the process of establishing a connection between computers or devices), and stronger password protections.

▨ **Endpoint Security:** The notion that every device, also called hosts, connected to a network should have some form of local security that is separate from any other security measure in place on the network or communications channel. The following safeguards are examples of endpoint security that should be implemented on local hosts:

- Antivirus and malware screening software

- Authentication and authorization mechanisms

- Auditing software

- Local host firewalls

- Host-based intrusion detection

- Prevention systems

▨ **System Hardening:** System hardening is a multipronged comprehensive security approach that reduces risk by minimizing the number of access points through which a company can be attacked. These access points are referred to as attack vectors and include all aspects of IT infrastructure, including applications, databases, operating systems, servers, and networking equipment. This gives attackers fewer opportunities to access and infiltrate an IT system.

- Examples of system hardening in the context of potential recommendations after a vulnerability scan by an IT consulting agency may include:

  —**Database Hardening:** Create different privilege levels so that there is a clear delineation between administrative users and users that have tiered need-to-know access. Also, data at rest needs to be encrypted.

  —**Endpoint Hardening:** Remove administrative rights for users on local devices so that endpoint users can only perform authorized functions. Restrict users from downloading certain files from the internet or email. Implement local firewalls and malware screening on all laptops. These hardening adjustments make it harder for users to inadvertently compromise the network.

  —**Network Hardening:** Revise the rules for the firewall so that it is configured to remove unused ports and block unnecessary protocols. This provides attackers with fewer options to infiltrate the network.

  —**Server Hardening:** Physically segregate servers in a secure facility, further separating backup servers geographically. If one server or group is attacked, not all will be compromised. Develop test procedures for servers connecting to the network for the first time, to increase the likelihood that administrative rights are set up properly. Perform tests on servers in operation after business hours to minimize functionality and service disruption.

■ **Media Access Control (MAC) Filtering:** This is a form of filtering in which an access point blocks access to unauthorized devices using a list of approved MAC addresses. A MAC address, also referred to as a physical or hardware address, is a unique identifier found on devices in a network that is used as an address for communicating with other devices on that network.

3.2.1 Service Auditor Consideration of Logical and Physical Access

Service auditors conducting a SOC 2® engagement may consider a company's organization controls related to network components in a scenario where the organization permits remote access by authorized employees only with multifactor authentication over an encrypted virtual private network connection. The service auditor would observe a remote login session to determine that the multifactor authentication over the virtual private network was required to access the network.

4 Authorization and Authentication

4.1 Authorization and Authentication in Security Operations

In addition to employing advanced cybersecurity applications and devices, organizations must also implement practices that complement these defense tools to thwart evolving threats. Some of the more prevalent practices include zero trust, least privilege, the need-to-know principle, and whitelisting. These concepts can be engineered into the architecture of an organization's IT and embedded in its policies.

4.1.1 Zero Trust

The concept of zero trust assumes that a company's network is always at risk, even after a user has been authenticated, and it shifts a company's cybersecurity focus away from one-time authentication to continuous authentication at every point of a user's interaction with a network. The National Institute of Standards and Technology (NIST) established the Zero Trust Network Architecture (ZTNA) model to help organizations implement continuous authentication principles through a zero-trust architecture (ZTA).

ZTA is designed to prevent data breaches and limit internal lateral movement by implementing a set of system design principles and a coordinated cybersecurity and system management strategy based on an acknowledgment that threats exist both inside and outside traditional network boundaries. The zero-trust security model eliminates implicit trust in any one element and instead requires continuous verification by focusing on users, assets, and resources in real time to determine access and other system responses.

While there are variations of ZTA outlined by NIST, the overarching tenets include the following:

■ All devices and data sources are considered resources, even those not directly managed by the organization.

■ All communications must be secure regardless of a network's location.

■ Access to company resources is granted on a per-session basis.

- Access is determined by using dynamic policies and other environmental or behavioral attributes.

- The company monitors and measures the integrity and security of all assets.

- All authorization and authentication mechanisms are dynamic and strictly enforced prior to granting access.

- Detailed information is collected about the current state of a company's assets, infrastructure, and communications to improve security.

NIST provides the following assumptions to implement the ZTA tenets:

- An organization's private network is not considered an implicit trust zone.

- Some devices on a company's network might not be owned or configurable by the company.

- No resource is inherently trusted.

- Some devices connecting to a company's infrastructure might not be company resources.

- Remote users should not trust local network connections.

- Workflows and assets involving several components of a company's infrastructure should have consistent security policies and structure.

4.1.2 Least Privilege

Least privilege is the notion that users and systems are granted the minimum authorization and system resources needed to perform a function. IT administrators should put safeguards in place so that privileges do not become excessive or allow privilege creep in which access to systems gradually increases over time as a person's job role evolves. This is common when an employee gets promoted or changes positions within the same company. System permissions are granted with the new role, but access from the prior role is never removed. This violates the concept of least privilege.

4.1.3 Need-to-Know

The need-to-know principle follows the idea that employees are only given what they must know to perform their job. The difference between need-to-know and least privilege is that need-to-know focuses on the data itself that is needed to perform the job, whereas least privilege focuses on the access needed to perform the job.

4.1.4 Allowlisting and Denylisting

Allowlisting (or application whitelisting) is the process of identifying a list of applications and application components that are authorized to run on an organization's systems and only allowing those programs to execute. Conversely, denylisting (or blacklisting) is the process used to identify a list of applications not authorized on a network and preventing those from running. These rules are enforced by automated software programs designed to prevent applications from executing unless they are on the whitelist.

Pass Key

Least privilege focuses on minimizing the access to system resources, whereas need-to-know focuses on minimizing the data accessed.

5   Identification and Authentication Techniques

5.1   Identification and Authentication

Identification and authentication are two separate concepts that occur in one multistep process when users validate their right to access systems, applications, or physical locations. Identification is the process of claiming or asserting one's identity, through means such as a username or identification card, and authentication is the process of validating that identity claim, which could be done by using a password or scanning identification cards with proprietary technology. First, a person's identity is claimed, and then it is authenticated.

Prior to establishing an identity to later be validated, a user must go through an initial registration process in which the user creates the identity. This is typically done by submitting the most foundational form of identification, such as social security cards in the United States, driver's licenses, or passports. Then secondary forms of identity can be created using that foundational identification.

5.2   Authentication Technologies

The most common forms of identification and authentication are usernames and passwords, respectively. However, there are various authentication technologies available to secure access to confidential data, applications, and networks, including the following:

- **Context-aware Authentication:** This form of authentication is used to identify mobile device users by using contextual data points such as time, geographic location of the user, point of access (mobile app, desktop browser, call center, etc.), or IP address.

- **Digital Signatures:** A digital signature is an electronic stamp of authentication that is usually encrypted and attached to a message for non-repudiation (proof of identity). These utilize cryptography, with the sender encrypting the message with a private key and the receiver decrypting the message with the sender's public key.

- **Single Sign-On (SSO):** A single sign-on (SSO) is a technique that allows users to authenticate one time for a single session using multiple resources or devices.

  - For instance, logging into an app on a smart TV may only require entering a one-time code displayed on the TV on an approved smartphone. This authenticates the user without requiring them to authenticate again during the session.

- **Multifactor Authentication:** This is an authentication method that uses two or more factors to validate someone's identity. It often combines knowledge with possession. For instance, a password is knowledge and a security fob with a changing PIN is a possession.

- **Personal Identification Numbers (PIN):** A PIN is a numeric code that a cardholder memorizes and uses as part of authenticating their identity. PINs are most effective when combined with other authentication factors, with the PIN serving as the factor the user knows and a physical device, token generator, or other factor as something that the user possesses. PINs should be changed regularly, not be duplicated across applications, be at least six characters, and have limited entry attempts.

- **Smart Cards:** These are plastic cards containing a microprocessor that enables the holder to process data or that acts as a certificate that can be used to purchase goods and services, enter restricted areas, or execute other activities that only the holder of the smart card can perform.

- **Token:** These are devices that generate fixed-digit passcodes that are carried with users as a form of multifactor or secondary authentication mechanism. The passcodes generated by the token are also stored on an authentication server so that when a passcode is entered for validation, it is confirmed against the server. Tokens may be synchronous or asynchronous.

  - Synchronous tokens are time-based and require the token and server to be synchronized so that they register with the same number at the time of validation.

  - Asynchronous tokens do not use clocks, but rather they create passcodes based on the same algorithm.

- **Biometrics:** This is an authentication technique that uses human physical characteristics or impressions to verify identity.

  - Common physical characteristics used for validation include facial recognition, fingerprint or palm scans, hand dimensions, voice recognition, iris or retina scans, heart or pulse patterns, keystroke patterns, and handwriting or signature dynamics.

5.3 Password Management

Strong password management is critical because it is both the most common form of authentication and the most common method of attack for attackers. Passwords can be in the form of a string of letters, numbers, or special characters. Despite being the most common form of authentication, passwords have the following weaknesses, some of which can be avoided.

- People often use passwords that are easily guessed, reuse passwords for multiple accounts, share passwords with others, never change passwords, or write down passwords because they are difficult to remember.

- Short passwords can be easily guessed by brute-force attacks, which are attacks used by attackers that perform rapid-fire password entry attempts that use all possible combinations of words and letters until the right combination is reached.

- Passwords saved by companies in databases accessible by the web are frequently breached by attackers.

To counter these weaknesses, password complexity standards are recommended. Passphrases may also be used, which are memorized sequences of words or other text that are utilized to authenticate a user's identity.

5.3.1 Password Complexity

The longer a password is, the more secure it is. This is based on the notion that guessing the correct combination of characters in a password becomes exponentially more time consuming when the number of characters is increased due to the number of potential combinations. For instance, a password that has only four characters can use all 26 letters (both upper and lower case) and digits zero through nine would result in 14,776,336 potential combinations. Increasing the number of characters to eight results in 218,340,105,584,896 combinations, which displays the added security of adding just four characters to a four-digit password.

NIST recommends having at least eight characters in a password per its standard, *NIST Special Publication 800-63B*, but many companies require 12 or more characters. Changing passwords frequently is also recommended and passwords are encouraged to be changed every 45 to 90 days.

5.3.2 Password Managers and Storage

Password storage and management applications are programs that store a user's passwords by using hashing rather than storing them as plaintext. Hashing is the process of converting passwords into illegible text using hash algorithms such as secure hash algorithms (SHAs). Hashed passwords are then stored in databases, and when a user enters a password, the hashing algorithm is computed using that word. The computed hash value is compared to the hash value stored in the database. If the two match, access is granted.

Additionally, to enhance security, two processes are frequently used along with hashing: salting and iteration count.

- Salting refers to the process of adding random strings of characters (commonly referred to as "salt") to the password input prior to running it through the hashing algorithms. The addition of a random string of characters makes cracking passwords significantly harder.

- The iteration count refers to the number of times a process is being repeated. In the context of hashing, it means the hashing algorithm could be applied multiple times to enhance security.

Hashed passwords are one-way, meaning they are not intended to be reversed, although it is possible. So, if an attacker gains access to a password database that only has hashed passwords, they must first determine which hashing algorithm was used. Then they can begin guessing, typically by using brute-force guessing software, which can then be converted to hash values and compared to the hash values in the database.

5.4 Provisioning

Provisioning is the process in identity management when an organization creates a user's account and provisions it with privileges based on their job role. This is often an automated yet protected process but it is critical in creating a valid identification that can be authenticated. It may be part of the employee onboarding process when other identification and background checks are performed, and no rights should be provisioned to individuals that do not meet company standards.

Prior to issuing system credentials and granting system access, the organization may register and authorize new internal and external users whose access is administered by the organization. For those users whose access is administered by the organization, user system credentials need to be removed when user access is no longer authorized.

In the context of a SOC 2® engagement, service auditors may inspect access request forms for a sample of new employees who received access to in-scope system components during a specified period. This procedure would be performed to determine that an access provisioning request was approved prior to access being provisioned.

5.5 Device Authentication

Validating a user's identity by verifying the device making a connection request is known as device authentication. The emphasis is not placed on the credentials or identity of the user, but rather the identity of a device, such as a unique IP address or MAC address. This technique is weak as a standalone authentication method but strengthens a multifactor approach in which a user is required to enter login credentials and use a valid device.

6   Definition and Purpose of Vulnerability Management

6.1   Vulnerability Management

NIST defines vulnerability as any weakness in the computational logic found in products or devices that could be exploited by a threat. Vulnerability management is a proactive security practice designed to prevent the exploitation of IT vulnerabilities that could potentially harm a system or organization. The practice involves identifying, classifying, mitigating, and fixing known vulnerabilities within a system. It is an integral part of computer and network security and plays an important role in IT risk management.

To meet its objectives, an organization may use detection and monitoring procedures to identify changes to configurations that result in the introduction of new vulnerabilities and susceptibilities to newly discovered vulnerabilities. An organization may also conduct periodic vulnerability scans designed to identify potential vulnerabilities or misconfigurations after any significant change in the environment. Subsequently, the organization should take action to remediate identified deficiencies on a timely basis.

6.2   Vulnerability Tools

Vulnerability management can be administered using tools such as vulnerability assessments and vulnerability scanners, as well as through the application of frameworks, such as the National Institute of Standards and Technology (NIST) Cybersecurity Framework.

6.2.1   Applying the NIST Cybersecurity Framework

The NIST Cybersecurity Framework (CSF) is often used in implementing vulnerability management solutions to achieve desired security results. The framework can be applied using its six functions as follows:

- **Govern:** Use this CSF to establish and monitor the organization's cybersecurity risk management strategy, expectations and policy.

- **Identify:** Use the CSF to identify resource vulnerabilities that are present in systems, data, assets, and employees. Apply the framework to understand the business environment in which those assets operate, and understand the policies established regarding those resources to define how governance is executed.

- **Protect:** Apply the framework to create safeguards against vulnerabilities by establishing measures to manage identity and access controls, keep assets secure, and inform employees of threats.

- **Detect:** Use the framework to define relevant activities that can identify vulnerabilities quickly. These activities may include searching for anomalies, performing continuous monitoring, and verifying that the results of protective measures are effective.

- **Respond:** Use the CSF to put activities in place that will react to discovered vulnerabilities. This may include analysis of the issue so that the appropriate response is delivered, executing mitigating activities to prevent the vulnerability from affecting other parts of the organization, and communicating to the organization what the issue is as well as the chosen response.

- **Recover:** This function of the framework can be used to help an organization transition from its current state in which the vulnerability exists to a state where the vulnerability is mitigated. Relevant activities may involve implementing a recovery plan, improvements, and delivering internal communications to the appropriate staff about the recovery.

6.2.2 Vulnerability Scanners

Vulnerability scanners are applications that test a company's systems for known security risks. The scanner works by checking results against a database of known threats. This database is periodically updated so that it is current with the most recent threats. Scanners work by scanning for open network ports that can be exploited, analyzing data packets transmitting across systems, identifying protocols being used, and fingerprinting, which identifies the type of operating system and application running on the victim's systems.

These same scanners can also be used against organizations by attackers to identify weaknesses and then exploit those weaknesses. Attackers often wait to launch attack campaigns after databases are updated and rolled out to customers. With some larger companies, updates are predictable, which makes this form of attack more dangerous because attackers can plan and be ready as soon as the update is announced.

6.2.3 Vulnerability Assessments

Vulnerability assessments are typically done as a part of an initial risk analysis, and then subsequently performed quarterly or annually after that. Vulnerability scanners are often used in these assessments and observed over time to determine whether certain threats still linger. In some cases, a company may not be able to implement a solution because it could hinder operations. Instead, the company continues to operate exposed until there is a solution that allows the company to both mitigate the vulnerability and operate in an efficient manner.

While there is significant value in the results of the assessment, there are also other ancillary benefits to the organization from going through the assessment process. This is because assessments involve observations of multiple IT processes and interviews with employees across the organization that may not normally be evaluated collectively. This aggregate view of the company allows management the opportunity to see how systems or processes in one part of the organization create vulnerabilities in other parts.

6.3 Common Vulnerabilities and Exposures Dictionary

The Common Vulnerabilities and Exposures (CVE) dictionary is a database of security vulnerabilities that provides unique identifiers for different vulnerabilities and risk exposures. As new vulnerabilities are discovered, they are added to the dictionary by the MITRE Corporation, which is the organization that maintains the dictionary.

The CVE dictionary helps standardize the recognition and naming of vulnerabilities that were once identified by various companies using differing names or descriptions. This made it difficult to manage security gaps because, prior to the CVE, there was often no effective vulnerability dictionary that companies could use in the effort to fight cyber threats. Now, CVE identifiers are used by various cybersecurity products and denoted as "CVE-Compatible" so that customers know the vulnerabilities that have been mitigated.

6.4 Patch Management

Patch management is an important part of minimizing security threats that works in conjunction with vulnerability management solutions. As bugs are discovered in applications, software vendors release updates, called patches, so that customers can correct those vulnerabilities. Effective patch management involves IT administrators assessing the update for applicability to their company, testing the patch on isolated systems, planning with management to implement the patch, deploying the patch, and validating that it was successfully implemented.

Service organizations may be expected to maintain a change management log and the patch management process is normally subject to inspection by service auditors during a SOC 2® engagement.

7   Layered Security in Cyberdefense

The purpose of layered security is to protect an organization by using a diversified set of security tactics so that a single cyberattack or security vulnerability does not compromise an entire system. Layered approaches typically combine physical access controls, logical and technical controls, and administrative controls to provide control redundancy. These redundancies are implemented to offset possible security defects that could arise in the event of a multipronged breach.

7.1   Defense-in-Depth

One of the most common layered security solutions is the defense-in-depth cybersecurity strategy. It focuses on a multilayered security approach that does not rely on technology alone, but rather it combines people, policies, technology, as well as both physical and logical access controls. These layers contribute to the defense-in-depth strategy as follows:

- **Personnel:** Organizations must have experts that can operate security functions and tools effectively to attempt to make sure multilayered defenses are effectively implemented. In some cases, only specific IT professionals will have the expertise to understand how all layers interact holistically.

- **Policies:** While technology is critical, policies governing how that technology should be used must also be created, implemented, and monitored over time to determine whether tools in place are working as designed.

- **Technology:** Technical controls applied in a defense-in-depth strategy include security solutions like intrusion detection and prevention systems, antivirus software, firewalls, and endpoint security.

- **Physical Access Controls:** This includes security measures like cameras, gates, locks, fences, badge-controlled access, and restricted access to climate-controlled devices.

- **Logical Access Controls:** These are rule-based controls that are carried out by software and hardware designed to prevent unauthorized access. Such controls are embedded in user authentication systems and software that require validation of identity through login credentials, multifactor authentication, and different permission-based logical access methods.

7.2   Redundancy and Diversification

Regardless of the type of layered security solution chosen, using two or more means of security to protect the same resource offers organizations additional, yet different, protective measures in the event that one layer fails. This eliminates having a single point of failure. Redundancy and diversity also help organizations counterattacks that target different weaknesses an organization might have.

Having duplication within duplication introduces even more security. For instance, a company's layered security solution may have a single process that is coupled with one access control. By further bifurcating either the process or the access control by introducing another person to perform one function, the overall security becomes more diverse and potentially more effective. This form of redundancy can be administered through:

- layering processes;

- isolating processes;

- concealing data; and

- segmenting hardware.

7.2.1   Process Layering and Isolation

Layering processes adds redundancy by breaking up an operation into smaller chunks that can be managed by different people, performed by a machine or computer, or completely isolated from other parts of the process. The redundancy allows diversity in security controls to prevent a single point failure. This may be done to protect critical pieces of an operation or sensitive information so that certain components are more protected than less important pieces of the process.

For instance, a bank may have one person grant access to a vault remotely, while another person physically removes the contents of the vault, while yet another person transports the contents to another branch, with all participants counting or reconciling the contents with the other employees.

Process isolation using a machine or computer involves segmenting processes using logical controls (such as virtual machines or containers coupled with access controls) to isolate different processes in a system to prevent them from influencing one another. This allows a security breach of a process to be contained in the virtual machine without spreading to other processes.

7.2.2   Abstraction and Concealment

Abstraction is the process of hiding the complexity of certain tasks so that only the relevant information to a specific person performing a function is presented. The primary intent of abstraction is to simplify complex tasks, but it also plays an important role in cybersecurity by limiting user access so they are only given access to the level of detail needed to perform the job. For instance, access controls and user rights may be assigned to a particular object, group of objects, or a type of privilege allowing a user to only access and perform certain functions. This allows security administrators to easily create and assign different levels of privileges to each user. Abstraction can be applied to both applications and networks in either cloud-based environments or locally managed environments.

Concealment is similar to abstraction, but its primary focus is on hiding data, whereas abstraction focuses more on removing underlying details so that only essential information is available to help the user manage a task more efficiently and more securely. Concealment is implemented by assigning users to a security level that must align with the same security level assigned to specific sets of data, sections of applications, or certain objects so that only those who need access get it.

7.2.3   Hardware Segmentation

Segmentation divides a network into smaller units, each governed by its own security policies and controls. It could be achieved through logical segmentation (using software-defined networking, virtualization technology, or access control policies), or network segmentation that relies heavily on physical hardware like routers.

For improved redundancy and diversification, having hardware segmentation (a subset of network segmentation) integrated with logical integration strengthens the organization's layered security. Specifically, hardware segmentation achieves the same goal as process isolation, but instead of enforcing separation logically, it is enforced physically with separate machines. This form of segmentation is not as common, but when it is used, it is typically applied to large organizations with a network that is distributed geographically.

8   Common Preventive, Detective, or Corrective Controls

Well-designed cybersecurity controls include policies, procedures, and technology that mitigate threats at all points of discovery and all stages of a counterattack. These controls can be grouped into the following categories: preventive controls, detective controls, and corrective controls. Authorization is defined by SOC 2® engagement guidance as the process of granting access privileges to a user, program, or process by a person who has authority to grant such access.

8.1   Preventive Controls

Preventive controls are designed to thwart malicious activity from ever occurring. They attempt to prevent attackers from accessing devices, applications, and networks by employing some of the following tactics:

- **Safeguarding Practices:** Strong preventive software and hardware controls should be coupled with well-designed policies and procedures, such as requiring strong passwords, using multifactor authentication, performing background checks, locking devices if unattended, and following strict guidelines regarding sensitive data.

- **Education and Training:** Informing employees about cybersecurity risks and the corporate tools in place to mitigate those risks serves as a preventive control that complements technical safeguards that have been deployed.

- **Regular Security Updates:** Broad and comprehensive security enhancements should occur regularly in order for an organization's physical and logical security measures to be protected against the latest cybersecurity threats.

- **Encryption:** Encrypting data both at rest and in transit involves the process of converting the data into an illegible format based on industry standards so that if the data is compromised or stolen, the hackers will not be able to decipher and use the data for any nefarious purposes.

- **Firewalls:** A firewall monitors and filters traffic based on a set of predefined rules so that only trusted parties and networks can connect or interact with an organization's network, which prevents threat actors from compromising the network.

- **Patches:** A patch is an update or modification to an existing software program that is typically released by an application's creator and serves as both a preventive and corrective control that is intended to resolve newly discovered design flaws, operating errors, or gaps that pose cybersecurity risks.

- **Physical Barriers:** Tangible barriers, or physical obstructions, are controls that are designed to both deter and prevent unauthorized physical access to an organization's IT infrastructure. Examples include locked doors and cabinets, access controls such as a badge entry system, security guards, fences, gates, and surveillance systems.

- **Device and Software Hardening:** Hardening refers to implementing security tools so that the totality of vulnerable points, or the surfaces that can be attacked, are reduced. Minimizing the number of vulnerabilities across hardware devices and software applications prevents some attacks from occurring.

- **Intrusion Prevention Systems (IPS):** An IPS is a network security solution that is intended to detect and stop a cyberattack before it reaches the targeted systems. It does this by receiving a direct feed of traffic so that all data coming into a network pass through the IPS, similar to a firewall.

8.1.1 Access Controls: Authorization Models

Access controls are security measures organizations put in place to allow access only to authorized employees. These controls can be applied as discretionary access controls, role-based access controls, rule-based access controls, policy-based access controls, and risk-adaptive access controls.

A **discretionary access control (DAC)** is a decentralized control that allows data owners, custodians, or creators to manage their own access to the data or object they own or created. With discretionary controls, owners can grant access to others based on their own judgment or delegate tasks to other custodians as the owner sees fit. Some other functions that a data owner enforcing a DAC can enforce include the following:

- Control the passing of information to other users or objects.

- Grant or change the security attributes of users.

- Choose the security attributes to be associated with newly created or revised objects.

- Change the rules governing access control.

In contrast, **mandatory access controls** are nondiscretionary controls that allow administrators to centrally manage and enforce rules consistently across an environment. This means access is not based on identity but rather on a general set of rules that governs the entire system. While nondiscretionary systems may be easier to manage, their limited set of rules makes them less flexible in terms of customization.

Role-based access controls administer access based on a user's job role instead of individually assigning permissions. Job roles are placed in categories that correspond with a specific level of access or privilege. If a user changes positions, the access level is then modified based on preexisting rules for that job role.

A **rule-based access control** manages access to areas, devices, or databases according to a predetermined set of rules or access permissions independent of the user's role or position within the organization. An administrator is tasked with setting the security permissions to allow access based on defined criteria.

The steps in the rule-based access control are:

- Access rules are created by the system administrator.

- Rules are integrated throughout the access control system.

- A user presents their access credentials.

- The control mechanism checks their credentials against the access rules.

- The user is either granted or denied access.

A **policy-based access control (PBAC)** uses a combination of user roles and policies consisting of rules to maintain and evaluate user access dynamically. PBAC is more like a framework to evaluate a user's access based on what is known about that user, such as their identity, role, clearance, operational need, and risk.

Policy-based controls are generally more flexible than rule-based controls because they allow for the analysis of theoretical privileges based on actual privileges. As organizations grow and policies change, PBACs can better accommodate the needs of a wider range of access control. Smaller organizations may be better suited to apply rule-based controls if there are only a few simple and fixed rules that need to be applied.

Risk-based access controls apply controls based on the risk level of the asset being accessed, the identity of the user, the intentions of accessing the asset, and the security risk that exists between the user and the system or asset being accessed. If high-risk systems are being accessed, they usually will have stricter security measures in place such as multifactor authentication, whereas lower-risk scenarios may only require a password.

8.1.2 Access Controls: Authorization Model Controls Used for Implementation

There are different control mechanisms that can be used to implement authorization model policies, including access control lists, access restrictions, and physical barriers.

An access control list (ACL) is a list of rules that outlines which users have permission to access certain resources, such as a file, folder, directory, or other IT resource. An ACL also administers account restrictions, which govern what type of action the user can execute using those resources, such as the ability to edit a file, apply read-only status, or execute a program. Access and account restrictions are enforced by controlling network traffic based on the rules defined in the ACL.

ACLs can be broad and filter all of an organization's network traffic, or they can be more focused and only filter access to specific files or directories for different users. These two types of ACL are defined as follows:

- **Filesystem ACL:** These ACLs grant or deny privileges in an operating system by restricting access to certain files, folders, and directories.

- **Networking ACL:** These ACLs are used to regulate the type of network traffic that is allowed to flow across a network by configuring routers, switches, and other network devices with an array of lists to enforce. Networking ACLs are not only used for controlling access, but also for improving network performance by restricting or channeling the flow of data.

Filesystem and networking ACLs can operate by identifying and controlling traffic using a variety of mechanisms and technologies.

ACLs are similar to firewalls in that they both filter traffic on a network, but the two are different in terms of their purpose and the way they function. ACLs are generally used to manage user access and permissions, whereas firewalls are intended to protect an organization from malicious attacks. Unless an ACL is "stateful," meaning it monitors the state of network traffic to evaluate details such as source and destination addresses, it does not have the ability to recognize where a data packet originated or other details about the connection to apply restrictions, whereas a firewall does. Stateful ACLs track the status of network connections as well as distinguish between legitimate packets that it allows to make connections and illegitimate packets that do not match known connections.

8.2 Detective Controls

Detective controls are designed to detect a threat event while it is occurring and provide assistance during investigations and audits after the event has occurred. Examples of detective controls include:

- **Network Intrusion Detection System (NIDS):** An NIDS is a security solution that monitors incoming traffic on all devices on a network by matching specific elements of that traffic to a library of known attacks and sending system alerts when events meeting predefined criteria are detected.

- **Antivirus Software Monitoring:** Antivirus software works by scanning files in real time and comparing them to a library of known viruses. Scheduled scans of systems should occur automatically and be performed on a regular basis. If viruses are detected, they should be removed, or at least quarantined, immediately. Viruses that can only be quarantined and not removed will require further action by the responsible IT personnel.

- **Network Monitoring Tools:** There are various tools available to monitor a network, such as packet sniffers, which analyze data packets being transmitted on a network; network performance monitoring (NPM) tools that measure network statistics (such as packet loss, system uptime, and availability); or Simple Network Management Protocol (SNMP), which is also used to measure network statistics and error rates.

- **Log Analysis:** Performing a log analysis involves the recording and monitoring of data to analyze it so that anomalies, trends, or patterns can be detected that may indicate that unauthorized events have occurred. This can be a manual or automated process.

- **Intrusion Detection Systems (IDS):** An IDS is a security solution that scans the environment to monitor and analyze network or system events for the purpose of finding and providing real-time or near real-time warnings of attempts to access system resources in an unauthorized manner. The key difference between an IDS and an IPS is that an IDS only detects an attack after it has started, but it is unable to prevent it.

Intrusion detection systems are used by organizations to provide continuous monitoring of the health of the client's environment and an early opportunity to prevent security breaches from worsening. A service auditor within the scope of a SOC 2® engagement may inspect intrusion detection system configurations to determine that continuous monitoring of the client's network was in place and that early prevention of potential security breaches was also in place.

8.3   Corrective Controls

Corrective controls are intended to fix known vulnerabilities as a result of recent security incidents, security self-assessments, or changes in industry practices. These controls become preventive or detective once they are put in place and operating effectively. Examples of corrective controls include:

- **Reconfigurations:** Modifying an application or system configuration to rectify known vulnerabilities can restore affected operations and prevent further damage. Examples include revamping firewall rules, retooling an operating system's settings, and altering access control settings.

- **Upgrades and Patches:** Security patches and software or application upgrades may be implemented to accomplish objectives such as enhancing system performance, adding new features, and plugging holes in a company's security.

- **Revised Policies and Procedures:** Periodically reviewing and revising organizational practices can eliminate some security issues without requiring the purchase of new technology or the modification of existing systems. Revisions may be as simple as splitting one job into two, adding an additional level of review, or changing the way in which sensitive data is handled.

- **Updated Employee Training:** Gaps in employee knowledge about the risk of certain cyberattacks and other forms of IT exploitation can be reduced or even eliminated by training employees to recognize the hallmarks of common fraud schemes, educating them on how to react when suspected fraud occurs, and teaching them how to change existing behavior to prevent future incidents.

- **Recovery and Continuity Plans:** Organizations should have a robust plan in place that quickly allows them to recover from a disaster or attack and continue operating so that the period in which normal business operations are interrupted is minimized.

- **Antivirus Software Removal of Malicious Viruses:** Most modern antivirus programs are designed to not only identify actual or potential viruses but also to expunge those viruses so that they are no longer a threat to the organization.

- **Virus Quarantining:** Isolating actual or suspected viruses removes the threat from the rest of a company's network and is usually accomplished in an automated manner via antivirus software or manually after suspicious activity has been flagged from the review of system logs.

NOTES

1 Security Assessments

Protecting the organization against cyberattacks is a critical part in achieving the goals of internal control. To effectively manage cyber risks, it is critical to follow the established risk management framework and assess and respond to threats on a continuous basis.

1.1 Risk Management Framework

Managing risk in an organization requires intricate planning and participation at all levels, from senior management to frontline employees. The National Institute of Standards and Technology (NIST) provides a framework for managing this risk in NIST Special Publication 800-39. The framework outlines a comprehensive process to manage risk by applying the following four components:

- **Risk Framework:** This involves defining, or framing, the environment in which risk-based decisions are made. The purpose of this component is to form a strategy that enables a company to assess, respond, and monitor risk. The framework requires that companies identify:
  - Risk assumptions
  - Risk constraints
  - Risk tolerance
  - Priorities and trade-offs

- **Assess Risk:** This component addresses the way companies assess risk in the context of the risk framework. The goal is to identify:
  - Threats to nations, organizations, individuals, assets, or operations
  - Vulnerabilities internal and external to organizations and entities
  - The harm that may occur given the potential for threats exploiting vulnerabilities
  - The likelihood that harm will occur

- **Respond to Risk:** The purpose of this component is to provide a consistent, organization-wide response based on the risk assessment results by:
  - Developing alternative courses of action for responding to risk
  - Evaluating the alternative courses of action
  - Determining appropriate courses of action consistent with organizational risk tolerance
  - Implementing risk responses based on the selected courses of action

- **Monitor Risk:** The purpose of this component is to evaluate and monitor risk over time by:
    - Determining the ongoing effectiveness of risk responses
    - Identifying risk-impacting changes to organizational information systems and the environments in which the systems operate
    - Verifying that planned risk responses are implemented and that information security requirements derived from, and traceable to, organizational missions/business functions, federal legislation, directives, regulations, policies, standards, and guidelines are satisfied

Pass Key

Security assessments and vulnerability assessments are related but distinct processes of cybersecurity. A vulnerability assessment focuses on technical weaknesses in a system, network, or application; whereas a security assessment is a comprehensive evaluation of an organization's security posture including examining its security infrastructure, policies, and procedures and testing security controls.

1.2   Security Assessment Engagements and Reporting

Security assessment engagements involve organizations addressing the second component of the risk management framework, which includes performing a risk assessment and testing controls to obtain data on the company's current state regarding information security capabilities. These engagements often result in the issuance of a Security Assessment Report (SAR) to management.

The fundamentals of how to perform an assessment as well as the key elements presented in a SAR are outlined extensively by the NIST in Special Publications 800-39 and 800-53A Rev 5.

1.2.1   Security Assessment Engagement Procedures

The first step in a security assessment engagement is defining assessment procedures, which is a set of objectives that have assessment objects and methods. An assessment object identifies the items being assessed as part of a specific control such as security specifications or job roles, whereas the methods define the nature of the actions to take. Assessment methods include the following:

- **Examination:** This is the process of analyzing, observing, and reviewing one or more assessment objects (job roles, security specifications, security activities, or relevant operational activities).
- **Interviewing:** This method involves having individual or group discussions to better understand, collect, and evaluate evidence.
- **Testing:** This method is the process of testing assessment objects that reflect how the object performs in its current state compared to a target or expected state.

Organizations must support these assessment methods by identifying the following:

- Tools, techniques, and methodologies needed to assess risk
- Risk assessment assumptions
- Constraints
- Roles and responsibilities
- Assessment data collection and processing methods
- Communication methods to the organization
- How assessments are conducted
- Frequency of assessments
- Sources and methods of collecting data on threats

1.2.2   Security Assessment Reports

Security assessment reports (SARs) are issued as evidence of controls complying, or not complying, with stated security goals and objectives. The NIST defines a security assessment report as a report that provides a disciplined and structured approach for documenting the findings of the assessor and the recommendations for correcting any identified issues or vulnerabilities in the security controls.

Assessment reports generally include detailed assessment findings as well as a summary that are used to determine the effectiveness of privacy and security controls. Determination statements are made throughout the report that assign a grade to each procedure performed by an assessor resulting in either a "satisfied (S)" or "other than satisfied (O)" rating.

A "satisfied" rating indicates the assessment objective was met and yielded an acceptable result. An "other than satisfied" rating indicates that an assessor could not obtain sufficient information that met the statements in the assessment procedure. This may be the result of either an anomaly in the operation or the implementation of a control.

SARs generally include the following key items:

- **Summary of Findings:** This introductory portion of a SAR has a synopsis of key findings and recommended actions to address weaknesses or deficiencies.
- **System Overview:** The overview of a SAR outlines the information management system being assessed, including hardware, software, personnel, and other relevant resources.
- **Assessment Methodology:** This part of a SAR explains the techniques and procedures utilized to perform the assessment.
- **Security Assessment Findings:** The findings section of a SAR discusses the gaps and deficiencies discovered during the assessment.
- **Recommendations:** This portion of the report provides prescriptive direction to remediate the deficiencies that were discovered.
- **Action Plan:** This final section of a SAR is a roadmap that covers the steps that should be taken to remediate the deficiencies.

Illustration 1   SAR Findings: Issue Documentation

Reference:	IA-XXX1

Risk Level: (Risk Level is High, Moderate, or Low)

Moderate

Ease-of-Fix: (Ease-of-Fix is Easy, Moderately Difficult, Very Difficult, or No Known Fix)

Easy

Estimated Work Effort: (Estimated Work Effort is Minimal, Moderate, Substantial, or Unknown; or a time estimate based on level of commitment and an adequate skill set)

Moderate

Description

ABC Co.'s "Identity and Access Management Policy," specifically Appendix A, establishes password management standards for authenticating ABC's system users based on level of assurance, system interface type, and impact to the company.

Scope

- Operating systems
- Microsoft 365 Suite
- Accounts payable automation
- Enterprise resource planning
- Human resources information system
- Project management
- Billing system
- Aurora databases

Findings: Other than satisfied (O)

The assessment team continued to identify multiple password management vulnerabilities. For example, we continued to find a significant number of weak passwords on major databases, applications, and networking devices at most of ABC's facilities.

Additionally, password parameter settings for network domains, databases, key financial applications, and servers were not consistently configured to enforce the company's password policy standards. Even though some improvements have been made, we continue to identify security weaknesses that were not remediated from prior years.

Many of these weaknesses can be attributed to ABC's ineffective enforcement of its company-wide information security risk management program and ineffective communication from senior management to the individual offices. The use of weak passwords is a well-known security vulnerability that allows malicious users to easily gain unauthorized access to mission-critical systems.

Recommended Corrective Action(s):

The assessment team recommended the chief information manager implement mechanisms to enforce company password policies and standards on all operating systems, databases, applications, and network devices.

Status: Corrective action needs to be executed

1.3   Security Assessment Evaluators

Security assessments are conducted by system auditors, developers, assessors, inspectors general, system integrators, or other system owners. If an assessment is being performed so others can have assurance regarding the operations and assertions made by a company, it usually means the AICPA's Service Organization Control (SOC) standards apply. For instance, a managed services provider (MSP) that provides information technology as a service may get a SOC report issued to give its clients assurance that its operations meet the standards claimed by management.

1.4   Security Assessment Process

The focus of the assessment process is to gather information to make objective conclusions about an organization's security and privacy controls in a cost-effective manner. This is done by considering the quality and maturity of a company's risk management process, and then tailor the assessment using the concepts, methods, and control objectives available in standards such as NIST 800-53A Rev 5.

The results of the assessments help organizations:

- Identify potential deficiencies in their risk management processes
- Identify security and privacy-related deficiencies in the security system's environment, then determine the appropriate responses
- Prioritize the responses to risks
- Support monitoring activities and system authorization decisions
- Inform budgeting and investing decision makers

1.5   Security Assessment Evidence

During the assessment process, evaluators obtain evidence from various sources, including previously conducted product and system assessments, documentation of system developmental activities, and documentation of operational activities. Product and system assessments are examinations, often conducted by third parties, to evaluate the security functions of an organization's products and their related configuration settings. Such assessments may have been performed to demonstrate compliance with regulations or with developer and vendor claims, but they can also be used as evidence to validate assertions in a SAR.

Evidence obtained from system developmental activities include artifacts produced by developers, operators, assessors, and other system owners during the system development life cycle. This may be in the form of design specifications, testing and code analysis, interviews with related employees, and other forms of documentation conducted by the company or third-party assessor that help provide evidence that the security function is trustworthy and reliable.

Similarly, evidence from the operational environment also contributes to the assurance of the security function by providing records of remediation efforts, incident reports from events such as a breach, and the results of continuous organizational monitoring. Specifically, this evidence helps an assessor determine the effectiveness of the following security functions and activities:

- Privacy and security controls currently deployed

- Change management practices regarding systems and operations

- Compliance with policies, regulations, and standards

The level of detail available from all sources of evidence can affect the type of testing, analysis, and evaluation performed. Artifacts with less coverage and depth provide a lower level of assurance and may require more rigorous, comprehensive, or focused testing. Conversely, artifacts with more depth may require less testing and may provide evidence that the security function is implemented correctly and completely, which indicates strength for a given system component.

2 Communication of Security Knowledge and Awareness

All employees play an important role in protecting a company's digital and physical assets, not just the IT department. As such, the need for educating and training programs is critical as the sophistication, scope, and number of cyberattacks increase each year. Organizations must prioritize and invest in these security awareness programs to minimize the cyber risk and the damages that cyberattacks can inflict upon an organization.

Conducting regularly scheduled security awareness training is encouraged or mandated by various information security frameworks and regulations. For instance, the information security standard-setting body, NIST, as well as GDPR, HIPAA, and SOC2®, emphasize the need for conducting regular security awareness and training programs for employees.

2.1 Security Awareness Delivery Methods

The source of IT security education and training content will vary by organization, but methods of communicating relevant security awareness information range from being fully outsourced to being managed solely in-house, or some combination of the two. Training provided in-house will require teaching tools, which will typically require resources acquired from a third party, unless content can be created internally.

Methods of course delivery can be individual or group sessions, as well as live or on-demand sessions. Live sessions may be in conducted in-person or remotely. Assessments of education content may include quizzes, examinations, case studies, or simulations. It is recommended that training methods be revised over time to optimize benefits. Adequate documentation of course planning and delivery methods should also be performed for consistency and evaluation purposes.

2.2   Organizational Job Roles Specific to Security Awareness

While every employee will have a unique role to play with respect to education regarding security awareness, there are generally three relevant categories of personnel with differing levels of responsibility:

- **Management:** Tasked with designing and evaluating security awareness programs or coordinating with third-party vendors hired to develop and/or perform the security awareness training.

- **Specialized IT Personnel:** Tasked with carrying out the policies set forth in security awareness programs. Specialized jobs include network security engineers, penetration testers, incident response analysts, and compliance analysts.

- **All Other Employees:** Tasked with following the security procedures based on their specific job roles.

Training should be provided at all stages of an employee's job, beginning with security training at new hire orientation, followed by refresher training courses that occur at least annually. Training should also be tailored to an employee's job role. Employees other than management and specialized roles should only be responsible for security practices relevant to a basic user role, such as training on identifying phishing emails or best practices on connecting remotely via a virtual private network.

Specialized roles may need initial and recurring training specific to certain functions like disaster recovery procedural training or content related to new regulations with which the organization must comply.

2.3   Components of a Successful Security Awareness Program

Hallmarks of a successful security awareness program include phishing simulations, program supporters and champions, regular employee engagement, and metrics to measure program success, such as the amount of money allocated to the program, the number of resources dedicated, and corrective action plans for any deficiencies discovered.

2.3.1   Phishing Simulations

Phishing simulations are designed to teach employees to recognize phony emails by sending messages that mirror actual phishing emails and other communications. When employees click a link or download an attachment in these simulated emails, the employee will receive a communication informing them they performed an action in violation of standard security protocols. The communication is designed to teach the person about phishing scams and may be in the form of a follow-up email or a direct communication from human resources or the IT department. The employee will often be required to complete additional security training.

Results of the phishing simulation programs are summarized with metrics and analyzed over time to evaluate employee awareness. Examples of those metrics may include the following:

- **Click Rate:** The percentage of employees who clicked on a phishing email link.

- **Re-click Rate:** The percentage of employees who failed the first campaign who click again.

- **Report Rate:** The percentage of employees who report phishing emails.

- **Non-responder Rate:** The percentage of employees who ignored the email and did not respond in any way.

- **Reply Rate:** The percentage of employees who replied to the phishing emails.

2.3.2 Security Program Champions

A program champion leading the effort of implementing a security platform is often needed. Preferably, a full task force would be ideal to lead such efforts. Key metrics for assessing the effectiveness of program champions include the following:

- **Employee Consultations:** This metric reports the number of times employees consult with a security program champion.

- **Security Behaviors (With and Without Champions):** This would involve capturing and comparing security awareness measures in departments that have champions versus those that do not.

- **Champion Density vs. Security Behaviors:** This would measure the degree of correlation and linear relationship of champion activity, or "density," among different departments and security behaviors. An example metric capturing this would be a correlation coefficient.

2.3.3 Employee Engagement

Measuring the level of employee engagement is yet another critical barometer for assessing a security training program. Some popular metrics include the following:

- Percentage of employees who completed training

- Average time taken per training session

- Count of employees who attended each training session

- Likelihood an employee would recommend the training to others

- Count of employees attending due to referrals

- Count of questions from employees about training content

- Count of employees requesting security information or visiting a related company intranet website

- Quantitative and qualitative metrics on social media interactions

4 Confidentiality and Privacy

1 Confidentiality vs. Privacy

While both confidentiality and privacy are terms that are often used interchangeably, the two terms are independent when it comes to cybersecurity.

- Privacy protects the rights of an individual and gives the individual control over what information they are willing to share with others.

- Confidentiality protects unauthorized access to information gathered by the company.

Alternatively, privacy requirements dictate the types of authorization granted to information. After the information is gathered adhering to the privacy requirements, confidentiality is required so that the information is only accessed by systems or individuals with the appropriate authority.

1.1 Confidentiality

The National Institute of Standards and Technology (NIST) defines confidentiality as preserving authorized restrictions on access and disclosure of data, including means for protecting personal privacy and proprietary information.

In addition to proprietary information, confidentiality requires organizations to protect all personal information that it collects or maintains during the course of normal business. To accomplish this, organizations must define and identify information that is deemed to contain personal information.

Personal identifiable information (PII) is defined as all data that can be used to identify an individual, including the following:

- Name, such as full legal name, maiden name, mother's maiden name, or alias

- Personal identification numbers, such as Social Security number (SSN), passport number, driver's license number, taxpayer identification number, or financial account or credit card number

- Address, such as street address or email address

- Personal characteristics, including photographic images, fingerprints, handwriting, or other biometric data

Well-designed cybersecurity programs typically attempt to minimize the amount of personal information used, collected, and stored. Only information that is critical to operations should be stored. Also, an organization should regularly review its storage of collected personal information to determine whether that information is still relevant and necessary for meeting critical business functions.

In order to protect confidentially and PII, organizations should:

- Review current holdings of personal information and confirm the data is accurate, relevant, timely, and complete.
- Reduce personal information gathered to the minimum necessary for critical business functions.
- Define the criteria of each authorization level and monitor the criteria and access list periodically.
- Establish a plan to purge personal information that is no longer required to perform critical business functions.

1.2 Privacy

The NIST defines privacy as the right of a party to maintain control and confidentiality of information about itself. Privacy is the process of protecting human autonomy and dignity. The NIST Privacy Framework is a tool for improving privacy through risk management procedures and communication methods employed throughout the organization.

The Privacy Framework's purpose is to help organizations manage privacy risks by:

- Considering privacy best practices as they design and deploy systems, products, and services that affect individuals.
- Communicating privacy practices to the rest of the organization.
- Encouraging cross-organizational workforce collaboration relating to user privacy and IT security.

The Privacy Framework approach to managing privacy risk requires the consideration of privacy events as potential problems individuals could experience at some stage during the life cycle of a data point. This could range from the collection to the disposal of data as it flows through systems and processes related to delivering products or services.

2 Methods of Protection of Confidential Data

Organizations should have a structured process to determine how information is handled in order to be in compliance in the following areas:

- Applicable legal, regulatory, and policy requirements
- Risks and effects of collecting, storing, and deleting information
- Identification and evaluation protections and alternative processes for handling information to mitigate potential privacy risks

Violation of these guidelines could subject the organization to potential litigation and monetary losses. To mitigate these risks, below are the common operational safeguards, privacy-specific safeguards, and security controls an organization can utilize to manage PII and proprietary information:

- **Data Collection**
  - **Creating Policies and Procedures:** Organizations should develop comprehensive policies and procedures for protecting the confidentiality of PII and proprietary information by defining:

    —the specific confidential data collected from both employees and customers;

    —how confidential data is collected, accessed, and retained;

—incident response;

—privacy in the development cycle;

—sharing rules; and

—consequences of violations.

- **Conducting Training:** Organizations should reduce the possibility that PII will be accessed, used, or disclosed inappropriately by requiring that all individuals receive appropriate training to understand the relevant guidelines and the repercussions of violating these guidelines.

Data Processing

- **De-identifying Personal Information:** Organizations should de-identify records by removing enough personal information such that the remaining information does not identify an individual.

  —For example, pseudonymization is a form of de-identification that would replace the name of a person visiting the doctor with a pseudonym, such as Patient 565 or Client AM.

  —Other types of de-identification, like anonymization, remove the ability to trace identifying data points to a person when full records are not necessary, such as for research studies or determining correlations and trends.

Data Storage

- **Using Access Enforcement:** Organizations should control access to personal information through access control policies and access enforcement mechanisms (e.g., access control lists).

- **Implementing Access Control for Mobile Devices:** Organizations should prohibit or strictly limit access to personal information from portable and mobile devices, such as laptops, cell phones, and personal digital assistants.

- **Auditing Events:** Organizations can monitor events that affect the confidentiality of personal information, such as inappropriate access to PII.

Data Transmission

Organizations should protect the confidentiality of information transmitted. This is commonly accomplished through encrypting the communications (i.e., VPN) or by encrypting the information before it is transmitted.

Data Deletion/Purging

Organizations should set up the policies to determine the data sets subject to be archived or purged.

2.1 Confidentiality During the System Development Life Cycle

When new systems are being developed, tested, and implemented, organizations often deploy methods that protect confidential data using data obfuscation. Obfuscation is the process of replacing production data or sensitive information with data that is less valuable to unauthorized users. The most common data obfuscation applications are:

▪ **Encryption:** Scrambles unencrypted data using cryptography so that it can generally only be deciphered with a key. There are various types of encryption methodologies, such as salting, that differ in the way in which keys are managed and transferred between users.

▪ **Tokenization:** Removes production data and replaces it with a surrogate value or token. Tokens can be generated using random number generators; by hashing, which transforms data using mathematical algorithms; or by encryption. Keys used to reverse the tokenization process are stored in a token vault, which is controlled using authorization and access controls. Tokenization is similar to encryption but it generally does not change the length or type of characters. Tokens are often used in credit card transactions at different stages within the payment clearing process.

▪ **Masking:** Swaps data with other like data so that the original identifying characteristics are disguised, or masked, while maintaining a similar structure to the unmodified data set. The modified data set's aggregate value remains intact, allowing insights and the data to be extracted. There are different forms of masking including shuffling, scrambling, substitution, nullifying, and masking out in which all or part of the data's value is swapped with a single character such as an asterisk.

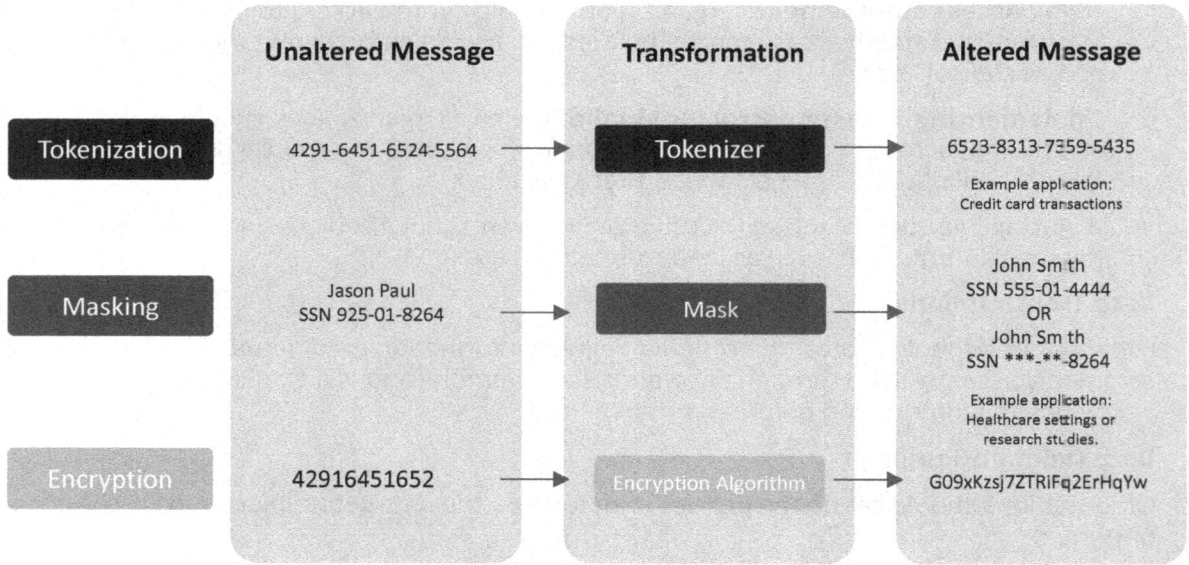

3   Data Encryption

3.1   The Fundamentals

Data is a critical asset to any business. Data breaches may result in a loss of sensitive data resulting in financial losses (e.g., litigation expenses), interruption of business operations (e.g., being unable to process customer orders or unable to work with suppliers), and damage to the company's reputation. To prevent loss of data and to reduce the risk that the attacker can extract information needed from the data obtained, data encryption plays a pivotal role as a defense mechanism against malicious cyberattacks.

Data encryption is a method of mitigating the risk of data breaches and data loss through the application of cryptography so that data is protected during its collection, processing, and storage. Cryptography involves applying an algorithm to transform, or encrypt, plaintext data into ciphertext. Prior to being encoded, data is referred to as plaintext, whereas after it is encoded and unreadable, it is called ciphertext. Ciphertext can only be decoded by using a key with the mathematically encoded algorithm, which offers the receiver nonrepudiation, or assurance, that the sender is who they say they are.

3.2   Encryption Methods

Encryption models can use different types of keys and different combinations of keys within one model. An organization may use encryption to supplement other measures used to protect data-at-rest when relevant protections are determined to be appropriate based on assessed risks. Keys can be public or private. Public keys are shared either publicly or with a group, and private keys are only known to one user. The following are the two most common encryption methods:

- **Symmetric Encryption:** Involves a single shared or private key for encryption and decryption of data within a group. The private key is used by all members in the group to both encrypt and decrypt data and can be in the form of a number, a letter, or a string of random numbers and letters. Symmetric encryption is commonly used by banks to encrypt sensitive customer data for time-sensitive transactions as decrypting needs to happen as quickly as the customer is performing a transaction.

    One drawback of symmetric encryption is that it does not facilitate non-repudiation because any person with the shared key can encrypt and decrypt messages. Therefore, there is no way to tell where a message originated. It is also difficult to scale because every combination of users in the group must each share private keys, and those keys must be generated each time participants leave a group.

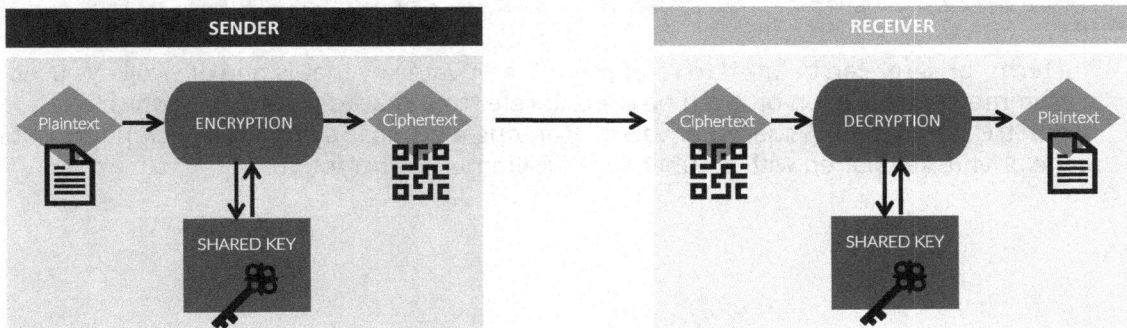

- **Asymmetric Encryption:** This data encryption method uses two keys, a public and private key. The public key is used to encrypt the message and the private key to decrypt it, or vice versa. Only the two opposite keys can be used in tandem for this form of encryption to work. Popular applications of asymmetric encryption include digital signing and blockchain.

  The primary weakness of asymmetric encryption is its speed of operation. They keys are generally longer, one is needed for both encryption and decryption, and the encryption algorithm is typically more complex. All of these factors require more computing power, which is time-consuming and could also lead to an increase in technology expense.

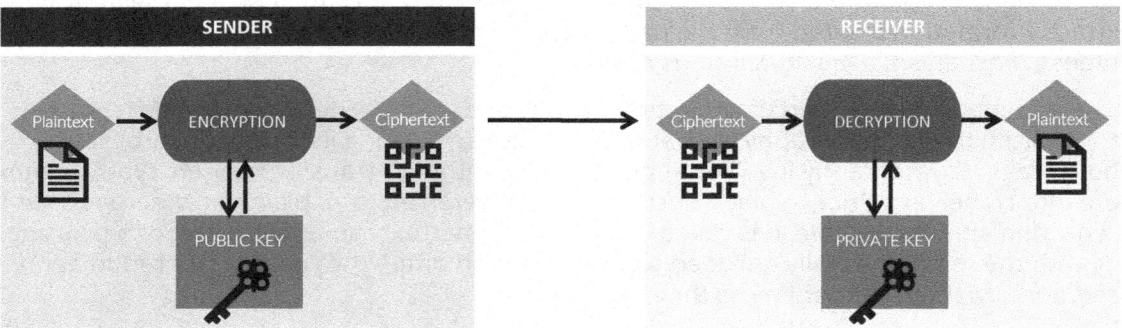

Hashing is often confused with encryption because it converts a message with variable lengths to a fixed-length message or code called a message digest or hash value. However, the effect of hashing is one-way, meaning it scrambles a message into code that cannot be unscrambled. Encryption is two-way because it can both be encrypted and decrypted.

One primary difference between encryption and hashing is their intended use. Encryption is intended for the secure transfer of data to maintain confidentiality, whereas hashing is intended to maintain the integrity of the data transmitting, validating that the message sent is from the true sender. Comparing two hash values will tell users that the message is legitimate.

Since hash values cannot be decrypted, hashing is often combined with encryption to securely transfer the message using encryption and then validate the authenticity of that message using hashing. The message is decrypted using either a public or private key, and the hash value received by the receiver can be compared to the hash value from the sender to ensure it is identical.

Pass Key

The term "private" can be used to refer to both a private key that is one of two keys used in asymmetric encryption or it can be used to refer to a shared private key, which is symmetric encryption. A shared private key among a group is symmetric encryption, but a single private key paired with a public key is asymmetric encryption.

3.3   Cipher Techniques

Ciphers are the result of applying encryption algorithms that encode unencrypted messages into an encrypted form. This generally results in a combination of numbers and letters that are meaningless and illegible to those without a key. Although some ciphers may seem simplistic, they are often difficult, if not impossible, to decrypt when combined with other cipher techniques unless using a key. Two common cipher techniques include:

▨   **Substitution Ciphers:** Are algorithms that replace each character of a plaintext message with another character. Very basic ciphers simply replace one letter or number with another using a key, while more complex ciphers involve mathematics to substitute. For example, using a cryptography technique known as the modulo function, letters or numbers can be converted into a number that is then used to decrypt a message.

▨   **Transposing Ciphers:** Are encryption techniques that rearrange the letters of a message to form unreadable ciphertext, often by using a matrix to perform columnar transposition. The following is an example of columnar transposition that works by using the key 3241:

•   The ciphertext is: ETVETLTWEMAE

The key is 3241. If using a three by four matrix, the code can be mapped as shown below.

3	2	4	1
E	E	T	M
T	T	W	A
V	L	E	E

Using the key to reorder the ciphertext in numerical sequence reveals the message "Meet at twelve."

1	2	3	4
M	E	E	T
A	T	T	W
E	L	V	E

There are various other types of ciphers, such as running key ciphers, which encrypt messages that are as long as the messages themselves; and block ciphers, which operate on chunks of a message and then apply encryption. The messages may also stream ciphers which operate on a single character, or a few, known as a stream. When used in combination with other ciphers, these forms of encryption can be difficult to decode.

4 Data Loss Prevention (DLP)

Data loss prevention (DLP) systems enable organizations to detect and prevent attempts by employees or unauthorized users to transfer sensitive information out of the organization electronically across multiple protocols, ports, and communication methods. DLP systems often use pattern-matching methods or word recognition technology to scan files for certain patterns, such as the way in which data is formatted or sequenced.

For example, systems designed to comply with regulatory standards, such as HIPAA, PCI-DSS, and GDPR, may deploy pattern-matching technology that searches for strings of 9-character numbers with dashes after the third number and fifth number to identify potential Social Security numbers. The software may then either prevent the message from being sent or encrypt it.

The main objectives and best practices of DLP are to develop a program to:

- Implement a centralized DLP program, with collaboration from various departments, which oversees data for the entire organization.

- Define and create enterprise data usage policies, report data loss incidents, and establish incident response capability to enable corrective actions to remediate violations.

- Evaluate the different forms of data, define the different levels of sensitivity, create an inventory of sensitive data, identify where sensitive data is stored, and manage data cleanup.

- Monitor the use of sensitive data, understand sensitive data usage patterns, and gain enterprise visibility.

- Enforce security policies to proactively secure data and prevent sensitive data from leaving an enterprise.

- Implement employee education programs.

Two common types of DLP systems include network-based DLP systems and endpoint-based DLP systems:

- **Network-Based DLP:** These types of DLP systems scan outgoing data that meet specific criteria and are transmitted using means such as email, file transfer protocols (ftp sites that facilitate file transfer), and direct messaging. Records of DLP policy violations are typically archived in a database that identifies the data moved and where it went on the network.

  - **Cloud-Based DLP:** These DLP systems apply the same protection as a network-based DLP but apply it to a cloud environment. Many organizations are migrating some functions, if not all computing functions, to a cloud-based (web-based) environment.

  - Data loss is prevented when transferring sensitive data across virtual machines and platforms rather than an organization's private on-premises network.

- **Endpoint-Based DLP:** These types of DLP systems scan files stored or sent to devices that might be outside of a network, such as a printer, USB drive, or any other device to which data can be transferred. Transferring data to such devices can be prevented by scanning for specific keywords, patterns, or file types, such as MP4 files.

Illustration 1   Network-Based Data Loss Prevention

Alice is the director of provider credentialing for North Pointe Hospital's billing department. She regularly sends records to insurance companies and other health care providers, which include sensitive data, such as Social Security numbers, dates of birth, and other personally identifying information. She typically encrypts emails that contain such information, but in a rush to meet a deadline, Alice forgets to encrypt an email containing dozens of provider records to an insurance company.

North Pointe recently purchased a subscription to an email DLP solution from the cybersecurity provider Clix Corp. This is a network-based DLP solution that auto-encrypts emails that an algorithm detects using pattern recognition applied to all emails that have North Pointe's domain, @northpointehospital.com. Operating as designed, this DLP solution automatically encrypted the email Alice forgot to send securely, minimizing the likelihood that these records would be exploited if intercepted.

4.1   Protecting Data at Rest

Storing sensitive data requires a robust storage infrastructure that provides sufficient physical security, adequate digital security, authorization, proper access controls, change management controls, backup, and recovery mechanisms. These safeguards should be in place so that data is protected as it is collected, processed, stored, transmitted, and purged.

- **Physical Security**: may be in the form of locked cabinets and closets, security cameras and badge entry-controlled entry/exit points, and tamper-evident seals.

- **Digital Security Controls:** include encrypted hard drives, encrypted USB drives, or secure file systems that are encrypted.

- **Authorization and User Access Controls:** include control mechanisms, such as role-based access controls, rule-based access controls, discretionary access controls, and multifactor authentication.

- **Change Management Controls:** these procedural controls require there to be processes in place for requesting changes to a system or data, review and approval, implementation, reversion, and documentation.

- **Backup and Recovery Mechanisms:** these redundancy defenses protect data so it is not lost and can be restored in the event of a disaster, cyberattack, or accidental deletion or modification.

4.2 Deleting Confidential Information

Removing and destroying confidential information at the end of its life cycle can be done through physical destruction, erasing, overwriting, and purging. Physical destruction involves the physical act of disassembling or changing the chemical construct of the data (i.e., through heat, pressure, or shredding).

Erasing is the performance of a delete operation of a file or its data. Overwriting, or clearing, involves preparing media for reuse by replacing the old data with unclassified data. Purging repeats the clearing process various times and may combine that process with another method, such as degaussing, which involves creating a strong magnetic field used to erase data on storage devices that use magnetism, such as magnetic tapes.

In some cases, data remanence may exist on storage devices that have been erased, overwritten, or treated so that confidential information is removed. This is common on media storage devices that use magnetism. When data is removed, a residual magnetic flux or imprint may remain. Even if degaussing is used, there are many tools available that can undelete or reverse the effects of wiping. Physical destruction may be the only means to completely purge confidential data.

5 Walk-Through of an Organization's Security, Confidentiality, and Privacy Procedures

5.1 Performing a Walk-Through

Effective security, confidentiality, and privacy policies and practices require a comprehensive strategy involving all departments within an organization. To enhance the likelihood that this strategy can be executed in the event of the examples below, performing periodic read-throughs and walk-throughs led by the IT departments or a joint task force of both IT and non-IT departments is necessary:

- Data breaches (confidentiality and privacy)
- Security incidents or disasters (security)

A read-through involves distributing security, confidentiality, and privacy procedures to members of both the IT departments and non-IT departments supporting the walk-through for review. The read-through lets an organization inform personnel of tactical and strategic procedures and review plans for obsolete information. A structured walk-through takes the read-through one step further by role playing/simulating a disaster scenario related to security or a confidentiality and privacy scenario in which an attacker is attempting to obtain data for personal gain and having team members use the procedures in place to prevent the attack and ensure the data leaked cannot be deciphered. Fire drills are less common but can be an effective way to test security policies and determine if employees understand emergency plans and follow proper protocols when they believe an emergency situation is occurring.

Walk-throughs are more commonly performed than fire drills and involve team members obtaining evidence about whether the documented policy requirement aligns with the observed procedures. Walk-throughs occur in phases starting with a planning and preparation phase, followed by obtaining an understanding of the process being evaluated, performing the walk-through, creating documentation, performing tests, and finally evaluating the procedures and reporting on their effectiveness.

The steps of performing a walk-through are:

1. **Plan and Prep**
   - Define the scope
   - Identify key controls and processes
   - Identify personnel

2. **Obtain an Understanding**
   - Review documentation
   - Interview personnel
   - Create notes

3. **Perform Walk-through**
   - Reperform processes
   - Verify results and effectiveness

4. **Create Documentation**
   - Create workpapers
   - Document procedures

5. **Test**
   - Test controls identified in walk-through
   - Obtain samples if needed

6. **Evaluate and Report**
   - Interpret results
   - Prepare a report to summarize findings
   - Provide recommendations

5.2   Walk-Throughs in Company Functions and Departments

Walk-throughs of documented IT security, confidentiality, and privacy policies should occur for all functions and departments within an organization, including the following:

- **Finance and Accounting:** Finance and accounting departments are the gatekeepers to a company's financial records.

  - For confidentiality and privacy, walk-throughs should focus on ensuring confidentiality and privacy policies are followed such that minimal PIIs are collected, and each user can only access the minimal level of PII and proprietary data to execute his or her job function.

  - For security, walk-throughs should focus on ensuring security policies are in place to only allow authorized employees access to systems that control any accounting functions that involve withdrawing or transferring cash, collecting or diverting payments, and reporting financial information.

- **Corporate Training and Education:** This may not be an individual department, but rather a function performed by multiple individuals from different departments. Walk-throughs should include:

  - viewing the security, confidentiality, and privacy content being delivered to employees and determining whether they are appropriate to their job roles;

  - employee acknowledgement of the policies and procedures;

  - attending courses delivered by trainers;

  - reviewing materials and assessments given to trainees; and

  - interviewing the training staff regarding plans for making revisions and updates to the training program.

- **Human Resources:** This department is considered the gatekeeper for onboarding newly hired employees and ultimately has access to an organization's systems.

  - For confidentiality and privacy, walk-throughs should focus on how human resources follow the policies and procedures to identify and collect PII, manage access to PIIs, and the process of handling violations.

  - For security, walk-throughs should focus on practices regarding background checks, defining security roles for both contractors and full-time employees, communicating security policies, monitoring employee activity, and processes for revoking access privileges as employees transfer positions or are terminated.

- **IT Risk Management:** This department is focused on identifying current and potential confidentiality and privacy risks so they can be eliminated, minimized, or transferred.

  - For confidentiality and privacy, walk-throughs should focus on identifying ways the department monitors the confidentiality and privacy controls, identifying and communicating potential violations.

  - For security, walk-throughs should focus on identifying ways the department tracks assets and systems that should be protected, identifies potential vulnerabilities and threats, assesses the operational and financial impact of risks, develops risk mitigation strategies, and periodically reviews risk management plans.

In relation to security, service auditors will perform procedures to understand how an entity communicates information through a security awareness training program. Procedures the service auditor may perform to obtain an understanding of the organization's communications may include reviewing documents related to the following:

- The service organization's security awareness and training programs

- The communication of the entity's code of conduct

- Employee handbooks

- Information security policies

- Incident notification procedures

- Other available documentation to understand the service organization's process for communicating to personnel their responsibilities for system security and other matters

6 Detect Deficiencies in a SOC 2® Engagement

Security, confidentiality, and privacy testing will take place with service organizations that are subject to System and Organization Controls (SOC) audits. During SOC 2® engagements, a service auditor evaluates the results of all procedures performed and conducts both a quantitative and qualitative analysis of whether identified description misstatements, deficiencies in the suitability of design, and, in a type 2 examination, the operating effectiveness of controls result in a description that is not presented in accordance with the description criteria or in controls that are not suitably designed or operating effectively.

Service auditors in a SOC 2® engagement will also perform a walk-through of the service organization's IT security, confidentiality, and privacy policies. General walk-through procedures to be performed by SOC 2® engagement service auditors include:

- Following a transaction, event, or activity from origination until final disposition through the service organization's system using the same documents used by service organization personnel.

  When considering confidentiality and privacy, the objective is to understand how PIIs and proprietary information are handled throughout the life cycle.

- Inquiry, observation, inspection of relevant documentation, and flowcharts, questionnaires, or decision tables to facilitate understanding the design of the controls.

- Inquiry about instances during the period in which controls did not operate as described or designed.

- Questioning variations in the process for different types of events or transactions.

An appropriately performed walk-through provides an opportunity to verify the service auditor's understanding of the flow of transactions and the design of the controls in relation to an organization's security, confidentiality, and privacy service commitments.

When performed properly, walk-throughs often provide evidence about whether controls included in the description were suitably designed and implemented and, in a type 2 examination, operated effectively.

When evaluating the results of procedures, the service auditor investigates the nature and cause of any identified description misstatements and deficiencies or deviations in the effectiveness of controls and determines the following:

- If the identified description misstatements result in either the failure to meet one or more of the description criteria or in a presentation that could be misunderstood by users if the service auditor's opinion was not modified to reflect the identified description misstatements.

- Whether identified deviations are within the expected rate of deviation and are acceptable or whether they constitute a deficiency.

- Whether the procedures that have been performed provide an appropriate basis for concluding that the control operated effectively throughout the specified period.

▪ Whether identified deficiencies are likely to have a pervasive effect on the achievement of the service organization's service commitments and system requirements based on the applicable trust services criteria.

▪ The magnitude of the effect of such deficiencies on the achievement of the service organization's service commitments and system requirements based on the applicable trust services criteria.

▪ Whether report users could be misled if the service auditor's opinion were not modified to reflect the identified deficiencies.

Factors that may be considered when determining whether the identified deviations may have a pervasive effect on other controls include the following:

▪ The effect that entity-level controls have on the operation of other controls. Deviations in entity-level controls often have a pervasive effect on other controls.

▪ The extent of the use of segmentation, a technique that enhances security by dividing networks or systems into multiple segments, across the service organization.

▪ The extent to which deficiencies in certain key controls have a pervasive effect on other controls.

If the service auditor identifies material description misstatements, material deficiencies in the suitability of design of controls, or, in a type 2 examination, deviations in the operating effectiveness of controls, the service auditor should modify the opinion. When modifying the opinion, the service auditor's understanding of the nature and cause of the description misstatements and deficiencies enables the service auditor to determine how to appropriately modify the opinion.

When incidents of fraud or suspected fraud are identified during the examination, the service auditor is expected to respond appropriately. Appropriate responses include the following:

▪ Discussing the matter with service organization senior management (and the engaging party, and other appropriate parties, unless senior management is suspected to have committed the fraud).

▪ For potential fraud involving senior management, communicating to those charged with governance and discussing with them the nature, extent, and timing of procedures necessary to complete the examination.

▪ Requesting that senior management consult with an appropriately qualified third party.

▪ Considering the implications of the matter in relation to other aspects of the engagement, including the service auditor's risk assessment and the reliability of written representations from service organization management.

▪ Obtaining legal advice about the consequences of different courses of action.

▪ Communicating with third parties.

▪ Withdrawing from the engagement.

1 Incident Response Plan Contents

An incident response plan (IRP) is the documentation of a set of procedures, people, and information to detect, respond to, and limit consequences of a cyberattack against an organization.

Organizations should have a formal and coordinated plan for responding to incidents, including a roadmap for implementing the incident response capabilities detailing the method of detection, response timeline, and incident response team's responsibilities. The plan should meet the unique requirements related to the organization, including the organization's mission, size, structure, and operational functions.

The contents included in an IRP are subject to the needs and risks associated with an organization. However, the National Institute of Standards and Technology (NIST) names the key elements that most policies contain, including the following:

- Mission
- Strategies and goals
- Senior management approval and statement of commitment
- Organizational approach to incident response
- Purpose and objectives of the policy
- Scope of the policy
- Metrics for measuring the incident response capability and its effectiveness
- Roadmap for maturing the incident response capability
- Definition of computer security incidents and related terms
- Organizational structure and definition of roles, responsibilities, and levels of authority
- Prioritization or severity ratings of incidents
- Internal and external communication methods

1.1   Incident Response Timeline

Robust IRPs require the recovery timeline to be charted when an incident occurs, clearly delineating the point at which the incident starts; when it is detected, contained, and eradicated; and when normal business operations are restored. This is often documented in the form of a Gannt chart, as follows:

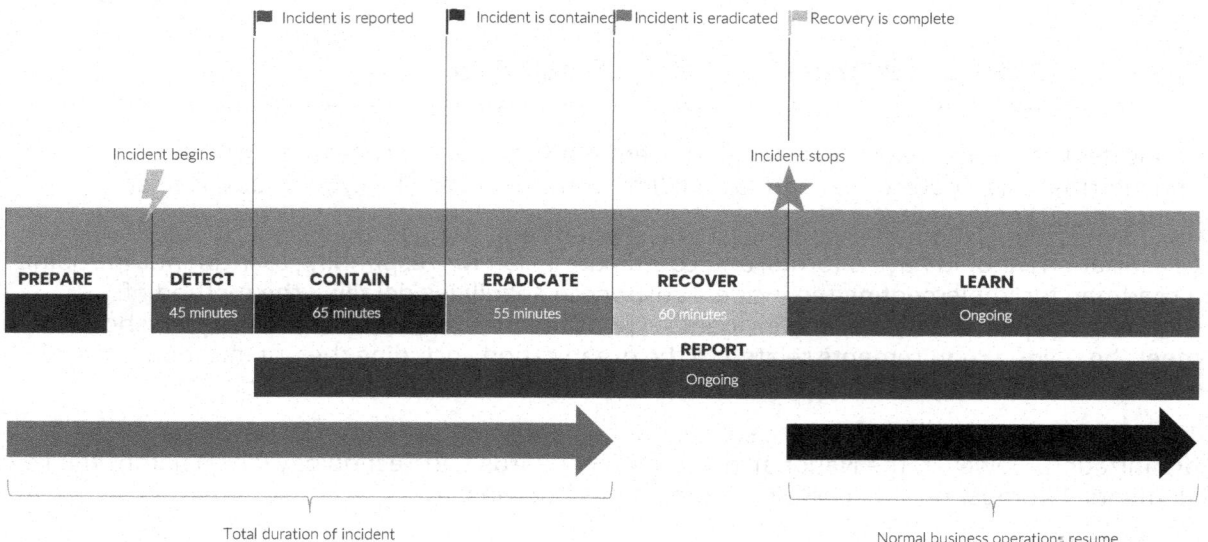

1.2   Method of Detection

The methods of detection deployed should be listed in the contents of an IRP. There are various mechanisms and forms of technology an organization may use to detect incidents or events, such as the following:

- Vulnerability scanning software
- Anomaly detection
- Endpoint detection and response (EDR) solutions
- File integrity monitoring
- Log analysis
- Intrusion detection systems (IDS)
- Intrusion prevention systems (IPS)
- Physical security monitoring
- Security information and event management solutions (SIEM)
- Threat intelligence software
- User behavior analytics (UBA) tools

1.3   Incident Response Personnel, Roles, and Responsibilities

The most critical component of an IRP is the human capital designated to respond to an incident. While an IRP's success depends on the participation and cooperation of individuals throughout the organization, it requires the assemblance of specialized employees with the right technical knowledge to handle each piece of the IRP. Guidance and support from senior management is also essential as they are the champions for incident response management in the organization.

Depending on an entity's size and business model, different structures may be better suited for adoption. NIST recommends the following models:

- **Centralized Incident Response Team:** In this model, a single incident response team is tasked with managing incidents across the organization. This approach is effective for smaller organizations and those with computing environments that aren't distributed geographically.

- **Distributed Incident Response Teams:** Organizations in this model have multiple incident response teams that are responsible for specific logical or physical segments of a company's network. This model is effective for organizations that have geographically widespread computing resources.

- **Coordinating Team:** A secondary function of either a distributed or centralized incident response team is coordinating with other departments without having authority over those teams.

NIST's *Computer Security Incident Handling Guide* recommends that organizations consider the following factors when selecting the appropriate structure and staffing models for incident response teams:

- **24/7 Availability:** Most organizations need incident response staff to be available 24/7 either by phone or on-site. Real-time availability helps minimize the impact of an attack because it shortens the amount of time it takes to discover and respond to an incident.

- **Full-Time vs. Part-Time Team Members:** The decision to staff an incident response team full time instead of part time depends on a number of factors, including available funding, other staffing needs or constraints, the industry in which the company operates, and the individual company's needs. Outsourcing to a virtual incident response team may be a viable alternative to hiring full-time staff.

- **Employee Morale:** Incident response work can be demanding because it often requires on-call responsibilities of most team members. This can make it easy for team members to become stressed, making it difficult for some organizations to find willing, available, and skilled people to hire, especially for roles that require 24-hour support. Segregating roles may be one option to combat this fatigue and be a morale booster.

- **Cost:** Cost is always a factor when deciding how to adequately staff an incident response team. The 24/7 availability requirement naturally makes it expensive. Because the incident response team works with so many facets of IT, its members require broader knowledge than most IT employees. They must also understand how to use incident response tools like digital forensics software.

- **Staff Expertise:** Incident handling requires a mixture of specialized knowledge and experience in both technical and nontechnical disciplines. Since IT professionals that specialize in cybersecurity must possess a deeper and up-to-date knowledge of intrusion detection, forensics, vulnerabilities, and exploits, it often makes sense to outsource this function to a managed services provider who can spread the expense across its client base.

While the main focus of an incident response team is intrusion detection, it is common for teams to perform additional duties to raise awareness of cybersecurity across the organization. They may include:

- **Education and Awareness:** The more employees outside of the IT team know about detecting, reporting, and responding to incidents, the less of a burden it will be on the incident response team. This information can be delivered using various mediums including workshops, company intranet sites, newsletters, posters, and other paraphernalia with security tips or reminders.

- **Advisory Distribution:** Issue cyber briefings or newsletters to inform the rest of the organization regarding new vulnerabilities and threats identified by the teams.

- **Information Sharing:** Incident response teams may participate in information sharing groups and manage the organization's incident information sharing efforts in the broader cybersecurity community. This may include sharing information related to past incidents, the response selected, the results of that response, as well as any company changes that resulted.

2 Responding to Cybersecurity Incidents in Accordance With the Incident Response Plan

Cybersecurity involves the safety of computer systems which includes the technology infrastructure supporting the computer systems (network, computers, etc.) and the digital data contained within.

2.1 Defining Cybersecurity Events and Incidents

An organization's IRPs must distinguish between recognizing and responding to an event versus a cybersecurity incident. Events may be benign, whereas incidents usually pose a threat to an organization's computer or network security. Discerning the difference between the two is critical because the responses may be vastly different. NIST defines these terms as follows:

- **Event:** An event is an observable occurrence in a system or network. Examples include a user connecting to a shared file server, a server receiving a request for a web page, a user sending an email, and a firewall blocking a connection attempt. Events also include cybersecurity changes that have an effect on an organization's operations, mission, manufacturing capabilities, or reputation.

- **Cybersecurity Event:** A cybersecurity change that may have an impact on organizational operations (including mission, capabilities, or reputation).

- **Adverse Event:** Any event with a negative consequence is defined as an adverse event, such as system crashes, packet floods, unauthorized use of system privileges, unauthorized access to sensitive data, and the execution of malware that destroys data. This includes both intentional and unintentional events, as well as human-inflicted and environmentally inflicted events.

- **Incident:** An incident is an occurrence that actually or potentially jeopardizes:

  - the confidentiality, integrity, or availability of an information system; or

  - the information that the system processes, stores, or transmits.

  An incident may also constitute a violation or imminent threat of violation of security policies, procedures, or acceptable use policies.

■ **Computer Security Incident:** This is a type of adverse event that is computer security-related and caused by malicious human intent, not by environmental or indirect human factors such as power failures or natural disasters. It is defined as any violation or imminent threat of computer security policies, acceptable use policies, or standard security practices. Examples include:

- an attacker flooding a web server with requests resulting in a site crash;

- deceiving users into opening phishing emails and downloading tools that infect the user's computer;

- an attacker holding a company's data hostage in a ransomware attack; and

- adverse events that are as seemingly harmless as exposing sensitive information to unintended parties because of careless use practices.

■ **Cybersecurity Incident:** A cybersecurity event that has been determined to have an impact on the organization prompting the need for response and recovery.

2.2 Steps in Responding to an Incident

Though incident response plans vary by organization and framework, there are seven widely recognized steps in responding to incidents, outlined below.

01	**PREPARATION**	Prepare for Incidents
02	**DETECTION**	Detect and Identify Incidents
03	**CONTAINMENT**	Contain the Incident From Spreading
04	**ERADICATION**	Eradicate Threats
05	**REPORTING**	Report and Communicate Status
06	**RECOVERY**	Recover and Restore Normal Operations
07	**LEARNING**	Learn and Improve

1. **Preparation:** The initial phase of incident response planning involves assembling key personnel, tools, and processes so the organization will be prepared to handle many scenarios. Tools and methods adopted in preparation typically include vulnerability assessment software, intrusion detection and prevention applications (vulnerability scanners), anti-malware software, and training for both end users and specialists directly involved in the response.

2. **Detection and Analysis/Identification:** The second phase concentrates on recognizing deviations from normal operations, evaluating those deviations, and correctly classifying them as either an acceptable event or a problematic cybersecurity incident.

3. **Containment:** Once a threat is correctly identified, the organization must contain it so that further damage is not incurred. This also allows the cybersecurity response team time to determine the best approach to eliminate the threat.

   - Containing a threat may include technical measures such as isolating a segment of a network, taking an exposed group of workstations out of use, or removing infected servers from production and rerouting those to backup or failover equipment.

   - Containment may also include nontechnical measures like informing employees so that certain routine operations still in progress might stop, preventing further proliferation of the incident.

4. **Eradication:** This phase targets the extraction of the threat and restoration of affected systems, which may be as simple as restoring infected files with clean backup copies or as complex as using specialized software and forensic analysis to help decrypt or remove infected files. System logging or network monitoring may also be performed company-wide to determine whether the breadth and depth of eradication efforts are adequate. A significant incident may require a system to be entirely rebuilt, resulting in the loss of critical data.

5. **Reporting:** This phase emphasizes communication of the incident to management, IT personnel, and affected employees. Messaging should be tailored to each of these employee groups, with information and next steps only given that are relevant to each group.

6. **Recovery:** The recovery step prioritizes returning an organization's normal IT operations to a fully functional state. This step should be performed using a phased approach with early days focused on increasing overall security and implementing immediate high-impact changes, followed by a more holistic long-term phase that may involve strategic changes such as a shift in infrastructure to prevent similar cybersecurity incidents from reoccurring.

7. **Post-Incident Activity/Lessons Learned:** The last step in responding to an incident involves learning and improving. Senior management and directly affected employees examine the incident, understand how it occurred, and develop ways to improve the response. Evaluating the response may involve measuring how long it took to perform each one of the six steps above and identifying areas in which missteps occurred. The incident response team may issue a report after this phase is completed and modify the IRP as necessary.

There are numerous popular frameworks that overlap with these seven overarching steps, including those issued by the SysAdmin, Audit, Network, and Security (SANS) Institute; NIST; and the International Organization for Standardization (ISO), among others.

2.2.1 SANS Institute Incident Response Plan

The SANS Institute is the largest cybersecurity training organization in the world. It divides incident response into six different phases in its *Incident Handlers Handbook* which include:

1. Preparation

2. Identification

3. Containment

4. Eradication

5. Recovery

6. Lessons learned

Guidance is given on applying different commands to identify unusual processes, files, and registry keys. The guide also explains methods used to scan for abnormal network activity and aberrations in scheduled tasks like reboots, unexplained accounts, and suspect user behavior.

2.2.2   NIST IRP

NIST separates the incident response process into four stages in its *Computer Security Incident Handling Guide*:

1. Preparation
2. Detection and analysis
3. Containment, eradication, and recovery
4. Post-incident activity

It also provides information on organizing incident response efforts such as providing guidance on developing policies and procedures, as well as recommendations on the composition of an incident response team. Detailed plans of action are also listed within the NIST guidance as four phases, and scenarios with applied guidance are in the appendix of the NIST *Computer Security Incident Handling Guide*.

2.2.3   International Organization for Standardization IRP

The International Organization for Standardization (ISO) has released standards that help companies across the globe respond to security incidents. These are known as the ISO/IEC 27000 family of standards, and they recommend that security incident management plans include the following activities:

- Evaluating event criteria and defining an incident
- Monitoring and detecting events by human or automated means
- Managing incidents to the end of their lifecycle
- Coordinating with authorities and handling evidence properly
- Performing a root cause analysis
- Reporting on all incident management activities

2.2.4   Other IRP Organizations and Frameworks

Various other organizations, both private and those affiliated with governments, have established frameworks that are either industry-specific or offer guidance to businesses and individuals across the globe. Some of those include the following:

- The Information Technology Infrastructure Library (ITIL), which is a library originally created by the British government but is now managed by a joint venture known as Axelos. ITIL outlines an incident management process that is integrated with service management principles, and they issue certifications that are often sought by third-party IT providers, which is why incident response is tied closely to serving clients.

- The United States Computer Emergency Readiness Team (US-CERT) is an organization that collaborates with government entities, academia, and the private sector to issue guidance related to incident response planning.

- The Payment Card Industry Data Security Standard (PCI-DSS) issues IRPs specific to responding to cybersecurity incidents related to payments and transactions.

2.2.5 IRPs Tailored to Specific Attacks

Many organizations have a multipronged IRP that is tailored to specific cybersecurity assaults. This means having several IRPs that are specifically designed to deal with a number of unique incidents, usually attacks the organization is most vulnerable to. IBM has identified attacks that are most often aligned with IRPs, which include the following in order of most frequently implemented:

- DDoS attacks
- Mobile code such as malware, spyware, viruses, trojans, and worms
- Phishing
- Insider incident
- Business email compromise
- Disaster recovery
- Supply chain attack
- Advanced persistent threats

2.3 Procedures to Test Whether a Company Follows Its Incident Response Plan

Once a formal IRP is put in place, organizations periodically test whether those plans respond as expected to both hypothetical and actual cybersecurity incidents. Some of the most common methods of testing include the following:

- **Simulations:** Also referred to as tabletop exercises, these are simulated events in which the response team either sits around a table and verbally walks through an incident as if it is happening in real time, or it could consist of exercises in which an employee or hired programmer actually executes an attack so that a response can be observed. The latter exercise is referred to as a "pen test," or penetration test.

  - Annual testing of the IRP may be performed using simulations to determine whether the incident response procedures are up to date and accurate. When updating the IRP, lessons learned from simulations and tabletop exercises are used to implement changes to reflect enhanced procedures when handling incidents.

  - A service auditor in the context of conducting a SOC 2® engagement may inspect documentation for the most recent IRP review to determine whether the plan was tested within the past year, and that drills conducted to simulate incidents were resolved and service availability was restored. Service auditors may also inspect the IRP for revision in response to the testing performed.

- **IRP Metrics:** Establishing metrics to which performance can be compared is a way companies can determine whether established procedures were followed during an incident or simulation. Example metrics include:

  - **Mean Time to Detect (MTTD):** The MTTD is the amount of time in minutes or hours that it takes an organization to detect a prior incident or one in progress. Higher average times indicate poorer detection capabilities and may result in incidents causing more significant impacts than organizations with a lower MTTD.

  - **Mean Time to Acknowledge (MTTA):** The MTTA is a metric used to determine the amount of time an organization takes to acknowledge an incident once it has occurred. It is measured as the difference between the point in time when an incident is reported and when it is recognized as an actual threat that requires a response.

- **Mean Time to Contain (MTTC):** Also referred to as the mean time to remediation, this is the average time it takes to stop and sequester an incident.

- **Mean Time to Repair (MTTR):** The MTTR refers to the amount of time it takes an organization to restore a system to the normal operational state that it was in prior to the event occurring, or to a target state of operations. The target state could be a full recovery, or it may be defined as minimal functionality that still permits normal business operations.

- **Mean Time Between Failures (MTBF):** This is the average time between consecutive incident failures. A higher MTBF metric indicates infrequent system failures and infers a more reliable and resilient network.

- **System Availability or Downtime:** This refers to the amount of time that a production system is completely or partially unusable. Most agreements with IT providers have a specified amount of system uptime they are required to meet, with applicable discounts or other penalties triggered if the uptime threshold is not met.

- **Service-Level Agreement Compliance:** This involves evaluating whether qualitative or quantitative specified performance levels in a service-level agreement with an IT provider were met.

- **Post-Incident Review:** Reviewing the chain of events post-incident with high scrutiny by senior management and security experts can evaluate how effective an IRP was and whether personnel and technology complied with the plan. This may involve analyzing logbooks, evaluating system configurations, interviewing employees involved, and performing further vulnerability testing.

- **Periodic Audits:** Performing regularly scheduled and unscheduled audits of incident response policies and reviews of those policies helps determine whether organizations are positioned to respond appropriately to incidents as they occur.

- **Continuous Monitoring:** Employing automated tools that constantly analyze system logs, network traffic, and unusual user behavior helps promote timely and adequate responses to incidents.

2.3.1 Indications an Organization Did Not Respond Appropriately

When evaluating whether an organization's IRP is designed appropriately or determining whether an actual response followed protocol, there are a number of indications that may reveal a subpar reaction. Such indications can be measured by the following:

- Increases in frequency of incidents or severity of incidents

- Time to identify or contain incidents

- Increases in data center downtime or IT infrastructure damage

- Cost of fines, attorneys, and consultants

- Decline in company reputation

3 Insurance as a Mitigation Strategy for a Security Incident

Cyber insurance policies are a relatively new form of insurance protection that help organizations hedge against cyberattacks by providing financial relief in the event of a successful attack. This relief can help with the cost of restoring data, the temporary disruption in business operations, lost revenues, and even managing public relations needs. As cyber threats evolve, insurance companies are carefully defining both their insurable losses and their requirements for issuing coverage.

3.1 Insurable Losses

Some of the most common losses related to a cyberattack that are typically covered by cyber insurance include:

- **Business Interruption Losses:** Lost revenue from operating delays that are due to the inability to access records, systems, or financial resources may be part of a cyber insurance policy.

- **Cyber Extortion Losses:** Coverage may include funds for ransom payments and fees to attorneys or IT experts for the cost of negotiating with attackers.

- **Incident Response Costs:** This includes the cost associated with the recovery of lost or stolen data by external IT experts or managed services providers. Reimbursable expenses usually include the cost of labor.

- **Replacement Costs for Information Systems:** If an attack results in corrupted software or physically damaged hardware, insurance may cover a partial or complete replacement of IT assets.

- **Litigation and Attorney Fees:** Cyberattacks often result in the need for consultations with attorneys to address lawsuits (especially class-action lawsuits) that arise from the attack or just to get legal advice on how to proceed after the initial attack in a way that minimizes future liability.

- **Reputational Damage:** Costs related to public relations, crisis management, and marketing to customers regarding a data breach may be covered by the policy. However, harm to a company's brand or the long-term impact that it may experience are unlikely to be covered costs.

- **Information or Identity Theft:** Insurance may cover the cost of losses related to an attacker using an employee's identity that stemmed from the attack.

3.2 Cyber Insurance Requirements for Applicants

Most cyber insurance companies require some up-front mitigating risk controls to be in place to minimize both the likelihood of an event and the impact if an event does occur. Some of those controls include the following:

- **Background Checks:** Understanding the criminal records of the employees given access to a company's systems is critical in protecting IT assets. This is usually an item on an application checklist.

- **Compliance With Regulations:** This includes attestation that the organization is compliant with applicable regulations such as HIPAA or PCI-DSS, especially for companies that collect individual health or financial data.

- **Disaster Recovery:** This includes the existence of a disaster recovery plan and regularly testing that the recovery mechanisms in place work.

- **Employee Training:** Educating employees on common schemes like phishing scams helps protect against cyberattacks. Implementing phishing tests or other security programs may reduce premiums.

- **Company Policies:** Insurance carriers often request copies of personnel policies that cover security as it relates to employees, customers, and vendors. These policies usually specify acceptable use and access to data, how company devices should be used, and prohibited practices by vendors and employees.

- **Independent Risk Assessment:** Usually performed by a third party, IT risk assessments help insurance companies ascertain weaknesses that could put the insured at risk for an incident.

- **Incident Response Plans:** Carriers typically look for IRP in place and how they deal with a cyber incident. For plans that are not robust in incident response planning, premiums may be higher.

- **IT Controls:** Standard IT security controls are part of any cybersecurity application checklist which generally include firewalls, intrusion detection or prevention systems, antivirus or endpoint software, controlled access to assets, and modern authentication tools such as multifactor authentication (MFA).

- **Mandatory Pen Testing:** Some insurers are making penetration testing a requirement as part of the application process. Companies with harder to intrude/penetrate systems may get a lower premium.

- **Loss History:** Carriers evaluating new clients typically review losses from any prior incidents and price the risk for that client based on those losses, as well as all of the other factors above.

NOTES

System and Organization Controls (SOC) Engagements

Module

1 Overview of SOC Engagements

Organizations often engage in business relationships with other entities to outsource key services and business operations. The organization utilizing the outsourced services is considered the user entity, and the outside organization providing services is known as the service organization. A service organization provides the user entity with the benefits of its personnel, expertise, equipment, and technology to operate tasks and functions that the user entity wishes to outsource.

Examples of the types of services provided by service organizations:

- **Outsourced Payroll Processors:** Service organizations that provide payroll services to user entities.

- **Cloud Service Providers:** Third-party organizations offering a cloud-based platform, infrastructure, application, or storage services.

- **Credit Card Processing Organizations:** Companies that process payments for merchants by offering an infrastructure that routes payment from customer banks or financial institutions to retailers.

- **Enterprise IT Outsourcing Services:** IT-managed service providers that manage, operate, and maintain user entities' IT data centers, infrastructure, and application systems.

- **Financial Technology (FinTech) Services:** Financial institutions that provide IT-based transaction processing services such as servicing loans, payment processing, and asset management.

- **Customer Support:** Organizations that provide customers of user entities online or telephonic customer support and service management.

User entities and business partners, entities with which another commercial entity has some form of alliance such as their external auditor, usually need information about the design, operation, and effectiveness of controls within the service organization's system. To support risk assessment procedures, user entities may request a System and Organizational Controls (SOC) report from the service organization. An independent CPA, referred to as the service auditor, performs a SOC examination in accordance with attestation standards issued by the American Institute of Certified Public Accountants (AICPA).

1.1 Types of SOC Engagements

SOC engagements assess the effectiveness of a service organization's controls. These engagements, which result in the issuance of a SOC report, promote reliance by third parties on service organizations.

There are three main types of SOC engagements including SOC 1®, SOC 2®, and SOC 3®:

- **SOC 1® for Service Organizations:** Internal Control over Financial Reporting (SOC 1® engagement). The examination and reporting on controls at a service organization that are likely to be relevant to user entities' internal control over financial reporting.

    SOC 1® reports are restricted to management of the service organization, user entities of the service organization's system, and the independent auditors of such user entities. It does not include potential users of the service organization.

- **SOC 2® for Service Organizations:** Trust Services Criteria (SOC 2® engagement). The examination and reporting on the security, availability, or processing integrity of a system, or the confidentiality or privacy of the information processed by the system (the AICPA's five trust services categories).

    SOC 2® reports are intended for use by those who have sufficient knowledge and understanding of the service organization, the services it provides, and the system used to provide those services, among other matters. Management and the service auditor should agree on the intended users of the report (specified parties).

    The expected knowledge of specified parties ordinarily includes the following:

    - The nature of the service provided by the service organization

    - Service organization's system interactions with user entities, subservice organizations, and other parties

    - Internal control and its limitations

    - Complementary user entity controls

    - Complementary subservice organizational controls

    - User entity responsibilities and their impact to effectively use the service organization's services

    - The applicable trust services criteria

    - The risks that may impact the service organization's service commitments and system requirements, and how controls address those risks

- **SOC 3® for Service Organizations:** Trust Services Criteria for General Use Report (SOC 3® engagement). Similar to the requirements and guidance for performing a SOC 2® engagement, the service auditor reports on whether controls within the system were effective to provide reasonable assurance that the service organization's service commitments and system requirements were achieved based on the applicable trust services criteria. The reporting requirements are different from a SOC 2® report; a SOC 3® report does not include a description of the system (detailed controls within the system are not disclosed), a description of the service auditor's tests of controls, and the results thereof.

    A SOC 3® report is ordinarily for general users who need assurance about the controls at a service organization relevant to security, availability, processing integrity, confidentiality, or privacy, but lack the knowledge and understanding for a SOC 2® report.

Other SOC engagements include the following:

- **SOC for Cybersecurity Engagement:** Examine and report on a description of the entity's cybersecurity risk management program and the effectiveness of controls with that program.

- **SOC for Supply Chain Engagement:** Examine and report on an entity's controls over the security, availability, processing integrity, confidentiality, or privacy of a system used to produce, manufacture, or distribute products.

1.1.1   Types of SOC Reports

At the completion of a SOC engagement, the practitioner issues a report showing the findings. SOC reports differ depending on the type of SOC engagement completed and whether the report issued is a Type 1 or Type 2 report.

- Type 1

  A report on the fairness of the presentation of management's description of the service organization's system and the suitability of the *design* of the controls to achieve the related control objectives included in the description *as of a specified date*.

- Type 2

  A report on the fairness of the presentation of management's description of the service organization's system and the suitability of the *design and operating effectiveness* of the controls to achieve the related control objectives included in the description *throughout a specified period*.

SOC 1® and SOC 2® reports can be issued as either Type 1 or Type 2 reports depending on the needs of the user, but a SOC 3® report is always issued as a Type 2 report.

Illustration 1   SOC 1® Use

Wyatt Co., a financial advising company, utilizes a third-party service provider named Database Inc. to process its sales contracts and store information about its clients. Wyatt Co.'s auditors want to ensure that the controls in place at Database Inc. are designed and operating effectively because control deficiencies at Database Inc. would negatively affect Wyatt Co. and its clients. Wyatt Co.'s auditors gain comfort by obtaining and reviewing the attestation to fairness of the controls and their operations within the System and Organization Controls (SOC 1®) Type 2 report because it gives them assurance that this has been in place over the last six months.

1.1.2   Contents of Type 1 and Type 2 SOC reports

The main components of a SOC report are consistent for both SOC 1® and SOC 2® engagements.

A service auditor's Type 1 report is typically comprised of the following:

- Management's description of the service organization's system.

- A written assertion by management of the service organization about whether, *as of a specified date*, based on the criteria:

  - Management's description of the system fairly presents the service organization's system that was designed and implemented.

  - The controls related to the control objectives stated in management's description of the system were suitably designed to achieve those control objectives.

- A report that expresses an opinion on the matters described above.

A service auditor's Type 2 report is comprised of the following:

- Management's description of the service organization's system.

- A written assertion by management of the service organization about whether, *throughout a specified period*, based on the criteria:

  - Management's description of the system fairly presents the service organization's system that was designed and implemented.

  - The controls related to the control objectives stated in management's description of the system were suitably designed and operated effectively to achieve those control objectives.

- A report that expresses an opinion on the matters described above *and* includes a description of the tests of controls and the results.

Pass Key

Key Differences Between Type 1 and Type 2 SOC Reports

A Type 1 report covers the system design as of a given point in time whereas a Type 2 report covers both the design and operating effectiveness over a period of time.

1.2   Summary of SOC Reports

Report Type	Subject Matter	Types	Purpose	Use of Report
SOC 1®	Assesses controls relevant to financial reporting.	Type 1 Type 2	Provides information and a service auditor's opinion about controls at a service organization likely relevant to financial reporting. Enables the user auditor to perform risk assessment procedures. Uses a Type 2 report as audit evidence that controls at the service organization are operating effectively.	Restricted to management of the service organization, user entities, and auditors.
SOC 2®	Assesses controls relevant to security, availability, processing integrity, confidentiality, or privacy.	Type 1 Type 2	Provides information and a service auditor's opinion about controls at a service organization relevant to security, availability, processing integrity, confidentiality, or privacy.	Restricted to management and other specified parties.
SOC 3®	Assesses controls relevant to security, availability, processing integrity, confidentiality, or privacy.	Type 2 only	Provides a service auditor's opinion about controls at a service organization relevant to security, availability, processing integrity, confidentiality, or privacy.	Not restricted. Users are interest parties.

2 Trust Services Criteria

2.1 Applicability of the Trust Services Criteria to SOC 2® and SOC 3® Engagements

Due to the nature of a system of internal controls, entities face certain risks that threaten their ability to achieve their objectives. Due to these inherent risks, entities are responsible for designing and implementing suitable controls to mitigate the risks. The AICPA's Assurance Services Executive Committee (ASEC) has established trust services criteria that set forth the outcomes that an entity's controls should meet to achieve the entity's unique objectives. This enables practitioners to evaluate and report on controls over the security, availability, processing integrity, confidentiality, or privacy of information and systems for SOC 2® and SOC 3® engagements. The report can be based on any of the five trust services categories, either individually or in combination. These categories include security, availability, processing integrity, confidentiality, and privacy.

The security category is addressed in most trust services engagements. Security controls are generally a primary area of focus for system users because organizations and their customers and business partners have an increased dependence on technology and concerns about cybersecurity risks and their impact on operational processes. Although uncommon, there may be circumstances in which the security category is not addressed by a trust services engagement.

2.2 Trust Services Criteria

2.2.1 Trust Services Categories

The five trust services categories can be remembered using the mnemonic "**CAPPS**":

- **Confidentiality:** Information designated as confidential is protected to meet the entity's objectives.

- **Availability:** Information and systems are available for operation and use to meet the entity's objectives.

- **Processing Integrity:** System processing is complete, valid, accurate, timely, and authorized to meet the entity's objectives.

- **Privacy:** Personal information is collected, used, retained, disclosed, and disposed of to meet the entity's objectives.

- **Security:** Information and systems are protected against unauthorized access; unauthorized disclosure of information; and damage to systems that could compromise the availability, integrity, confidentiality, and privacy of information or systems and affect the entity's ability to meet its objectives.

2.2.2 Application and Use of the Trust Services Criteria

The trust services criteria were designed to provide flexibility in application and use for a variety of different subject matters. The types of subject matter a practitioner may be engaged to report on using the trust services criteria include the following:

- SOC for cybersecurity engagement—the effectiveness of controls within an entity's cybersecurity risk management program to achieve the entity's cybersecurity objectives using the trust services criteria relevant to security, availability, and confidentiality as control criteria.

- SOC 2® engagement:

  Type 1: Same subject matter as a Type 2 SOC 2® engagement; however, a Type 1 SOC 2® report does not contain an opinion on the operating effectiveness of controls nor a detailed description of tests of controls performed by the service auditor and the results of those tests.

  Type 2: The suitability of design and operating effectiveness of controls included in management's description of a service organization's system relevant to one or more of the trust services criteria over security, availability, processing integrity, confidentiality, or privacy throughout a specified period to achieve the entity's objectives based on those criteria. A Type 2 SOC report includes an opinion on the operating effectiveness of controls, and a detailed description of tests of controls performed by the service auditor and the results of those tests.

- SOC 3® engagement—the design and operating effectiveness of a service organization's controls over a system relevant to one or more of the trust services criteria over security, availability, processing integrity, confidentiality, and privacy. A SOC 3® report contains an opinion on the operating effectiveness of controls but does not include a detailed description of tests of controls performed by the service auditor and the results of those tests.

- The suitability of design and operating effectiveness of controls of an entity, other than a service organization, over one or more systems relevant to one or more of the trust services categories of security, availability, processing integrity, confidentiality, or privacy (e.g., a SOC for supply chain engagement).

- The suitability of the design of an entity's controls over security, availability, processing integrity, confidentiality, or privacy to achieve the entity's objectives based on the related trust services criteria.

3 The COSO Framework Overview and Alignment to the Trust Services Criteria

3.1 Overview of the COSO Framework

The AICPA has aligned the trust services criteria with the COSO (Committee of Sponsoring Organizations of the Treadway Commission) *Internal Control—Integrated Framework* (the COSO framework), a widely accepted control framework utilized by entities to establish and implement an effective system of internal control. The COSO framework includes five components that are supported by 17 principles. The trust services criteria have been aligned to the 17 COSO principles, but include additional criteria.

3.1.1 Control Environment

COSO principles 1 through 5 relate to the control environment, which cover control from the perspective of the board and management through integrity, ethics, the proper corporate structure, and establishing an environment that holds employees accountable.

1. The entity demonstrates a commitment to integrity and ethical values.

2. The board of directors demonstrates independence from management and exercises oversight of the development and performance of internal control.

3. Management establishes, with board oversight, structures, reporting lines, and appropriate authorities and responsibilities in the pursuit of objectives.

4. The entity demonstrates a commitment to attract, develop, and retain competent individuals in alignment with objectives.

5. The entity holds individuals accountable for their internal control responsibilities in the pursuit of objectives.

3.1.2 Risk Assessment

COSO principles 6 through 9 relate to the risk assessment component of the COSO framework. They focus on identifying risk, considering the potential for fraud, and understanding changes that could impact internal controls.

6. The entity specifies objectives with sufficient clarity to enable the identification and assessment of risks relating to objectives.

7. The entity identifies risks to the achievement of its objectives across the entity and analyzes risks as a basis for determining how the risks should be managed.

8. The entity considers the potential for fraud in assessing risks to the achievement of objectives.

9. The entity identifies and assesses changes that could significantly impact the system of internal control.

3.1.3 Control Activities

COSO principles 10 through 12 relate to the control activities implemented and designed to ensure the proper application of policies and procedures that help ensure management directives and control objectives are met.

10. The entity selects and develops control activities that contribute to the mitigation of risks to the achievement of objectives to acceptable levels.

11. The entity also selects and develops general control activities over technology to support the achievement of objectives.

12. The entity deploys control activities through policies that establish what is expected and procedures that put policies into action.

    The trust services criteria expand on principle 12 by adding four common criteria referred to as the trust services supplemental criteria:

    - **Logical and Physical Access Controls:** Relates to how an entity restricts, provides, and removes access and prevents unauthorized access.

    - **System Operations:** Relates to how an entity detects and mitigates processing deviations, including logical and physical security deviations.

    - **Change Management:** Relates to how an entity manages changes and prevents unauthorized changes from being made.

    - **Risk Mitigation:** Relates to how an entity manages risk mitigation activities arising from potential business disruptions and the use of vendors and business partners.

3.1.4 Information and Communication

COSO principles 13 through 15 focus on obtaining, generating, and controlling information and communication.

13. The entity obtains or generates and uses relevant, quality information to support the functioning of internal control.

14. The entity internally communicates information, including objectives and responsibilities for internal control, necessary to support the functioning of internal control.

15. The entity communicates with external parties regarding matters affecting the functioning of internal control.

3.1.5 Monitoring Activities

COSO principles 16 and 17 relate to monitoring activities, which outline how an organization should conduct ongoing evaluations of control activities and communicate internal control deficiencies.

16. The entity selects, develops, and performs ongoing and/or separate evaluations to ascertain whether the components of internal control are present and functioning.

17. The entity evaluates and communicates internal control deficiencies in a timely manner to those parties responsible for taking corrective action, including senior management and the board of directors, as appropriate.

3.2 Alignment of the Trust Services Criteria and the COSO Principles

The trust services criteria consist of:

▨ criteria common to all five of the trust services categories (common criteria); and

▨ additional specific criteria for the availability, processing integrity, confidentiality, and privacy categories.

3.2.1 Overview

Trust Services Category	Common Criteria	Additional Category-Specific Criteria
Security	✓	N/A, common criteria is suitable with no additional criteria
Availability	✓	A series
Processing Integrity	✓	PI series
Confidentiality	✓	C series
Privacy	✓	P series

3.2.2 Additional Criteria for Availability (A Series)

The additional criteria for availability focus on an entity's ability to ensure all systems are continuously available as needed by maintaining and monitoring processing capacity, identifying and responding to threats, and ensuring a recovery plan is in place and tested.

▨ **A1.1:** The entity maintains, monitors, and evaluates current processing capacity and use of system components to manage capacity demand and to enable the implementation of additional capacity to meet entity objectives.

▨ **A1.2:** The entity ensures systems are available by identifying environmental threats, designing detection measures, implementing protection mechanisms and alerts, responding to environmental threats, communicating threat events, performing data backup, ensuring there is offsite storage, implementing an alternate infrastructure, and considering data recoverability to meet entity objectives.

▨ **A1.3:** The entity tests its recovery plan procedures to ensure system recovery meets entity objectives.

3.2.3 Additional Criteria for Processing Integrity (PI Series)

The additional criteria for processing integrity include considerations related to creating, using, and communicating quality information so that objectives will be met regarding product/service specifications, controls for completeness and accuracy, productivity, and system specifications.

- **PI1.1:** The entity obtains or generates, uses, and communicates relevant, quality information regarding processing objectives to support the use of products and services.

- **PI1.2:** The entity implements policies and procedures over system inputs to result in products, services, and reporting that meet entity objectives.

- **PI1.3:** The entity implements policies and procedures over system processing to result in products, services, and reporting that meet entity objectives.

- **PI1.4:** The entity implements policies and procedures to make available or deliver output completely, accurately, and timely that meet entity objectives.

- **PI1.5:** The entity implements policies and procedures to store inputs, items in processing, and outputs completely, accurately, and timely in accordance with system specifications to meet the entity's objectives.

3.2.4 Additional Criteria for Confidentiality (C Series)

The additional criteria for confidentiality relate to ensuring confidential information is handled appropriately.

- **C1.1:** The entity identifies and maintains confidential information to meet the entity's confidentiality objectives.

- **C1.2:** The entity disposes of confidential information to meet the entity's confidentiality objectives.

3.2.5 Additional Criteria for Privacy (P Series)

The additional criteria for privacy relate to collecting personal data, obtaining consent when collecting and using that data, using data for specific purposes only, managing access to individuals' data responsibly, disclosing policies to third parties and individuals properly, maintaining complete and accurate records, and monitoring and enforcing practices in place.

- **P1.0:** Notice and Communication of Objectives Related to Privacy

- **P2.0:** Choice and Consent

- **P3.0:** Collection

- **P4.0:** Use, Retention, and Disposal

- **P5.0:** Access

- **P6.0:** Disclosure and Notification

- **P7.0:** Quality

- **P8.0:** Monitoring and Enforcement

NOTES

1 Forming the Opinion in a SOC Engagement

The service auditor should form an opinion about the subject matter of the engagement. When forming the opinion, the service auditor should evaluate:

- the sufficiency and appropriateness of the evidence obtained; and
- whether uncorrected misstatements, individually or in the aggregate, are material.

In a SOC engagement, the service auditor forms an opinion about whether the subject matter is in accordance with (or based on) the criteria, in all material respects, or the assertion is fairly stated in all material respects. The opinion of the service auditor focuses on:

- Fair presentation of management's description of the service organization's system.
- The suitability of the design of the controls related to the control objectives stated in management's description.
- The effective operation of the controls stated in management's description (Type 2 only).

The overall objectives of a SOC 1® and SOC 2® engagement are consistent, however, the subject matter for which an opinion is being formed is different. In a SOC 1® engagement, the service auditor forms an opinion regarding the controls at a service organization relevant to the user entities' internal control over financial reporting. In a SOC 2® engagement, the service auditor forms an opinion regarding the controls at a service organization relevant to one or more of the five trust services criteria, which include security, availability, processing integrity, confidentiality, and privacy.

2 Types of Opinions in a SOC Engagement

When a service auditor concludes a SOC 1® or SOC 2® engagement, the report will contain the service auditor's opinion pertaining to the controls examined. The service auditor reaches his or her opinion by determining whether:

- The description of the controls is presented fairly by management.
- The controls are designed effectively.
- The controls operate as intended over a specified period of time (Type 2 only).

The opinions of the service auditor in a SOC engagement depend on the facts and circumstances of the evidence gathered throughout the engagement and may include an:

- unmodified (unqualified) opinion;
- qualified opinion;
- adverse opinion; or
- disclaimer of an opinion.

2.1   Unmodified (Unqualified) Opinion

An unmodified opinion is the service auditor's opinion that, in all material respects, based on the criteria described in management's assertion:

1.   Management's description of the system fairly presents the system that was designed and implemented.

- SOC 1®: Management's description of the service organization's system fairly presents the service organization's system that was designed and implemented as of a specified date (Type 1) or throughout the specified period (Type 2).

- SOC 2®: Management's description of the service organization's system presents the service organization's system that was designed and implemented in accordance with the description criteria, as of a specified date (Type 1) or throughout the specified period (Type 2).

2.   The controls stated in management's description of the system were suitably designed.

- SOC 1®: The controls related to the control objectives statement in management's description of the service organization's system were suitably designed to achieve the control objectives as of the specified date (Type 1) or throughout the specified period (Type 2).

- SOC 2®: The controls stated in management's description were suitably designed to provide reasonable assurance that the service organization's service commitments and system requirements were achieved based on the applicable trust services criteria as of the specified date (Type 1) or throughout the specified period (Type 2).

3.   The controls stated in management's description of the system operated effectively (Type 2 only).

- SOC 1®: The controls related to the control objectives stated in management's description of the system operated effectively throughout the specified period to achieve the control objectives.

- SOC 2®: The controls stated in management's description of the system operated effectively throughout the specified period to provide reasonable assurance that the service organization's service commitments and system requirements were achieved based on the applicable trust services criteria.

If the application of complementary user entity controls is necessary to achieve the related control objectives stated in management's description of the service organization's system, a statement to that effect has been made.

If the application of complementary subservice organization controls is necessary to achieve the related control objectives stated in management's description of the service organization's system, a statement to that effect has been made.

2.2   Modifications to the Service Auditor's Opinion

The service auditor is required to modify the opinion when either of the following circumstances exist and, in the service auditor's professional judgment, the effect of the matter is or may be material:

- The service auditor is unable to obtain sufficient appropriate evidence to conclude that the subject matter is in accordance with (or based on) the criteria, in all material respects.

- The service auditor concludes, based on evidence obtained, that the subject matter is not in accordance with (or based on) the criteria, in all material respects.

The service auditor's opinion should be modified, and the service auditor's report should include a description of the matter or matters giving rise to the modification, if the service auditor concludes any of the following:

- SOC 1® engagement:

    - Management's description of the service organization's system is not fairly presented, in all material respects.

    - The controls are not suitably designed to provide reasonable assurance that the control objectives stated in management's description of the service organization's system would be achieved if the controls operated effectively, in all material respects.

    - The controls did not operate effectively throughout the specified period to achieve the related control objectives stated in management's description of the service organization's system, in all material respects (Type 2 only).

    - The service auditor is unable to obtain sufficient and appropriate evidence.

- SOC 2® engagement:

    - Management's description of the service organization's system does not present the system designed and implemented throughout the period in accordance with the description criteria, in all material respects.

    - The controls are not suitably designed to provide reasonable assurance that the service organization's service commitments and system requirements would be achieved based on the applicable trust services criteria if the controls operated effectively, in all material respects.

    - The controls did not operate effectively throughout the specified period to provide reasonable assurance that the service organization's service commitments and system requirements were achieved based on the applicable trust services criteria, in all material respects (Type 2 only).

    - The service auditor is unable to obtain sufficient and appropriate evidence.

The service auditor determines whether a qualified opinion, an adverse opinion, or a disclaimer of opinion is appropriate depending on the following:

- The nature of the matter giving rise to the modification (that is, whether the subject matter of the engagement is presented in accordance with [or based on] the criteria, in all material respects, or, in the case of an inability to obtain sufficient appropriate evidence, may be materially misstated).

- The service auditor's professional judgment about the pervasiveness of the effects, or possible effects, of the matter on the subject matter of the engagement.

2.2.1 Types of Modified Opinions

There are three types of modified opinions:

- **Qualified Opinion:** A qualified opinion states that except for the effects of the matter(s) giving rise to the modification, the description is presented in accordance with the description criteria and the controls were suitably designed and operating effectively (Type 2), in all material respects.

- **Adverse Opinion:** An adverse opinion states that the description misstatements, either individually or in the aggregate, are material and pervasive, or deficiencies in the design or operation of controls are material and pervasive.

- **Disclaimer of Opinion:** A disclaimer of opinion states that the auditor does not express an opinion.

2.2.2 Summary of Modified Opinions

The chart below summarizes the nature of matters giving rise to the service auditor's opinion modification:

Nature of Matter Giving Rise to the Modification (SOC 1®)	Nature of Matter Giving Rise to the Modification (SOC 2®)	Service Auditor's Professional Judgment About the Pervasiveness of the Effects (or Possible Effects) on the Opinion on the Description, on the Suitability of the Design of Controls, and on the Operating Effectiveness of Controls	
		Material but Not Pervasive	*Material and Pervasive*
Scope limitation: An inability to obtain sufficient appropriate evidence.	Scope limitation: An inability to obtain sufficient appropriate evidence.	Qualified opinion	Disclaimer of opinion
Material misstatements: The description is materially misstated. **OR** The controls are not suitably designed to achieve one or more of the related control objectives stated in management's description of the service organization's system. **OR** The controls are not operating effectively to achieve one or more of the related control objectives stated in management's description of the service organization's system.	Material misstatements: The description is materially misstated. **OR** The controls are not suitably designed to provide reasonable assurance that one or more of the service organization's service commitments or system requirements were achieved based on the applicable trust services criteria. **OR** The controls are not operating effectively to provide reasonable assurance that one or more of the service organization's service commitments or system requirements were achieved based on the applicable trust services criteria.	Qualified opinion	Adverse opinion

3   Contents of the Auditor's Report for a SOC Engagement

The SOC report includes the following key components:

1. Management's description of the system

2. Management's assertion

3. Independent service auditor's report

4. Auditor's tests of controls and results of tests

3.1 Management's Description of the System

3.1.1 SOC 1® Purpose and Common Sections of Management's System Description

A SOC 1® engagement is an examination to report on a service organization's controls relevant to user entities' internal control over financial reporting.

The service organization's management is responsible for documenting the description of the service organization's system. The description must provide sufficient information to allow a user auditor to understand how the service organization's processing affects the user entity's financial statements and to assess the risk of material misstatement of the user entity's financial statements. The form and extent of the description are determined by management and may depend on the size and complexity of the service organization.

Common sections of a system description subject to SOC 1® engagements include:

- Types of services provided—defined scope of services provided and the classes of transactions processed.

- Procedures performed—procedures, within both manual and automated systems, by which services are provided, including procedures to initiate, authorize, record, process, correct, and transfer transactions to reports and other information for user entities.

- System functionality—how the system captures and addresses significant events and conditions (other than transactions).

- Subservice organizations—services performed by entities the service organization uses to provide services to the user entity, including whether the carve-out method or the inclusive method has been used, and any complementary subservice organizational controls necessary to meet control objectives.

- Controls—a description of the control objective and design to achieve those objectives, including the frequency, timing, person or parties responsible for performance, and the source of information to which the control is applied.

- Information on other aspects of the control environment, risk assessment process, information and communication, control activities, and monitoring activities that are relevant to the services provided.

- Prepare reports—process to prepare reports and other information for user entities.

- Deficiencies in information—if applicable, information used in the performance of the procedures (if applicable, related accounting records and supporting information) to initiate, authorize, record, process, and report transactions. This includes the correction of incorrect information and how information is transferred to the report, and other information prepared for user entities.

- Complementary user entity controls (CUECs)—controls that must be implemented by the user entity to meet control objectives.

- Relevant details of changes to the service organization's system during the period covered by the description (Type 2 only).

- The description does not omit or distort information relevant to the system and is prepared to meet the common needs of a broad range of user entities and their auditors, and thus may not include every aspect that a user entity may consider important in its own particular environment.

3.1.2 SOC 2® Purpose and Common Sections of Management's System Description

A SOC 2® engagement is an examination of a service organization's description of its system, the suitability of the design of controls, and in a Type 2 engagement, the operating effectiveness of controls relevant to security, availability, processing integrity, confidentiality, and privacy.

The service organization's management is responsible for presenting a description of the system to enable report users, such as user entities, business partners, or other relevant parties, to understand the system and the processing and flow of data throughout and from the system. The description is to be prepared in accordance with specific criteria and describes the procedures and controls in place to manage risk.

Common sections of a system description subject to a SOC 2® engagement include:

- Types of services provided—types of services provided by service organizations, including the services that are the focus of the engagement.

- Principal service commitments and system requirements—the commitments made to user entities and the system requirements required to achieve such commitments.

  - Service commitments—declarations made by service organization management to user entities and others (such as user entities' customers) about the system used to provide the service.

  - System requirements—specifications regarding how the system should function to meet the service organization's service commitments to user entities and others (such as user entities' customers), to meet the service organization's commitments to vendors and business partners, to comply with relevant laws and regulations and guidelines of industry groups (such as business or trade associations), and to achieve other objectives of the service organization that are relevant to the trust services category or categories addressed by the description.

- Components of the system used to provide the services—infrastructure, software, people, procedures, and data.

- Identified system incidents—incidents that were the result of controls that were not suitably designed or operating effectively or that resulted in a significant failure in the achievement of one or more service commitments and system requirements. The nature, extent (or effect), and timing of the system incident and its disposition (based on management's judgment) that occurred as of the date of the description (Type 1) or during the period of time covered by the description (Type 2).

- Applicable trust services criteria—the trust services criteria being reported on, including applicable controls in place to provide reasonable assurance that the service commitments and system requirements were achieved.

- Complementary user entity controls (CUECs)—the controls implemented by the user entity that are necessary, in combination with controls at the service organization, to provide reasonable assurance that the service commitments and system requirements would be achieved.

▪ Subservice organizations—a subservice organization used by the service organization and the controls at the subservice organization are necessary, in combination with controls at the service organization, to provide reasonable assurance that the service commitments and system requirements would be achieved.

  • Inclusive method—nature of the service provided, controls with clear differentiation between controls at the service organization and subservice organization, portions of the system attributable to the subservice organization along with relevant aspects (e.g., infrastructure, software, people, procedures, data).

  • Carve-out method— management does not include a description of the controls that operate only or primarily at the subservice organization. However, the description should contain details regarding the nature of the service provided, types of controls along with the applicable trust services criteria that are intended to be met by the complementary subservice organization controls (CSOCs), the subservice organization's responsibilities for implementing the CSOCs, and an indication that the related service commitments and system requirements can only be achieved if the CSOCs are suitably designed and operating effectively.

▪ Irrelevant specific criteria—explanations for why specific trust services criteria are not relevant for the service organization's system.

▪ Details of system and control changes during the period that are relevant to the service organization's service commitments and system requirements (Type 2 only).

3.1.3 Management's Description of the Entity's Cybersecurity Risk Management Program

An entity's cybersecurity risk management program is a set of policies, processes, and controls designed to:

▪ protect information and systems from security events that could compromise the achievement of the entity's cybersecurity objectives; and

▪ detect, respond to, mitigate, and recover from, on a timely basis, security events that are not prevented.

The categories of description criteria include the following:

1. Nature of business and operations

2. Nature of information at risk

3. Cybersecurity risk management program objectives (cybersecurity objectives)

4. Factors that have a significant effect on inherent cybersecurity risks

5. Cybersecurity risk governance structure

6. Cybersecurity risk assessment process

7. Cybersecurity communications and the quality of cybersecurity information

8. Monitoring of the cybersecurity risk management program

9. Cybersecurity control processes

The cybersecurity risk management examination is predicated on the concept that management is responsible for developing and presenting a description of the entity's cybersecurity risk management program, making an assertion about whether the description is presented in accordance with the description criteria, and making an assertion about the effectiveness of the controls within the program based on a set of control criteria.

3.2   Management's Assertions

In a SOC engagement, the service auditor is required to request a written assertion from management.

In a SOC 1® or SOC 2® engagement, management's assertion addresses whether:

1. Management's description of the system fairly presents the system that was designed and implemented.

    - SOC 1®: Management's description of the service organization's system fairly presents the service organization's system that was designed and implemented as of a specified date (Type 1) or throughout the specified period (Type 2).

    - SOC 2®: Management's description of the service organization's system presents the service organization's system that was designed and implemented in accordance with the description criteria, as of a specified date (Type 1) or throughout the specified period (Type 2).

2. The controls stated in management's description of the system were suitably designed.

    - SOC 1®: The controls related to the control objectives statement in management's description of the service organization's system were suitably designed to achieve the control objectives as of the specified date (Type 1) or throughout the specified period (Type 2).

    - SOC 2®: The controls stated in management's description were suitably designed to provide reasonable assurance that the service organization's service commitments and system requirements were achieved based on the applicable trust services criteria as of the specified date (Type 1) or throughout the specified period (Type 2).

3. The controls stated in management's description of the system operated effectively (Type 2 only).

    - SOC 1®: The controls related to the control objectives stated in management's description of the system operated effectively throughout the specified period to achieve the control objectives.

    - SOC 2®: The controls stated in management's description of the system operated effectively throughout the specified period to provide reasonable assurance that the service organization's service commitments and system requirements were achieved based on the applicable trust services criteria.

In a SOC 3® engagement, management's assertion addresses whether:

- the controls within the system were effective throughout the specified period to provide reasonable assurance that the service organization's service commitments and system requirements were achieved based on the applicable trust services criteria, including a description of the boundaries of the system and the service organization's principal service commitments and system requirements.

Management's assertions are included in the SOC report along with the description of the service organization's system in the service auditor's report. If management refuses to provide a written assertion, the service auditor is required to withdraw from the engagement when withdrawal is possible under applicable laws and regulations. If law or regulation does not allow the service auditor to withdraw, the service auditor should disclaim an opinion on the description, the suitability of design of controls in a Type 1 engagement, and the operating effectiveness of controls in a Type 2 engagement.

3.2.1 Summary of Management Assertions by Engagement Type

Management's Assertions by SOC Engagement and Report Type			
Report Type	*SOC 1®*	*SOC 2®*	*SOC 3®*
Type 1	• Management's system description • Management's written assertion about whether the description fairly presents the system, **AND** the controls were suitably designed to achieve control objectives	• Management's system description • Management's written assertion about whether the description fairly presents the system, **AND** the controls related to the applicable trust services criteria were suitably designed to meet those criteria	
Type 2	• Management's system description • Management's written assertion about whether the description fairly presents the system that was designed and implemented throughout the specified period, **AND** the controls were suitably designed throughout the period to achieve control objectives, **AND** the controls operated effectively throughout the period to achieve control objectives	• Management's system description • Management's written assertion about whether the description fairly presents the system that was designed and implemented throughout the specified period, **AND** the controls were suitably designed throughout the period to achieve applicable trust services criteria, **AND** the controls operated effectively throughout the period to meet applicable trust services criteria	• Management's description of the service organization's system boundaries and copy of its privacy notice if addressing the privacy principle • Management's written assertion concerning whether effective controls over the system related to applicable trust services criteria

4 Contents of the Service Auditor's Report for a SOC 1® Engagement

4.1 Contents of the SOC 1® Report

The SOC 1® report includes the following key components:

1. **Management's Description of the System**

   Management's description of the system as of a specified date (Type 1) or throughout the specified period (Type 2).

2. **Management's Assertion**

   Management assertion that addresses whether, based on the criteria in a management's assertion:

   * Management's description of the service organization's system fairly presents the service organization's system that was designed and implemented as of a specified date (Type 1) or throughout the specified period (Type 2).

   * The controls related to the control objectives stated in management's description of the service organization's system were suitability designed to achieve those control objectives as of the specified date (Type 1) or throughout the specified period (Type 2).

   * The controls related to the control objectives stated in management's description of the service organization's system operated effectively to achieve those control objectives (Type 2 only).

3. **Independent Service Auditor's Report**

   The service auditor's opinion about whether:

   * Management's description of the service organization's system fairly presents the service organization's system that was designed and implemented as of a specified date (Type 1) or throughout the specified period (Type 2).

   * The controls related to the control objectives stated in management's description of the service organization's system were suitability designed to achieve those control objectives as of the specified date (Type 1) or throughout the specified period (Type 2).

   * The controls related to the control objectives stated in management's description of the service organization's system operated effectively to achieve those control objectives (Type 2 only).

4. **Auditor's Tests of Controls and Results of Tests**

   Description of the service auditor's tests of controls and results thereof (Type 2 only).

4.1.1 Elements of the Service Auditor's SOC 1® Report

The elements to be included in a service auditor's SOC 1® report include:

Independent Service Auditor's SOC 1® Report	
Title	A title that includes the word *independent*.
Addressee	An appropriate addressee as required by the circumstances of the engagement.
Scope	Identification of the following:
	• Management's description of the service organization's system, the function performed by the system, and the period to which the description relates.
	• The criteria against which the fairness of the presentation of the description and the suitability of the design and operating effectiveness (Type 2) of the controls to achieve the related control objectives stated in the description were evaluated.
	• Any information included in a document containing the service auditor's report that is not covered by the service auditor's report.
	• Any services performed by a subservice organization and whether the carve-out method or the inclusive method was used in relation to them.
	If the carve-out method was used, a statement that:
	— Management's description of the service organization's system excludes the control objectives and related controls of the relevant subservice organizations.
	— Certain control objectives specified by the service organization can be achieved only if complementary subservice organization controls assumed in the design of the service organization's controls are suitably designed and operating effectively.
	— The service auditor's procedures do not extend to such complementary subservice organization controls.
	If the inclusive method was used, a statement that:
	— Management's description of the service organization's system includes the subservice organization's specified control objectives and related controls, and that the service auditor's procedures included procedures related to the subservice organization.
	• A statement that the controls and control objectives included in the description are those that management believes are likely to be relevant to user entities' internal control over financial reporting, and the description does not include those aspects of the system that are not likely to be relevant to user entities' internal control over financial reporting.
	If management's description of the service organization's system refers to the need for complementary user entity controls, a statement that:
	— The service auditor has not evaluated the suitability of the design or operating effectiveness of complementary user entity controls, and that the control objectives stated in the description can be achieved only if complementary user entity controls are suitably designed and operating effectively, along with the controls at the service organization.
Service Organization's Responsibilities	• A reference to management's assertion and a statement that management is responsible for:
	— Preparing the description of the service organization's system and the assertion, including the completeness, accuracy, and method of presentation of the description and assertion.
	— Providing the services covered by the description of the service organization's system.
	— Specifying the control objectives and stating them in the description of the service organization's system.
	— Identifying the risks that threaten the achievement of the control objectives.

(continued) Service Organization's Responsibilities	— Selecting the criteria. — Designing, implementing, and documenting controls that are suitably designed and operating effectively to achieve the related control objectives stated in the description of the service organization's system.
Service Auditor's Responsibilities	A statement that the service auditor is responsible for expressing an opinion on the fairness of the presentation of management's description of the service organization's system and on the suitability of the design and operating effectiveness (Type 2) of the controls to achieve the related control objectives stated in the description based on the service auditor's examination. A statement that: • The examination was conducted in accordance with attestation standards established by the AICPA. • The standards require the service auditor to plan and perform the examination to obtain reasonable assurance about whether, in all material respects, based on the criteria in management's assertion, management's description of the system is fairly presented and the controls are suitably designed and operating effectively (Type 2), as of the specified date (Type 1) or throughout the specified period (Type 2), to achieve the related control objectives. • The service auditor believes the evidence obtained is sufficient and appropriate to provide a reasonable basis for the service auditor's opinion. A statement that an examination of management's description of a service organization's system and the suitability of the design and operating effectiveness (Type 2) of the service organization's controls to achieve the related control objectives stated in the description involves: • Performing procedures to obtain evidence about the fairness of the presentation of the description and the suitability of the design and operating effectiveness (Type 2) of the controls to achieve the related control objectives stated in the description based on the criteria in management's assertion. • Assessing the risks that management's description of the service organization's system is not fairly presented and that the controls were not suitably designed or operating effectively (Type 2) to achieve the related control objectives. • Evaluating the overall presentation of management's description of the service organization's system, suitability of the control objectives stated in the description, and suitability of the criteria specified by the service organization in its assertion. • Testing the operating effectiveness of those controls that management considers necessary to provide reasonable assurance that the related control objectives stated in management's description of the service organization's system were achieved (Type 2 only).
Inherent Limitations	A description of the inherent limitations of controls, including that projecting to the future any evaluation of the fairness of the presentation of management's description of the service organization's system or conclusions about the suitability of the design or operating effectiveness (Type 2) of the controls to achieve the related control objectives is subject to the risk that controls at a service organization may become ineffective.
Description of Tests of Controls (Type 2 only)	A reference to a description of the service auditor's tests of controls and the results, including: • The controls that were tested. • Whether the items tested represent all or a selection of items in the population. • The nature of the tests in sufficient detail for user auditors to determine the effect of such tests on their risk assessment. • Any identified deviations in the operation of controls included in the description, the extent of testing performed by the service auditor that identified deviations (including the number of items tested), and the number and nature of deviations noted (even if, on the basis of tests performed, the service auditor concludes that the related control objective was achieved).

(continued) Description of Tests of Controls (Type 2 only)	• When applicable, if the work of the internal audit function has been used in a test of controls to obtain evidence, a description of the internal auditor's work and the service auditor's procedures with respect to that work.
Other Matter (Type 1 only)	A statement that the service auditor did not perform any procedures regarding the operating effectiveness of controls and, therefore, expresses no opinion thereon.
Opinion	The service auditor's opinion on whether, in all material respects, based on the criteria described in management's assertion: • Management's description of the service organization's system fairly presents the service organization's system that was designed and implemented as of the specified date (Type 1) or throughout the specified period (Type 2). • The controls related to the control objectives stated in management's description of the service organization's system were suitably designed to provide reasonable assurance that the control objectives would be achieved if the controls operated effectively as of the specified date (Type 1) or throughout the specified period (Type 2). • The controls operated effectively to provide reasonable assurance that the control objectives stated in management's description of the service organization's system were achieved throughout the specified period (Type 2 only). • If the application of complementary user entity controls is necessary to achieve the related control objectives stated in management's description of the service organization's system, a statement to that effect. • If the application of complementary subservice organization controls is necessary to achieve the related control objectives stated in management's description of the service organization's system, a statement to that effect.
Restricted Use	An alert, in a separate paragraph, that restricts the use of the report. The alert should state: • The report, including the description of tests of controls and results (Type 2), is intended solely for the information and use of management of the service organization, user entities of the service organization's system as of the specified date (Type 1) or during some or all of the period covered by the report (Type 2), and the auditors who audit and report on such user entities' financial statements or internal control over financial reporting. • The report is not intended to be, and should not be, used by anyone other than the specified parties.
Service Auditor's Signature	The manual or printed signature of the service auditor's firm.
Service Auditor's City and State	The city and state where the service auditor practices.
Date of the Service Auditor's Report	The date of the report. The report should be dated no earlier than the date on which the service auditor has obtained sufficient appropriate evidence on which to base the service auditor's opinion, including evidence that: • management's description of the service organization system has been prepared; • management has provided a written assertion; and • the attestation documentation has been reviewed.

Pass Key

Key Differences Between SOC 1® Type 1 and Type 2 Reports

The main differences between a SOC 1® Type 1 and SOC 1® Type 2 report relate to the addition of expanded language to include the operating effectiveness of control in a Type 2 report. The only section that is fully unique to a Type 2 report (excluded from Type 1 reports) is the reference to the description of the service auditor's tests of controls and the related results.

4.1.2   Sample Report: SOC 1® Type 1 Report

Independent Service Auditor's Report on XYZ Service Organization's Description of Its [*type or name of*] System and the Suitability of the Design of Controls

To: XYZ Service Organization

Scope

We have examined XYZ Service Organization's description of its [*type or name of*] system titled "XYZ Service Organization's Description of Its [*type or name of*] System" for processing user entities' transactions [*or identification of the function performed by the system*] as of [*date*] (description) and the suitability of the design of the controls included in the description to achieve the related control objectives stated in the description, based on the criteria identified in "XYZ Service Organization's Assertion" (assertion). The controls and control objectives included in the description are those that management of XYZ Service Organization believes are likely to be relevant to user entities' internal control over financial reporting, and the description does not include those aspects of the [*type or name of*] system that are not likely to be relevant to user entities' internal control over financial reporting.

Service Organization's Responsibilities

In [*section number where the assertion is presented*], XYZ Service Organization has provided an assertion about the fairness of the presentation of the description and suitability of the design of the controls to achieve the related control objectives stated in the description. XYZ Service Organization is responsible for preparing the description and assertion, including the completeness, accuracy, and method of presentation of the description and assertion, providing the services covered by the description, specifying the control objectives and stating them in the description, identifying the risks that threaten the achievement of the control objectives, selecting the criteria stated in the assertion, and designing, implementing, and documenting controls that are suitably designed and operating effectively to achieve the related control objectives stated in the description.

(continued)

(continued)

Service Auditor's Responsibilities

Our responsibility is to express an opinion on the fairness of the presentation of the description and on the suitability of the design of the controls to achieve the related control objectives stated in the description, based on our examination.

Our examination was conducted in accordance with attestation standards established by the American Institute of Certified Public Accountants. Those standards require that we plan and perform the examination to obtain reasonable assurance about whether, in all material respects, based on the criteria in management's assertion, the description is fairly presented, and the controls were suitably designed to achieve the related control objectives stated in the description as of [*date*]. We believe that the evidence we obtained is sufficient and appropriate to provide a reasonable basis for our opinion.

An examination of a description of a service organization's system and the suitability of the design of controls involves:

■ Performing procedures to obtain evidence about the fairness of the presentation of the description and the suitability of the design of the controls to achieve the related control objectives stated in the description, based on the criteria in management's assertion.

■ Assessing the risks that the description is not fairly presented and that the controls were not suitably designed to achieve the related control objectives stated in the description.

■ Evaluating the overall presentation of the description, suitability of the control objectives stated in the description, and suitability of the criteria specified by the service organization in its assertion.

Inherent Limitations

The description is prepared to meet the common needs of a broad range of user entities and their auditors who audit and report on user entities' financial statements and may not, therefore, include every aspect of the system that each individual user entity may consider important in its own particular environment. Because of their nature, controls at a service organization may not prevent, or detect and correct, all misstatements in processing or reporting transactions [*or identification of the function performed by the system*]. Also, the projection to the future of any evaluation of the fairness of the presentation of the description, or conclusions about the suitability of the design of the controls to achieve the related control objectives, is subject to the risk that controls at a service organization may become ineffective.

(continued)

(continued)

Other Matter

We did not perform any procedures regarding the operating effectiveness of controls stated in the description and, accordingly, do not express an opinion thereon.

Opinion

In our opinion, in all material respects, based on the criteria described in XYZ Service Organization's assertion:

a. The description fairly presents the [*type or name of*] system that was designed and implemented as of [*date*].

b. The controls related to the control objectives stated in the description were suitably designed to provide reasonable assurance that the control objectives would be achieved if the controls operated effectively as of [*date*].

Restricted Use

This report is intended solely for the information and use of management of XYZ Service Organization, user entities of XYZ Service Organization's [*type or name of*] system as of [*date*], and their auditors who audit and report on such user entities' financial statements or internal control over financial reporting and have a sufficient understanding to consider it, along with other information, including information about controls implemented by user entities themselves, when assessing the risks of material misstatement of user entities' financial statements. This report is not intended to be, and should not be, used by anyone other than the specified parties.

[*Service auditor's signature*]
[*Service auditor's city and state*]
[*Date of the service auditor's report*]

4.1.3   Sample Report: SOC 1® Type 2 Report

Independent Service Auditor's Report on XYZ Service Organization's Description of Its [*type or name of*] System and the Suitability of the Design and Operating Effectiveness of Controls

To: XYZ Service Organization

Scope

We have examined XYZ Service Organization's description of its [*type or name of*] system titled "XYZ Service Organization's Description of Its [*type or name of*] System" for processing user entities' transactions [*or identification of the function performed by the system*] throughout the period [*date*] to [*date*] (description) and the suitability of the design and operating effectiveness of the controls included in the description to achieve the related control objectives stated in the description, based on the criteria identified in "XYZ Service Organization's Assertion" (assertion). The controls and control objectives included in the description are those that management of XYZ Service Organization believes are likely to be relevant to user entities' internal control over financial reporting, and the description does not include those aspects of the [*type or name of*] system that are not likely to be relevant to user entities' internal control over financial reporting.

Service Organization's Responsibilities

In [*section number where the assertion is presented*], XYZ Service Organization has provided an assertion about the fairness of the presentation of the description and suitability of the design and operating effectiveness of the controls to achieve the related control objectives stated in the description. XYZ Service Organization is responsible for preparing the description and assertion, including the completeness, accuracy, and method of presentation of the description and assertion, providing the services covered by the description, specifying the control objectives and stating them in the description, identifying the risks that threaten the achievement of the control objectives, selecting the criteria stated in the assertion, and designing, implementing, and documenting controls that are suitably designed and operating effectively to achieve the related control objectives stated in the description.

Service Auditor's Responsibilities

Our responsibility is to express an opinion on the fairness of the presentation of the description and on the suitability of the design and operating effectiveness of the controls to achieve the related control objectives stated in the description, based on our examination.

(continued)

(continued)

Our examination was conducted in accordance with attestation standards established by the American Institute of Certified Public Accountants. Those standards require that we plan and perform the examination to obtain reasonable assurance about whether, in all material respects, based on the criteria in management's assertion, the description is fairly presented, and the controls were suitably designed and operating effectively to achieve the related control objectives stated in the description throughout the period [*date*] to [*date*]. We believe that the evidence we obtained is sufficient and appropriate to provide a reasonable basis for our opinion.

An examination of a description of a service organization's system and the suitability of the design and operating effectiveness of controls involves:

- Performing procedures to obtain evidence about the fairness of the presentation of the description and the suitability of the design and operating effectiveness of the controls to achieve the related control objectives stated in the description, based on the criteria in management's assertion.

- Assessing the risks that the description is not fairly presented and that the controls were not suitably designed or operating effectively to achieve the related control objectives stated in the description.

- Testing the operating effectiveness of those controls that management considers necessary to provide reasonable assurance that the related control objectives stated in the description were achieved.

- Evaluating the overall presentation of the description, suitability of the control objectives stated in the description, and suitability of the criteria specified by the service organization in its assertion.

Inherent Limitations

The description is prepared to meet the common needs of a broad range of user entities and their auditors who audit and report on user entities' financial statements and may not, therefore, include every aspect of the system that each individual user entity may consider important in its own particular environment. Because of their nature, controls at a service organization may not prevent, or detect and correct, all misstatements in processing or reporting transactions [*or identification of the function performed by the system*]. Also, the projection to the future of any evaluation of the fairness of the presentation of the description, or conclusions about the suitability of the design or operating effectiveness of the controls to achieve the related control objectives, is subject to the risk that controls at a service organization may become ineffective.

Description of Tests of Controls

The specific controls tested, and the nature, timing, and results of those tests are listed in [*section number where the description of tests of controls is presented*].

(continued)

(continued)

Opinion

In our opinion, in all material respects, based on the criteria described in XYZ Service Organization's assertion:

a. The description fairly presents the [*type or name of*] system that was designed and implemented throughout the period [*date*] to [*date*].

b. The controls related to the control objectives stated in the description were suitably designed to provide reasonable assurance that the control objectives would be achieved if the controls operated effectively throughout the period [*date*] to [*date*].

c. The controls operated effectively to provide reasonable assurance that the control objectives stated in the description were achieved throughout the period [*date*] to [*date*].

Restricted Use

This report, including the description of tests of controls and results thereof in [*section number where the description of tests of controls is presented*], is intended solely for the information and use of management of XYZ Service Organization, user entities of XYZ Service Organization's [*type or name of*] system during some or all of the period [*date*] to [*date*], and their auditors who audit and report on such user entities' financial statements or internal control over financial reporting and have a sufficient understanding to consider it, along with other information, including information about controls implemented by user entities themselves, when assessing the risks of material misstatement of user entities' financial statements. This report is not intended to be, and should not be, used by anyone other than the specified parties.

[*Service auditor's signature*]
[*Service auditor's city and state*]
[*Date of the service auditor's report*]

5 Contents of the Service Auditor's Report for a SOC 2® Engagement

5.1 Contents of the SOC 2® Report

The SOC 2® report includes the following key components:

1. **Management's Description of the System**

   Management's description of the system as of a point in time (Type 1) or throughout a period of time (Type 2) in accordance with the description criteria.

2. **Management's Assertion**

   Management assertion that addresses whether:

   - The description of the service organization's system as of a point in time (Type 1) or throughout a period of time (Type 2) is presented in accordance with the description criteria.

   - The controls stated in the description were suitably designed as of a point in time (Type 1) or throughout a period of time (Type 2) to provide reasonable assurance that the service organization's service commitments and system requirements were achieved based on the applicable trust services criteria.

   - The controls stated in the description operated effectively throughout a period of time to provide reasonable assurance that the service organization's service commitments and system requirements were achieved based on the applicable trust services criteria (Type 2 only).

3. **Independent Service Auditor's Report**

   The service auditor's opinion about whether:

   - The description of the service organization's system as of a point in time (Type 1) or throughout a period of time (Type 2) is presented in accordance with the description criteria.

   - The controls stated in the description were suitably designed as of a point in time (Type 1) or throughout a period of time (Type 2) to provide reasonable assurance that the service organization's service commitments and system requirements were achieved based on the applicable trust services criteria.

   - The controls stated in the description operated effectively throughout a period of time to provide reasonable assurance that the service organization's service commitments and system requirements were achieved based on the applicable trust services criteria (Type 2 only).

4. **Auditor's Tests of Controls and Results of Tests**

   Description of the service auditor's tests of controls and results thereof (Type 2 only).

5.1.1　Elements of the Service Auditor's SOC 2® Report

The elements to be included in a service auditor's SOC 2® report include:

Independent Service Auditor's SOC 2® Report	
Title	A title that includes the word *independent*
Addressee	An appropriate addressee as required by the circumstances of the engagement.
Scope	An identification or description of the subject matter or assertion being reported on, including the point in time or period of time (Type 2) to which the measurement or evaluation of the subject matter or assertion relates. • Any services provided by, along with controls at, a subservice organization and whether the carve-out method or the inclusive method was used in relation to them. An identification of the criteria against which the subject matter was measured or evaluated: • In a SOC 2® engagement, the description is evaluated against the *description criteria* and the suitability of design and operating effectiveness of controls (Type 2) is evaluated against the trust services criteria relevant to the categories addressed by the engagement (*applicable trust services criteria*). • A reference to both sets of criteria should be included in the scope paragraph of the service auditor's report.
Service Organization's Responsibilities	A statement that identifies the responsible party and its responsibility for the subject matter in accordance with (or based on) the criteria or for its assertion.
Service Auditor's Responsibilities	A statement that the service auditor's responsibility is to express an opinion on the subject matter or assertion, based on the service auditor's examination. A statement that: • The service auditor's examination was conducted in accordance with attestation standards established by the AICPA. • Those standards require that the service auditor plan and perform the examination to obtain reasonable assurance about whether the subject matter is in accordance with the criteria, in all material respects. • The service auditor believes the evidence the service auditor obtained is sufficient and appropriate to provide a reasonable basis for the service auditor's opinion. A description of the nature of an examination engagement.
Inherent Limitations	A statement that describes significant inherent limitations, if any, associated with the measurement or evaluation of the subject matter against the criteria.
Description of Tests of Controls (Type 2 only)	A description of the procedures performed by the service auditor and the results of those procedures.
Other Matter (Type 1 only)	A statement that the service auditor did not perform any procedures regarding the operating effectiveness of controls stated in the description and, accordingly, does not express an opinion thereon.
Opinion	The service auditor's opinion about whether the subject matter is in accordance with (or based on) the criteria, in all material respects.
Restricted Use	An alert, in a separate paragraph, that restricts the use of the report and should: • State that the service auditor's report is intended solely for the information and use of the specified parties.

Restricted Use (continued)	• Identify the specified parties for whom use is intended. • State that the report is not intended to be, and should not be, used by anyone other than the specified parties.
Service auditor's signature	The manual or printed signature of the service auditor's firm.
Service auditor's city and state	The city and state where the service auditor practices.
Date of the service auditor's report	The date of the report.

Pass Key

Key Differences Between SOC 2® Type 1 and Type 2 Reports

The SOC 2® report elements would be tailored to exclude all references to the operating effectiveness of controls when performing a Type 1 engagement. The Type 1 report would not include a description of the service auditor's tests of controls and related results.

5.1.2   Describing Test of Controls and Results in a SOC 2® Engagement

A service auditor's SOC 2® report for a Type 2 engagement should contain a reference to the description of the service auditor's tests of controls and the results of such tests.

Information required to be described includes:

- Controls that were tested.
- Whether the items tested represent all, or a selection of, the items in the population.
- The nature of the tests performed in sufficient detail to enable report users to determine the effect of such tests on their risk assessments.

If deviations were identified, the following information would also be included:

- The number of items tested
- The number and nature of deviations
- Causative factors (optional)

If the work of the internal audit function has been used in the tests of controls to obtain evidence, the service auditor is required to include a description of the internal auditor's work and the service auditor's procedures with respect to the work of the internal auditor.

5.1.3   Sample Report: Service Auditor's Report for a SOC 2® Type 1 Engagement

Independent Service Auditor's Report

To: XYZ Service Organization

Scope

We have examined XYZ Service Organization's (XYZ's) accompanying description of its [*type or name*] system titled [*insert title of management's description*] as of [*date*] (description) based on the criteria for a description of a service organization's system in DC section 200, *2018 Description Criteria for a Description of a Service Organization's System in a SOC 2® Report* (AICPA, *Description Criteria*) (description criteria) and the suitability of the design of controls stated in the description as of [*date*], to provide reasonable assurance that XYZ's service commitments and system requirements were achieved based on the trust services criteria relevant to security, availability, processing integrity, confidentiality, and privacy (applicable trust services criteria) set forth in TSP section 100, *2017 Trust Services Criteria for Security, Availability, Processing Integrity, Confidentiality, and Privacy* (AICPA, *Trust Services Criteria*).

Service Organization's Responsibilities

XYZ is responsible for its service commitments and system requirements and for designing, implementing, and operating effective controls within the system to provide reasonable assurance that XYZ's service commitments and system requirements were achieved. XYZ has provided the accompanying assertion titled [*insert the title of the attached management assertion*] (assertion) about the description and the suitability of design of controls stated therein. XYZ is also responsible for preparing the description and assertion, including the completeness, accuracy, and method of presentation of the description and assertion; providing the services covered by the description; selecting the applicable trust services criteria and stating the related controls in the description; and identifying the risks that threaten the achievement of the service organization's service commitments and system requirements.

Service Auditor's Responsibilities

Our responsibility is to express an opinion on the description and on the suitability of design of controls stated in the description based on our examination. Our examination was conducted in accordance with attestation standards established by the American Institute of Certified Public Accountants. Those standards require that we plan and perform our examination to obtain reasonable assurance about whether, in all material respects, the description is presented in accordance with the description criteria and the controls stated therein were suitably designed to provide reasonable assurance that the service organization's service commitments and system requirements were achieved based on the applicable trust services criteria. We believe that the evidence we obtained is sufficient and appropriate to provide a reasonable basis for our opinion.

(continued)

(continued)

An examination of the description of a service organization's system and the suitability of the design of controls involves the following:

- Obtaining an understanding of the system and the service organization's service commitments and system requirements.

- Assessing the risks that the description is not presented in accordance with the description criteria and that controls were not suitably designed.

- Performing procedures to obtain evidence about whether the description is presented in accordance with the description criteria.

- Performing procedures to obtain evidence about whether controls stated in the description were suitably designed to provide reasonable assurance that the service organization achieved its service commitments and system requirements based on the applicable trust services criteria.

- Evaluating the overall presentation of the description.

Our examination also included performing such other procedures as we considered necessary in the circumstances.

Inherent Limitations

The description is prepared to meet the common needs of a broad range of report users and may not, therefore, include every aspect of the system that individual users may consider important to meet their informational needs.

There are inherent limitations in any system of internal control, including the possibility of human error and the circumvention of controls. The projection to the future of any conclusions about the suitability of the design of controls is subject to the risk that controls may become inadequate because of changes in conditions or that the degree of compliance with the policies or procedures may deteriorate.

Other Matter

We did not perform any procedures regarding the operating effectiveness of controls stated in the description and, accordingly, do not express an opinion thereon.

Opinion

In our opinion, in all material respects,

a. The description presents XYZ's [*name or type*] system that was designed and implemented as of [*date*], in accordance with the description criteria.

b. The controls stated in the description were suitably designed as of [*date*], to provide reasonable assurance that XYZ's service commitments and system requirements would be achieved based on the applicable trust services criteria, if its controls operated effectively as of that date.

(continued)

(continued)

Restricted Use

This report is intended solely for the information and use of XYZ, user entities of XYZ's [*type or name*] system as of [*date*], business partners of XYZ subject to risks arising from interactions with the [*type or name*] system, practitioners providing services to such user entities and business partners, prospective user entities and business partners, and regulators who have sufficient knowledge and understanding of the following:

- The nature of the service provided by the service organization

- How the service organization's system interacts with user entities, business partners, subservice organizations, and other parties

- Internal control and its limitations

- User entity responsibilities and how they may affect the user entity's ability to effectively use the service organization's services

- The applicable trust services criteria

- The risks that may threaten the achievement of the service organization's service commitments and system requirements and how controls address those risks

This report is not intended to be, and should not be, used by anyone other than these specified parties.

[*Service auditor's signature*]
[*Service auditor's city and state*]
[*Date of the service auditor's report*]

5.1.4 Sample Report: Service Auditor's Report for a SOC 2® Type 2 Engagement

Independent Service Auditor's Report

To: XYZ Service Organization

Scope

We have examined XYZ Service Organization's (XYZ's) accompanying description of its [*type or name*] system titled [*insert title of management's description*] throughout the period [*date*] to [*date*] (description) based on the criteria for a description of a service organization's system in DC section 200, *2018 Description Criteria for a Description of a Service Organization's System in a SOC 2® Report* (AICPA, *Description Criteria*) (description criteria) and the suitability of the design and operating effectiveness of controls stated in the description throughout the period [*date*] to [*date*] to provide reasonable assurance that XYZ's service commitments and system requirements were achieved based on the trust services criteria relevant to security, availability, processing integrity, confidentiality, and privacy (applicable trust services criteria) set forth in TSP section 100, *2017 Trust Services Criteria for Security, Availability, Processing Integrity, Confidentiality, and Privacy* (AICPA, *Trust Services Criteria*).

Service Organization's Responsibilities

XYZ is responsible for its service commitments and system requirements and for designing, implementing, and operating effective controls within the system to provide reasonable assurance that XYZ's service commitments and system requirements were achieved. XYZ has provided the accompanying assertion titled [*insert the title of the attached management assertion*] (assertion), about the description and the suitability of design and operating effectiveness of controls stated therein. XYZ is also responsible for preparing the description and assertion, including the completeness, accuracy, and method of presentation of the description and assertion; providing the services covered by the description; selecting the applicable trust services criteria and stating the related controls in the description; and identifying the risks that threaten the achievement of the service organization's service commitments and system requirements.

Service Auditor's Responsibilities

Our responsibility is to express an opinion on the description and on the suitability of design and operating effectiveness of controls stated in the description based on our examination. Our examination was conducted in accordance with attestation standards established by the American Institute of Certified Public Accountants. Those standards require that we plan and perform our examination to obtain reasonable assurance about whether, in all material respects, the description is presented in accordance with the description criteria and the controls stated therein were suitably designed and operated effectively to provide reasonable assurance that the service organization's service commitments and system requirements were achieved based on the applicable trust services criteria. We believe that the evidence we obtained is sufficient and appropriate to provide a reasonable basis for our opinion.

(continued)

(continued)

An examination of the description of a service organization's system and the suitability of the design and operating effectiveness of controls involves the following:

- Obtaining an understanding of the system and the service organization's service commitments and system requirements

- Assessing the risks that the description is not presented in accordance with the description criteria and that controls were not suitably designed or did not operate effectively

- Performing procedures to obtain evidence about whether the description is presented in accordance with the description criteria

- Performing procedures to obtain evidence about whether controls stated in the description were suitably designed to provide reasonable assurance that the service organization achieved its service commitments and system requirements based on the applicable trust services criteria

- Testing the operating effectiveness of controls stated in the description to provide reasonable assurance that the service organization achieved its service commitments and system requirements based on the applicable trust services criteria

- Evaluating the overall presentation of the description

Our examination also included performing such other procedures as we considered necessary in the circumstances.

Inherent Limitations

The description is prepared to meet the common needs of a broad range of report users and may not, therefore, include every aspect of the system that individual users may consider important to meet their informational needs.

There are inherent limitations in the effectiveness of any system of internal control, including the possibility of human error and the circumvention of controls.

Because of their nature, controls may not always operate effectively to provide reasonable assurance that the service organization's service commitments and system requirements are achieved based on the applicable trust services criteria. Also, the projection to the future of any conclusions about the suitability of the design and operating effectiveness of controls is subject to the risk that controls may become inadequate because of changes in conditions or that the degree of compliance with the policies or procedures may deteriorate.

Description of Tests of Controls

The specific controls we tested, and the nature, timing, and results of those tests are listed in section XX.

(continued)

(continued)

Opinion

In our opinion, in all material respects,

a. The description presents XYZ's [*name or type*] system that was designed and implemented throughout the period [*date*] to [*date*] in accordance with the description criteria.

b. The controls stated in the description were suitably designed throughout the period [*date*] to [*date*] to provide reasonable assurance that XYZ's service commitments and system requirements would be achieved based on the applicable trust services criteria if its controls operated effectively throughout that period.

c. The controls stated in the description operated effectively throughout the period [*date*] to [*date*] to provide reasonable assurance that XYZ's service commitments and system requirements were achieved based on the applicable trust services criteria.

Restricted Use

This report, including the description of tests of controls and results thereof in section XX, is intended solely for the information and use of XYZ, user entities of XYZ's [*type or name*] system during some or all of the period [*date*] to [*date*], business partners of XYZ subject to risks arising from interactions with the [*type or name*] system, practitioners providing services to such user entities and business partners, prospective user entities and business partners, and regulators who have sufficient knowledge and understanding of the following:

- The nature of the service provided by the service organization

- How the service organization's system interacts with user entities, business partners, subservice organizations, and other parties

- Internal control and its limitations

- User entity responsibilities and how they may affect the user entity's ability to effectively use the service organization's services

- The applicable trust services criteria

- The risks that may threaten the achievement of the service organization's service commitments and system requirements and how controls address those risks

This report is not intended to be, and should not be, used by anyone other than these specified parties.

[*Service auditor's signature*]
[*Service auditor's city and state*]
[*Date of the service auditor's report*]

1 Overview of the Carve-out and Inclusive Methods

When conducting a SOC engagement, the service auditor may need to consider outsourced functions that are performed for the service organization by other organizations. For SOC 1® engagements, a vendor used by a service organization is considered a subservice organization if:

- The services provided by the vendor are likely relevant to user entities' internal control over financial reporting.

- Controls implemented at the subservice organization are necessary to achieve the control objectives stated in management's description of the service organization's system. These controls are referred to as complementary subservice organization controls (CSOCs).

For SOC 2® and SOC 3® engagements, a vendor used by a service organization is considered a subservice organization only if:

- The services provided by the vendor are relevant to report users' understanding of the service organization's system as it relates to the applicable trust services criteria.

- Controls at the subservice organization are necessary, in combination with the service organization's controls, to provide reasonable assurance that the service commitments and system requirements are achieved. These controls are referred to as CSOCs.

A subservice organization may be a separate entity that is external to the service organization or may be a related entity, such as a subsidiary of the parent company that owns the service organization. Service organization management is responsible for determining whether it uses a subservice organization.

If the service organization uses a subservice organization, management is responsible for determining whether to carve out or include the subservice organization's controls within the scope of the engagement. The two methods are defined as follows:

- **Carve-out Method:** Method of addressing the services provided by a subservice organization in which the CSOCs of the subservice organization are excluded from the description of the service organization's system and from the scope of the engagement.

   This method identifies:

   1. The nature of the services performed by the subservice organization.

   2. The types of controls expected to be performed at the subservice organization that are necessary, in combination with controls at the service organization, to provide reasonable assurance that the control objectives stated in management's description of the service organization's system (SOC 1®) or the service organization's service commitments and system requirements (SOC 2®) were achieved. These may include logical access controls, controls relevant to the completeness and accuracy of processing transactions, or controls relevant to accurate and complete reporting.

   3. The controls at the service organization used to monitor the effectiveness of the subservice organization's controls.

- **Inclusive Method:** Method of addressing the services provided by a subservice organization in which the description of the service organization's system includes a description of:

    1. The nature of the services provided by the subservice organization.

    2. The components of the subservice organization's system used to provide services to the service organization, including the subservice organization's controls that are necessary, in combination with controls at the service organization, to provide reasonable assurance that the control objectives stated in management's description of the service organization's system (SOC 1®) or the service organization's service commitments and system requirements (SOC 2®) were achieved.

When a service organization uses multiple subservice organizations, it may prepare its description using the carve-out method for one or more subservice organizations and the inclusive method for others.

An inclusive report generally provides more information for report users and is most useful in the following circumstances:

- The services provided by the subservice organization are extensive.

- A Type 1 or Type 2 report that meets the needs of report users is not available from the subservice organization.

- Information about the subservice organization is not readily available from other sources.

Management may determine that the carve-out method is most practical in the following circumstances:

- The challenges entailed in implementing the inclusive method are sufficiently onerous, and it is not practical to use the inclusive method.

- The service auditor is not independent of the subservice organization. (When the inclusive method is used, the SOC 2® engagement covers the service organization and the subservice organization, and the service auditor must be independent of both entities.)

- A Type 1 or Type 2 service auditor's report on the subservice organization, meeting user needs, is available.

- The service organization is unable to obtain contractual or other commitment from the subservice organization regarding its willingness to be included in the SOC 2® engagement.

The subservice organization's services and controls can have a pervasive effect on the service organization's system. In these situations, management and the service auditor would consider whether the use of the carve-out method may result in a description of the service organization's system that is so limited that it is unlikely to be useful to the intended users of the report.

When making this determination, consideration of the following factors should be considered:

- The significance of the portion of the system functions performed by the subservice organization.

- The complexity of the services and the types of controls that would be expected to be implemented by the subservice organization.

- The extent to which the achievement of the service organization's service commitments and system requirements based on the applicable trust services criteria depends on controls at the subservice organization.

- The number of applicable trust services criteria that would not be met if the types of controls expected to be implemented at the subservice organization were not implemented.

- The ability of the intended users of the report to obtain sufficient appropriate evidence about the design and, in a Type 2 engagement, the operating effectiveness of controls at the subservice organization (e.g., the availability of a SOC report for the subservice organization).

When the subservice organization's services and controls have a pervasive effect on the service organization's system, management would not be able to use the carve-out method.

1.1   Impact of the Carve-out and Inclusive Methods in a SOC Report

When a service organization uses a subservice organization, the service auditor's report is required to identify any services performed by the subservice organization and whether the carve-out method or inclusive method was used in relation to them.

If the carve-out method was used, the service auditor's report should include a statement indicating:

- Management's description of the service organization's system excludes the control objectives and related controls at relevant subservice organizations.

- Certain control objectives specified by the service organization can be achieved only if complementary subservice organization controls assumed in the design of the service organization's controls are suitably designed and operating effectively.

- The service auditor's procedures do not extend to such complementary subservice organization controls.

If the inclusive method was used, the service auditor's report should include a statement that management's description of the service organization's system includes the subservice organization's specified control objectives and related controls, and that the service auditor's procedures included procedures related to the subservice organization.

1.1.1   Complementary User Entity Controls (CUECs)

For SOC 1® and SOC 2® engagements, complementary user entity controls (CUECs) are controls that are necessary to be implemented by the user entity, in combination with the service organization's controls, to provide reasonable assurance that the control objectives stated in management's description of the service organization's system (SOC 1®) or the service organization's service commitments and system requirements (SOC 2®) were achieved. When CUECs are identified, management of the service organization is required to ensure that the system description contains certain disclosures about those controls, including a statement that user entities are responsible for implementing those CUECs.

In some instances, a service organization's controls cannot provide reasonable assurance that its service commitments and system requirements were achieved without the user entity performing certain activities in a defined manner.

In these cases, the service organization expects the user entity to implement necessary controls and to perform them completely and accurately in a timely manner. Management of the service organization identifies such CUECs in their system description.

Common examples of CUECs include:

- Security monitoring
- Managed service provider (MSP) environment changes
- Encrypted financial data
- Physical access controls
- Authorization policies

A service organization's controls are usually able to provide reasonable assurance that the service organization's service commitments or system requirements were achieved without the implementation of CUECs because the service organization restricts its service commitments and system requirements to those matters that are its responsibility and that it can reasonably perform.

Example 1   CUEC

Encrypted Financial Data: A service organization has a business relationship with a user entity that operates as a bank, which sends large amounts of data to the service organization. A CUEC within the service organization's report might say that user entities must send data in an encrypted manner using encryption or request that the service organization provide a secure transmission method.

For SOC 1® reports, any relevant CUECs that ensure control objectives are met should be described in the system description. It is recommended that a statement be made, if applicable, that a service organization's controls could only be achieved if CUECs are designed and operating effectively.

For SOC 2® reports, a service organization's system descriptions should also include relevant CUECs and a statement that user entities are responsible for those controls. The report should also state that the engagement did not include an evaluation of whether the CUECs were evaluated for design suitability or operating effectiveness.

SOC 2® reports should also include language about how CUECs interact with the service organization's controls. In some cases, separate SOC 2® reports may exist for subservice organizations that outline relevant CUECs and potentially fall within the scope of the service entity's controls.

Pass Key

Key Differences Between CSOC and CUEC

CSOCs are controls that a subservice organization must execute in order for a service organization's controls to function effectively, whereas CUECs are controls a user entity must employ for the service organization's controls to function. In both scenarios, the service organization relies on other entities (vendor or client) for their own controls to work properly.

1.1.2   Impact of Complementary User Entity Controls (CUECs) and Complementary Subservice Organization Controls (CSOCs) on the SOC report

If the application of complementary user entity controls or complementary subservice organization controls (or both) are considered necessary to achieve the related control objectives stated in management's description of the service organization's system (SOC 1®) or the service organization's service commitments and system requirements (SOC 2®), the auditor's report must include a statement to that effect in the opinion section of the report.

1.1.3 Sample Report: SOC 1® Type 2 Report (Service Organization Uses Carve-out Method for Subservice Organization, Service Organization Requires Complementary User Entity Controls and Complementary Subservice Organization Controls)

To: XYZ Service Organization

Scope

We have examined XYZ Service Organization's description of its [*type or name of*] system titled "XYZ Service Organization's Description of Its [*type or name of*] System" for processing user entities' transactions [*or identification of the function performed by the system*] throughout the period [*date*] to [*date*] (description) and the suitability of the design and operating effectiveness of the controls included in the description to achieve the related control objectives stated in the description, based on the criteria identified in "XYZ Service Organization's Assertion" (assertion). The controls and control objectives included in the description are those that management of XYZ Service Organization believes are likely to be relevant to user entities' internal control over financial reporting, and the description does not include those aspects of the [*type or name of*] system that are not likely to be relevant to user entities' internal control over financial reporting.

Example Service Organization uses Computer Subservice Organization, a subservice organization, to provide hosting services. The description includes only the control objectives and related controls of Example Service Organization and excludes the control objectives and related controls of the subservice organization. The description also indicates that certain control objectives specified by Example Service Organization can be achieved only if complementary subservice organization controls assumed in the design of Example Service Organization's controls are suitably designed and operating effectively, along with the related controls at Example Service Organization. Our examination did not extend to controls of the subservice organization, and we have not evaluated the suitability of the design nor operating effectiveness of such complementary subservice organization controls.

The description indicates that certain control objectives specified in the description can be achieved only if complementary user entity controls assumed in the design of Example Service Organization's controls are suitably designed and operating effectively, along with related controls at the service organization. Our examination did not extend to such complementary user entity controls and we have not evaluated the suitability of the design or operating effectiveness of such complementary user entity controls.

(continued)

(continued)

Service Organization's Responsibilities

Same as standard SOC 1® report.

Service Auditor's Responsibilities

Same as standard SOC 1® report.

Inherent Limitations

Same as standard SOC 1® report.

Description of Tests of Controls

Same as standard SOC 1® report.

Opinion

In our opinion, in all material respects, based on the criteria described in XYZ Service Organization's assertion:

a. The description fairly presents the [type or name of] system that was designed and implemented throughout the period [*date*] to [*date*].

b. The controls related to the control objectives stated in the description were suitably designed to provide reasonable assurance that the control objectives would be achieved if the controls operated effectively throughout the period [*date*] to [*date*], **and the subservice organization and user entities applied the complementary controls assumed in the design of Example Service Organization's controls throughout the period January 1, 201X, to December 31, 201X.**

c. The controls operated effectively to provide reasonable assurance that the control objectives stated in the description were achieved throughout the period [*date*] to [*date*], **if complementary subservice organization and user entity controls assumed in the design of Example Service Organization's controls operated effectively throughout the period January 1, 201X, to December 31, 201X.**

Restricted Use

Same as standard SOC 1® report.

[*Service auditor's signature*]
[*Service auditor's city and state*]
[*Date of the service auditor's report*]

1.1.4 Sample Report: SOC 1® Type 2 Report (Using the Inclusive Method, Complementary User Entity Controls Are Required)

To: XYZ Service Organization

Scope

We have examined XYZ Service Organization's description of its [*type or name of*] system **and ABC Subservice Organization's description of its application maintenance and support services, both of which are included in** titled "XYZ Service Organization's Description of Its [*type or name of*] System" for processing user entities' transactions [*or identification of the function performed by the system*] throughout the period [*date*] to [*date*] (description) and the suitability of the design and operating effectiveness of **XYZ Service Organization's and ABC Subservice Organization's** controls included in the description to achieve the related control objectives stated in the description, based on the criteria identified in "XYZ Service Organization's Assertion" **and "ABC Subservice Organization's Assertion"** (assertion). **ABC Subservice Organization is a subservice organization that provides application maintenance and support services to XYZ Service Organization. XYZ Service Organization's description includes a description of ABC Subservice Organization's application maintenance and support services used by XYZ Service Organization to process transactions for user entities, including controls relevant to the control objectives stated in the description.** The controls and control objectives included in the description are those that management of XYZ Service Organization **and management of ABC Subservice Organization** believe are likely to be relevant to user entities' internal control over financial reporting, and the description does not include those aspects of the [*type or name of*] system that are not likely to be relevant to user entities' internal control over financial reporting.

The description indicates that certain control objectives specified in the description can be achieved only if complementary user entity controls assumed in the design of XYZ Service Organization's controls are suitably designed and operating effectively, along with related controls at the service organization and the subservice organization. Our examination did not extend to such complementary user entity controls and we have not evaluated the suitability of the design or operating effectiveness of such complementary user entity controls.

(continued)

(continued)

Service Organization's Responsibilities

In [*section number where the assertion is presented*], XYZ Service Organization *and ABC Subservice Organization* has **have provided** an **their** assertions about the fairness of the presentation of the description and suitability of the design and operating effectiveness of the controls to achieve the related control objectives stated in the description. XYZ Service Organization **and ABC Subservice Organization** is **are** responsible for preparing the description and **their** assertions, including the completeness, accuracy, and method of presentation of the description and assertion; providing the services covered by the description; specifying the control objectives and stating them in the description; identifying the risks that threaten the achievement of the control objectives; selecting the criteria stated in the assertion; and designing, implementing, and documenting controls that are suitably designed and operating effectively to achieve the related control objectives stated in the description.

Service Auditor's Responsibilities

Our responsibility is to express an opinion on the fairness of the presentation of the description and on the suitability of the design and operating effectiveness of the controls to achieve the related control objectives stated in the description, based on our examination.

Our examination was conducted in accordance with attestation standards established by the American Institute of Certified Public Accountants. Those standards require that we plan and perform the examination to obtain reasonable assurance about whether, in all material respects, based on the criteria in management's assertion, the description is fairly presented, and the controls were suitably designed and operating effectively to achieve the related control objectives stated in the description throughout the period [*date*] to [*date*]. We believe that the evidence we obtained is sufficient and appropriate to provide a reasonable basis for our opinion.

An examination of a description of a service organization's system and the suitability of the design and operating effectiveness of controls involves:

- Performing procedures to obtain evidence about the fairness of the presentation of the description and the suitability of the design and operating effectiveness of the controls to achieve the related control objectives stated in the description, based on the criteria in management's assertion.

- Assessing the risks that the description is not fairly presented and that the controls were not suitably designed or operating effectively to achieve the related control objectives stated in the description.

- Testing the operating effectiveness of those controls that management considers necessary to provide reasonable assurance that the related control objectives stated in the description were achieved.

(continued)

(continued)

- Evaluating the overall presentation of the description, suitability of the control objectives stated in the description, and suitability of the criteria specified by the service organization *and subservice organization* in *their* its assertions.

Inherent Limitations

The description is prepared to meet the common needs of a broad range of user entities and their auditors who audit and report on user entities' financial statements and may not, therefore, include every aspect of the system that each individual user entity may consider important in its own particular environment. Because of their nature, controls at a service organization *or subservice organization* may not prevent, or detect and correct, all misstatements in processing or reporting transactions [*or identification of the function performed by the system*]. Also, the projection to the future of any evaluation of the fairness of the presentation of the description, or conclusions about the suitability of the design or operating effectiveness of the controls to achieve the related control objectives, is subject to the risk that controls at a service organization *or subservice organization* may become ineffective.

Description of Tests of Controls

Same as standard SOC 1® report.

Opinion

In our opinion, in all material respects, based on the criteria described in XYZ Service Organization's assertion *and ABC Subservice Organization's assertion:*

a. The description fairly presents the [*type or name of*] system *and ABC Subservice Organization's application maintenance and support services* that was *were* designed and implemented throughout the period [*date*] to [*date*].

b. The controls *of XYZ Service Organization and ABC Subservice Organization* related to the control objectives stated in the description were suitably designed to provide reasonable assurance that the control objectives would be achieved if the controls operated effectively throughout the period [*date*] to [*date*], *and user entities applied the complementary user entity controls assumed in the design of XYZ Service Organization's controls throughout the period January 1, 201X, to December 31, 201X.*

c. The controls *of XYZ Service Organization and ABC Subservice Organization* operated effectively to provide reasonable assurance that the control objectives stated in the description were achieved throughout the period [*date*] to [*date*] *if complementary user entity controls assumed in the design of XYZ Service Organization's controls operated effectively throughout the period January 1, 201X, to December 31, 201X.*

Restricted Use

Same as standard SOC 1® report.

[*Service auditor's signature*]
[*Service auditor's city and state*]
[*Date of the service auditor's report*]

1.1.5 Sample Report: Service Auditor's SOC 2® Report for a Type 2 Engagement (Carved-out Controls of a Subservice Organization and Complementary Subservice Organization and Complementary User Entity Controls)

Independent Service Auditor's Report

To: XYZ Service Organization

Scope

We have examined XYZ Service Organization's (XYZ's) accompanying description of its [*type or name*] system titled [*insert title of management's description*] throughout the period [*date*] to [*date*] (description) based on the criteria for a description of a service organization's system in DC section 200, *2018 Description Criteria for a Description of a Service Organization's System in a SOC 2® Report* (AICPA, *Description Criteria*) (description criteria) and the suitability of the design and operating effectiveness of controls stated in the description throughout the period [*date*] to [*date*] to provide reasonable assurance that XYZ's service commitments and system requirements were achieved based on the trust services criteria relevant to security, availability, processing integrity, confidentiality, and privacy (applicable trust services criteria) set forth in TSP section 100, *2017 Trust Services Criteria for Security, Availability, Processing Integrity, Confidentiality, and Privacy* (AICPA, *Trust Services Criteria*).

XYZ uses a subservice organization to provide application maintenance and support services. The description indicates that complementary subservice organization controls that are suitably designed and operating effectively are necessary, along with controls at XYZ, to achieve XYZ's service commitments and system requirements based on the applicable trust services criteria. The description presents XYZ's controls, the applicable trust services criteria, and the types of complementary subservice organization controls assumed in the design of XYZ's controls. The description does not disclose the actual controls at the subservice organization. Our examination did not include the services provided by the subservice organization, and we have not evaluated the suitability of the design or operating effectiveness of such complementary subservice organization controls.

The description indicates that complementary user entity controls that are suitably designed and operating effectively are necessary, along with controls at XYZ, to achieve XYZ's service commitments and system requirements based on the applicable trust services criteria. The description presents XYZ's controls, the applicable trust services criteria, and the complementary user entity controls assumed in the design of XYZ's controls. Our examination did not include such complementary user entity controls and we have not evaluated the suitability of the design or operating effectiveness of such controls.

Service Organization's Responsibilities

Same as standard SOC 2® report.

(continued)

(continued)

Service Auditor's Responsibilities

Same as standard SOC 2® report.

Inherent Limitations

Same as standard SOC 2® report.

Description of Tests of Controls

Same as standard SOC 2® report.

Opinion

In our opinion, in all material respects:

a. The description presents XYZ's [*name or type*] system that was designed and implemented throughout the period [*date*] to [*date*] in accordance with the description criteria.

b. The controls stated in the description were suitably designed throughout the period [*date*] to [*date*] to provide reasonable assurance that XYZ's service commitments and system requirements would be achieved based on the applicable trust services criteria, if its controls operated effectively throughout that period ***and if the subservice organization and user entities applied the complementary controls assumed in the design of XYZ's controls throughout that period.***

c. The controls stated in the description operated effectively throughout the period [*date*] to [*date*] to provide reasonable assurance that XYZ's service commitments and system requirements were achieved based on the applicable trust services criteria, ***if complementary subservice organization controls and complementary user entity controls assumed in the design of XYZ's controls operated effectively throughout that period.***

Restricted Use

This report, including the description of tests of controls and results thereof in section XX, is intended solely for the information and use of XYZ, user entities of XYZ's [*type or name*] system during some or all of the period [*date*] to [*date*], business partners of XYZ subject to risks arising from interactions with the [*type or name*] system, practitioners providing services to such user entities and business partners, prospective user entities and business partners, and regulators who have sufficient knowledge and understanding of the following:

- The nature of the service provided by the service organization
- How the service organization's system interacts with user entities, business partners, subservice organizations, and other parties
- Internal control and its limitations

(continued)

(continued)

- ◼ ***Complementary user entity controls and complementary subservice organization controls and how those controls interact with the controls at the service organization to achieve the service organization's service commitments and system requirements***

- ◼ User entity responsibilities and how they may affect the user entity's ability to effectively use the service organization's services

- ◼ The applicable trust services criteria

- ◼ The risks that may threaten the achievement of the service organization's service commitments and system requirements and how controls address those risks

This report is not intended to be, and should not be, used by anyone other than these specified parties.

[Service auditor's signature]
[Service auditor's city and state]
[Date of the service auditor's report]

1.1.6 Sample Report: Service Auditor's SOC 2® Report for a Type 2 Engagement (Subservice Organization Presented Using the Inclusive Method and Complementary User Entity Controls)

Independent Service Auditor's Report

To: XYZ Service Organization

Scope

We have examined XYZ Service Organization's (XYZ's) accompanying description of its [*type or name*] system, ***including application maintenance and support services provided by and controls operated by ABC Subservice Organization (ABC),*** titled [*insert title of management's description*] throughout the period [*date*] to [*date*] (description) based on the criteria for a description of a service organization's system in DC section 200, *2018 Description Criteria for a Description of a Service Organization's System in a SOC 2® Report* (AICPA, *Description Criteria*) (description criteria) and the suitability of the design and operating effectiveness of controls, ***including the controls designed by XYZ and operated by ABC,*** stated in the description throughout the period [*date*] to [*date*] to provide reasonable assurance that XYZ's service commitments and system requirements were achieved based on the trust services criteria relevant to security, availability, processing integrity, confidentiality, and privacy (applicable trust services criteria) set forth in TSP section 100, *2017 Trust Services Criteria for Security, Availability, Processing Integrity, Confidentiality, and Privacy* (AICPA, *Trust Services Criteria*).

(continued)

(continued)

ABC is an independent subservice organization providing application maintenance and support services to XYZ. The description includes those elements of the application maintenance and support services provided to XYZ and the controls designed by XYZ and operated by ABC that are necessary for XYZ to achieve its service commitments and system requirements based on the applicable trust services criteria.

The description indicates that complementary user entity controls that are suitably designed and operating effectively are necessary, along with controls at XYZ, to achieve XYZ's service commitments and system requirements based on the applicable trust services criteria. The description presents XYZ's controls, the applicable trust services criteria, and the complementary user entity controls assumed in the design of XYZ's controls. Our examination did not include such complementary user entity controls, and we have not evaluated the suitability of the design or operating effectiveness of such controls.

Service Organization's Responsibilities

Same as standard SOC 2® report.

Subservice Organization's Responsibilities

ABC has provided the accompanying assertion titled "Assertion of ABC Subservice Organization Management," (ABC assertion) about the description and the controls stated therein. ABC is responsible for preparing the portion of the description related to the application maintenance and support services provided to XYZ and the ABC assertion, including the completeness, accuracy, and method of presentation of the description and assertion; providing the services covered by the description; and implementing, operating, and documenting controls designed by XYZ, which enable XYZ to achieve its service commitments and system requirements.

Service Auditor's Responsibilities

Same as standard SOC 2® report.

Inherent Limitations

Same as standard SOC 2® report.

Description of Tests of Controls

Same as standard SOC 2® report.

Opinion

In our opinion, in all material respects:

a. The description presents XYZ's [*name or type*] system that was designed and implemented throughout the period [*date*] to [*date*] in accordance with the description criteria.

(continued)

(continued)

b. The controls stated in the description were suitably designed throughout the period [*date*] to [*date*] to provide reasonable assurance that XYZ's service commitments and system requirements would be achieved based on the applicable trust services criteria, if its controls operated effectively throughout that period, ***and if the user entities applied the complementary controls assumed in the design of XYZ's controls throughout that period.***

c. The controls stated in the description operated effectively throughout the period [*date*] to [*date*] to provide reasonable assurance that XYZ's service commitments and system requirements were achieved based on the applicable trust services criteria, ***if complimentary user entity controls assumed in the design of XYZ's controls operated effectively throughout that period.***

Restricted Use

This report, including the description of tests of controls and results thereof in section XX, is intended solely for the information and use of XYZ, user entities of XYZ's [*type or name*] system during some or all of the period [*date*] to [*date*], business partners of XYZ subject to risks arising from interactions with the [*type or name*] system, practitioners providing services to such user entities and business partners, prospective user entities and business partners, and regulators who have sufficient knowledge and understanding of the following:

■ The nature of the service provided by the service organization

■ How the service organization's system interacts with user entities, business partners, subservice organizations, and other parties

■ Internal control and its limitations

■ ***Complementary user entity controls and complementary subservice organization controls and how those controls interact with the controls at the service organization to achieve the service organization's service commitments and system requirements***

■ User entity responsibilities and how they may affect the user entity's ability to effectively use the service organization's services

■ The applicable trust services criteria

■ The risks that may threaten the achievement of the service organization's service commitments and system requirements and how controls address those risks

This report is not intended to be, and should not be, used by anyone other than these specified parties.

[*Service auditor's signature*]
[*Service auditor's city and state*]
[*Date of the service auditor's report*]

2   Impact of Modified Opinions on the SOC Report

The service auditor's report will need to be modified accordingly when a modified opinion is necessary based on the professional judgment of the service auditor.

2.1   Qualified Opinion

The service auditor expresses a qualified opinion in the following circumstances:

▦ SOC 1® engagement:

- If the misstatements in management's description of the service organization's system or deficiencies in the suitability of the design or operating effectiveness (Type 2) of the controls are limited to one or more, but not all, aspects of the description of the service organization's system or control objectives and do not affect the service auditor's opinion on other aspects of the description of the service organization's system or other control objectives.

▦ SOC 2® engagement:

- The service auditor concludes that description misstatements, either individually or in the aggregate, are material but not pervasive, or deficiencies in the design or operation (Type 2) of controls are material but not pervasive.

- The service auditor is unable to obtain sufficient appropriate evidence on which to base the opinion, and the service auditor has concluded that the possible effects on the subject matter of undetected description misstatements or deficiencies, if any, could be material but not pervasive to the subject matter.

2.1.1   Elements of Service Auditor's SOC 1® Report: Qualified Opinion

When the service auditor has determined that a qualified opinion is appropriate, the service auditor's SOC 1® report will include:

Qualified Opinion SOC 1® Report	
Title	Same as standard SOC 1® report.
Addressee	Same as standard SOC 1® report.
Scope	Same as standard SOC 1® report.
Service Organization's Responsibilities	Same as standard SOC 1® report.
Service Auditor's Responsibilities	Same as standard SOC 1® report.
Inherent Limitations	Same as standard SOC 1® report.
Description of Tests of Controls (Type 2 only)	Same as standard SOC 1® report.
Other Matter (Type 1 only)	Same as standard SOC 1® report.

Qualified Opinion	A separate paragraph, before the opinion paragraph, that provides a description of the matters giving rise to the modification.
	In addition, the service auditor's opinion paragraph should be amended as follows:
	In our opinion, *except for the matter referred to in the preceding paragraph,* in all material respects, based on the criteria described in [*service organization's*] assertion in section 2, ...
Restricted Use	Same as standard SOC 1® report.
Service Auditor's Signature	Same as standard SOC 1® report.
Service Auditor's City and State	Same as standard SOC 1® report.
Date of the Service Auditor's Report	Same as standard SOC 1® report.

2.1.2 Elements of Service Auditor's SOC 2® Report: Qualified Opinion Due to Material Misstatements

When material misstatements in the description or deficiencies in the design or operation of controls are identified, the service auditor generally expresses a qualified opinion if:

1. The identified misstatements in the description of the service organization's system are limited to one or more, but not all, aspects of the description.

2. The identified deficiencies in the suitability of the design or operating effectiveness (Type 2) of the controls result in the failure of the controls to provide reasonable assurance that one or more, but not all, of its service commitments and system requirements were achieved based on the applicable trust services criteria.

3. The identified misstatements and deficiencies do not otherwise affect the service auditor's opinion on other aspects of the description of the service organization's system or on whether controls were suitably designed or operated effectively (Type 2).

When the service auditor has determined that a qualified opinion is appropriate because of material misstatements or deficiencies, the service auditor's SOC 2® report will include:

Qualified Opinion Due to Material Misstatements SOC 2® Report	
Title	Same as standard SOC 2® report.
Addressee	Same as standard SOC 2® report.
Scope	Same as standard SOC 2® report.
Service Organization's Responsibilities	Same as standard SOC 2® report.
Service Auditor's Responsibilities	The service auditor's responsibility paragraph should be amended to state that the service auditor believes that the evidence the service auditor has obtained is sufficient and appropriate to provide a basis for the service auditor's qualified opinion.
Inherent Limitations	Same as standard SOC 2® report.
Description of Tests of Controls (Type 2 only)	Same as standard SOC 2® report.
Other Matter (Type 1 only)	Same as standard SOC 2® report.
Qualified Opinion	A separate paragraph, before the opinion paragraph, that provides a description of the matters giving rise to the modification.
	In addition, the service auditor's opinion paragraph should be amended as follows:
	In our opinion, *except for the effects of matters giving rise to the modification*, the description is presented in accordance with the description criteria and the controls were suitably designed and operating effectively (Type 2) to provide reasonable assurance that the service organization's service commitments and system requirements were achieved based on the applicable trust services criteria, in all material respects.
Restricted Use	Same as standard SOC 2® report.
Service Auditor's Signature	Same as standard SOC 2® report.
Service Auditor's City and State	Same as standard SOC 2® report.
Date of the Service Auditor's Report	Same as standard SOC 2® report.

2.1.3 Elements of Service Auditor's SOC 2® Report: Qualified Opinion Due to Scope Limitations

The service auditor should express a qualified opinion when unable to obtain sufficient appropriate evidence on which to base the opinion and the service auditor has concluded that the possible effects on the subject matter of undetected description misstatements or deficiencies, if any, could be material but not pervasive to the subject matter.

When the service auditor determines that a qualified opinion is appropriate because of scope limitations, the service auditor's SOC 2® report will include:

Qualified Opinion Due to Scope Limitations SOC 2® Report	
Title	Same as standard SOC 2® report.
Addressee	Same as standard SOC 2® report.
Scope	Same as standard SOC 2® report.
Service Organization's Responsibilities	Same as standard SOC 2® report.
Service Auditor's Responsibilities	The service auditor's responsibility paragraph should be amended to state that the service auditor believes that the evidence the service auditor has obtained is sufficient and appropriate to provide a basis for the service auditor's *qualified* opinion.
Inherent Limitations	Same as standard SOC 2® report.
Description of Tests of Controls (Type 2 only)	Same as standard SOC 2® report.
Other Matter (Type 1 only)	Same as standard SOC 2® report.
Qualified Opinion	A separate paragraph, before the opinion paragraph, that provides a clear explanation of the matters giving rise to the modification. In addition, the service auditor's opinion paragraph should be amended as follows: In our opinion, *except for the possible effects of the matters giving rise to the modification*, the description is presented in accordance with the description criteria and the controls were suitably designed and operating effectively (Type 2) to provide reasonable assurance that the service organization's service commitments and system requirements were achieved based on the applicable trust services criteria, in all material respects. If the service auditor also concludes there were material misstatements in the description or material deficiencies in the suitability of design or operating effectiveness of controls, the service auditor should include, in separate paragraphs of the report, a clear explanation of both: • the scope limitation; and • the matters that caused the description, suitability of design, or operating effectiveness of controls to be materially misstated.
Restricted Use	Same as standard SOC 2® report.
Service Auditor's Signature	Same as standard SOC 2® report.
Service Auditor's City and State	Same as standard SOC 2® report.
Date of the Service Auditor's Report	Same as standard SOC 2® report.

2.2 Adverse Opinion

A practitioner should issue an adverse opinion when he or she concludes that the description misstatements, either individually or in the aggregate, are material and pervasive, or deficiencies in the design or operation of controls are material and pervasive.

2.2.1 Elements of Service Auditor's SOC 1® Report: Adverse Opinion

The service auditor expresses an adverse opinion if the misstatements in management's description of the service organization's system or deficiencies in the suitability of the design or operating effectiveness of the controls are material and pervasive throughout the description or across all or most of the control objectives.

When the service auditor has determined that an adverse opinion is appropriate, the service auditor's SOC 1® report will include:

Adverse Opinion SOC 1® Report	
Title	Same as standard SOC 1® report.
Addressee	Same as standard SOC 1® report.
Scope	Same as standard SOC 1® report.
Service Organization's Responsibilities	Same as standard SOC 1® report.
Service Auditor's Responsibilities	Same as standard SOC 1® report.
Inherent Limitations	Same as standard SOC 1® report.
Description of Tests of Controls (Type 2 only)	Same as standard SOC 1® report.
Other Matter (Type 1 only)	Same as standard SOC 1® report.
Adverse Opinion	A separate paragraph, before the opinion paragraph, that provides a description of the matters giving rise to the modification. In addition, the service auditor's opinion paragraph should be amended as follows: In our opinion, **because of the matter referred to in the preceding paragraph**, in all material respects, based on the criteria described in [*name of service organization's*] assertion in section 2: • The description **does not** fairly present the [*type or name of system*] that was designed and implemented throughout the period. • The controls related to the control objectives stated in the description were **not** suitably designed to provide reasonable assurance that the control objectives would be achieved if the controls operated effectively throughout the period [*date*] to [*date*].

Adverse Opinion (continued)	• The controls tested, which were those necessary to provide reasonable assurance that the control objectives stated in the description were achieved, **did not** operate effectively throughout the period from [*date*] to [*date*].
Restricted Use	Same as standard SOC 1® report.
Service Auditor's Signature	Same as standard SOC 1® report.
Service Auditor's City and State	Same as standard SOC 1® report.
Date of the Service Auditor's Report	Same as standard SOC 1® report.

2.2.2 Elements of Service Auditor's SOC 2® Report: Adverse Opinion

The service auditor expresses an adverse opinion if the description misstatements in the description of the service organization's system or deficiencies or deviations in the suitability of the design or operating effectiveness of the controls are material and pervasive throughout the description or prevent the achievement of all or most of the service organization's service commitments and system requirements based on the applicable trust services criteria.

When the service auditor has determined that an adverse opinion is appropriate, the service auditor's SOC 2® report will include:

Adverse Opinion SOC 2® Report	
Title	Same as standard SOC 2® report.
Addressee	Same as standard SOC 2® report.
Scope	Same as standard SOC 2® report.
Service Organization's Responsibilities	Same as standard SOC 2® report.
Service Auditor's Responsibilities	The service auditor's responsibility paragraph should be amended to state: We believe that the evidence we obtained is sufficient and appropriate to provide a reasonable basis for our **adverse** opinion.
Inherent Limitations	Same as standard SOC 2® report.
Description of Tests of Controls (Type 2 only)	Same as standard SOC 2® report.
Other Matter (Type 1 only)	Same as standard SOC 2® report.

Adverse Opinion	A separate paragraph, before the opinion paragraph, that provides a clear explanation of the matters giving rise to the modification.
	In addition, the service auditor's opinion paragraph should be amended as follows:
	In our opinion, **because of the significance of the matter(s) referred to in the preceding paragraph**, in all material respects:
	a. The description of the [*name or type*] system **does not** present the system that was designed and implemented throughout the period [*date*] to [*date*] in accordance with the description criteria.
	b. The controls stated in the description were **not** suitably designed throughout the period [*date*] to [*date*] to provide reasonable assurance that the service organization's service commitments and system requirements would be achieved based on the applicable trust services criteria.
	c. The controls stated in the description **did not** operate effectively throughout the period [*date*] to [*date*] to provide reasonable assurance that the service organization's service commitments and system requirements were achieved based on the applicable trust services criteria.
Restricted Use	Same as standard SOC 2® report.
Service Auditor's Signature	Same as standard SOC 2® report.
Service Auditor's City and State	Same as standard SOC 2® report.
Date of the Service Auditor's Report	Same as standard SOC 2® report.

2.3   Disclaimer of Opinion

A disclaimer of opinion should be issued when the service auditor is unable to obtain sufficient appropriate evidence on which to base the opinion, and the service auditor concludes that the possible effects on the subject matter of undetected misstatements could be both material and pervasive.

In these situations, the service auditor's opinion should be modified, and the service auditor's report should include a separate paragraph containing a clear description of the matters that give rise to the modification. In a disclaimer of opinion, that paragraph describes the items in question in which the examination did not comply with the attestation standards.

When disclaiming an opinion:

- The first sentence of the service auditor's report is revised to state, "We were engaged to examine."

- The standards under which the service auditor conducts an examination are identified in the first paragraph of the report rather than the second.

- The report omits statements:

  - Indicating what those standards require of the practitioner.

  - Indicating that the practitioner believes the evidence obtained is sufficient and appropriate to provide a reasonable basis for the service auditor's opinion.

  - Describing the nature of an examination engagement.

2.3.1 Sample Report Language When a Disclaimer of Opinion Is Issued

We were engaged to examine XYZ Company's description of its medical claims processing system titled "XYZ Company's Description of its Medical Claims Processing System" for processing medical claims throughout the period *[date]* to *[date]* (description) and the suitability of the design and operating effectiveness of the controls included in the description to achieve the related control objectives stated in the description, based on the criteria identified in "XYZ Service Organization's Assertion" (assertion).

XYZ Company's management is responsible for the fairness of the presentation of the description and the suitability of the design and operating effectiveness of the controls included in the description. Our responsibility is to express an opinion on the fairness of the presentation of the description and the suitability of the design and operating effectiveness of the controls included in the description, based on conducting the examination in accordance with attestation standards established by the American Institute of Certified Public Accountants.

Attestation standards established by the American Institute of Certified Public Accountants require that we request certain written representations from management, including a representation that all relevant matters are reflected in the measurement or evaluation of the fairness of the presentation of the description of the service organization's system and the suitability of design and operating effectiveness of controls. **We requested that management provide us with such a representation, but management refused to do so.**

Because of the limitation on the scope of our examination discussed in the preceding paragraph, the scope of our work was not sufficient to enable us to express, and we do not express, an opinion on whether XYZ Company's description of its medical claims processing system throughout the period *[date]* to *[date]* is fairly presented or on whether the controls included in the description were suitability designed and operating effectively to achieve the related control objectives stated in the description, based on the criteria identified in XYZ Company's assertion, in all material respects.

2.4   Report Paragraphs Describing Matters Giving Rise to Modification

When a service auditor concludes that a modified opinion is appropriate based on the evidence obtained during a SOC engagement, a separate paragraph should be added to the service auditor's report to explain the matter giving rise to the modification.

2.4.1   The Description Includes Controls That Have Not Been Implemented

The below language is an example of a separate paragraph that would be added when the description includes controls that have not been implemented:

> The accompanying description of the XYZ System states that Example Service Organization uses operator identification numbers and passwords to prevent unauthorized access to its system. Our testing determined that operator identification numbers and passwords are used in applications A and B, but are not used in applications C and D.

2.4.2   Controls That Are Not Suitably Designed

The below language is an example of a separate paragraph that would be added to the auditor's report preceding the opinion paragraph, when the auditor concludes the controls are not suitably designed:

> The accompanying description of ABC Service Organization's system states on page 8 that ABC Service Organization's system supervisor makes changes to the systems only if the changes are authorized, tested, and documented. The procedures, however, do not include a requirement for approval of the change before the change is placed into operation. As a result, controls were not suitably designed or operating effectively throughout the period [date] to [date] to provide reasonable assurance that the service organization's service commitments and system requirements were achieved based on trust services criterion CC8.1, The entity authorizes, designs, develops or acquires, configures, documents, tests, approves, and implements changes to infrastructure, data, software, and procedures to meet its objectives.

NOTES

1 Understanding Service Organization Management's Responsibilities

The service auditor, when auditing the service organization, is required to establish, prior to acceptance of the SOC engagement, an understanding with service organization management about its responsibilities and the responsibilities of the service auditor. The decisions a service organization's management makes prior to engaging the service auditor can affect the nature, extent, and timing of procedures the service auditor performs.

The service auditor should also establish communication with management of the service organization. The service auditor should determine the appropriate person(s) within the service organization's management or governance structure with whom to interact. This should include the service auditor's consideration of which person(s) has the appropriate responsibilities for, and knowledge of, the relevant matters.

1.1 SOC 1® Engagements

For SOC 1® engagements, management of the service organization is responsible for the following during the engagement:

- Defining the scope of the engagement, including:

  - Which services (including the classes of transactions processed), functions performed, business units, functional areas, or applications are likely to be relevant to user entities' internal control over financial reporting.

  - Management also considers whether the service organization has any contractual obligations to provide a Type 1 or Type 2 report to one or more of its user entities, including the frequency with which such a report is to be issued and the period that will be covered by the report.

  - In the case of a recurring or existing engagement, the prior report provides a useful starting point for defining the scope of the engagement.

- The report type (Type 1 or Type 2).

- Determining the as of date (Type 1) or specified period (Type 2) of the engagement.

- If services provided to a service organization by other entities are likely to be relevant to user entities' internal control over financial reporting, and if so, identifying these other entities as subservice organizations.

  Whether subservice organizations will be presented using the carve-out or inclusive method in the description of the service organization's system.

- Preparing a description of the system, including the completeness, accuracy, and method of presentation of the description.

- Having a reasonable basis for its assertion.

- Selecting the criteria to be used, stating them in the assertion, and determining that the criteria are appropriate for management's purposes.

- Specifying and stating the control objectives, whether any control objectives are specified by law, regulation, or another party, including the party specifying the control objectives.

- Identifying the risks that threaten the achievement of the stated control objectives and designing, implementing, and documenting controls that are suitably designed and operating effectively to provide reasonable assurance that stated control objectives will be met.

- Preparing a written assertion that accompanies management's description of the service organization's system and providing both to the user entities.

- Providing the service auditor with access to all relevant information (records, documentation, service-level agreements, internal audit, or other reports), additional information that the service auditor may request, and personnel to obtain relevant evidence.

- Providing the service auditor with written representations at the conclusion of the engagement.

- If the service auditor plans to use internal auditors to provide direct assistance, providing the service auditor with written acknowledgment that internal auditors providing direct assistance to the service auditor will be allowed to follow the service auditor's instructions and that the service organization will not intervene in the work the internal auditor performs for the service auditor.

- Disclosing to the service auditor:

  - Incidents of noncompliance with laws and regulations, fraud, or uncorrected misstatements that are clearly not trivial and that may affect one or more user entities and whether such incidents have been communicated appropriately to affected user entities.

  - Knowledge of any actual, suspected, or alleged intentional acts that could adversely affect the presentation of the description of the service organization's system, or the completeness or achievement of the control objectives stated in the description.

  - Any deficiencies in the design of controls of which management is aware.

  - All instances in which controls have not operated as described.

  - Any events subsequent to the period covered by the description of the service organization's system, up to the date of the service auditor's report, that could have a significant effect on management's assertion.

1.2 SOC 2® Engagements

For SOC 2® engagements, management of the service organization is responsible for the following prior to engaging the service auditor:

- Defining the scope of the engagement, including:

  - The services provided to user entities (which will establish the subject matter of the engagement).

  - The system used to provide services.

  - The report type (Type 1 or Type 2).

  - Identifying risks of business partners or services to the service organization related to the system.

- Determining the as of date (Type 1) or specified period (Type 2) of the engagement.

- If services are provided to the service organization by other entities, evaluating the effect of those services on the achievement of service commitments and system requirements, and concluding whether those entities are subservice organizations.

  Whether subservice organizations will be presented using the carve-out or inclusive method in the description of the service organization's system. If a subservice organization is to be presented using the inclusive method, obtaining agreement from subservice organization management to participate in the engagement.

- Selecting the trust services category or categories to be included in the scope of the engagement.

- Specifying the principal service commitments made to user entities and the necessary system requirements to operate the system.

- Specifying the principal system requirements related to commitments made to business partners.

- Identifying and analyzing risks that could prevent the service organization from achieving its service commitments and system requirements.

- Designing, implementing, operating, monitoring, and documenting controls that are suitably designed and operating effectively (Type 2), to provide reasonable assurance about the service organization's ability to achieve their service commitments and system requirements based on the applicable trust services criteria.

Management of the service organization is also responsible for the following during the SOC 2® engagement:

- Preparing a description of the system and its assertion, including the completeness, accuracy, and method of presentation of the description and assertion.

- Having a reasonable basis for its assertion.

- Identifying the risks that threaten the service organization's achievement of its service commitments and system requirements stated in the description.

- Providing a written assertion that accompanies management's description of the service organization's system and providing both to report users.

- Designing, implementing, and documenting controls that are suitably designed and operating effectively (Type 2), to provide reasonable assurance that the service commitments and system requirements will be achieved based on the applicable trust services criteria.

- Providing the service auditor with access to all relevant information (records, documentation, service-level agreements, internal audit, or other reports), additional information that the service auditor may request, and personnel to obtain relevant evidence.

- Providing the service auditor with written representations at the conclusion of the engagement.

- If the service auditor plans to use internal auditors to provide direct assistance, providing the service auditor with written acknowledgment that internal auditors providing direct assistance to the service auditor will be allowed to follow the service auditor's instructions and that the service organization will not intervene in the work the internal auditor performs for the service auditor.

- Disclosing to the service auditor:

  - Incidents of noncompliance with laws and regulations, fraud, or uncorrected misstatements that are clearly not trivial and that may affect one or more user entities and whether such incidents have been communicated appropriately to affected user entities.

  - Knowledge of any actual, suspected, or alleged intentional acts that could adversely affect the presentation of the description of the service organization's system, the suitability of design of its controls, or the operating effectiveness of controls (Type 2).

  - Any deficiencies in the design of controls of which management is aware.

  - All instances in which controls have not operated as described.

  - All identified system incidents that resulted in a significant impairment of the service organization's achievement of its service commitments and system requirements as of the date of the description (Type 1) or during the period of time covered by the description (Type 2).

  - Any events subsequent to the period covered by the description of the service organization's system, up to the date of the service auditor's report, that could have a significant effect on management's assertion.

1.3 SOC 3® Engagements

For SOC 3® engagements, the responsibilities of management of the service organization are substantially the same as those for a SOC 2® engagement, *except* that management does not prepare a system description. During acceptance and planning, management's responsibilities include:

- Defining the scope of the engagement, including:

  - The services provided to user entities (which will establish the subject matter of the engagement).

  - The system used to provide services.

  - The report type (Type 2).

  - Identifying risks of business partners or services to the service organization related to the system.

  - Determining the period to be covered by the engagement.

  - If services are provided to the service organization by other entities, evaluating the effect of those services on the achievement of service commitments and system requirements, and concluding whether those entities are subservice organizations.

    Whether subservice organizations will be presented using the carve-out or inclusive method in the description of the service organization's system. If a subservice organization is to be presented using the inclusive method, obtaining agreement from subservice organization management to participate in the engagement.

  - Selecting the trust services category or categories to be included in the scope of the engagement.

- Specifying the principal service commitments made to user entities and the necessary system requirements to operate the system.

- Identifying and analyzing risks that could prevent the service organization from achieving its service commitments and system requirements.

- Designing, implementing, monitoring, and documenting effective controls to provide reasonable assurance of achieving the service organization's service commitments and system requirements based on the applicable trust services criteria.

- Identifying subservice organizations and determining whether to present them under the inclusive or carve-out method.

  If using the carve-out method, identifying complementary subservice organization controls (CSOCs).

- Providing a written assertion that discloses:

  - The boundaries of the system.

  - The service organization's principal service commitments and system requirements.

2   Objectives and Planning Considerations for a Service Auditor

Planning a SOC engagement requires the service auditor to obtain an understanding of key areas and formulate assessments of risk relevant to the engagement. The planning requirements of a service auditor for SOC 1®, SOC 2®, and SOC 3® engagements are similar.

2.1   Objectives of the Service Auditor

The objectives of the service auditor are to:

- Obtain reasonable assurance about whether, in all material respects, based on suitable criteria:

  - Management's description of the service organization's system fairly presents the system that was designed and implemented throughout the specified period (Type 2) or as of a specified date (Type 1).

  - The controls related to the control objectives stated in management's description of the service organization's system were suitably designed throughout the specified period (Type 2) or as of a specified date (Type 1).

  - When included in the scope of the engagement, the controls operated effectively to provide reasonable assurance that the control objectives stated in management's description of the service organization's system were achieved throughout the specified period (Type 2 only).

- Report in accordance with the service auditor's findings.

2.2   Responsibilities of the Service Auditor

During planning of any SOC engagement, the service auditor is responsible for:

- Determining whether to accept or continue the engagement.

- Agreeing on engagement terms.

- Reaching an understanding with management regarding a written assertion.

During planning of a SOC 1® engagement, the service auditor is also responsible for:

- Assessing the risk of material misstatement.

- Obtaining an understanding of the service organization's system and assessing the suitability of the criteria used by management in preparing its system description.

During planning of SOC 2® and SOC 3® engagements, the service auditor is also responsible for:

- Establishing an overall strategy for the engagement.

  Sets the scope, timing, and direction of the engagement and guides the development of the engagement plan, including the consideration of materiality and the identification of the risks of material misstatement (SOC 2®).

- Performing risk assessment procedures.

  Includes understanding of the service organization's system and how the system controls were designed, implemented, and operated to provide reasonable assurance that the service organization's service commitments and system requirements are achieved based on the applicable trust services criteria (SOC 2®).

2.2.1 Agreeing to Engagement Terms

A SOC engagement is an example of an assertion-based examination engagement, and relevant engagement standards apply.

The service auditor and the service organization should agree upon the engagement terms, such as:

- The objectives and scope of the engagement.

- The responsibilities of the service auditor and the responsible party (likely management of the service organization), including the responsibility of management to provide a representation letter.

- The identification of the criteria used to measure, evaluate, or disclose information about the subject matter.

- Acknowledgement that the engagement will be conducted in accordance with attestation standards established by the AICPA and the inherent limitations of an engagement.

The service auditor should request that management provide a written assertion.

2.3 Independence Considerations

Independence is required in an engagement to report on controls at a service organization. The independence assessment process may address matters such as scope of services, fee arrangements, firm and individual financial relationships, firm business relationships, and alumni and familial relationships with the client and client personnel.

The service auditor is not required to be independent of each user entity.

2.3.1 Service Organization and Service Auditor

The service auditor needs to be independent with respect to the responsible party (or parties), as defined in those standards. The responsible party is most often the service organization.

2.3.2 Subservice Organization and Service Auditor

If the service organization uses a subservice organization, and management elects to use the inclusive method to present certain information about the subservice organization in its description of the service organization's system, subservice organization management is also a responsible party. As a result, the service auditor should also be independent of the subservice organization.

2.3.3   Service Auditor Lacks Independence

When the service auditor is not independent but is required by law or regulation to accept the engagement and report on the subject matter, the service auditor should disclaim an opinion and should specifically state that the service auditor is not independent. The service auditor is neither required to provide, nor precluded from providing, the reasons for the lack of independence, but should include all reasons if any are given.

2.4   Materiality Considerations

The services auditor is required to consider materiality during risk assessment and to determine the nature, extent, and timing of procedures necessary to obtain sufficient appropriate evidence to support an opinion in the SOC engagement. Materiality definitions and interpretations vary between SOC 1® and SOC 2® engagements but in both cases, the service auditor is required to reassess materiality if the auditor obtains new information that would have caused the auditor to assess the initial materiality differently.

2.4.1   Materiality in a SOC 1® Engagement

In a SOC 1® engagement, the service auditor's consideration of materiality should include the fair presentation of the description of the service organization's system. The concept of materiality in the context of the fair presentation of the description relates to the information being reported on, not the financial statements of user entities. Materiality relates to qualitative factors, such as whether significant aspects of the processing have been included in the description or if relevant information has been omitted or distorted.

Materiality with respect to the operating effectiveness of controls for a Type 2 report includes the consideration of quantitative and qualitative factors, such as:

- Quantitative: the tolerable and observed rate of deviations
- Qualitative: the nature and cause of deviations

Example 1   Materiality in a SOC 1® Engagement

The service organization is responsible for implementing general IT controls. The service organization's application controls cannot function without the underlying general IT controls; therefore, the general IT controls would be considered material to the description of the service organization's system and would be included in the service organization's description of its system.

2.4.2   Materiality in a SOC 2® Engagement

In the SOC 2® engagement, materiality can be described as the likelihood and magnitude of the risks that threaten the achievement of the service organization's service commitments and system requirements and whether the controls the service organization has designed, implemented, and operated were effective in mitigating those risks to an acceptable level based on the applicable trust services criteria.

- The service auditor should consider the nature of threats and the likelihood and magnitude of the risks arising from those threats to the achievement of the service organization's service commitments and system requirements based on the applicable trust services criteria.

- The service auditor's consideration of materiality is a matter of professional judgment and is affected by the service auditor's perception of the common information needs of the broad range of report users as a group.

- When considering materiality, the service auditor typically considers whether misstatements in the description or deficiencies in the suitability of design of controls, and the operating effectiveness of controls (Type 2), could reasonably be expected to influence the relevant decisions made by the broad range of report users.

- If the engagement has been designed to meet the informational needs of a specific subset of such SOC 2® report users, and the report is restricted to those specific users, the service auditor considers the possible effect of such misstatements on the decisions that may be made by that specific subset of report users.

2.4.3 Misstatements in a SOC Engagement

The following are common terms used when discussing misstatements related to the different subject matters in a SOC engagement:

- **Description Misstatement:** The term used when describing errors or omissions in the description of the service organization's system.

- **Deviation or Exception:** Identified misstatements resulting from the failure of a control to operate in a specific instance. A deviation could result in a deficiency.

- **Deficiency in the Design:** When a control necessary to meet control objectives is missing or improperly designed so that even if it operates as designed, control objectives would not be achieved.

- **Deficiency in the Operating Effectiveness:** When a properly designed control fails to operate as designed or when the person performing the control does not possess the competency necessary to perform the control effectively.

The service auditor accumulates misstatements related to each of the subject matters of the engagement. These include the description, the suitability of design of controls, and the operating effectiveness of controls (Type 2). Misstatements or deficiencies related to a specific subject matter in the service auditor's opinion could affect the other subject matters in the opinion.

Example 2	Misstatements in a SOC Engagement

Brown Corp., a service organization that provides server hosting for the user entity's emails, included the following controls in its description:

- Secured room with locks and a security system where email data is stored and maintained

- Backup power system for when power outages occur

- Daily file backups to external servers in another state

It was determined that the security system included in the description was never implemented by the service organization, which would compromise the operating effectiveness of the organization's controls to ensure that the email data is safely stored. This control that was not implemented may affect the relevance of design controls, as unauthorized personnel may have access to email data since the security system was not implemented.

---

3 Risk Assessment in a SOC Engagement

3.1 Understanding the System, System Requirements, and Service Commitments in a SOC 2® Engagement

In a SOC 2® engagement, a system is defined as the infrastructure, software, procedures, and data that are designed, implemented, and operated by people to achieve one or more of the organization's specific business objectives in accordance with management-specified requirements. The system components are comprised of the following categories:

■ **Infrastructure:** Individual physical or virtual resources, or a collection of resources, that support a service organization's environment. This may include physical structures or hardware such as buildings, servers, switches, file storage devices, surveillance equipment, mobile devices, and internally or externally connected networks.

■ **Software:** Applications and programs that support the operations of an IT system such as operating systems, middleware, database structures and retrieval mechanisms, external web-based applications, internally shared applications, and details describing those systems or how they function.

■ **People:** The employees, contractors, subcontractors, and managers who govern, manage, operate, secure, and use the system. Common personnel include developers, system end users, vendors, and managers.

■ **Data:** The type of information used by personnel and systems, information describing that data such as data dictionaries, and information mapping the flow of data and where it is stored.

■ **Procedures:** The automated or manual business procedures that are related to services and products offered, including the activities that initiate, authorize, perform, deliver, and report on those procedures.

3.1.1 Boundaries of the System

The boundaries of a system need to be clearly defined and communicated to report users in a SOC engagement. The system boundaries are the specific aspects of a service organization's infrastructure, software, people, procedures, and data necessary to provide its services. When systems for multiple services share aspects, infrastructure, software, people, procedures, and data, the systems will overlap, but the boundaries of each system will differ.

■ A financial reporting system is bounded by the components of the system related to financial transaction initiation, authorization, recording, processing, and reporting.

■ The boundaries of a system related to processing integrity may extend to other operations such as risk management, internal audit, information technology, or call center processes.

■ In a SOC 2® engagement that addresses the confidentiality and privacy criteria, the system boundaries cover, at a minimum, all the system components as they relate to the life cycle of the confidential and personal information within well-defined processes and informal ad hoc procedures.

3.1.2 Service Commitments and System Requirements

A service organization's system of internal control is evaluated by using the trust services criteria to determine whether such controls provide reasonable assurance that its business objectives and sub-objectives were achieved. Objectives and sub-objectives relate primarily to the following:

- The achievement of service commitments made to user entities related to the system used to provide the services and the system requirements necessary to achieve those commitments.

  Service commitments may be established for many different aspects of the service being provided, including the following:

  - Specifics of an algorithm used in a system calculation

  - The hours the system will be available

  - Published password standards

  - Encryption standards used to encrypt stored customer data

  Service commitments may also be established for one or more of the trust services categories addressed by the description.

- Compliance with laws and regulations regarding the provision of the services by the system.

- The achievement of the other objectives the service organization has for the system.

System requirements may also define how the system should function to meet the service commitments, comply with laws and regulations, and achieve other objectives. Examples include requirements such as:

- Workforce member fingerprinting and background checks established in government banking regulations

- System edits that restrict the values accepted for system input, which are defined in application design documents

- Maximum acceptable intervals between periodic reviews of workforce member logical access as documented in the security policy manual

- Data definition and tagging standards, including any associated metadata requirements (e.g., Simple Object Access Protocol), established by industry groups or other bodies

- Business processing rules and standards established by regulations (e.g., Health Insurance Portability and Accountability Act)

System requirements may result from the service organization's commitments related to one or more of the trust services categories.

3.1.3 Assessing the Suitability of the Service Commitments and System Requirements

A service organization's management is responsible for achieving its service commitments and system requirements, as well as for disclosing the principal system requirements and service commitments in the system description in a manner that allows SOC 2® report users to understand how the controls operate and how management and the service auditor evaluated the suitability of the controls' design and operating effectiveness (Type 2). The service commitments that a service organization makes to user entities may differ based on the needs of the user entities. Management does not need to disclose every service commitment to every user entity. Management should disclose those that are relevant to the common needs of the broad range of SOC 2® report users.

When deciding whether the disclosures stated in the description are appropriate, the service auditor should consider whether:

- The service commitments are presented in sufficient detail for report users to understand the relationship between the controls implemented by the service organization, the service commitments, and system requirements.

- The description summarizes the principal service commitments that are common to such report users when the SOC 2® report is designed for a broad range of users.

In addition to describing only controls that have been implemented, the description should provide sufficient details about each control to enable report users, particularly user entities and business partners, to understand how each control may affect their interactions with the service organization.

Illustration 1	Suitability of the Service Commitments and System Requirements

CompuGain Inc. is a payment processing company that allows its clients to process payments using credit cards, debit cards, and mobile phones over its payment network. Retail Xtra Co. signs up with CompuGain because of the payment processor's ability to maintain consumer privacy when processing transactions over its network. Due to the focus on the trust services criterion of Privacy, Retail Xtra ensures that the following stipulations (service commitments) are outlined in its service-level agreement:

- CompuGain will obtain a customer's consent before processing a payment and transferring information.

- CompuGain will provide a brief privacy notice to customers prior to completing a transaction at the time of purchase.

- CompuGain will respond to requests from Retail Xtra's customers regarding past transactions within 10 days of receiving the request.

3.2   Risk Assessment Considerations of the Service Organization

In a SOC engagement, risk assessment begins with the service organization identifying and assessing the types, likelihood, and impact of risks that affect the preparation of the description, the suitability of design of controls, and the operating effectiveness of controls (Type 2) within the system. How an entity both identifies and manages risks could affect its ability to meet its commitments and control objectives.

These risks may include:

- Intentional and unintentional internal and external acts

- Identified threats and vulnerabilities to, and deficiencies of, the system

- The use of subservice organizations that store, process, or transmit sensitive information on the service organization's behalf

- The type of employee personnel with access to the system

- A lack of CUECs or CSOCs, when those controls are considered necessary

3.2.1   Inherent Risk Factors

In all SOC engagements, risk assessment primarily focuses on inherent risks (i.e., the risks present before the consideration of controls) that affect the preparation of the description of the system and the effectiveness of the service organization's controls. Some of the risk factors considered in an organization's risk assessment process include the following:

- **Changes in the Operating Environment:** Newly promulgated regulations or standards may require new controls or existing ones to be revised.

- **New Personnel:** New personnel performing manual controls could increase the risk that controls do not operate effectively.

- **New or Revamped Information Systems:** New IT systems could affect control functions and user entities.

- **Rapid Growth:** An increase in customers could reduce the effectiveness of certain controls.

- **New Technology:** New software or other technology may perform similar functions differently, which could affect user entities.

- **New Business Models, Products, or Activities:** Diverting resources to new activities could impact certain controls at the service organization.

- **Corporate Restructurings:** Changes in ownership or internal structure may affect reporting responsibilities or the resources that serve user entities.

- **Expanded Foreign Operations:** Organizations that use employees in foreign locations may have difficulty responding to changes in user requirements.

- **New Accounting Standards:** Implementing new accounting pronouncements in software and controls may affect user entities.

- **Changes in Economic Conditions:** Slowing economic growth may impact the range of services offered.

3.3   Risk Assessment Considerations of a Service Auditor

In a SOC engagement, the service auditor must perform risk assessment procedures that are sufficient to enable the auditor to identity and assess the risk of material misstatement and provide a basis for designing and performing procedures that are responsive to the risks. In a Type 1 or Type 2 engagement, the risk of material misstatement relates to the risk that, in all material respects, based on the criteria in management's assertion:

1.   Management's description of the service organization's system is not fairly presented;

2.   The controls are not suitably designed to provide reasonable assurance that the control objectives stated in management's description of the service organization's system would be achieved if the controls operated effectively; and

3.   The controls did not operate effectively throughout the specified period to achieve related control objectives stated in management's description of the service organization's system (Type 2 only).   '

3.3.1   Performing Risk Assessment Procedures

As part of the risk assessment, the service auditor should obtain an understanding of the service organization's system, including controls within the system. That understanding should include the service organization's processes and procedures used to:

*   prepare the description of the service organization's system, including the determination of the control objectives;

*   identify the controls designed to achieve control objectives;

*   assess the suitability of the design of the controls; and

*   assess the operating effectiveness of controls (Type 2 only).

If the service organization has an internal audit function, the service auditor's understanding of the service organization's system should include the following:

*   The nature of the internal audit function's responsibilities and how the internal audit function fits into the service organization's organizational structure

*   The activities performed or to be performed by the internal audit function as it relates to the service organization

The service auditor's risk assessment procedures to obtain an understanding of the service organization's system may include the following, in some combination:

*   Inquiring of service organization management, those charged with governance, and others within the service organization who, in the service auditor's judgment, may have relevant information.

*   Observing operations and inspecting documents, reports, and printed and electronic records of transaction processing.

*   Inspecting a selection of agreements between the service organization and its user entities and business partners.

*   Reperforming the application of a control.

*   Reading relevant reports received from regulators, internal auditors, or other specialists (SOC 2®).

Service auditors may accomplish risk assessment procedures through the performance of a walk-through. Additionally, risk assessment procedures may be performed concurrently with procedures performed to obtain information about whether the system description is presented in accordance with the description criteria and whether the controls were suitably designed and operated effectively to meet the control objectives.

The service auditor should also perform risk assessment procedures to identify any fraud risk or risk of noncompliance with laws or regulations. Risks could include management override of controls, misappropriation of assets, or the creation of false or misleading documents or records.

1 Overview

Once the service auditor has accepted the engagement and completed the initial planning and risk assessment, the next phase of the engagement involves obtaining an understanding of the system defined by the service organization, performing tests of controls and obtaining evidence, and the consideration of subsequent events.

Key areas of engagement performance once initial risk assessment procedures are complete:

1. Respond to the assessed risks.

2. Evaluate whether management's description of the service organization's system is fairly presented in accordance with the description criteria.

3. Obtain and evaluate evidence regarding the suitability of the design of controls.

4. Obtain and evaluate evidence regarding the operating effectiveness of controls (Type 2 only).

5. Evaluate the results of the procedures.

6. Form the opinion.

2 Responding to the Assessed Level of Risk

The service auditor is required to obtain sufficient audit evidence to reduce attestation risk to an acceptably low level. This evidence enables the service auditor to obtain reasonable assurance and to draw conclusions on which to base the service auditor's opinion.

When performing a SOC engagement, the service auditor is required to design and implement overall responses to address the assessed risks of material misstatement for the subject matter; and design and perform further procedures whose nature, extent, and timing are based on, and responsive to, the assessed risks of material misstatement.

Assessment of the risks of material misstatement is impacted by several factors, including:

- materiality considerations;

- the service auditor's understanding of the effectiveness of the control environment; or

- other components of internal control related to the service provided to user entities and business partners.

The control environment or other components of the system of internal control may impact the effectiveness of specific system controls. Ineffective aspects of the control environment or other components of the service organization's system of internal control may cause the service auditor to design and perform further procedures whose nature, extent, and timing are based on, and responsive to, the higher assessed risks related to the ineffective aspects of the control environment or other components of internal control.

Example 1	**Audit Procedures Based on Risk Assessment**

The service auditor observes a business process that rewards employees with a compensation incentive for reaching targeted outcomes. If the service auditor assesses a high risk of manipulation of controls to misstate the actual outcomes, due to the employees' desire to reach the incentive, it is likely that the service auditor will increase the testing of controls, the sample population used for testing, or both.

Overall responses by the service auditor to address the assessed risks of material misstatement may include:

- Maintaining a culture of professional skepticism with the engagement team.

- Assigning more experienced staff or using specialists as needed.

- Providing additional supervision over audit procedures.

- Incorporating elements of unpredictability in the selection of procedures to be performed.

- Making changes to the nature, extent, or timing of procedures (e.g., selecting different types of procedures, or changing the extent and timing of those procedures).

3   Evaluating Management's Description

3.1   SOC 1®: Evaluating Whether Management's Description of the Service Organization's System Is Fairly Presented

The service auditor is required to obtain and read management's description of the service organization's system and evaluate whether those aspects of the description that are included in the scope of the engagement are presented fairly, in all material respects, based on the suitable criteria in management's assertion, including whether:

- The control objectives stated in management's description of the service organization's system are reasonable in the circumstances.

- Controls identified in management's description of the service organization's system were implemented.

- Complementary user entity controls and complementary subservice organization controls, if any, are adequately described.

- The services performed by a subservice organization, if any, are adequately described, including whether the carve-out method or the inclusive method has been used in relation to them.

The attributes of suitable criteria for evaluating the fair presentation of management's description includes:

- Whether management's description of the service organization's system presents how the service organization's system was designed and implemented, including the following information about the service organization's system, if applicable:

  - The types of services provided, including, as appropriate, the classes of transactions processed.

- The procedures, within both automated and manual systems, by which services are provided.

- The information used in the performance of the procedures, including, if applicable, related accounting records and supporting information involved in initiating, authorizing, recording, processing, and reporting transactions.

- How the service organization's system captures and addresses significant events and conditions other than transactions.

- The process used to prepare reports and other information for user entities.

- Services performed by a subservice organization.

- The specified control objectives and controls designed to achieve those objectives.

- Other aspects of the service organization's control environment, risk assessment process, information and communications, control activities, and monitoring activities that are relevant to the services provided.

- Whether management's description of the service organization's system includes relevant details of changes to the service organization's system during the period covered by the description (Type 2 only).

- Whether management's description of the service organization's system does not omit or provide misleading information relevant to the service organization's system, while acknowledging that management's description of the service organization's system is prepared to meet the common needs of a broad range of user entities and their auditors, and may not include every aspect of the service organization's system that each individual user entity may consider important in its own particular environment.

The service auditor should also consider and assess the adequacy of the level of detail of the description, the nature of the user entities, and available documentation from the service organization such as a policy and procedures manual, legal contracts, and any process narratives.

Through inquiries and other procedures, the service auditor should also determine whether the service organization's system has been implemented.

3.1.1 Performing Procedures to Obtain Evidence

Procedures the service auditor may perform to evaluate whether the description of the service organization's system is fairly presented typically include a combination of the following:

- Considering the nature of the user entities and how the services provided by the service organization are likely to affect them.

- Reading contracts with user entities to gain an understanding of the service organization's contractual obligations.

- Observing the procedures performed by service organization personnel.

- Reviewing the service organization's policy and procedure manuals and other documentation of the system (e.g., flowcharts and narratives).

- Performing walk-throughs of transactions through the service organization's system.

A description is not fairly presented if:

- the description states or implies that controls are being performed when they are not being performed; or

- the description inadvertently or intentionally omits relevant controls performed by the service organization that are not suitably designed or operating effectively.

3.2 SOC 2®: Evaluating Whether the Description Presents the System That Was Designed and Implemented in Accordance With the Description Criteria

The service auditor should obtain and read the description of the service organization's system and perform procedures to determine whether the description is presented in accordance with the description criteria. Determining whether the description of a service organization's system is presented in accordance with the description criteria involves comparing the service auditor's understanding of the service provided to user entities to the system through which service is provided based on the trust services category or categories included in the scope of the engagement.

A description of a service organization's system in a SOC 2® engagement is presented in accordance with the description criteria when it does the following:

- Describes the system that the service organization has implemented.

- Includes information about each description criterion, to the extent it is relevant to the system being described.

- Does not inadvertently or intentionally omit or distort information that is likely to be relevant to report users' decisions.

A description is not presented in accordance with the description criteria if:

- the description states or implies that certain IT components exist when they do not;

- the description states or implies that certain processes and controls have been implemented when they are not being performed; or

- the description contains statements that cannot be objectively evaluated.

Determining whether the description is presented in accordance with the description criteria also involves evaluating whether each stated control has been implemented. A control has been implemented when it has been placed into operation. If a service auditor concludes that certain controls stated in the description have not been implemented, the service auditor may request that the service organization delete those controls from the description. If management does not modify the description accordingly, the service auditor should consider the impact on his or her conclusion about the description and on the presentation of the service auditor's report.

3.2.1 Performing Procedures to Obtain Evidence

The service auditor performs multiple procedures to obtain evidence about whether the description presents the system that was designed and implemented in accordance with the description criteria, including some combination of the following:

- Discussing with management and other service organization personnel the content of management's assertion and the description.

- Reading the service organization's annual report.

- Reading the service organization's service commitments and system requirements to determine whether they are appropriate for the specific engagement circumstances.

- Inspecting documentation supporting the service organization's risk assessment (including plan for mitigating risks).

- Observing controls performed by service organization personnel.

- Reading contracts with user entities and business partners, as well as marketing materials distributed to user entities and business partners or posted on the service organization's website.

- Reading documents to understand the service organization's risk governance structure and processes (board minutes, organization charts, communications).

- Reading documents to understand the organization's process for communicating responsibilities for system security to service organization personnel (employee handbooks, code of conduct).

- Reading internal audit reports, third-party assessments, audit committee presentations, and other documentation related to the service organization's monitoring activities.

- Reading sample contracts with subservice organizations and vendors.

- Reading incident response and recovery plan documentation to understand the service organization's processes for recovering from identified system events.

3.2.2 Walk-throughs and Other Procedures

Performing walk-throughs provide evidence about whether the controls within the system have been implemented. Walk-through procedures include:

- Following a transaction, event, or activity from origination until final disposition through the service organization's system using the same documents used by service organization personnel.

- Inquiry, observation, inspection of relevant documentation, and flowcharts, questionnaires, or decision tables to facilitate understanding the design of the controls.

- Inquiry about instances during the period in which controls did not operate as described or designed.

- Questioning variations in the process for different types of events or transactions.

An appropriately performed walk-through provides an opportunity to verify the service auditor's understanding of the flow of transactions and the design of the controls. When performed properly, walk-throughs often provide evidence about whether controls included in the description were suitably designed and implemented and operated effectively (Type 2).

3.2.3 Evaluation of Description Disclosures

The service auditor should evaluate whether the description is misleading within the context of the engagement based on the evidence obtained. The service auditor should consider whether additional disclosures are necessary to supplement the description.

Additional disclosures may include:

- Significant interpretations made in applying the criteria in the engagement circumstances.

- Subsequent events, depending on their nature and significance.

If the service auditor believes that the description is misstated or otherwise misleading, the service auditor should ask management to amend the description. If service organization management refuses to amend the description, the service auditor must consider the effect on the opinion about the description.

4 Performing Tests of Controls and Other Procedures in a SOC 2® Engagement

In addition to obtaining evidence that the description presents the system that was designed and implemented in accordance with the description criteria, the service auditor must also obtain evidence that the controls were suitably designed and operated effectively during the specified period (Type 2).

4.1 Procedures to Obtain Evidence About the Suitability of the Design of Controls

The evidence gathered by the service auditor when obtaining an understanding of the service organization's system and the related controls, as well as when determining if the description is fairly presented is useful when assessing the suitability of the design of the controls.

To supplement such evidence, the auditor may perform a combination of the following procedures:

- Inquiry of service organization personnel about the design and operation of controls or system events.

- Inspection of documents.

- Additional walk-throughs.

- Reading applicable supporting system documentation.

- Determining whether attacks, vulnerability exploitations, emerging risks, or threats have been adequately addressed.

When evaluating the suitability of the design of the controls, the service auditor should consider the frequency of the control, the competence and authority of the individual performing the control, the precision and sensitivity of tasks within the control, and any evidence that may contradict the assertion that the control is functioning as designed.

4.2 Obtaining Evidence About the Operating Effectiveness of Controls in a Type 2 Engagement

If controls are suitably designed, they have the potential to meet the applicable trust services criteria, thereby enabling the service organization's controls to provide reasonable assurance that the service organization's service commitments and system requirements were achieved.

- Suitably designed controls operate as designed by individuals who have the necessary authority and competence to perform the controls.

- Controls that operate effectively provide reasonable assurance of achieving the service organization's service commitments and system requirements based on the applicable trust services criteria.

In the Type 2 engagement, the service auditor tests the operating effectiveness of the controls stated in the description based on the applicable trust services criteria. The service auditor performs tests of controls to obtain evidence about the operating effectiveness of controls.

The evidence obtained from the tests of controls relates to how the controls were applied, the consistency with which they were applied, and by whom or in what manner they were applied.

◼ If a service organization uses the inclusive method to present the services and controls of a subservice organization, the service auditor also applies tests of controls to the controls at the subservice organization.

The service auditor is responsible for determining the nature, extent, and timing of procedures necessary to obtain sufficient and appropriate evidence about the operating effectiveness of controls throughout the engagement period.

◼ **Nature:** How controls are tested.

◼ **Extent:** The number of procedures performed and the size of the sample.

◼ **Timing:** When the controls are tested and the frequency of testing.

A combination of controls is necessary when more than one control is required to address a risk that would prevent the service organization from achieving one or more of its service commitments and system requirements.

4.2.1 Nature of Test of Controls

The nature and objectives of tests to evaluate the operating effectiveness of controls are different from those performed to evaluate the suitability of the design of controls. When designing and performing tests of controls, the service auditor will often do the following:

◼ Make inquiries and perform other procedures such as inspection, observation, or reperformance to obtain evidence about the following:

⚬ How the control was applied.

⚬ The consistency with which the control was applied throughout the period.

⚬ By whom or by what means the control was applied.

◼ Determine whether the controls to be tested depend on other controls and, if so, whether it is necessary to obtain evidence supporting the operating effectiveness of those other controls.

◼ Evaluate and determine an effective method for selecting the items to be tested to meet the objectives of the procedure.

The service auditor must consider the reliability of evidence obtained by evaluating the completeness and accuracy of information and determining whether it is sufficiently precise to meet their needs.

4.2.2 Extent of Test of Controls

The extent of the service auditor's testing refers to the size of the sample tested or the number of observations of a control activity.

◼ The extent of testing is based on the service auditor's professional judgment after considering:

⚬ The tolerable rate of deviation

⚬ The expected rate of deviation

⚬ The frequency with which the control operates

⚬ The relevance and reliability of the evidence that can be obtained to support the conclusion that the controls are operating effectively

⚬ The length of the testing period

- The significance of the control to the achievement of the service organization's service commitments and system requirements based on the applicable trust services criteria

- The extent to which audit evidence is obtained from tests of other controls that support the achievement of those service commitments and system requirements based on the applicable trust services criteria

4.2.3 Timing of Test of Controls

The following are factors that are relevant to the service auditor's determination of the timing of tests of controls:

- The period of time during which the information will be available:

  - Electronic files may be overwritten after a period of time.

  - Procedures may occur only at certain times during the period.

  - Certain procedures may need to be performed after the end of the period, such as reviewing reconciliations that are generated after the end of the period.

- Whether the control leaves evidence of its operation and, if not, whether the control should be tested through observation.

- The significance of the control being tested.

The service auditor may perform tests of controls at interim dates, at the end of the engagement period, or after the engagement period if the tests relate to controls that were in operation during the period but do not leave evidence until after the end of the period. When tests are performed at an interim date, the service auditor should determine what procedures are necessary to obtain evidence about the control performance through the end of the period.

4.3 Reporting Failures, System Incidents, and Concerns

Service auditors should gain an understanding of processes in place to report system failures, system incidents, and complaints by either external or internal system users by inquiring of management about the controls in place. Management is responsible for identifying the nature, extent, and timing of system incidents in the service organization's system description, making that an ideal place to start reviewing for such incidents. Service auditors may consider information related to the following in gaining an understanding and obtaining evidence:

- Quarterly or annual board meetings should involve discussions of incident responses and escalation plans for unforeseen events. Minutes from board meetings should indicate communication of such failures to senior management and the board of directors, as well as the incident response plan resulting from a significant event.

- Inquiries about third-party administered whistleblower hotlines available to internal and external users to understand whether management monitors workforce and customer complaints as well as sanction personnel who violate the code of conduct. Verification and testing of operability can be performed by test-dialing the hotline, reviewing operating procedures related to complaint intake, and documenting system failures.

- External and internal system users should be provided with documented responsibilities, policies, and procedures related to security commitments, including instructions on how to report and escalate security failures, system incidents, concerns, and complaints. A common place for documentation around policies, procedures, and communication plans to be in place is on a company's intranet for employees, customer portal, and websites. Changes, security alerts, and known issues should be documented and communicated to internal and external system users.

- Management monitors and provides training to personnel.

- External and internal system users are provided with a description of its system, system boundaries, and system processes that include infrastructure, software, people, processes and procedures, and data. A common place for this documentation is on a company's intranet for internal users, and internet for external users.

- Agreements are established with service providers and business partners that include clearly defined terms, conditions, and responsibilities for service providers and business partners.

- Planned changes to system components are reviewed, approved, and scheduled internally, then communicated (along with potential impact) to internal and external users. A common place for this documentation is the IT maintenance schedule and communications for internal users, and the customer portal or website for external users.

5   Evaluating the Results of Procedures in a SOC 2® Engagement

Sufficient evidence is necessary to support the service auditor's opinion and report. The service auditor must consider all information and evidence obtained during the engagement. This should include evidence from all sources (both internal and external) as well as evidence that both corroborates or contradicts management's assertions.

- The absence of information should be considered by the service auditor as evidence.

- If the evidence is not sufficient and appropriate based on the professional judgment of the service auditor, additional procedures should be performed to gather additional evidence.

If the service auditor is unable to obtain necessary further evidence, the service auditor should consider the implications for the service auditor's opinion.

The service auditor must evaluate the results of all procedures performed and must conduct both quantitative and qualitative analyses. Analysis must also be performed on deviations in the operating effectiveness of controls resulting in a description that is not presented in accordance with the description criteria or in controls that are not suitably designed or operating effectively (Type 2 only).

When evaluating the results of procedures, the service auditor investigates the nature and cause of any identified description misstatements and deficiencies or deviations in the effectiveness of controls and determines the following:

- Whether the identified description misstatements result in either the failure to meet one or more of the description criteria or in a presentation that could be misunderstood by users if the service auditor's opinion were not modified to reflect the identified description misstatements.

- Whether identified deviations are within the expected rate of deviation and are acceptable or whether they constitute a deficiency.

- If deviations are within the expected rate of deviation, whether the procedures that have been performed provide an appropriate basis for concluding that the control operated effectively throughout the specified period.

- Whether identified deficiencies are likely to have a pervasive effect on the achievement of the service organization's service commitments and system requirements based on the applicable trust services criteria or whether they are likely to affect only one of them.

- Whether:
  - a previously tested control (or combination of controls) provides sufficient appropriate evidence about whether controls operated effectively; or
  - additional testing of the control or other controls is necessary to determine whether the controls were effective throughout the period.

    If the service auditor is unable to apply additional procedures to the selected items, the service auditor should consider the reasons for this limitation and conclude on whether those selected items are deviations from the prescribed policy or result in a limitation of the scope of the engagement.

- The magnitude of the effect of such deficiencies on the achievement of the service organization's service commitments and system requirements based on the applicable trust services criteria.

- Whether report users could be misled if the service auditor's opinion were not modified to reflect the identified deficiencies.

- Considerations of any known or suspected fraud or noncompliance with laws or regulations.

If the service auditor identifies material description misstatements, material deficiencies in the suitability of design of controls, or deviations in the operating effectiveness of controls (Type 2), the service auditor should modify the opinion. When modifying the opinion, the service auditor's understanding of the nature and cause of the description misstatements and deficiencies enables the service auditor to determine how to appropriately modify the opinion.

6 Subsequent Events and Subsequently Discovered Facts

6.1 Nature of Subsequent Events

Transactions or events may occur after the engagement period, but prior to the date of the service auditor's report, that could have a significant effect on the description, the suitability of design of controls, and the operating effectiveness of controls (Type 2), or on management's assertion. In these circumstances, disclosure of those events and transactions in the description may be necessary to prevent report users from being misled.

The service auditor is required to inquire of management about whether it is aware of any such events. If such events exist, the service auditor should apply appropriate procedures to obtain evidence regarding the events.

The service auditor may obtain evidence by inquiring about the operating effectiveness of controls by inspecting the following:

- Relevant internal auditors' reports issued during the subsequent period

- Other practitioners' reports issued during the subsequent period

- Relevant regulatory agencies' reports issued during the subsequent period

- Reports on other professional engagements for that entity

6.1.1   Subsequent Events Likely to Affect a SOC Report

The following examples are likely to affect system descriptions or management's assertions in a SOC engagement. After the period covered by an engagement, the service organization's management discovered:

- During the last quarter of the period covered by the service auditor's report, the IT director provided all of the programmers with access to the production data files, enabling them to modify data.

- A confidentiality breach occurred during the period covered by the service auditor's report (SOC 2®)

- The signatures on a number of non-automated trade execution instructions submitted during the engagement period that appeared to be authenticated by signature verification had been forged (SOC 1®).

- A defalcation occurred at the service organization (SOC 1®).

6.1.2   Subsequent Events Unlikely to Affect a SOC Report

Not all subsequent events are likely to impact a SOC report, as the event or underlying situation may not have existed until after the period covered by the report. In these circumstances, the service auditor may conclude that there is no impact on the description, suitability of the design of controls, or operating effectiveness of controls (Type 2). However, some subsequent events may be sufficiently important or significant to warrant disclosure by management in the system description or by the service auditor in the service auditor's report.

Examples of subsequent events that warrant disclosure include when the service organization:

- was acquired by another company.

- experienced a major operational disruption that was caused by weather or a natural disaster.

- made significant changes to its information systems, including either a system conversion or outsourcing a portion of its operations.

6.1.3   Impact of Subsequent Events on the SOC Report

Upon becoming aware of a subsequent event that is of significance, a service auditor should request that management disclose the event in either management's assertions or the description of the service organization's system.

If management refuses to disclose an event, that if undisclosed, would mislead report users, the practitioner should consider taking the following actions:

- Modifying the auditor's report and disclosing the event.

- Withdrawing from the engagement.

6.2   Subsequently Discovered Facts After the Issuance of a SOC Report

The service auditor is not required to perform any procedures regarding the description, the suitability of design of controls, the operating effectiveness of controls (Type 2), or management's assertion after the date of the service auditor's report. However, the service auditor is responsible for responding appropriately to facts that become known after the date of the report.

The service auditor should, using professional judgment, determine whether the subsequently discovered facts, had they been known as of the report date, may have caused the service auditor to revise the report.

- The service auditor determines whether the facts existed at the date of the report and, if so, whether persons who would attach importance to these facts are currently using, or likely to use, the report.

  The service auditor may do this through discussions with management and other appropriate parties and through the performance of additional procedures that the service auditor considers necessary to determine whether the description, assertion, and service auditor's report need revision or whether the previously issued report continues to be appropriate.

- The service auditor may determine it is necessary to notify persons currently using or likely to use the service auditor's report depending on factors such as the time elapsed since the date of the report and when the issuance of a subsequent report is imminent.

7 Obtaining Written Representations From Management

The service auditor is required to obtain written representations from the management of the service organization. Such representations are intended to confirm explicit or implicit representations given to the service auditor, indicate and document the continuing appropriateness of those representations, and reduce the possibility of a misunderstanding between the service auditor and management. The service auditor should determine the appropriate individuals within the service organization's management or governance structure based on their responsibilities and knowledge of the subject matter of the engagement.

The written representations should be as of the date of the issued SOC report and should address the subject matter and periods covered by the service auditor's opinion. The service auditor would not ordinarily be able to issue the report until the service auditor had received the representation letter. If a subservice organization is used and the inclusive method is used for management's description of the system, written representations should be obtained from the subservice organization as well.

7.1 Content of Written Representations

The written representations should do the following:

- Include management's assertion about the subject matter based on the criteria.
- State that:
  - All relevant matters are reflected in the measurement or evaluation of the subject matter or assertion.
  - All known matters contradicting the subject matter or assertion and any communications from regulatory agencies or others affecting the subject matter have been disclosed to the service auditor (including communications received between the end of the period addressed in the written assertion and the date of the service auditor's report).
- Acknowledge responsibility for:
  - the subject matter and assertions;
  - selecting the criteria; and
  - determining that such criteria are appropriate for management's purposes.

- State that any known subsequent events related to the subject matters of the report that would have a material effect on the subject matter or assertion have been disclosed to the service auditor.

- State that management has provided the service auditor with all relevant access and information.

- State that management believes the effects of uncorrected misstatements (description misstatements and deficiencies) are immaterial, individually and in the aggregate, to the subject matter.

- State that management has disclosed to the service auditor:

  - All deficiencies in internal control relevant to the engagement of which it is aware.

  - Its knowledge of any actual, suspected, or alleged fraud or noncompliance with laws or regulations affecting the subject matter.

  - All other matters deemed appropriate by the service auditor (e.g., changes to the service organization's controls).

  - Instances of noncompliance with laws and regulations or uncorrected misstatements attributable to the service organization (SOC 2®), including those that may affect one or more user entities (SOC 1®).

  - Knowledge of any actual, suspected, or alleged fraud by management or the service organization's employees that could adversely affect:

    —The fairness of the presentation of management's description of the service organization's system or the completeness or achievement of the control objectives stated in the description (SOC 1®).

    —The description of the service organization's system or the achievement of the service organization's service commitments or system requirements (SOC 2®).

  - Identified system incidents that resulted in a significant impairment of the service organization's achievement of its service commitments and system requirements as of the date of the description (Type 1) or during the period of time covered by the description (Type 2) (SOC 2®).

- State that significant assumptions used in making any material estimates are reasonable (SOC 1®).

7.2 Written Representations Not Provided

If management does not provide one or more of the requested representations, or the service auditor concludes that there is sufficient doubt about the competence, integrity, ethical values, or diligence of those providing the written representations, or the service auditor concludes that the written representations are otherwise not reliable, the service auditor should:

- discuss the matter with the appropriate party;

- reevaluate the integrity of those from whom the representations were requested or received and evaluate the effect that this may have on the reliability of representations and evidence in general; and

- if any of the matters are not resolved to the practitioner's satisfaction, take appropriate action.

Failure by management to provide written representations to the service auditor may constitute a scope limitation. In such cases, if the matters remain unresolved, the service auditor may be precluded from issuing an unmodified opinion. Depending on the circumstances, the service auditor may withdraw from the engagement if permitted by law or regulation.

NOTES

NOTES

NOTES

NOTES